JAVASCRIPT™
HOW-TO

THE DEFINITIVE JAVASCRIPT PROBLEM-SOLVER

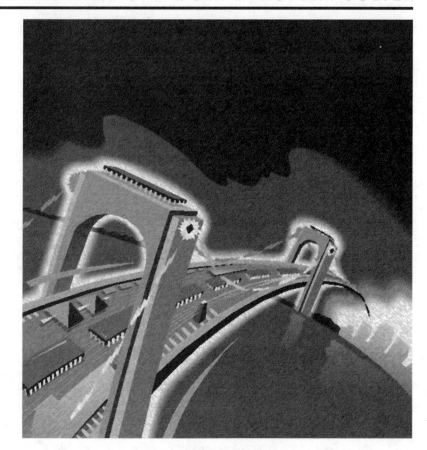

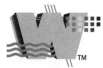

Waite Group Press™
A Division of
Sams Publishing
Corte Madera, CA

George Pickering, Shelley Powers, Ron Johnson

Publisher: Mitchell Waite
Associate Publisher: Charles Drucker

Acquisitions Manager: Jill Pisoni
Acquisitions Editor: Joanne Miller

Editorial Director: John Crudo
Project Editor: Laura E. Brown
Content Editor: Russ Jacobs
Technical Editors: Brian Stoler, Allen Bunch, Mitch Lieberman
Software Specialist: Dan Scherf

Production Director: Julianne Ososke
Production Manager: Cecile Kaufman
Production Editor: Kelsey McGee
Senior Designer: Sestina Quarequio
Designer: Karen Johnston, Jil Weil
Copy Editor: Elizabeth Leahy/Creative Solutions

Cover Illustration: Don Baker
Illustrations: Casey Price, Marvin Van Tiem
Production: Kevin Fulcher, Ayanna Lacey, Lisa Pletka, Dana Rhodes, Andrew Stone

© 1996 by The Waite Group, Inc.®
Published by Waite Group Press™, 200 Tamal Plaza, Corte Madera, CA 94925.

Waite Group Press™ is a division of Sams Publishing.

All terms mentioned in this book that are known to be trademarks, registered trademarks, or service marks are listed below. In addition, terms suspected of being trademarks, registered trademarks, or service marks have been appropriately capitalized. Waite Group Press™ cannot attest to the accuracy of this information. Use of a term in this book should not be regarded as affecting the validity of any trademark, registered trademark, or service mark.

The Waite Group® is a registered trademark of The Waite Group, Inc. Waite Group Press™ and The Waite Group logo are trademarks of The Waite Group, Inc. JavaScript™, Netscape, Navigator, and Navigator Gold are trademarks of Netscape Communications Corporation. Java and Sun are trademarks of Sun Microsystems, Inc. Microsoft, Windows, Windows NT, and Windows 95 are trademarks or registered trademarks of Microsoft Corporation. UNIX is a registered trademark of AT&T. Macintosh is a registered trademark of Apple Computer, Inc. All other product names are trademarks, registered trademarks, or service marks of their respective owners.

Printed in the United States of America
96 97 98 99 • 10 9 8 7 6 5 4 3 2 1

Library of Congress Cataloging-in-Publication Data
Pickering, George, 1967-
  JavaScript how-to / George Pickering, Shelley Powers, Ron Johnson.
      p.   cm.
  Includes index.
  ISBN 1-57169-047-6
  1. JavaScript (Computer program language) I. Powers, Shelley. II. Johnson, Ron, 1954- . III. Title.
QA76.73.J39P53   1996
005.2--dc20   96-31609
                                                                                    CIP

DEDICATION

To my lovely wife, Padma, who makes every day so beautiful. And to my son, whose life represents the special love Padma and I share.

—George Pickering

I wish to dedicate this book, as always, to Rob and to Zoe. I also wish to extend this dedication to the great teachers I had at Yakima Valley Community College and Central Washington University in Washington State. Years ago they provided the base that I have been able to successfully build upon.

—Shelley Powers

For Ivar and Marylin, who introduced me to these wonderful things called computers!

—Ron Johnson

George Pickering is a senior software engineer with Intuit's Interactive Insurance Services Division in Alexandria, Virginia. George is leading the development of several intranet systems that support the Quicken Financial Network's Insuremarket site (www.insure-market.com). He holds a B.S. in decision support systems from Virginia Polytechnic Institute, an M.S. in software engineering administration from Central Michigan University, and is currently pursuing an M.S. in computer science from The Johns Hopkins University. His interests are Geographic Information Systems (GIS), Internet technologies, and relational databases.

Shelley Powers has worked professionally for several years in the Northwest, and for the last two years has been a consultant, first working for a consulting company and now as an independent with her own company, YASD. Shelley is a Microsoft Certified Product Specialist as well as a PowerSoft Certified Professional–Associate Level, and is experienced with several client/server tools, Internet and Web development, and relational databases. She is also coauthor of *PowerBuilder 5 How-To* (Waite Group Press, 1996). Shelley has worked for years with Windows, including Windows 95 and NT, as well as UNIX. She specializes now in Web application development, and her Web site can be seen at http://www.yasd.com.

Ron Johnson works for TASC, Inc. in Reston, Virginia, managing a project that uses HTML, Java, and JavaScript to implement an information management system for a large-scale program. Ron holds a B.S. and M.S. in computer and systems engineering from Rensselaer Polytechnic Institute and is currently working toward an M.S. in computer science from The Johns Hopkins University. Ron's interests include signal processing, Java, and VRML. You can e-mail Ron at rejohnso@rest.tasc.com.

TABLE OF CONTENTS

CONTENTS

ACKNOWLEDGMENTS

We wish to thank our project editor, Laura Brown, for putting up with two first-time authors. Also, thanks to our content editor, Russ Jacobs, and technical editors, Brian Stoler, Allen Bunch, and Mitch Lieberman, for providing excellent comments that increased the book's quality.

George Pickering wishes to thank his grandparents, Ernest and Laura Brooks, for paying for his education, without which he would not have been able to write this book. Also, thanks to his managers, Sheri Meffle and Robert Freeland, for their support of the book and George's desire to push JavaScript technology to the "edge of the envelope" in their intranet systems.

Shelley Powers wishes to thank Alec Plumb from Netscape for testing some of the JavaScript code between beta releases of version 3.0 of Netscape Navigator, and reassuring her that it does still work.

Ron Johnson would like to thank his family and friends for their support and understanding.

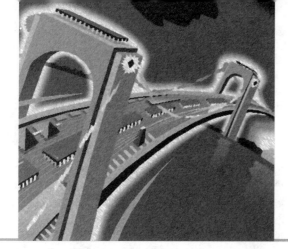

INTRODUCTION

About This Book

The original concept of the World Wide Web (WWW) was a set of tools for quickly transferring documents using the Internet. The original Web browser, NCSA Mosaic, was built to allow users to easily request and view WWW-based documents. The HyperText Markup Language (HTML) was used to specify formatting requirements for text within one of these documents.

User interaction with HTML documents was limited to links and forms that submitted HyperText Transfer Protocol (HTTP) requests back to the Web server. HTTP requests could be used to download static documents or execute server side processes through the Common Gateway Interface (CGI). This meant that the browser was heavily dependent on the server for any processing needs.

The new generation of Web browsers has been designed to reduce this dependency. The JavaScript language, developed by Netscape Communications Corporation, allows Web developers to specify small programs that can be embedded inside an HTML document. JavaScript programs are executed on the client machine. An interpreter, built into the Web browser, converts JavaScript code into executable content. JavaScript can be used to develop data validation and dynamic document creation functions.

JavaScript How-To examines the capabilities and syntax of the JavaScript language. Each chapter presents the conceptual, semantic, and syntactic aspects of the JavaScript language required to solve real world problems encountered in developing Internet and intranet systems. Other JavaScript-related topics, including LiveConnect, frames, and cookies, are also discussed. The organization of the book provides an effective index for locating solutions to problems you will encounter when developing a JavaScript-enhanced HTML document.

The designers of JavaScript wanted a simple language that could be used by a wide range of developers. The language empowers Web developers to quickly build state-of-the-art interactive pages. Unlike its sister environment Java, JavaScript does not require an in-depth knowledge of computer programming in order to implement interactive pages.

Although JavaScript is a relatively easy language to use, there are many advanced concepts that require some experience with the environment. *JavaScript How-To* was developed for readers of all skill levels. The complexity level is given at the start of each How-To. The chapters are organized so that they present an evolutionary approach to teaching JavaScript concepts. The early How-To's are typically easy, allowing you to build a solid foundation of the basic JavaScript concepts.

Defining the complexity of each How-To allows you to determine whether or not you have the necessary prerequisites to tackle the example. If you encounter an advanced problem but feel your experience is not at that level, read the other How-To's in the chapter to gain a solid foundation in a particular topic area. When you complete the foundation How-To's, proceed to the advanced areas.

What You Need to Use This Book

You must have access to a JavaScript-friendly Web browser in order to run the JavaScript programs you develop. *JavaScript How-To* focuses on the capabilities of the Netscape 2.0 and 3.0 browsers. Although some examples may work on another browser, other examples require the Netscape browser. Since you can download the latest version of the Netscape browser (for free), the authors recommend you acquire this software from the Netscape Communications Corporation Home Page (www.netscape.com).

This recommendation is based on the fact that portability issues are rapidly becoming a major issue in Internet systems development. As browsers implement new capabilities in an effort to distinguish their product from other competitors, different JavaScript capabilities may arise. Because JavaScript technology belongs to Netscape, the amount of language variance should be minimal. This depends on the license agreement signed by other vendors.

Even exclusive use of Netscape browsers does not preclude the impact of portability problems. New versions of the Navigator browser are being released every four or five months. Each new version brings minor tweaking of the JavaScript environment. For example, the LiveConnect technology was added in Netscape Version 3.0 as a way to link JavaScript/Java/Plug-Ins. To account for portability issues, each How-To is branded with a version indicator (either 2.0 or 3.0). This indicates which Netscape Navigator version can be used to run the example. At the time of publishing, the latest version of Netscape was Version 3.0 b5.

How This Book Is Organized

Each chapter covers one broad topic encountered by Web developers building simple and complex interactive pages. At the beginning of a chapter, you will be presented with a list of questions that are answered by the How-To's in the chapter. A brief explanation is provided that previews the material covered in each How-To. These descriptions, along with the chapter description, provide a high-level overview of the topic area. This background is needed to understand how all the concepts are tied together. Since most How-To's build on concepts presented in previous How-To's, these descriptions will indicate the direction being taken by the chapter.

It is as though you are getting a glimpse of the final jigsaw puzzle before the authors present you with the individual pieces (jumbled up, of course) that comprise the puzzle. Don't worry—the individual How-To's follow the background information. The How-To's will give step-by-step instruction needed to construct small sections of the overall puzzle. When you finish the last How-To, you should have an excellent view of the final puzzle, including the techniques used to construct the puzzle. You can then proceed to your own puzzle (work-related, school-related, personal) with the confidence of being able to quickly finish the job.

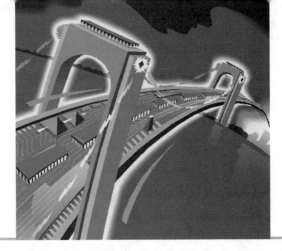

INSTALLATION

The CD-ROM bundled with *JavaScript How-To* includes all sample JavaScript code created in the book. The code is organized by chapter in CHXX directories at the root of the CD. What follows are directions for copying files to your hard drive for Windows 3.x, Windows NT, Windows 95, Macintosh, and UNIX.

> **NOTE**
>
> The PC installation instructions assume your CD-ROM drive is D: and C: is your hard drive. If your system is set up differently, please substitute the appropriate drive letters. For UNIX users, the instructions assume you're using the mount point /cdrom. If this isn't the mount point you will be using, please substitute accordingly. In all cases, the mount point must exist or an error will occur. To create the mount point directory, use the mkdir command and remount the CD-ROM.

Windows 3.x and Windows NT 3.51

1. Open the File Manager.

2. In File Manager, locate the drive you want to copy to and click on it.

3. If you have a directory to copy the files to, skip to Step 4. Otherwise, create a new directory by selecting File, Create Directory. Type

`javascrp`

or a directory name of your choice, and press ENTER or click the OK button.

4. Click on JAVASCRP or the directory you've created.

5. Double-click on the D: drive icon. You should see chapter directories. Drag the contents to the destination drive. If you want to copy only a few directories, control-click on them and drag them to the destination drive.

> **NOTE**
>
> When Windows copies a CD-ROM, it does not change the Read-only attribute for the files it copies. You can view the files, but you cannot edit them until you remove the attribute. To do this, select the topmost directory with the files in it. In File Manager, select File, Properties and click on the Read-only checkbox to deselect it. Then click OK.

Windows 95 and Windows NT 4.0

The easiest way to copy files in Windows 95 or Windows NT 4.0 is by using the Desktop.

1. Double-click on the My Computer icon. Your drives will appear in a window on the desktop.

2. Double-click on your hard drive and create a new folder, such as JavaScript How-To, by selecting File, New, Folder from the window menu. A folder called *New Folder* will be created on your hard drive with the name highlighted. Type in the name you want and press (ENTER).

3. Go back to your drive window and double-click on the icon that represents your CD-ROM. You will see a window that has chapter folders in it.

4. Select the directories you want to copy (control-click on the folders if you're not copying all of them) and drag your selection to the directory you've created on your hard drive.

> **NOTE**
>
> When Windows copies a CD-ROM, it does not change the Read-only attribute for the files it copies. You can view the files, but you cannot edit them until you remove the attribute. To do this, select the topmost directory with the files in it. In the folder, right-click on the file or folder and select Properties; click on the Read-only checkbox to deselect it. Then click OK.

Macintosh

1. Double-click on your hard drive and create a new folder, such as JavaScript How-To, by selecting File, New Folder from the menu. A folder called *untitled folder* will be created on your hard drive with the name highlighted. Type in the name you want and press (ENTER).

2. Double-click on your CD-ROM drive's icon. You will see a window that has chapter folders in it.

3. Select the directories you want to copy (shift-click on the folders if you're not copying all of them) and drag your selection to the directory you've created on your hard drive.

UNIX

Some versions of UNIX only mount the CD-ROM if it is inserted before the machine is booted. If your UNIX platform automatically mounts CD-ROMs, skip to Step 2.

1. While it is not necessary to be logged in as root, it may help in the mounting process. A few typical commands to mount a CD-ROM at the UNIX prompt are

```
mount /dev/cdrom /cdrom
mount -tiso9660 /dev/cdrom /cdrom
mount -f hsfs /dev/cdrom /cdrom
```

If none of these commands work, you may be working with a non-standard implementation of UNIX. Please contact your systems administrator for further assistance.

2. Create and move into a directory that you would like to copy the files into, such as javascript_how-to, by typing

```
mkdir javascript_how-to
cd javascript_how-to
```

3. Copy all of the source code to your local drive by typing

```
cp /cdrom/* .
```

or copy individual directories of source code by typing

```
cp /cdrom/ch?/* .
```

where ch? is the name of the directory that corresponds to the chapter that you want to copy.

CHAPTER 1
ADDING INTERACTIVE CONTENT TO A WEB PAGE

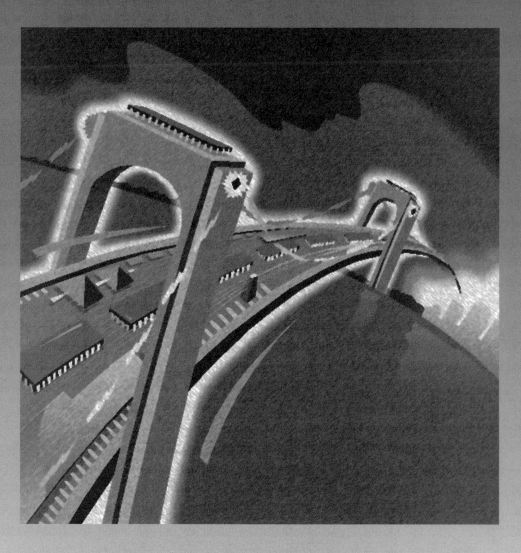

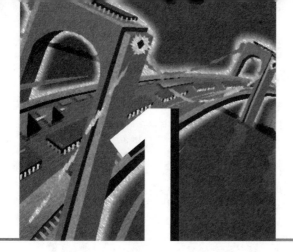

1

ADDING INTERACTIVE CONTENT TO A WEB PAGE

How do I...

JavaScript, developed by Netscape Communications (Netscape), is one of several initiatives in the commercial marketplace designed to add interactive content or functionality to Hypertext Markup Language (HTML) documents. The only interactive content in HTML 2.0 and 3.0 are hypertext links and fill-out forms, which rely on the Common Gateway Interface (CGI) to remotely execute functionality that resides on the HTTP server. This approach is inefficient in that it results in additional load on the server.

JavaScript is an easy-to-use, object-based language that reduces an HTML document's dependency on the server for its processing power. World Wide Web (Web) developers can use the language as a quick way to add "spice" to their Web pages. JavaScript gives developers great power by allowing them to trap user events and dynamically build HTML documents "on the fly."

1.1 Embed JavaScript code inside an HTML document

In this How-To, you will learn how to embed JavaScript code inside an HTML document. After creating your first JavaScript-enhanced document, you will learn how to run your JavaScript application using the Netscape Navigator (Navigator) Web browser.

1.2 Establish an event handler for an HTML input element

Because user interaction with input forms is asynchronous, most Graphical User Interface (GUI)-based languages and toolkits establish a series of callbacks which notify the application when an event has occurred. In this How-To, you will learn how to establish an event handler. Event handlers execute a series of JavaScript statements when an event occurs.

1.3 Receive notification of an error in the JavaScript code

Because human beings are notorious for making errors, error detection is an important capability of any programming environment. This How-To will explain how Netscape notifies developers of errors inside a piece of JavaScript code.

1.4 Make older browsers ignore JavaScript code

At the time of this publishing, only Navigator 2.0 and Microsoft Internet Explorer (Explorer) 3.0 supported the JavaScript language. HTML documents should be portable, meaning they can be viewed on all Web browsers. This How-To will show you how to hide JavaScript code from older Web browsers which do not support JavaScript.

1.5 Access JavaScript objects without altering existing HTML documents

This How-To will teach you how to use the new Uniform Resource Locator (URL) tag *mocha* to execute JavaScript expressions without altering existing HTML documents. The mocha tag can be used to determine the output of JavaScript expressions or obtain information on documents you download over the Web.

1.6   Get information about the Web browser being used

When a document is loaded into Netscape, the JavaScript environment automatically creates a series of objects representing key pieces of the document. One of these objects, called Navigator, contains information about the Web browser being used to view the document. This How-To will describe the properties of the Navigator object.

COMPLEXITY
BEGINNING

1.1   How do I...
Embed JavaScript code inside an HTML document?

COMPATIBILITY:

Problem

HTML documents have limited capabilities for supporting user interaction. The primary approach is to rely on the server for all processing needs. The server-side approach is inefficient in terms of network traffic and server utilization. I understand that JavaScript can be used to add interactive content to a Web page. How can I embed JavaScript code inside my HTML document so that certain types of functionality, such as data validation, will be processed on the client machine?

Technique

JavaScript code is embedded within an HTML document. The <SCRIPT> tag was created to distinguish JavaScript code from the rest of the document. A closing </SCRIPT> tag marks the end of a JavaScript code segment. As additional Web-based scripting languages are developed, the <SCRIPT> tag will be used to represent any executable content embedded within an HTML document. To provide support for future languages, the <SCRIPT> tag contains a LANGUAGE attribute. This attribute is used to specify the scripting language of the code located inside the <SCRIPT> container. For <SCRIPT> containers which contain JavaScript code, the LANGUAGE attribute should be set to JavaScript. Besides JavaScript, the <SCRIPT> container can also contain VBScript code, which is recognized by Explorer 3.0. The LANGUAGE attribute is optional. In Netscape, JavaScript is the default language as no LANGUAGE attribute is provided. The following code represents a <SCRIPT> container that contains JavaScript code.

```
<SCRIPT LANGUAGE="JavaScript">
</SCRIPT>
```

Please note that the language parameter is set to "JavaScript" and not "Javascript". The interpreter is case sensitive. The <SCRIPT> container can contain a combination of variable declarations, function declarations, and JavaScript statements. Variable declarations and JavaScript statements are automatically executed, while function execution is delayed until a call is made to the function.

> **NOTE**
>
> Variable declarations must precede the first reference to the variable inside a JavaScript statement.

Running a JavaScript Application

JavaScript applications are run when the host document is loaded into a browser that supports the JavaScript language. HTML documents are loaded into Netscape by typing the URL into the Location field or loading a local file using the File/Open File menu options. In some versions of Navigator, the execution of JavaScript code can be turned off. This is normally done through the Options/Security Preference option. When JavaScript is disabled, the browser will ignore all <SCRIPT> containers.

Executing a JavaScript Application

JavaScript is an interpreted language. Interpreted languages are those whose source code is transformed into machine-dependent binary code at runtime by a program known as the interpreter. The JavaScript interpreter is contained within the Netscape browser. This means the JavaScript code will be executed when the browser loads the document into memory. When the document is loaded, any embedded JavaScript code is automatically converted to binary code and executed on the host or client machine. JavaScript code can reside anywhere in an HTML document. If there are multiple blocks of JavaScript code in the same HTML document, each block will be analyzed in order, starting from the topmost block. JavaScript code inside functions or event handlers is executed when these modules are invoked.

Steps

This example creates a simple JavaScript-enhanced HTML document that contains a variable declaration, function declaration, and a JavaScript code segment. The document uses multiple <SCRIPT> containers.

From Navigator 2.0 or Explorer 3.0, use the File/Open menu option to load the HTML document HT0101.HTM into memory. The HTML file is located on the accompanying compact disk (CD). The document displayed in Figure 1-1 will appear on the screen. This document displays the current date.

1. Open your favorite editor and use the following code to create a JavaScript-enabled HTML document.

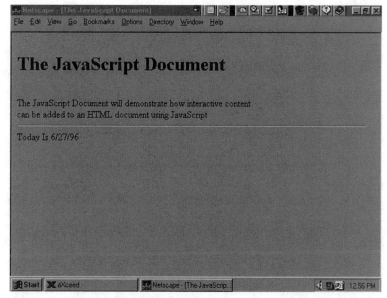

Figure 1-1 The JavaScript document

```
<HTML>
<HEAD> <TITLE> The JavaScript Document </TITLE>
<HEAD>
<BODY>
<BR>
<H1> The JavaScript Document </H1>
<BR>
The JavaScript Document will demonstrate how interactive content <BR>
can be added to an HTML document using JavaScript
<BR>
<HR>
</BODY>
</HTML>
```

2. Inside the <HEAD> container, use the code below to create a JavaScript code fragment. This code defines a function named *popup*. This function displays an alert dialog to the user.

```
<SCRIPT LANGUAGE="JavaScript">
function popup() {
alert("Thanks For Coming");
}
</SCRIPT>
```

3. After the <BODY> tag, use the following code to create a second JavaScript code segment. This code will declare a global variable named *today*. This variable is a Date object, which is assigned the current date and time. This definition means that the today variable will belong to the current Window object.

```
<SCRIPT LANGUAGE="JavaScript">
today = new Date();
</SCRIPT>
```

4. Immediately following the <HR> tag, add a third <SCRIPT> container. This container will reference the today variable defined in Step 3. The JavaScript code will use the Document object's Write method to insert dynamic text into the body of the document. This text displays the current date to the user.

```
<SCRIPT LANGUAGE="JavaScript">
document.write("Today Is " + (today.getMonth()+1) +
             "/" + today.getDate() + "/" + today.getYear());
</SCRIPT>
```

5. Save the JavaScript-enhanced HTML document created in Steps 1–4 as HT0101.HTM.

6. Type the URL of the HT0101.HTM document into the Location field. This field is located at the top of the Netscape browser. The URL will indicate which source code file the browser should load into memory. You can also use the File/Open File menu options to load a local file from disk.

How It Works

When the HTML document is loaded into memory, the interpreter will analyze each JavaScript code block starting with the topmost block. As the browser begins to lay out the document, the first <SCRIPT> container is encountered. Because this code contains a function declaration, no code is executed by the interpreter. Next, the browser comes across the second <SCRIPT> container, created in Step 3. This container declares the global variable today. The memory for the variable is allocated and the object is initialized to the current date and time. Initialization occurs inside the Date constructor. Constructors are functions that initialize JavaScript objects. Next, the third JavaScript code block is analyzed and dynamic text written to the document's body. This code uses the today variable to display today's date.

Comments

The Internet was conceived as a tool that links computers residing in different locations. Networking allows one computer to pass messages and information to another computer. In its original form, the Internet could hardly be considered a success. It was primarily used by the educational and defense communities as a means of transferring files and remotely logging into computers.

In the late 1980s, the foundations of what is now known as the World Wide Web (Web) began to take form. The Web used Internet technology to pass scientific documents between geographically dispersed computers. The Hypertext Transfer Protocol (HTTP) was devised as the underlying communication mechanism for the

Web. HTML was chosen to identify text formatting in documents that would be served over the Web. HTML uses a set of tags to specify formatting requirements for a section of text. The following represents a simple HTML document:

```
<html>
<head> <title>Welcome Message </title> </head>
<body>
<b> Welcome To The Web </b>
</body>
</html>
```

Notice how the text "Welcome To The Web" is contained inside a set of <B> tags. The <B> tags indicate that this text should be represented as bold characters on the screen.

Soon after the creation of the Web, the National Center for Supercomputing Applications (NCSA) began to develop Mosaic, the original Web browser. Mosaic was a GUI tool that allowed users to specify the URL for a particular document. A URL serves to notify the HTTP daemon or Web server which document a client wishes to view. Mosaic was designed to understand HTML tags so the document which was served could be viewed in its proper format.

Following the success of Mosaic, several companies began to develop their own version of a Web browser. One of these companies, Netscape, was founded by the developers who built the Mosaic browser. Since its founding in 1994, Netscape has pioneered many of the advancements in browser technology. Some of these advancements include frames and client-side data persistence. Netscape has also worked to establish a programming environment that adds interactive content to Web pages. Traditionally, HTML documents are static, stateless objects, dependent on server-side processing power. JavaScript represents the first enhancement of this environment. Along with Sun's Java Developers Kit and Microsoft's ActiveX, JavaScript represents the first generation of Web development tools that allow developers to build fully functional Web-based applications.

COMPLEXITY
BEGINNING

1.2   How do I...
Establish an event handler for an HTML input element?

COMPATIBILITY:

Problem

How do I establish a JavaScript event handler that is tied to a particular HTML input element?

Technique

There are two methods for embedding JavaScript code inside an HTML document. How-To 1.1 discussed JavaScript code embedded inside the body of an HTML document. This code is executed when the document is loaded into the browser. Event handlers represent a second mechanism for embedding JavaScript code inside a document. Event handlers are fragments of JavaScript code that are executed whenever a predefined event, like a button click, occurs. Event handlers are tied to specific input elements. This means that a form could possess several instances of a specific input element with different event handlers, one for each element, registered for the same event. Table 1-1 describes all the event handlers that the JavaScript language supports. Individual event handlers are discussed, in detail, in Chapter 8, "Form Elements," Chapter 9, "Event Handling," and Chapter 10, "Form Methods."

EVENT HANDLER	INVOKED WHEN
onBlur	User removes input focus from an input element
onClick	User clicks on a form element or link
onChange	User changes the value property of a text, textarea, or selected element
onFocus	User moves input focus to an input element
onLoad	User loads a document in a Web browser
onMouseOver	Mouse pointer is positioned over a link or anchor
onSelected	User selects a form element's input field
onSubmit	Form is submitted to the HTTP server
onUnload	A document is unloaded from a Web browser

Table 1-1 JavaScript event handlers

Event handlers are registered inside the <INPUT> tag. The handler is linked to a specific event occurring within the input element. The standard format for registering an event handler is:

```
eventHandler="JavaScript Code"
```

Notice that an event handler contains a specific reference to the event. It also contains a quoted string which contains a JavaScript statement that will be executed when the event occurs. Because the event handler is linked to a specific input object, the *this* variable can be used, inside the handler, to reference the host input element. This variable can be used as a shortcut for accessing the host object's properties.

The JavaScript code that comprises an event handler can contain multiple statements separated by a semicolon (;). Typically, these statements will invoke functions, defined elsewhere in the document. The syntax for establishing an onClick event handler, tied to the user clicking a push button, would look like this:

```
<input type="button" value="Click Me" onClick="alert('Here')">
```

In addition to input elements, event handlers can be registered for other objects such as a form or hypertext link. Not all event handlers apply to the entire set of input elements. Table 1-2 shows which event handlers apply to each JavaScript object type.

EVENT HANDLER	TEXTFIELD	TEXTAREA	SELECT	BUTTON	LINK	RESET	SUBMIT	CHECKBOX	WINDOW	FORM
onBlur	X	X	X							
onClick				X	X	X	X	X		
onChange	X	X	X							
onFocus	X	X	X							
onLoad									X	
onMouseOver					X					
onSelected										
onSubmit							X			X
onUnload									X	

Table 1-2 Event handler/object matrix

Steps

This example creates a document that contains several event handlers. Event handlers are established for a button, submit, and link object. This code is meant as a sampling of the various types of event handlers. Each handler displays an alert dialog indicating that the event handler has been invoked.

From Navigator 2.0 or Explorer 3.0, use the File/Open menu option to load HT0102.HTM into memory. Click on the Click Me button, and the alert dialog in Figure 1-2 will appear on the screen. Click on the OK button to dismiss the dialog from the screen. Move your mouse over the top of the Click On Me link. An alert dialog displays with the message You Are Over A Link. Activate the submit button and the alert You Submitted A Form displays.

1. Open an editor and create an HTML input form based on the objects specified in Table 1-2.

```
<html>
<head> <title> The Event Handler Document </title>
</head>
<body>
<form name="ErrorHandler" onSubmit="window.alert('You Submitted A Form')">
<input type="button" name="click" value="Click Me"
 onClick="youClick()">
<input type="submit">
<br>
```

continued on next page

continued from previous page

```
<input type="text" name="change"
 onChange="window.alert('You Have Changed The Text Field')">
<br>
</form>
<a href="test.htm" onMouseOver="window.alert('You Are Over A Link')">
Click On Me </a>
</body>
</html>
```

2. Create the JavaScript function youClick, which will display an alert dialog indicating that a button has been clicked. The youClick method will be called from the Click button's onClick event handler.

```
<script language="JavaScript">
<!-- Support For Old Browsers
function youClick() {
window.alert("You Clicked A Button");
}
<!-- Support For Old Browser -->
</script>
```

3. Save the HTML input form under the name EventHandler.HTM.

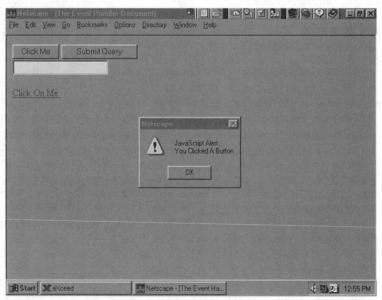

Figure 1-2 The EventHandler form following the activation of the Click Me button

How It Works

This example demonstrates how to set up an event handler. The event handlers will be registered when the EventHandler form is loaded into the browser. Event handlers are registered by code located inside the <INPUT> tag used to create an input element. As a user interacts with the form, event handlers will be "kicked off" when an event occurs that has a registered handler.

Comments

Event handlers are a common part of many GUI toolkits. In Motif, the *XtAppAddCallback* function is used to register event handlers, known as callbacks, for a particular widget. With the Microsoft Windows Software Developer's Kit (SDK), a window or dialog procedure is invoked when an event occurs. The *message*, *wParam*, and *lParam* parameters, which are passed to window and dialog procedures, indicate the type of event that occurred. In Java, events result in a call to the eventHandler method, which belongs to the component superclass. Because most graphical objects inherit from the component class, this method is the central point for determining the type of event that occurred.

COMPLEXITY:
BEGINNING

1.3 How do I...
Receive notification of an error in the JavaScript code?

COMPATIBILITY:

Question

In JavaScript, as in most programming languages, there is a pre-defined set of programming rules, also known as syntax, which I must follow. How will I be notified when I make a JavaScript syntax error?

Technique

In compiled languages, syntax errors are detected by the compiler during the process when the source code is converted into an executable. This means that developers have the opportunity to fix syntax errors before the application is run.

Because JavaScript is an interpreted language, there is no compilation process to detect syntax errors before a document is loaded into a browser.

Types of Errors

There are two types of errors which may be found in JavaScript code: syntax errors and runtime errors. Syntax errors normally result from the program violating a JavaScript rule. These errors are detected by the interpreter when the document is loaded into memory. Syntax errors in functions and event handlers will also be detected during the document load process.

Runtime errors are located during normal program execution. These errors typically result from problems with how an object is used. The object may hold the wrong type of data or contain an incomplete object type specification. Table 1-3 shows some common syntax and runtime errors.

ERROR	FOUND DURING	POTENTIAL PROBLEM
object is not defined	Runtime	An attempt was made to access an invalid property. Either the variable assigned a value of a different type or property does not exist in the current object type definition. Verify the type of object which is accessing the invalid property. If the object type is correct, verify that you are trying to access a valid property for this object type.
attribute cannot be set	Runtime	Program tried to assign a value to an undeclared by assignment variable. Precede the variable with the "var" keyword to declare the variable.
object has no properties	Runtime	Could result from trying to access a member function from a variable that is not an object. This may be caused by passing an unexpected type object to a function.
object is not a function	Runtime	Input NAME attribute matches a function name.
object is not a numeric	Runtime	Used a non-numeric variable inside a mathematical literal operation.
missing variable name	Document Load	Attempted to use an improper variable name.
syntax error	Document Load	Generic, catch-all error message.
missing function name	Document Load	Attempted to execute a function that has not been declared.
missing formal parameter	Document Load	Did not close a parameter list with a) character.
missing operator in	Document Load	String not enclosed inside double quotes.
expression		Function not enclosed inside parentheses.

Table 1-3 Common JavaScript errors

Error Notification

When an error is detected, the browser will display an error dialog. Error dialogs contain the following information: the type of error which occurred, the source code line where the error is located, the approximate location of the error within the statement, and a brief description of the rule that was violated. Error dialogs are application modal. You must click on the OK button to dismiss the error dialog.

Event Handler Errors

The problem is that errors made when setting up event handlers, such as misspelling the name of the event which invokes the handler, will be ignored by the JavaScript interpreter. The reason why these errors are not detected is because the error handler straddles the fence between HTML and JavaScript. Although they are part of the JavaScript language, they are not part of the interpreter's syntax check. Similar to the way browsers ignore tags which they do not understand, a browser will simply ignore an event handler which it does not recognize or which is not appropriate for a particular input element.

Steps

This example will create a document that contains a seeded syntax error. This error will be detected by the JavaScript interpreter when the document is loaded into the browser.

From Navigator 2.0 or Explorer 3.0, use the File/Open menu option to load HT0103.HTM into memory. Notice the error dialog in Figure 1-3 appear on the screen. This dialog indicates that a syntax error has occurred because of incorrect usage of the string concatenation operator (+).

1. Open an editor and create an HTML document like the one below. The Compute Salary button contains an event handler which calls the *computeRaise* function. This function is defined in Step 2. This button also contains an invalid event handler.

```
<html>
<head><title> The Error Document </title>
</head>
<body>
<br>
<form>
Old Salary <input type="text" name="salary"> <br>
Raise Percentage <input type="text" name="raise"> <br>
<input type="button" name="ComputeSalary" value="Compute Salary"
onLoad="window.alert('Here')"
onClick="computeRaise(form.salary.value, form.raise.value)">
</form>
</body>
</html>
```

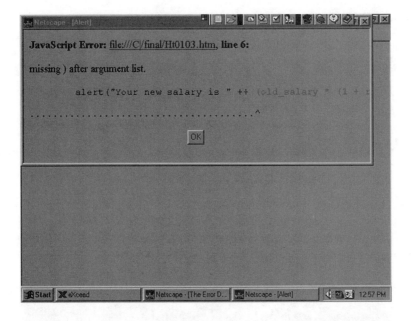

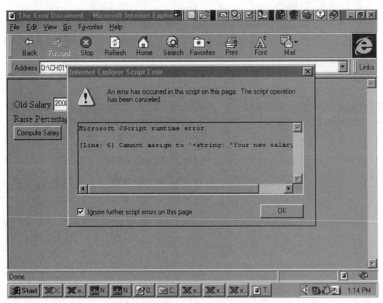

Figure 1-3 A JavaScript syntax error alert dialog

2. Inside the <HEAD> container, use the following code to create the computeRaise function. This function contains a seeded JavaScript syntax error because the string concatenation binary operator (+) is not in the middle of two operands.

```
<SCRIPT LANGUAGE="JavaScript">
function computeRaise(old_salary, raise)
{
alert("Your new salary is " +++++++ (old_salary * (1 + raise)));
}
</SCRIPT>
```

3. Store the document as HT0103.HTM.

How It Works

When HT0103.HTM is loaded into the browser, it is checked for syntax. This check locates a syntax error inside the computeRaise function. This error stems from an incorrect use of the string concatenation operator. The error checking does not check the correctness of event handler definitions. This is why the event handler syntax error is not caught by the JavaScript interpreter. This error is the result of creating an improper event handler for a Button object. The interpreter is designed to catch JavaScript syntax errors as opposed to errors in the HTML document. Because the error handlers are attributes of the HTML input elements, the interpreter does not analyze this part of the code. The browsers were implemented to ignore labels and attributes that they do not recognize. This is their way of allowing vendors to add new labels while still making these enhanced documents viewable from any browser.

When the JavaScript syntax error is introduced in Step 5, the browser notifies the user of the error when the document is loaded into memory. The interpreter detects the error and displays an Alert dialog. The user is required to activate the OK button on the Error dialog to acknowledge that he or she has seen the error. If multiple Errors had been introduced, the interpreter would have displayed multiple Alert dialogs, one for each syntax error, to the user.

Comments

Web developers should implement a process of Quality Assurance (QA) for their JavaScript-enhanced HTML documents. In the past, QA for HTML documents could be as simple as loading the document into a browser and checking its aesthetic effect. However, JavaScript is a programming language and will require a more rigorous question and answer process.

COMPLEXITY:
BEGINNING

1.4 How do I...
Make older browsers ignore JavaScript code?

COMPATIBILITY:

Question

Because older browers don't support JavaScript, I would like to use JavaScript in non-critical areas, such as scrolling the status bar message, of my HTML documents. How can I make these older browsers ignore any JavaScript code that I add to my HTML document?

Technique

Because JavaScript was designed to be embedded inside an HTML document, its designer had to devise a way to allow JavaScript-enhanced documents to be properly viewed using older browsers. Older browsers were designed to read ASCII text documents, with embedded HTML tags, and display the properly formatted text in the browser's document viewing area. Because JavaScript code is ASCII text, like the HTML document, the older browsers would treat the JavaScript code like the rest of the document, by simply displaying it in the document viewing area. Figure 1-4 demonstrates how older browsers react to the following JavaScript code:

```
<html>
<head> <title> The Navigator Document </title> <head>
<body>
<script language="JavaScript">
document.write("You Are Using <b>" + navigator.appName
                              + " </b> Version <b>"
                              + navigator.appVersion
                              + "</b> To View This Document");
</script>
<br>
<h1> The Navigator Document </h1>
<br>
The Navigator Document will demonstrate how to get information about the
web browser <br>
being used to view this HTML document.
</body>
</html>
```

Notice how the JavaScript code is treated like any other text contained within the document.

Another constraint placed on the designers of JavaScript was that they had to use an existing capability in the older browsers to hide the JavaScript code. As these browsers were already in the field, their capabilities were established. The designers could not specify how another browser, which does not support JavaScript, should be implemented to ignore the text inside the <SCRIPT> tags.

The only ASCII text in an HTML document that older browsers are designed to ignore is comments. Comments are indicated by their enclosure inside a pair of HTML comment tags. A standard HTML comment would look like this:

```
<!-- Comments -->
```

In HTML 1, comments must be contained on a single line. However, HTML 2 and 3 support multi-line comments. JavaScript's designers used this enhancement to their advantage by recommending that all JavaScript code be embedded inside HTML comments. The only JavaScript-related code to remain outside the comment block is the <SCRIPT> tags used to indicate the beginning and ending of the JavaScript code in an HTML document. The <SCRIPT> tag can be excluded from the comment block because all browsers were implemented to ignore tags that they do not understand.

```
<script>
<!-- Hide From Older Browers
document.write("You Are Using <b>" + navigator.appName
                            + " </b> Version <b>"
                            + navigator.appVersion
                            + "</b> To View This Document");
<!-- Ending Hiding -->
</script>
```

Because JavaScript should be included inside HTML documents, Netscape Navigator version 2.0 was implemented to ignore any HTML comments contained with the <SCRIPT> tags. By using HTML comments, developers can be assured that their code will provide backwards compatibility with older browsers while allowing newer browsers to interpret and execute JavaScript code.

> **NOTE**
> You must include both the beginning (<!--) and ending (-->) comment tags, or your JavaScript code will not be hidden. Furthermore, if you do not include, for a second time, the beginning tag (<!--) on the same line as the ending indicator (-->), Netscape will issue a JavaScript error.

Why Portability Is a Problem

One of the key issues in software development is to develop portable code that can be run on a large number of platforms and environments. Portability is a key issue because vendors provide additional capabilities with their implementation of a particular technology. These capabilities are meant to distinguish that product from its competitors in the marketplace. The classic example of this phenomenon is the numerous versions of the UNIX operating system.

Portability problems are also caused by new versions of a product. Newer versions typically contain enhanced functionality that is not present in the older version of the software. Because migration between versions is a gradual process, multiple versions of a product must be supported for a short period of time.

Recently, portability has become an issue for the Web. As vendors implement different capabilities into their Web browser products in an attempt to distinguish their products in the marketplace, the need for Web standards has arisen. Standards are a way of reducing variability by ensuring that vendors implement a core set of functionality.

The development of the JavaScript language represents Netscape's attempt to discriminate its product by providing client-side interactive content to the Web. Although Netscape is currently trying to incorporate JavaScript into the work of several Web-oriented standards bodies, at the time of publishing, only the Navigator 2.0 browser was JavaScript-friendly.

Steps

The following example modifies HT0101.HTM, created in How-To 1.1, for the purpose of making this document portable to older browsers.

From a browser other than Navigator 2.0 or Explorer 3.0, load HT0101.HTM into memory. The document in Figure 1-4 displays on the screen. Make the following modifications to this document. Reload this document into the browser. The screen now changes to the document in Figure 1-5.

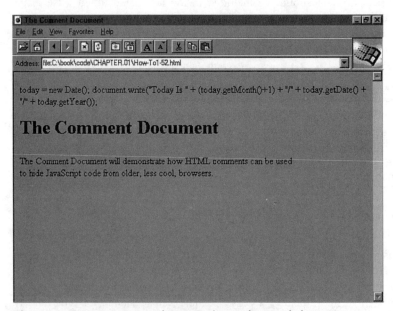

Figure 1-4 Uncommented JavaScript-enhanced document displayed using the Microsoft Explorer browser

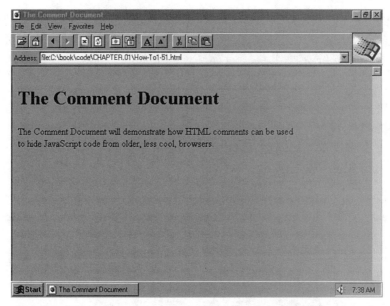

Figure 1-5 Commented JavaScript-enhanced document displayed using the Microsoft Explorer browser

This example will make modifications to the HT0101.HTM document. Add HTML comments inside the <SCRIPT> tags. This causes older browsers to ignore the JavaScript code.

```
<script language="JavaScript">
<!-- Begin Hiding
today = new Date();
document.write("Today Is " + (today.getMonth()+1) +
              "/" + today.getDate() + "/" + today.getYear());
<!-- Ending Hiding -->
</script>
```

UNCOMMENTED JAVASCRIPT CODE

If you have access to a browser other than Netscape Navigator 2.0, save the document as Comment.HTM and minimize the editor on the screen. Pull up the older browser and open the Comment.HTM file. Notice how the older browser lays out the top of the document where the JavaScript code is stored. The JavaScript code appears at the top of the document.

How It Works

Other browsers are designed to ignore ASCII text contained within HTML comments. This allows browsers that are not JavaScript-friendly to properly display a JavaScript-enhanced document. Navigator is designed to ignore HTML comments within <SCRIPT> tags.

Comment

JavaScript code that is not encased inside an HTML comment can be run without incident on JavaScript-friendly browsers. Despite this fact, you should make every effort to place HTML comment indicators around your JavaScript code. Making your HTML document portable requires a little extra effort on your part; however, it makes a significant difference to users that are not on the "bleeding edge" of technology.

COMPLEXITY:
BEGINNING

1.5 How do I...
Access JavaScript objects without altering existing HTML documents?

COMPATIBILITY:

Problem

Because Web browsers automatically instantiate JavaScript objects to hold information about a wide variety of browser-related objects, how can I access their properties and methods without altering an existing HTML document?

Technique

A URL is used to specify the location of a file–usually an HTML document or ASCII text file–that a user wishes to access. The standard format for a URL is

```
tag://host.domain[:port]/path/filename
```

The URL's prefix, known as a scheme or tag, is used to identify the type of interaction the browser will have with the server. Table 1-4 describes the most common URL tags.

URL TAG	DESCRIPTION
file	Standard file
http	HTML document

URL TAG	DESCRIPTION
news	Usenet newsgroup
gopher	Gopher server
telnet	Telnet session
wais	Wide Area Information Server

Table 1-4 Common URL tags

In order to support the JavaScript environment, Netscape created a new tag, known as mocha. The mocha tag can be used to access the methods and properties of JavaScript objects without altering an existing HTML document. It can also be used to execute a syntactically correct JavaScript expression. This capability exists because the mocha tag is being used to send a JavaScript expression to the interpreter for execution. Like JavaScript expressions embedded inside an HTML document, the interpreter will flag any syntax errors and display them to the user. An example of a URL that uses the mocha tag and JavaScript to invoke the current window's alert method is

```
mocha:window.alert("Hello World!");
```

As you will learn in How-To 2.2, there are two different implementations of alert dialogs. One implementation, like the Windows 95 version of Netscape 2.0, supports modal alert dialogs, while other implementations, like the Solaris 2.4 version of Netscape 2.0, have implemented modeless alert dialogs. You can use the mocha tag to identify the modality of the alert dialogs displayed using your favorite JavaScript-friendly browser.

A second use of the mocha tag is to reference the properties of the JavaScript objects automatically created when a document is loaded. For example, if you are curious about the date a page loaded from another site was last modified, you can see the date by entering this URL

```
mocha:document.lastModified;
```

The date when this document was last modified now appears on the screen. In addition to accessing the properties and methods of the predefined Web objects, mocha can also be used to invoke JavaScript functions embedded in the current document. By selecting the Document Source option from Navigator's View menu, you have the ability to look at the HTML and JavaScript code used to create the current document. Any JavaScript function, including those that require parameters, can be invoked using the mocha tag. This capability allows you to see the output of JavaScript functions given a canned parameter list.

The URL-Based Calculator

Because the mocha tag will allow users to execute syntactically correct JavaScript statements, JavaScript-knowledgeable users can take advantage of this capability to have access to a crude URL-based calculator. As you will see in Chapter 5, JavaScript implements a rich set of mathematical operators and functions. These operators can be combined to form complex mathematical functions. Through the mocha tag, power users have realtime access to these functions without the need to create an HTML document. The following URL will display the value 20 in the browser's viewing area:

```
mocha:((10*1.5) + 51.1
```

Steps

1. Bring up Navigator 2.0 browser.

2. Type the following URL into the Location text field and see the name of your browser appear in the viewing area.

```
mocha:navigator.appName
```

3. Type the following URL into the Location text field and see the answer, 11, appear in the viewing area.

```
mocha:33/3
```

4. Type the following URL into the Location text field, and an error dialog will display on the screen. The error results from the mocha URL attempting to execute an invalid JavaScript expression.

```
mocha:*10
```

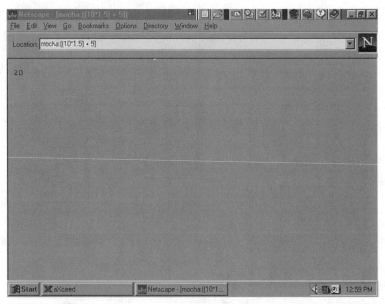

Figure 1-6 Output of a JavaScript expression invoked from a mocha-tagged URL

5. Open an editor and create an HTML document like the one below.

```
<html>
<head><title> The Mocha Document </title>
</head>
<body>
<form>
Old Salary <input type="text" name="salary"> <br>
Raise Percentage <input type="text" name="raise"> <br>
<input type="button" name="ComputeSalary" value="Compute Salary"
onClick="computeRaise(form.salary.value, form.raise.value)">
</form>
</body>
</html>
```

6. Create the function *computeRaise,* which will display the new salary based on two input parameters, the old salary and the raise percentage.

```
<script language="JavaScript">
<!-- Hide
function computeRaise(old_salary, raise)
{
alert("Your new salary is " + (old_salary * (1 + raise)));
}
<!-- End Hide -->
</script>
```

7. Store the document as HT0105.HTM.

8. Load HT0105.HTM into your open Netscape browser.

9. Type the following URL into the Location text field and see an alert dialog with the message, Your new salary is 13200, pop up on the screen.

```
mocha:computeRaise(12000,.1)
```

How It Works

The mocha tag is used to execute JavaScript expressions without having to develop a JavaScript application. This tag is also used to execute a JavaScript function inside the loaded HTML document. The JavaScript interpreter is used to execute expressions following the mocha tag. If the expression contains a syntax error, an error dialog is displayed to the user.

Comments

The mocha tag is very helpful in debugging JavaScript code!

COMPLEXITY:
BEGINNING

1.6 How do I...
Get information about the Web browser being used?

COMPATIBILITY:

In the future, JavaScript will be supported by a large number of Web browsers. How can I get information, such as browser name and version, about the Web browser being used to display my JavaScript-enhanced document?

Technique

As you learned in How-To 1.1, JavaScript automatically instantiates a set of objects when an HTML document is loaded into memory. One of these objects, known as the Navigator object, contains information about the Web browser being used to view the JavaScript-enhanced document. Figure 1-7 shows the properties belonging to the Navigator object. Although the Navigator object is named after the Netscape browser (which is only natural because Netscape created JavaScript and currently has the only JavaScript-friendly browser on the market), this object will be used to hold information for any browser that supports the JavaScript language.

The Navigator properties are read-only. This means that any attempt to change their values will result in an error message, generated when you try to set the *appName* property, similar to, You are using Netscape cannot set by assignment.

Navigator

PROPERTIES	METHODS	EVENT HANDLERS
appCodeName	NONE	NONE
appName		
appVersion		
userAgent		

Figure 1-7 The Navigator object

The appName property contains the browser's name. For Navigator 2.0, set appName to Netscape, while for Explorer 3.0, set appName to Microsoft Internet Explorer As other browsers start to support JavaScript, appName will be set to a browser-specific label.

The *appVersion* property holds two important pieces of information: the browser version and the operating system that the browser is running under. For the Windows 95 version of Navigator, this property is set to 2.0 (Win95,1). The *appCode* property contains the code name of the browser (for example, "mozilla"), and the *userAgent* property contains a browser's user agent header, a concatenation of the appName, appVersion, and appCode properties.

Steps

This example will display a page that has the browser information displayed as part of the document's content.

From Navigator 2.0 or Explorer 3.0, use the File/Open menu option to load HT0106.HTM into memory. The document in Figure 1-8 will appear on the screen.

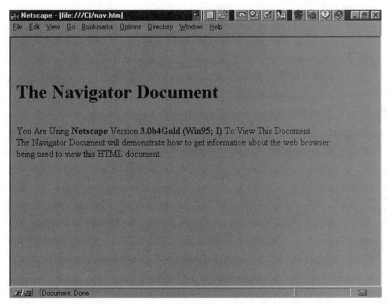

Figure 1-8 The Navigator document when viewed with Navigator

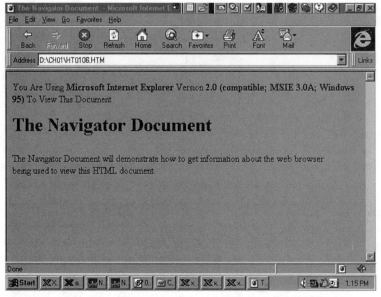

Figure 1-9 The Navigator document when viewed within Explorer

1. Open an editor and use the following HTML code to begin the creation of an HTML document.

```
<html>
<head> <title> The Navigator Document </title> </head>
<body>
<br>
<h1> The Navigator Document </h1>
<br>
The Navigator Document will demonstrate how to get information about the
web browser <br>
being used to view this HTML document.
</body>
</html>
```

2. Add the following JavaScript code underneath the <BODY> tag. This code displays the browser information to the user inside a dynamic HTML statement.

```
<script language="JavaScript">
<!-- Hide From Older Browers
document.write("You Are Using <b>" + navigator.appName
                                + " </b> Version <b>"
                                + navigator.appVersion
                                + "</b> To View This Document");
<!-- Ending Hiding -->
</script>
```

3. Save the HTML document under the name HT0106.HTM.

How This Works

As we learned in How-To 1.1, the browser lays out documents in a sequential, top-down fashion. Therefore, when the Navigator document is loaded in Netscape, the browser sets the document's title and then begins to lay out the body of the document. The first body of the document is a JavaScript expression that dynamically creates text, using the current document's Write method, to display the browser's name and version. To gain access to the browser's information, the appName and appVersion properties of the Navigator object are referenced. As the Navigator object has been created prior to the browser analyzing this part of the document, the browser's information is available to the JavaScript expression. Notice how the string concatenation operator (+) is used to combine a string literal and the Navigator's properties, which are also strings. String concatenation is discussed in Chapter 5.

Comments

As more browsers adopt the JavaScript language, the Navigator object will be the key to handling the unique capabilities of certain browsers. Already, in Netscape 3.0, the Navigator object can be used to interface with Java applets only if the browser version equals 3.0. This condition is needed because Navigator 3.0 is the only browser that supports LiveConnect, the JavaScript/Java integration tool. LiveConnect is discussed in Chapter 16, "LiveConnnect."

CHAPTER 2
COMMUNICATING WITH THE USER

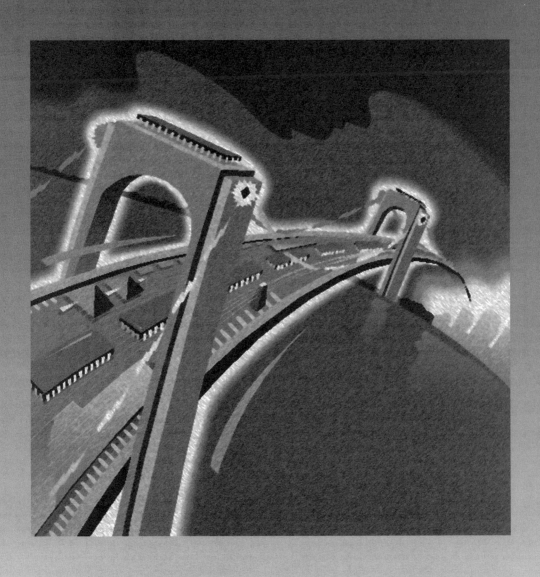

COMMUNICATING WITH THE USER

How do I...

2.1 **Display a message in the browser's status bar?**

2.2 **Alert the user when a problem occurs?**

2.3 **Confirm the user's desire to initiate an action?**

2.4 **Prompt the user to enter a value?**

An effective user interface should provide informative feedback about user actions. If the user submits a form without entering data into all mandatory fields, the form validation function must be able to detect the error and communicate to the user the type of error that occurred. This chapter will discuss the built-in mechanisms JavaScript provides to allow a Hypertext Markup Language (HTML) document to communicate with the user. These built-in mechanisms allow JavaScript to display messages to a user in either the World Wide Web (Web) browser's status bar or a popup dialog.

2.1 Display a message in the browser's status bar

During the loading of an HTML document, you probably have noticed a series of status messages displayed in the lower-left corner of the Web browser. The area where these status messages are displayed is the status bar. JavaScript gives application developers the ability to display default and transient messages inside the Web browser's status bar. This How-To will demonstrate how to use the status bar to display context-sensitive Help messages to the user. The How-To will also show you how to set up a default message that will be visible inside the status bar when transient messages, such as a context-sensitive Help messages, are not being displayed.

2.2   Alert the user when a problem occurs

Have you ever been watching your favorite television show when the announcer comes on and says, "We interrupt our regularly scheduled broadcast to bring you this late-breaking news story"? After the anchor relays the news story to the audience, the announcer comes back on and says, "And now back to the program." This interaction demonstrates a real-world example of how television networks alert the general public whenever a problem occurs anywhere in the world. This How-To will show you how to display an Alert dialog that will notify users of late-breaking problems that occur during their interactions with an input form.

2.3   Confirm the user's desire to initiate an action

Computer programs are developed to automate the decision-making process. Occasionally, a problem arises that requires an operator to make a manual decision. This How-To will demonstrate how to display a Confirm dialog that will verify the user's desire to initiate an action. Confirm dialogs can be used to let the user make a go/no-go decision.

2.4   Prompt the user to enter a value

This How-To will show you how to pop up a prompt dialog for the purpose of acquiring additional information from the users. Additional information may be required in order for a JavaScript function to proceed with data manipulation.

COMPLEXITY
BEGINNING

2.1   How do I...
Display a message in the browser's status bar?

COMPATIBILITY:

Problem

I would like to display context-sensitive Help messages in the browser's status bar. How can I do this?

Technique

The status bar is the long, thin text area located at the bottom of the Web browser's client window. Figure 2-1 shows where the status bar is located on the screen.

The purpose of the status bar is to provide an area where transient messages can be displayed to the user. Transient messages are low-priority, informative messages that reside in the status bar for a short period of time. You probably have seen the status bar used to display percentage-complete messages during the loading of an HTML document, or the uniform resource locator (URL) of a hypertext link when the mouse is positioned over it. Through JavaScript, application developers have access to the status bar as an area where context-sensitive Help messages can be displayed to the user.

As you will recall from Chapter 1, "Adding Interactive Content to a Web Page," the JavaScript environment automatically creates objects in memory to hold information about important browser objects. One such object, the Window object, represents the Web browser's current window. All browser-related objects are aggregates of the Window object. Figure 2-2 shows the properties that belong to the Window object.

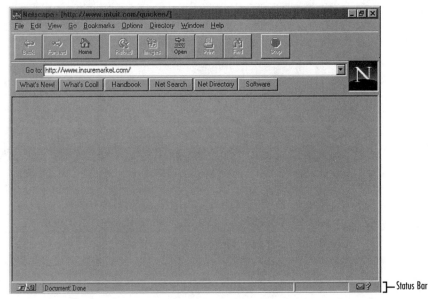

Figure 2-1 The browser's status bar

```
                        Window

  PROPERTIES           METHODS              EVENT HANDLERS

  defaultStatus        alert("msg");        onLoad()
  frames[x]            close();             onUnload()
  parent               confirm("msg");
  self                 open(URL, "name",
  status                 "options");
  top                  prompt("msg","default");
  window               setTimeOut("expire",
                         time);
                       clearTimeOut(ID);
```

Figure 2-2 The Window object

The browser's status bar is set by assigning a value to the window's status property. When a new value is assigned to the status property, that value is immediately displayed inside the status bar. An existing status message will be displaced when the status property is assigned a new value. An example of how to display the message, Please Enter Your Full Name (Last, First, MI), in the status bar is

```
window.status='Please Enter Your Full Name (Last, First, MI)';
```

Because the JavaScript environment automatically instantiates the Web browser's window, the reference to the Window object is optional. The following code performs exactly the same as the previous example.

```
status='Please Enter Your Full Name (Last, First, MI)';
```

> **NOTE**
>
> An important point to remember about setting the status bar message is that a `true` value must be returned if the status property is set inside an `onMouseOver` event handler. If a `true` value is not returned, the status message will not display.

One important consideration when using the status bar is the restrictions a terminal places on message length. The status bar is a single-line text area with no scrolling capabilities. Therefore, messages should be designed to contain less than 80 characters. If a message exceeds the status bar's length, the Web browser will display as many characters as can be seen in the status bar.

Because the status message is enclosed by either single or double quotes, the escape character ('\') must be used to display an embedded single or double quote inside the status message. The escape character ('\') is used in combination with another character to represent a special character inside a string. Because quotes are used to indicate the end of a string, an embedded quote would be viewed by the JavaScript interpreter as the string termination character. If a quote is preceded by an escape character, the interpreter recognizes the special character as a quote instead of a string termination character. The following code will display the status message Please Select Your Overall Evaluation Of Waite's Book:

```
window.status='Please Select Your Overall Evaluation Of Waite\'s Book';
```

The single quote (\') and double quote (\") characters are the only special characters that can be used in status bar messages. Because the status bar is a single-line display, the status property cannot support messages that use the new-line (\n) or return (\r) special characters.

The Default Status Message

The current window's *defaultStatus* property is used to set up a default status message that will be displayed whenever the status bar is empty. Because status messages are transient or temporary in nature, there will be periods when the status bar will be empty. To fill the void, a value can be assigned to the window's defaultStatus property. If no status messages have been established, the defaultStatus message will be displayed in the status bar. An important point to remember is that status messages take precedence over defaultStatus messages. Default messages are immediately displaced when a status message is established. An example of how to set the message, Thank You For Reading The JAVASCRIPT HOW-TO Book, as a default message is:

```
window.defaultStatus='Thank You For Reading The JAVASCRIPT HOW-TO Book';
```

> **NOTE**
>
> Because of a bug in Netscape Navigator, the defaultStatus message may not be displayed on the screen. This problem appears inside the Windows 95 version of Navigator 2.X. The problem does not appear inside some of the UNIX versions of Navigator.

Steps

This example will construct a simple HTML input form that will capture reader reaction to the *JavaScript How-To* book. The feedback form will be submitted to the publisher, Waite Group Press, for consideration in the next release of this work. This form uses status messages, in addition to field labels, to help users gain a better understanding of the type of information they are being asked to provide.

From Navigator 2.0 or Explorer 3.0, use the File/Open File menu option to load HT0201.HTM into memory. The form shown in Figure 2-3 will appear. Click inside the Name text field, and the Help message, Please Enter Your Full Name (Last, First, MI), will appear as the status bar message. Pull down the Rating selection choice list, and the Help message Please Select Your Overall Evaluation Of Waite's Book now appears as the status bar message. Now move the mouse over the Waite Group Press Home Page. The status message now displays This Is The Publisher Of The Book.

> **NOTE**
>
> The following description will apply if you are viewing this example inside a Navigator version that does not contain the defaultStatus bug.

When the HT0201.HTM document is loaded into the Web browser, the onLoad event handler is activated, establishing a default status message for the browser. The default message will remain displayed even when another document, other than the one that created the default message, is displayed in the browser. If no other message is displayed in the status bar, then the Web browser will automatically show the default message. As the user clicks inside one of the text fields or pulls down the select list, the *onFocus* event handler, which displays the Help message for the appropriate element, is activated. Because the status message is dependent on the element that currently has the input focus, a Help message for each input element can be established. When the focus is removed from the element, the Help message is removed, and the default message fills the vacancy left inside the status bar.

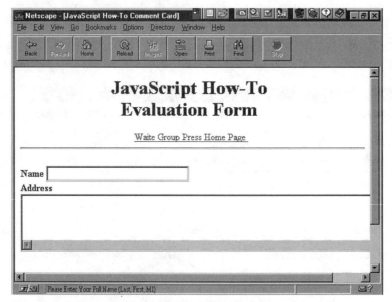

Figure 2-3 The status bar form

1. Using your favorite editor, create a new JavaScript-enhanced document using the following HTML code.

```
<HTML>
<HEAD> <TITLE> JavaScript How-To Comment Card </TITLE> </HEAD>
<BODY BGCOLOR=#FFFFFF>
<CENTER> <H1> JavaScript How-To <br> Evaluation Form </H1>
<A HREF="test.htm"> Waite Group Press Home Page </A>
</CENTER>
<HR>
<FORM NAME="StatusBar">
<B> Name </B>
<INPUT TYPE="text" NAME="FullName" SIZE=30>
<BR>
<B> Address </B>
<TEXTAREA NAME="Address" ROWS=4 COLS=80>
</TEXTAREA>
<BR> <BR>
<B> Overall Evaluation </B>
<SELECT NAME="Rating">
<OPTION SELECTED> Excellent, Brain Food!!!
<OPTION> OK, Average, The Norm, Nuttin' Special
<OPTION> Terrible, Where's The Beef?
</SELECT>
<BR> <BR>
<CENTER>
<INPUT TYPE="reset" VALUE="Clear Comments">
<INPUT TYPE="submit" VALUE="Submit Comments">
</FORM>
</BODY>
</HTML>
```

2. Inside the <HEAD> container, use the following code to create a <SCRIPT> container.

```
<SCRIPT LANGUAGE="JavaScript">
<!-- Hide JavaScript Code From Older Browsers
/* *********************************************************
 *    Function -  setHelp
 *    Parameter - message :          Message String That Will Be
                                     Displayed Inside The Browser's
 *                                   Status Bar
 *    Description -                  This Function Is Used To Set
 *                                   Browser's Status Bar Message
 * ********************************************************* */
function setHelp(message) {
    status = message;
}
<!-- End Hiding -->
</SCRIPT>
```

3. Add the onLoad event handler to the <BODY> tag. The onLoad event handler will assign the default message, Thank You For Reading The JAVASCRIPT HOW-TO Book, to the current window's defaultStatus property.

```
<BODY BGCOLOR=#FFFFFF
onLoad="window.defaultStatus='Thank You For Reading The JAVASCRIPT ⇐
HOW-TO Book';">
```

4. Add the onFocus event handler to the *FullName* text element. The onFocus event handler will assign the Help message, Please Enter Your Full Name (Last, First, MI), to the current window's status property whenever the FullName element receives the input focus.

```
<INPUT TYPE="text" NAME=FullName SIZE=30
onFocus="setHelp('Please Enter Your Full Name (Last, First, MI)')">
```

5. Add the onFocus event handler to the Address textarea element. The onFocus event handler will assign the help message, Please Enter Your Home Address, to the current window's status property whenever the Address element receives the input focus.

```
TEXTAREA NAME-Address ROWS-4 COLS-80
onFocus="window.status='Please Enter Your Home Address';">
```

6. Add the onFocus event handler to the Rating select element. The onFocus event handler will assign the Help message, Please Select Your Overall Evaluation Of Waite's Book, to the current window's status property whenever the Rating element receives the input focus.

```
<SELECT NAME="Rating"
onFocus="setHelp('Please Select Your Overall Evaluation Of Waite\'s ⇐
Book');">
```

```
<A HREF="test.htm"
onMouseOver="status='This Is The Publisher Of The Book'; return true;"> ⇐
Waite Group Press Home Page </A>
```

7. Save the HTML input form under the name HT0201.HTM. In Navigator, use the File/Open File menu option to execute the JavaScript application by loading HT0201.HTM into the browser.

How It Works

The Window object's status property is used to set up context-sensitive Help messages for the reader feedback form. This property is set inside event handlers invoked when the user is getting ready to change an input's VALUE attribute. When the status property is set, the new message displaces the old message inside the browser's status bar.

Comments

Although each input element can be preceded with a one- or two-word label, users may require additional information to understand the nature of the data they are being asked to provide. Because of real estate restrictions and to prevent bombarding the user with a wealth of information, element labels should remain small but effective methods for communicating with the user. By augmenting the information contained in the element label with a context-sensitive Help message, the probability of extracting accurate, complete information from the user will increase.

COMPLEXITY
BEGINNING

2.2   How do I...
Alert the user when a problem occurs?

COMPATIBILITY: NAVIGATOR 2.X   NAVIGATOR 3.X

Problem

Many user input forms have built-in functional and data dependencies (also known as business rules) that define a set of interactive rules a user must follow. When a problem arises, such as the user leaving a mandatory field blank, how do I notify the user that a problem has occurred?

Technique

JavaScript provides an Alert dialog that can be used to warn a user that an error condition exists. The Alert dialog is displayed upon a call to the Window object's alert method. This method takes a single parameter, specifying the message that will be contained inside the dialog. Messages can take the form of strings, numbers, dates, object properties, or a combination of these data types. An example call to the Alert method is:

```
window.alert('The Value Is Incorrect');
```

As indicated in How-To 2.1, the persistence of the current window is assumed by JavaScript, meaning that the Window object reference is optional in the method invocation statement. This statement is logically equivalent to the above code.

```
alert('The Value Is Incorrect');
```

ELEMENT	DESCRIPTION
Icon	Displays an Alert icon, such as an exclamation mark
Text	Displays the message "JavaScript Alert"
Text	Displays the message sent in through the Alert function's only parameter
Button	OK button, which the user must click to acknowledge the alert

Table 2-1 Alert dialog elements

Table 2-1 shows the elements contained within an Alert dialog. Alert dialogs contain a text field used to communicate the problem to the user and a push button which the user clicks to indicate that he or she has seen the message. Application programmers should use Alert dialogs to notify a user about any error. Alert dialogs cannot assist in error correction. This type of dialog presents users with a single course of action, acknowledging that they have seen the message, so the capability does not exist for a user to choose between multiple courses of action. This style of interaction is in contrast to confirmation dialogs, discussed in How-To 2.3, which allow users to make simple go/no-go decisions.

MODALITY

Dialog boxes can be defined as either *modal* or *modeless.* When a modal dialog box is displayed, the user cannot interact with other windows belonging to the same application. This type of modality is known as *application-modal.* An operator must acknowledge an application-modal dialog box, typically by clicking the OK button, before continuing its interaction with the program. With application-modal dialog boxes, users can interact with windows belonging to other desktop applications. Some dialog boxes, called *system-modal* dialog boxes, do not allow access to any other window, including those belonging to other applications.

Some graphical user interface (GUI) toolkits, such as Motif, allow Alert dialogs or message boxes to be defined as either modal or modeless. An inconsistency exists in the methods Web browsers have used to implement Alert dialogs. Some Web browsers, such as the Windows 95 Navigator 2.0, define Alert dialogs to be application-modal while the Solaris 2.4 Navigator 2.0 defines Alert dialogs to be modeless.

The modality of an Alert dialog will affect the control flow of a JavaScript program. If the Alert dialog is defined to be modal, then a call to the Alert method will block until the user activates the OK button. This means that two successive calls to the Alert method will result in one Alert dialog being displayed to the user. Once the user acknowledges the first alert by clicking the OK button, the first alert will be replaced by a second alert.

If the Alert dialog is defined to be modeless, then successive calls to the Alert method will result in two dialogs being simultaneously displayed to the user. This is because the Alert method does not block when modeless alerts have been implemented. Play around with alerts to determine your favorite Web browser's implementation of Alert dialog modality.

Multi-Line Error Messages

By using the new-line character (\') or the return character (\"), embedded inside the Alert dialog's message parameter, Alert dialogs can be coaxed to display multi-line error messages. The new-line character (\n) and the return character (\r) are JavaScript special characters discussed in Chapter 5, "Language Syntax." These characters should be used to specify the location in the error message where the line break will occur. For example, the message string

```
alert("\nERROR\nPlease Enter Your Name");
```

will display the Alert dialog shown in Figure 2-4. The return character (\r) could be substituted for the new-line character (\n) without affecting the way the Alert message in Figure 2-4 is displayed.

Steps

This example will modify the reader feedback form, created in How-To 2.1. Waite Group Press does not want anonymous reaction to the book. Therefore, a reader must enter his or her name and address before the form will be submitted to the server. If the reader fails to provide either piece of information, an Alert dialog box will pop up on the screen. The dialog will indicate that a created input field is blank and must contain data before the feedback is sent to the server.

From Navigator 2.0 or Explorer 3.0, use the File/Open menu option to load HT0202.HTM into memory. Click the Submit Comments button and the Alert dialog in Figure 2-4 will appear on the screen. Click the OK button to acknowledge the alert. Enter text into both the Name and Address elements. Once again, activate the Submit Comments buttons, and you will notice that the form is successfully submitted to the server. All input elements have been reset to their initial state.

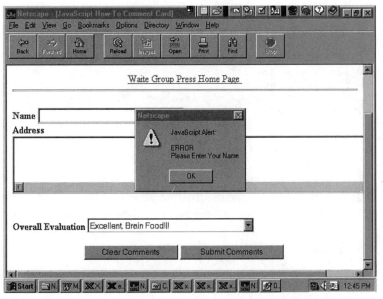

Figure 2-4 The Alert form with multi-line Alert dialog

1. Open an editor and load in the JavaScript How-To Comment Card created in How-To 2.1. This document was saved under the file name HT0201.HTM. The remaining steps will add a form validation function to this document. This function will be invoked when the reader clicks the Submit Comments button.

2. Inside the <SCRIPT> container, add a second JavaScript function named *verifyInput*. The verifyInput function will check the *FullName* text element and the Address textarea element to make sure that the user has entered information in both fields. If either field is empty, an Alert dialog will be displayed to the user. Only when information has been entered into both fields will the form be submitted to the server.

> **NOTE**
>
> The input form does not contain a Submit button. A regular button is used to submit a form. If a Submit button were used, a form with blank fields would still be sent to the server. By using a button instead of a Submit element, only valid data is submitted.

```
/* **********************************************************
 *    Function -    verifyInput
 *    Parameter -   form :         Reference To The Input Form
 *    Description -                This Function Will Verify That
 *                                 Information Has Been Entered
 *                                 Into The Full Name And Address
 *                                 Fields Before The Form Is
 *                                 Submitted To The Server
 * ********************************************************** */

function verifyInput(form) {
      if (form.FullName.value.length == 0)
           alert("\nERROR\n\Please Enter Your Name");
      else if (form.Address.value.length == 0)
           alert("\nERROR\nPlease Enter Your Address");
      else
           form.submit();
}
```

3. Add an onClick event handler to the Submit Comments button. The handler will call the verifyInput function, created in Step 2, when the user clicks this button.

```
<INPUT TYPE="button" VALUE="Submit Comments"
 onClick="verifyInput(this.form)">
```

4. Save the HTML input form under the name HT0202.HTM. In Navigator, use the File/Open File menu option to execute the JavaScript application by loading HT0202.HTM into the browser.

How It Works

The Submit Comments button will be used to submit the reader's feedback to the Waite Group Press server. This button was implemented as a button, instead of a Submit element. This allows data validation to occur before the form is submitted.

When the user activates the Submit Comments button, the onClick event handler is fired. This handler calls the verifyInput() function, declared inside the header's <SCRIPT> container. A single parameter, referencing the Comment form, is passed to this function. This allows this function easier access to the form's input elements.

The verifyInput function first checks the FullName text field to verify that its value attribute has a length greater than zero. If this test fails, the Window object's Alert method is called. Only if the first test is successful will the function validate that data has been entered into the Address element. This means that the verifyInput function will only display a single error, but multiple problems may exist in the form. If all validation tests are successful, the Form object's Submit method is used to programmatically submit the comments to the server.

The Alert messages follow a standard format with the word ERROR displayed on the top line and the detailed message immediately below. The new-line (\n) character indicates a line break in an error message. The new line causes a multi-line error message to appear inside the dialog.

Comments

Error trapping is a fundamental principle in user interface design. However, the fact that a screen detects and prevents errors is only half of the solution. Alert dialogs should be used to indicate that a problem has occurred and what steps the user must take to correct the problem. Cryptic error messages such as Error! and Improper User Action should be avoided.

COMPLEXITY
BEGINNING

2.3 How do I...
Confirm the user's desire to initiate an action?

COMPATIBILITY:  NAVIGATOR 2.X   NAVIGATOR 3.X

Problem

Computer programs are written for the purpose of automating the decision-making process. However, there are times when I need the user to make a go/no-go decision. How can I make the user choose between two options?

Technique

Confirmation dialogs allow the user to decide between two options. By activating the OK button, the user indicates a positive response to the question being asked. Clicking the Cancel button represents a negative response. The ability for a user to make a choice by activating either push button underlies the differences between the Confirm dialog and the Alert dialog, discussed in How-To 2.2. This difference is reinforced in users' minds by the fact that the Confirm dialog presents a question mark icon, versus the Alert dialog's exclamation mark icon, to indicate that the application is asking a question that requires them to make a decision. Table 2-2 lists the elements contained inside a Confirm dialog.

ELEMENT	DESCRIPTION
Icon	Displays a Confirm icon, such as a question mark
Text	Displays the message "JavaScript Confirm"
Text	Displays the message sent in through the confirm function's only parameter
Button	OK button, which the user may click to indicate a positive or go decision
Button	Cancel button, which the user may click to indicate a negative or no-go decision

Table 2-2 Confirm dialog elements

To display a Confirmation dialog to the user, the current window's Confirm method must be invoked. This method requires a single parameter representing the Confirmation message or question being asked of the user. Like the Alert dialog's message, Confirmation messages can be defined as strings that can contain embedded special characters to indicate line breaks in multi-line messages. Messages can also take the form of numbers, dates, object properties, or a combination of these data types. Confirmation dialogs are defined as application-modal, which means that the Confirm method will block until the user makes a decision. An example call to the Confirm method is:

```
window.confirm('The Value Is Incorrect');
```

As indicated in How-To 2.1, the persistence of the current window is assumed by JavaScript, meaning that the Window object reference is optional in the method invocation statement. This code will also display a Confirm dialog.

```
confirm('The Value Is Incorrect');
```

To indicate the user's response to the Confirmation message, the Confirm method returns a Boolean value. This value can be referenced inside a conditional predicate to determine whether or not a block of code should be executed. A true value indicates that the user clicked on the OK button. This indicates a positive response to the confirmation message. Negative responses are indicated by activating the Cancel button. This will result in the Confirm method returning a false value to the calling function.

The following code demonstrates how to invoke the Confirm method. A Confirm dialog is used to verify the user's intention to clear an input form. The output of the Confirm function is referenced inside the *if* statement's predicate. This means that the form will be cleared only if a positive response is indicated by the user.

```
if (confirm("Are You Sure You Want To Clear The Form") == true) {
    form.FullName.value = "";
    form.Address.value = "";
    form.Rating.selectedIndex = 0;
}
```

Steps

This example will modify the Reader Feedback form, created in How-To 2.1 and 2.2. A common capability, provided with many input forms, allows users to reset the form to its initial state. This functionality can be implemented by using a *Reset* HTML element. The problem is that the Reset function is a catastrophic event, which means that it will result in loss of data. If the user accidentally clicks a Reset button, no verification is used to confirm the user's intentions. Waite Group Press wants to provide a Reset button in its JavaScript How-To Comment Card. To keep users happy, the Reset button must confirm the user's intentions before "blowing away" any data.

From Navigator 2.0 or Explorer 3.0, use the File/Open menu option to load HT0203.HTM into memory. Type text into both the Name and Address text fields. When you click on the Clear Comments button, the Confirm dialog in Figure 2-5 will display on the screen. Try to click on any of the buttons in the Web browser's toolkit and notice that you are prevented from interacting with the rest of the application. This means that the Confirm dialog is modal and will not allow further interaction with the Web browser or Confirm input form until either the OK or Cancel button is activated. Activate the Cancel button, and the Confirm dialog is removed from the screen. All input elements remain uncleared. Once again, click on the Clear Comments button. This time, activate the OK button. The input elements have been cleared or reset to their initial state.

1. Open an editor and load in the JavaScript How-To Comment Card modified in How-To 2.2. This document was saved under the file name HT0202.HTM. The remaining steps will add a Reset validation function to this document. This function will be invoked when the reader clicks on the Clear Comments button.

2. Add a JavaScript function named *verifyClear* to the <SCRIPT> container. The verifyClear function will prompt the user to reverify his or her desire to clear all form elements. If the user responds by clicking the Cancel button, the Confirm dialog will close, and the form will remain unchanged. If the OK button is activated, the Confirm dialog will close, and the elements will be reset to their initial state.

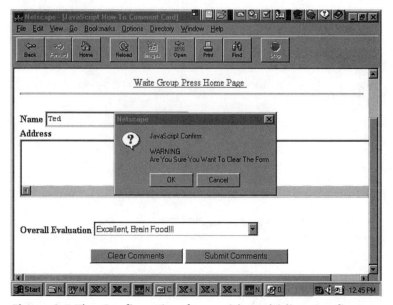

Figure 2-5 The Confirmation form with multi-line Confirm dialog

```
/* **********************************************************
 *    Function -     verifyClear
 *    Parameter -   form :     Reference To The Input Form
 *    Description -       This Function Will Verify The
 *                        User's Intention To Clear The
 *                        Form
 * ********************************************************** */

function verifyClear(form) {
   if (confirm("\nWARNING\nAre You Sure You Want To Clear The Form") ==
               true) {
      form.FullName.value = "";
      form.Address.value = "";
      form.Rating.selectedIndex = 0;
   }
}
```

3. Add an onClick event handler to the Clear Comments button. The handler will call the verifyClear function defined in Step 2.

```
<INPUT TYPE="button" VALUE="Clear Comments"
 onClick="verifyClear(this.form)">
```

4. Save the HTML input form under the name HT0203.HTM. In Navigator, use the File/Open File menu option to execute the JavaScript application by loading HT0203.HTM into the browser.

How It Works

The Clear Comments button will be used to reset the JavaScript How-To Comment Card. This button was implemented as a button instead of a Reset element. This allows confirmation to occur before the form reset takes place.

When the user activates the Clear Comments button, the onClick event handler is fired. This handler calls the verifyClear() function, declared inside the header's <SCRIPT> container. A single parameter, referencing the Comment form, is passed to this function, allowing this function easier access to the form's input elements. The verifyClear function invokes the Window object's Confirm method. The Confirmation message, WARNING Are You Sure You Want To Clear The Form, is displayed inside the dialog. A *conditional* is used to check the user's reaction to the Confirm message. If the user selects the OK button, the conditional is true. This executes the code block that resets the form.

Comments

Experienced GUI developers use Confirm dialogs to verify the user's intention to perform an action that could result in a loss of information. The classic example of this situation is reverifying the user's desire to exit a form when unsaved changes are present.

COMPLEXITY
BEGINNING

2.4   How do I...
Prompt the user to enter a value?

COMPATIBILITY:

Problem

I may wish to prompt the user for information in addition to what the user provides on an input form. How can I do this?

Technique

JavaScript has implemented a Prompt dialog, which can be used to get additional information from a user. These dialogs contain a text field where users can enter the information they are being asked to provide. The ability for a user to enter text through this dialog distinguishes the Prompt dialog from the Alert and Confirm dialogs. These dialogs also contain a message to indicate the type of information being requested from the user, an OK push button, and a Cancel push button.

ELEMENT	DESCRIPTION
Text	Displays the message "JavaScript Prompt"
Text	Displays the message sent through the Prompt function's first parameter
TextField	User-entered information, defaults to Prompt function's second parameter or <undefined>
Button	OK button, which the user may click to indicate a value has been entered
Button	Cancel button, which the user may click to indicate a value will not be entered

Table 2-3 Prompt dialog elements

To display a Prompt dialog on the screen, the current window's Prompt method must be called. Because Prompt dialogs are defined as application-modal, the Prompt method will block waiting for the user's response (either clicking the OK or Cancel button). The Prompt method requires at least one parameter representing the dialog's message. The Prompt message should notify users about the type and format of the information they are being asked to provide.

The Prompt method's second parameter, which is optional, specifies a default value that will be displayed to the user. This parameter should be used in instances where a default response, such as N/A, should be used if the user does not wish to provide any information. If the second parameter is omitted from the *Method Invocation* statement, then the prompt will display the string <undefined> in its text field. Given this fact, it is probably desirable to pass the *at null* string ("") as the second parameter to the Prompt method.

As opposed to Alert and Confirm dialog messages, Prompt messages cannot contain embedded special characters to create multi-line messages. Prompt messages are limited to a single line. The Prompt message will display strings, numbers, dates, object properties, or a combination of these data types. An example call to the Prompt method, which displays the string <undefined> as the default value, is:

```
window.prompt('Please Enter Your Phone Number');
```

As indicated in How-To 2.1, the persistence of the current window is assumed by JavaScript, meaning that the Window object reference is optional in the method invocation statement.

```
prompt('Please Enter Your Phone Number');
```

If you wish to set a default value for the Prompt dialog text field, then use this syntax:

```
prompt('Please Enter Your Phone Number', 18006969696);
```

Notice that the second or default value parameter, like the message or first parameter, will accept a wide range of data types.

The Prompt method returns the value entered by the user into the Prompt dialog's text field, provided that the OK button is used to end interaction with the dialog. If the user selects the Cancel button, then a null value is returned. Even if the user enters text into the field and then activates the Cancel button, a null value will still be returned. If the OK button is chosen before any information is entered into the Prompt dialog's text field, then an empty string will be returned.

The example that follows demonstrates how to use the Prompt method's Return value to set a field only when the user responds to the request for additional information:

```
if (prompt("Could We Have Your Phone Number","") != null) {
    form.Phone.value = hold;
}
```

Notice how the Prompt method is checked to ensure that the *form.Phone.value* property will only be set if the user has clicked the OK button on the Prompt dialog. This check prevents a null field from being submitted to the server.

Steps

This example will modify the Reader Feedback form, created in How-To 2.1-2.3. In an effort to improve the quality of the *JavaScript How-To* book, Waite Group Press will perform random phone surveys of readers. Only readers who provide negative feedback about the book will be surveyed. Because Waite wants to contact only a subset of the reader population, only readers who select the "Terrible" option from the Overall Evaluation menu will be prompted for their phone numbers. This will occur before the comments are submitted to the server. Readers have the option of submitting negative comments without having to give out their phone numbers.

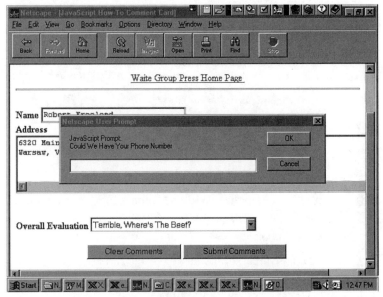

Figure 2-6 The Prompt dialog for readers' phone numbers

In Navigator 2.0 or Explorer 3.0, use the File/Open menu option to load HT0204.HTM into memory. Enter text into both the Name and Address elements. If you fail to enter data into these fields, an Alert dialog will be displayed when you submit the form. After entering data into both fields, activate the Submit Comments button. The Prompt dialog in Figure 2-6 will appear on the screen. Enter your phone number into the text field and click the OK button. The form is successfully submitted to server. All input elements have been reset to their initial state.

1. Open an editor and load in the JavaScript How-To Comment Card modified in How-To 2.3. This document was saved under the file name HT0203.HTM. The remaining steps will add a Prompt dialog to the verifyInput function. This function will be invoked when the reader clicks the Submit Comments button.

2. Replace the verifyInput with the following code which implements a new verifyInput function. The new function still validates that data has been entered in both the FullName and Address text fields. If the form passes validation, the program checks to see the reader's overall evaluation of the JavaScript How-To book. If the evaluation is negative, the reader is prompted to enter his or her phone number. Phone number entry is optional.

```
function verifyInput(form) {
    var hold;
    if (form.FullName.value.length == 0)
        alert("\nERROR\n\Please Enter Your Name");
    else if (form.Address.value.length == 0)
        alert("\nERROR\nPlease Enter Your Address");
    else {
        if (form.Rating.selectedIndex == 2) {
            hold = prompt("Could We Have Your Phone Number","");
            if (hold != null) {
                form.Phone.value = hold;
            }
        }
        form.submit();
    }
}
```

3. Add an onClick event handler to the Submit Comments button. The handler will call the verifyInput function, created in Step 2.

```
<INPUT TYPE="hidden" NAME="Phone" VALUE="Not Provided">
```

4. Save the HTML input form under the name HT0204.HTM. In Navigator, use the File/Open File menu option to execute the JavaScript application by loading HT0204.HTM into the browser.

How It Works

When the user clicks on the Submit Comments button, the onClick event handler is fired. This handler invokes the new verifyInput function, defined in Step 2. If data has been entered into the FullName and Address text fields, then the function will analyze the user's selection in the Overall Evaluation menu. If Option 3 was selected, indicating that the book was "Terrible," the user is presented with a Prompt dialog that asks for his or her home phone number.

The Window object's Prompt method is used to display the Prompt dialog. Although the Prompt method requires a single parameter, two parameters are passed to this method. By passing the *space string* ("") as the optional second parameter, the Prompt dialog will be displayed with an empty input field. If the user chooses not to enter a phone number, he or she will press the Cancel button. This will cause the Prompt method to return a null value to the verifyChange function. If the OK button is selected, the Prompt function returns the text entered into the input area. The return value is placed in a hidden field so that it can be submitted to the server. A hidden field is needed because JavaScript variables cannot be submitted to the server. If the Cancel button is selected, the hidden field's default value, "Not Provided," is submitted.

Comments

This chapter has introduced several techniques that allow JavaScript programs to communicate with the user. When you are designing a JavaScript-enabled HTML document, spend some design time considering when communication with the user is necessary. Then make that sure you apply the proper technique to meet the specific need. Not all communication techniques can be used in every situation. Just imagine the Help messages in How-To 2.1 being implemented as alerts instead of status messages. Users would grow weary closing alert dialogs as they traverse through the form. Just remember, many software programs are not used because they implement a bad user interface.

CHAPTER 3
DOCUMENTS

3

DOCUMENTS

How do I...

3.1   **Open and close a document?**

3.2   **Change a document's title and heading?**

3.3   **Change a document's background and foreground colors?**

3.4   **Change the color of active and visited links?**

3.5   **Identify the date a document was last modified?**

3.6   **Get the URL of a document?**

3.7   **Move backward and forward through previously viewed documents?**

JavaScript has a set of predefined objects that you can create and/or reference directly in your code. Of the objects that are basic to Web pages, the Document object provides the content of the page, which is all of the page except for the window frame, tool bars, and menu bars. Some of the properties of the Document object are themselves objects: the History object contains a list of Web pages that the user has visited in the current session; the Location object contains information such as the URL and protocol that identifies where the current document is located. With these objects and their associated properties, methods, and events, you can programmatically change a Web page title based on its background color, or move to the previously displayed page. You can open a new document and write HTML commands directly to it, or you can open a popup window and display another Web page in addition to the one currently open.

3.1 Open and close a document

The browser will automatically open your document when the document URL (Uniform Resource Locator), embedded as a hypertext link, is clicked. However, there may be times when you will want to be able to open a document based on some other criteria. This How-To describes how to programmatically open, write HTML commands to, and close a document.

3.2 Change a document's title and heading

The document title is shown at the top of the browser and listed under the menu item that displays which Web pages have been visited during the current session. This How-To demonstrates how to programmatically set the title of a document.

3.3 Change a document's background and foreground colors

You can set the background color of a document at any time before or after the document is displayed, but you can only set the foreground, or document text, color before the document is displayed. This How-To demonstrates how to set both of these attributes.

3.4 Change the color of active and visited links

The user of a browser such as Netscape Navigator can define what the colors are for links, visited links, and active links. You can change these attributes using JavaScript but you must make these changes before the document is displayed. This How-To demonstrates how to change each of these link colors within a specific document.

3.5 Identify the date a document was last modified

As a courtesy to those people viewing your Web page, you will want to place the date that your document was last modified into your page. This How-To provides a simple *scriplet* to do this for your document.

3.6 Get the URL of a document

The Location object, a property of the Window object, provides the parts of the URL for the Window/Document that makes up the Web page. This How-To demonstrates how to access this object and display it programmatically.

3.7 Move backward and forward through previously viewed documents

The History object, another object that is a property of the Window object, has associated methods to traverse back and forth through windows that have been viewed during the current session. This How-To provides code samples using these History object methods.

3.1 How do I...
Open and close a document?

COMPATIBILITY:

Problem

Based on selections my Web page readers may make, I want to be able to open a new document in order to send it new HTML commands. I also want the browser to implement those commands. How can I open and close a Document object using JavaScript?

Technique

JavaScript contains several built-in objects, one of which is the Document object. This object has several methods associated with it, such as Open, Close, Write, and writeln. In this example you will create three HTML documents: the first will create a frameset with two frames and will open HTML files into these frames; the second will be a blank HTML file that contains nothing more than the basic HTML <HEAD> and <BODY> tags; and the third will contain the code that will open, write to, and close a new document. The new document, which contains the blank HTML document, will be created in the window frame.

Steps

Open the OPENPRNT.HTM document in your browser. The page has two frames, with two buttons in the top frame as shown in Figure 3-1. The bottom frame is blank. Click the Open Document button in the top frame, and you'll notice no difference in the window. Now click the Close Window button. The second frame now contains the words Second Document! Reload the original document and click the Open Document button three times. When you click the Close Window button you will see that the Second Document! text is repeated three times, as shown in Figure 3-2.

The steps to create these windows follow.

1. Create a basic blank HTML file containing the following code:

```
<HTML>
<HEAD><TITLE> Working Window </TITLE></HEAD>
<BODY></BODY>
</HTML>
```

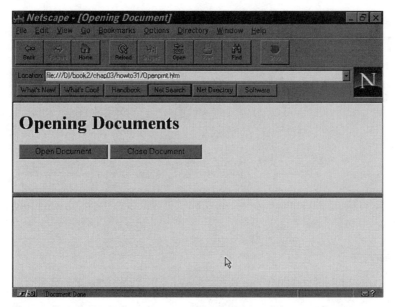

Figure 3-1 Opening a document window with two frames

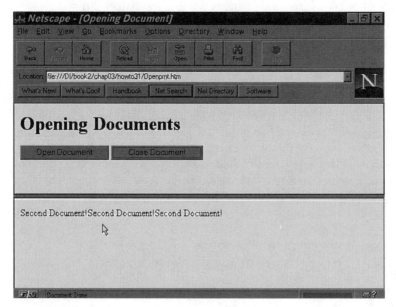

Figure 3-2 Opening a document window with writing in second frame

2. Close this file and call it BLANK.HTM.

3. Create a new HTML file.

4. In this file type in code that will create an HTML document with two frames. Open the BLANK.HTM file you created in one frame, and an HTML file you will be creating in the following steps in the other. Close and save the results as OPENPRNT.HTM.

```
<HTML>
<HEAD>
<TITLE>Opening Document</TITLE>
</HEAD>

<FRAMESET ROWS="50%, 50%">
    <FRAME SRC=open.htm NAME="Open">
    <FRAME SRC=blank.htm NAME="workFrame">
</FRAMESET>

</HTML>
```

5. Create a third HTML file. Type in the standard HTML and TITLE tags and the <JavaScript> tag. The last line on the code will hide the JavaScript code from browsers that cannot read it.

```
<HTML>
<HEAD><TITLE> Opening a Document </TITLE>
<SCRIPT LANGUAGE="JavaScript">
<!--- hide script from old browsers
```

6. Next you will create a JavaScript function that will write the words Second Document! to this document. Note that the words will not display until the document is closed.

```
// create display window for document
//
// Open document and write to stream
function OpenDocument() {
parent.workFrame.document.write
    ("Second Document!")
  }
```

7. Create a second JavaScript function called CloseDocument and type in code to close the newly opened document. This will flush the queue containing all of the Write or Writeln commands to the opened document and will force the document to display. Also type in the closing JavaScript tag.

```
// Close document, flush stream (output)
function CloseDocument() {
   parent.workFrame.document.close()
   }

// end hiding from old browsers -->
</SCRIPT>
<H1> Opening Documents </H1>
</HEAD>
```

8. In the BODY HTML document section create a form with two input buttons. The first button will call the OpenDocument function when the button is clicked and the second button will call the CloseDocument function when clicked. Type in the closing HTML tags.

```
<BODY>
<FORM NAME="DocumentForm" >
<INPUT TYPE="button" VALUE="Open Document"
      onClick="OpenDocument()">
<INPUT TYPE="button" VALUE="Close Document"
      onClick="CloseDocument()">
</FORM>
</BODY>
</HTML>
```

9. Close the document and call it OPEN.HTM. Test your code by opening the OPENPRNT.HTM document in your browser.

10. Without redirecting the Write() and Writeln() methods, the contents of the existing document would be cleared. Test this by opening the file OPEN-ME.HTM in your browser.

11. Click the Open Document button and notice that the form, including the two buttons, have disappeared. The document in the current window was the document that the Open() method was directed against, which cleared the document of its existing contents. Because the button that would normally call the Close() method is now gone, there is no way to issue the flush, the queue action that would cause the new stream contents to display.

12. Test this by creating an empty HTML document.

13. Create the HEAD and begin the JavaScript section by typing the following code:

```
<HTML>
<HEAD><TITLE> Opening a Document </TITLE>

<SCRIPT LANGUAGE="JavaScript">
<!--- hide script from old browsers
```

14. Add a JavaScript function that will open a document and write the string Hello! to it. Note that the document is not prefaced with the name of another window, which means that the results will be directed to the current document in the current window.

```
// create display window for document
//
// Open document and write to stream
function OpenDocument() {
   document.open("text/html")
   document.write
      ("Second Document!")
   }
```

15. Create a second function that will close the document and flush the queue. Also type in the code to close the JavaScript section.

```
// Close document, flush stream (output)
function CloseDocument() {
   document.close()
   }

// end hiding from old browsers -->
</SCRIPT>
```

16. Create the BODY section with a form and two buttons.

```
<H1> Opening Documents </H1>
</HEAD>
<body>
<FORM NAME="DocumentForm" >
<INPUT TYPE="button" VALUE="Open Document"
      onClick="OpenDocument()">
<INPUT TYPE="button" VALUE="Close Document"
      onClick="CloseDocument()">
</FORM>
</BODY>
</HTML>
```

17. Close and save the file as OPENME.HTM.

How It Works

The document Open Document method will open a stream that will collect your Write and Writeln function calls. If you use this method with the document that is currently open in the window displayed on-screen, these functions will clear the existing document contents.

The results of the Write and Writeln function calls will not be visible until this stream is flushed or displayed. This occurs when you use FONT style tags such as <SMALL> or <CENTER>, or when you close the document using the Close method. Additionally Document:Done is displayed in the status bar.

The Open() method for a document can take an optional mimetype such as image/gif or the name of a plug-in. These techniques will be detailed in Chapter 15, "Advanced Features."

Comments

When creating a new document programmatically, be aware of when a document layout occurs. If you are changing the document foreground color (the default text color) you will want to make this change prior to any Write() or Writeln() function calls that might flush the stream.

COMPLEXITY
INTERMEDIATE

3.2 How do I...
Change a document's title and heading?

COMPATIBILITY: NAVIGATOR 2.X   NAVIGATOR 3.X

Problem

I want my Web page to be as interactive as possible—I may change a document's contents based on the actions of a person viewing it. But when I change the contents, the document title that appears in the browser title bar is no longer representative of the document contents. How can I change the document title when I change the document contents?

Technique

The Title property of the document is normally a read-only property. To change this value you must write out the HEAD tags using the Write() or Writeln() methods, and place the TITLE tags within the head section. After that you can write HTML tag values for the rest of the new document display.

Steps

From your browser open the TITLE.HTM file. The Web page contains a heading and a button, as shown in Figure 3-3. Click the button. Notice that the button disappears, the heading has changed, and document title, in the browser's title bar, has changed, too, as shown in Figure 3-4. Select the Go menu item and notice that the name of the document has changed in this list as well.

The steps to create this Web page using JavaScript follow.

1. Create a new HTML file and call it TITLE.HTM.

2. Type in the standard HTML and HEAD tags with the TITLE tag as shown in the listing below.

```
<HTML>
<HEAD><TITLE> Old Title </TITLE>
```

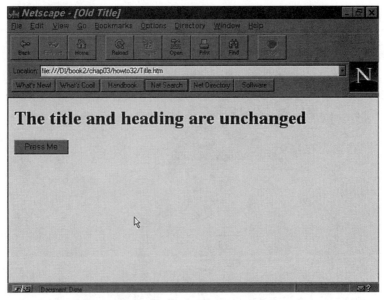

Figure 3-3 Title document before title property is changed

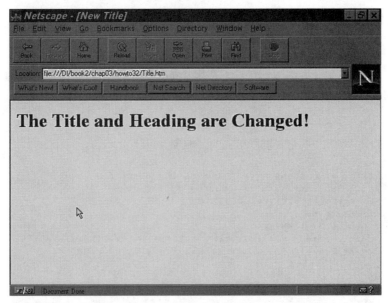

Figure 3-4 Title document after both title and heading have been changed

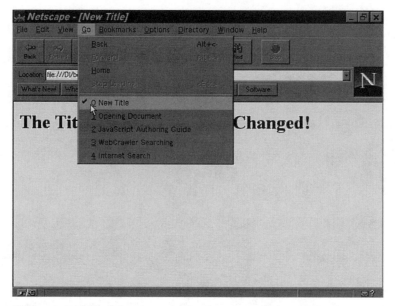

Figure 3-5 Title document with changed title in visited document list

3. Next, type in the JavaScript tag and the Comments marker.

```
<SCRIPT LANGUAGE="JavaScript">
<!--- hide script from old browsers
```

4. Create a function that will write out the head and body tags and a new heading for the document. Notice that the Writeln command writes out the heading (<H1></H1>) tags as well as the heading. If these tags are not all text that follows, the beginning <H1> tag would become part of the header. Type in the ending for the JavaScript section.

```
//writetitle
// function will change the title on the document
// when the user presses the button in the form
function writetitle(title, heading) {
    document.open();
    document.write("<HTML>");
    document.write("<HEAD><TITLE>" + title + "</TITLE></HEAD>");
    document.write("<BODY><H1>" + heading + "</H1></BODY>");
    }

// end hiding from old browsers -->
</SCRIPT>
```

5. Finally, type in code that will close the HEAD section, start the BODY section, and create a form with one button. The button onClick event will first call the writetitle JavaScript function and then the writehead JavaScript function. There can be more than one function called in response to an event if the events are separated by a semicolon (;).

```
</HEAD>

<BODY>
<H1> The title and heading are unchanged </H1>

<FORM>
<INPUT TYPE="button" VALUE="Press Me" onClick=
   "writetitle('New Title','The Heading has Changed!')">
</FORM>
</BODY>
</HTML>
```

6. Close and save your new HTML document. Test the document by opening it in your browser.

How It Works

The Title property is a read-only property that can only be changed when the document is redisplayed. You must create an HTML that includes the TITLE tags using the document Write or Writeln methods. When the current document is modified using this technique, the existing contents are cleared, as demonstrated by the example you just created.

Comments

Normally you will not want to modify the Title property, but will instead want to create a new window and a new document. When you change the document title or clear the existing document, you have lost the ability to return to the document using the History object. The person viewing your document will also have lost the ability to return to the previous document.

COMPLEXITY

INTERMEDIATE/ADVANCED

3.3 How do I...
Change a document's background and foreground colors?

COMPATIBILITY: NAVIGATOR 2.X   NAVIGATOR 3.X

Problem

To make my Web page more interactive and colorful, I would like to be able to change the document background or text color using JavaScript. How can I do this?

Technique

The foreground color is equivalent to the Text attribute defined in the BODY section of the document. The background color is equivalent to the *bgColor* attribute. Both of these properties can be set by the user in the Preferences property sheets in the Colors sheet.

Using JavaScript you can change the background color attribute (bgColor) of the document at any time. However, the default text color that is defined, the *fgColor* document attribute, can only be changed before the document is displayed or laid out.

Steps

Open the HTML file COLRPRNT.HTM in your browser. The window is divided into two frames with a button and a heading in the top frame as shown in Figure 3-6. Click the Change Colors button and now the top frame is peach-colored! In addition, the words, Hello World!, are displayed below in blue. Click the button again. The top frame is now gray and the text in the second frame is red as shown in Figure 3-7.

1. Create a basic blank HTML file containing the following code:

```
<HTML>
<HEAD><TITLE> Working Window </TITLE></HEAD>
<BODY></BODY>
</HTML>
```

2. Close this file and call it BLANK.HTM.

3. Create a new HTML file.

4. In the new file type in a FRAMESET tag to create two separate frames out of the document. Name one of the frames "BgFg" and set its source to BGFG.HTM. Name the second frame "workFrame" and set its source to BLANK.HTM, which is the document you just created.

```
<HTML>
<HEAD>
<TITLE>Changing Colors</TITLE>
</HEAD>
<FRAMESET ROWS="50%, 50%">
   <FRAME SRC=bgfg.htm NAME="BgFg">
   <FRAME SRC=blank.htm NAME="workFrame">
</FRAMESET>
</HTML>
```

5. Close and save the document as COLRPRNT.HTM. Create a third document.

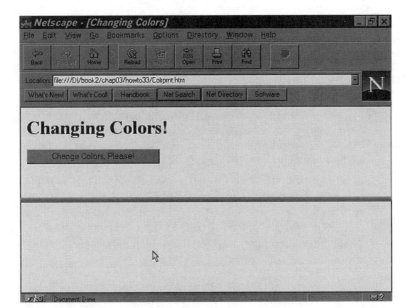

Figure 3-6 Changing colors before modifications

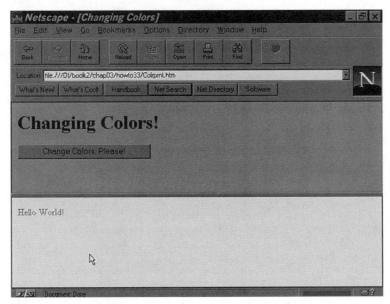

Figure 3-7 Changing colors after modifications

CHAPTER 3
DOCUMENTS

6. In this document create the HEAD section and create a JavaScript section.

```
<HTML>
<BASE </BASE>
<HEAD><TITLE> Changing Document Background/Foreground Colors </TITLE>
<SCRIPT LANGUAGE="JavaScript">
<!--- hide script from old browsers
```

7. Create a JavaScript function called *ChangeColors*. This function will open a document into the workFrame. It will then compare the existing document color. If the color is silver, as denoted by the hexadecimal value #ffdab0, the background color of the existing document—the bgColor attribute—will be set to peach (#FFDAB9), and the text color of the new document—the fgColor attribute—will be set to red (#FF0000). Otherwise the bgColor attribute will be set to silver (#C0C0C0), and the fgColor attribute will be set to blue (#0000FF). Finally, the new document will be closed to force the layout of the document.

```
// ChangeColors
// ChangeColors will allow the user to
// change the background and foreground color of the new document
// each time the Change Colors, Please! button is pressed
// Background color is changed by using the Hexidecimal
// notation
//
function ChangeColors() {
    parent.workFrame.document.open()
    parent.workFrame.document.write
       ("<HEAD><TITLE>Message window</TITLE></HEAD>")
    if (document.bgColor == "#ffdab9") {
    parent.workFrame.document.fgColor="#FF0000"
    document.bgColor="#C0C0C0"
    }
    else   {
    parent.workFrame.document.fgColor="#0000FF"
    document.bgColor="#FFDAB9"
    }
    parent.workFrame.document.write
       ("Hello World!")
    parent.workFrame.document.close()
  }
```

8. Close the JavaScript and HEAD tag section and create the BODY section. Create a form and an input button. The onClick button event will trigger the ChangeColors JavaScript function call.

```
// end hiding from old browsers -->
</SCRIPT>

<H1> Changing Colors! </H1>
</HEAD>
<body TEXT="#00ff00" >
<FORM NAME="ColorForm" >
<INPUT TYPE="button" VALUE="Change Colors, Please!"
      onClick="ChangeColors()">
```

```
</FORM>

</BODY>
</HTML>
```

9. Close your third document and name it BGFG.HTM. Test your Web page by opening COLRPRNT.HTM in your browser.

How It Works

The Document object has several properties such as the background and text colors, but not all can be changed at one time. In this example you were able to change the existing document background color easily. However, you had to set the other document up for a new display in order to change the text color.

Colors are hexadecimal values of the format *rrggbb* or *#rrggbb* and are known as RGB (Red-Green-Blue) values. The first two characters are the red colors, the second two are the green, and the third two are the blue. With this you can represent a blue-green color like aqua as *00ffff*. The saturation or purity of the color is determined by the size of the number, with a larger number signifying more color saturation. You can also specify the color as a named value in some circumstances. Netscape has a list of named values defined for colors, which can be found in the *JavaScript Authoring Guide* currently located at

`http://home.netscape.com/eng/mozilla/2.0/handbook/javascript/index.html`.

Comments

Note that some RGB values will not show up properly as text or may not show to expectations, depending on your computer's video card. You would be safest to stay with pure hues and only use a combination of 0s and Fs, such as 00ff00 or ffffff.

COMPLEXITY

INTERMEDIATE/ADVANCED

3.4 How do I...
Change the color of active and visited links?

COMPATIBILITY: NAVIGATOR 2.X   NAVIGATOR 3.X

Problem

I am using an unusual background for one of my Web pages and I want to override the user's standard colors for the links with my own. I am concerned that with this background some link colors will not show up well. However, I also allow the user to specify an option to allow the document to display without the background, and I do not want to override the colors in this case. How can I use JavaScript to change my link colors?

Technique

The Document object has the linkColor property for non-visited links, the vlinkColor property for visited links, and the alinkColor property to color links when you have clicked but not released the mouse button. None of these properties can be changed after the document has been displayed. However, they can be changed programmatically using JavaScript—after the document is opened but before it is displayed.

Steps

Open LINKPRNT.HTM in your browser. The page consists of two frames with a button, a heading in the first frame, and a blank document in the second as shown in Figure 3-8. Click the button and the second frame now has text and a link as shown in Figure 3-9. Notice the colors for the links as listed in the text above the link. Because the location has never been visited before, it should be red, regardless of your default link colors. Click the button again and notice that the background color of the top frame has changed and that the link color in the bottom frame is now blue. If you were to click the link and hold the mouse button, you would find that the color of the link matches what is written for the Active link. After you release the mouse button the colors of the link reflect the visited link color. The steps to create this type of Web page follow.

1. Create a basic blank HTML file containing the following code:

```
<HTML>
<HEAD><TITLE> Working Window </TITLE></HEAD>
<BODY></BODY>
</HTML>
```

2. Close this file and call it BLANK.HTM.

3. Create a new HTML file that contains two separate frames. Name one of the frames "Link" and set its source to LINK.HTM. Name the second frame "workFrame" and set its source to BLANK.HTM.

```
<HTML>
<HEAD>
<TITLE>Changing Link Colors</TITLE>
</HEAD>
<FRAMESET ROWS="50%, 50%">
   <FRAME SRC=link.htm NAME="Link">
   <FRAME SRC=blank.htm NAME="workFrame">
</FRAMESET>
</HTML>
```

4. Close and save the document as LINKPRNT.HTM.

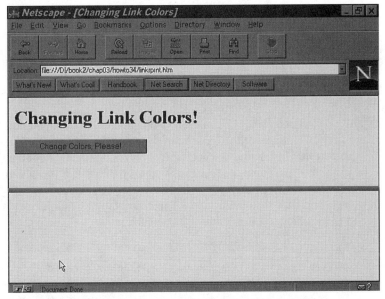

Figure 3-8 Changing link colors before modification

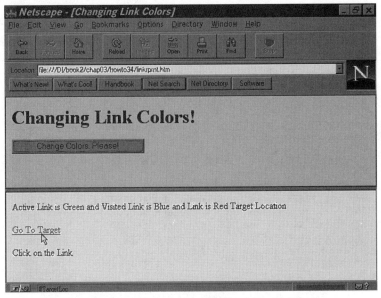

Figure 3-9 Changing link colors after modification

5. Create a third document and add the HTML below to start both the HEAD
section and a JavaScript section.

```
<HTML>
<BASE </BASE>
<HEAD><TITLE> Changing Link Colors </TITLE>
<SCRIPT LANGUAGE="JavaScript">
<!--- hide script from old browsers
```

6. Type in the following code to create a function called ChangeColors. The
code will create an HREF location in the document, modify the link colors,
and create a link to the newly generated location. The colors of the links
will switch each time the user clicks a button that will be created in Step 7.
Note that the code writes out new HEAD and TITLE sections for the document and changes the link colors. The colors currently active will be
displayed in a text string in the document.

```
// ChangeColors will allow the user to
// change the link colors of the document
// each time the Change Colors, Please! button is pressed
// Background color is changed by using the Hexidecimal
// notation
//
// ChangeColors will also display the changes in a popup window
function ChangeColors() {
    var RefString="Target Location"
    var LinkString = "Go To Target"
    var URLString = "#TargetLoc"
    parent.workFrame.document.open()
    parent.workFrame.document.write
      ("<HEAD><TITLE>Message window</TITLE></HEAD>")
  if (document.bgColor == "#ffdab9") {
    parent.workFrame.document.alinkColor="#FF0000"
    parent.workFrame.document.linkColor="#0000FF"
    parent.workFrame.document.vlinkColor="#00FF00"
    document.bgColor="#C0C0C0"
    parent.workFrame.document.writeln
      ("<p>Active Link is Red and Visited Link is Green and Link is Blue")
    }
  else    {
    parent.workFrame.document.alinkColor="#00FF00"
    parent.workFrame.document.vlinkColor="#0000FF"
    parent.workFrame.document.linkColor="#FF0000"
    document.bgColor="#FFDAB9"
    parent.workFrame.document.writeln
      ("<p>Active Link is Green and Visited Link is Blue and Link is Red")
    }
    parent.workFrame.document.writeln
    ("<p>" + RefString.anchor('TargetLoc'))
    parent.workFrame.document.writeln
    ("<p> " + LinkString.link(URLString))
    parent.workFrame.document.writeln
      ("<p>Click on the Link </BODY>")
    parent.workFrame.document.close()
  }
```

```
// end hiding from old browsers -->
</SCRIPT>
```

7. Finally, type in code that will create a standard HTML form with one button. The onClick event of the button will generate a call to the new ChangeColors function.

```
<H1> Changing Link Colors! </H1>
</HEAD>
<body linkColor=000000 >
<FORM NAME="ColorForm" >
<INPUT TYPE="button" VALUE="Change Colors, Please!"
     onClick="ChangeColors()">
</FORM>
</BODY>
</HTML>
```

8. Close and save the window as LINK.HTM and test your code by loading the LINKPRNT.HTM document in your browser.

How It Works

Every hypertext link has three colors associated with it: the link color, the followed or visited link color, and the active link color. The visited and link colors can be set in the preferences of the browser. You can use JavaScript to set these colors for a document that has not been displayed by setting the Document vLinkColor, aLinkColor, and LinkColor attributes. The format for colors can be found in the How It Works section of How-To 3.3.

COMPLEXITY
BEGINNING

3.5 How do I..
Identify the date a document was last modified?

COMPATIBILITY:

Problem

I want to place at the bottom of my Web page the date the document was last modified, but I don't want to hard code this value. How can I do this?

Technique

One of the simplest and most effective uses of JavaScript is to display the modification date *of* the document *in* the document. This display is usually placed at the bottom of the document in small italic script.

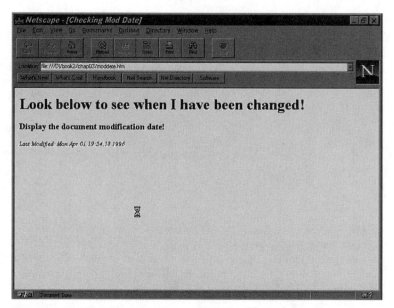

Figure 3-10 Checking Mod Date HTML display showing LastModified attribute

Steps

Open the MODDATE.HTM file in your browser. The page displayed contains a heading, a text string in larger font, and the modification date at the bottom in a small, italicized font, as shown in Figure 3-10. The steps to display the *LastModified* document attribute are listed below.

1. Create a new HTML document and type in the following HEAD section. This code will create the title and a heading.

```
<HTML>
<HEAD><TITLE> Checking Mod Date </TITLE>
<H1> Look below to see when I have been changed! </H1>
</HEAD>
```

2. Type in the HTML code to create the document BODY section, including a JavaScript section that writes out the document LastModified attribute.

```
<body>
<p><BIG><B>Display the document modification date!</B></BIG>
<SCRIPT LANGUAGE="JavaScript">
<!--- hide script from old browsers
document.write ("<p><SMALL><EM>Last Modified: " +
        document.lastModified + "</EM></SMALL>")
// end hiding from old browsers -->
</SCRIPT>
```

```
</BODY>
</HTML>
```

3. Close and save the file as MODDATE.HTM. Test your code by opening the file in your browser.

How It Works

The LastModified attribute is one of several that can be used to test values or to display directly in the Web page. Note that these attributes are contained in JavaScript objects and must be accessed in a JavaScript language block.

Comments

JavaScript does not have to be included in functions and does not have to be placed in the HEAD section. A browser processes the script by scanning the document once for JavaScript functions, images, plug-ins, and other embedded objects. It also processes the HEAD section before the BODY. It then loads the document and processes the HTML and non-function JavaScript in the order in which it appears in the document.

COMPLEXITY
BEGINNING

3.6 How do I...
Get the URL of a document?

COMPATIBILITY:

Problem

As a courtesy to viewers of my Web page, I want to print the URL of my document in my document. How can I display the document URL?

Technique

The document has Location as one of its properties. This value can be accessed and printed out. The value will display the complete URL of the document. In addition, one of the standard JavaScript objects is the Location object. Location is a property of the Window and contains the protocol, hostname, port, pathname, search, and hashname (anchor name) of the document. As with the property values of other objects, Location properties can be printed out directly in the document. However, unlike the Document.Location property, the Location object properties can be changed.

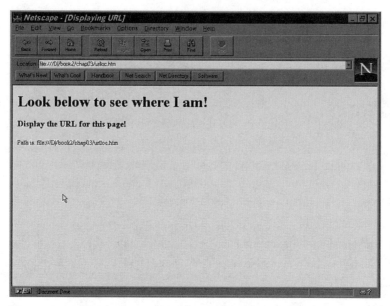

Figure 3-11 Displaying URL showing the HTML file location

Steps

Open the file URLLOC.HTM in your browser. The page will display a bold heading, a text string, and a smaller string showing the URL of the document as shown in Figure 3-11. To do this with your own Web page follow the steps below.

1. Create a new HTML file and type in the following HEAD section statements.

```
<HTML>
<HEAD><TITLE> Displaying URL </TITLE>
<H1> Look below to see where I am! </H1>
</HEAD>
```

2. Type the statements to create the BODY section of the document, including a JavaScript section that will write out the Document.Location property. Include the following:

```
<body>
<p><BIG><B>Display the URL for this page!</B></BIG>
<SCRIPT LANGUAGE="JavaScript">
<!--- hide script from old browsers
document.write ("<p><SMALL>Path is: " + document.location + "</SMALL>")
// end hiding from old browsers -->
</SCRIPT>
</BODY>
</HTML>
```

3. Close and save the document as URLLOC.HTM and open the file in your browser to test.

4. You can also print out the properties of the Location object. To do this, edit the document you just created.

5. Replace the *document.write* statement you just created with the following.

```
document.write ("<p><SMALL>Path is: " + location.protocol
                + "//"
                + location.hostname
                + ":"
                + location.port
                + " " + "</SMALL>")
```

6. Close and test the document with the modification. The results should look similar to those shown in Figure 3-12.

How It Works

The Location object consists of several properties such as Protocol, Hostname, Port, Hashname, HREF (full URL), Search, and Target. The URL of the current window can be changed by assigning a new value to the Location object.

The Document object also contains a read-only Location property and the full URL of the object. This is handy for writing out the URL of a document.

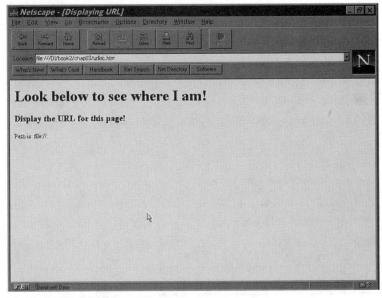

Figure 3-12 Location using the Location object

3.7 How do I...
Move backward and forward through previously viewed documents?

COMPATIBILITY:  NAVIGATOR 2.X   NAVIGATOR 3.X

Problem

I want those who visit my Web page to be able to move backward or forward to other Web pages that have been visited in the current session. What object and methods should I use?

Technique

The History object in JavaScript maintains a linked list of URLs visited in the current session. With this object you can use the published methods of Back() and Forward() and Go() to move forward, backward, or to go to a specific URL.

Steps

Open the file MOVE.HTM in your browser. This simple Web page consists of two buttons (as shown in Figure 3-13) that will allow you to navigate forward from this page or backward from this page to other URLs that have been visited in the current session. Follow the steps below to re-create this page.

1. Create an empty HTML file.

2. Start a HEAD and JavaScript function by typing the following code.

```
<HTML>
<HEAD><TITLE> Moving between Windows </TITLE>
<SCRIPT LANGUAGE="JavaScript">
<!--- hide script from old browsers
// JavaScript Global Variables

// JavaScript Functions
```

3. Create a function called *MoveForward* that will access the History object and move forward in the URL linked list.

```
// MoveForward()
// Function will move Forward in previously viewed documents
function MoveForward() {
   history.forward()
   }
```

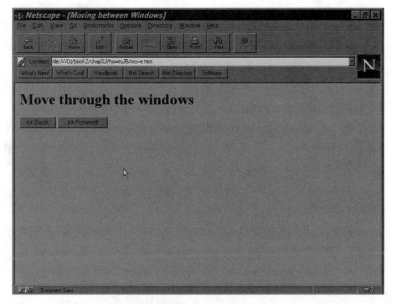

Figure 3-13 The MOVE.HTM page with two move buttons

4. Create a second function called *MoveBack* that will access the History object and move backward in the URL linked list.

```
// MoveBack()
// Function will move Back in previously viewed documents
function MoveBack() {
   history.back()
   }
```

5. Type in the code to end the JavaScript and the HEAD sections.

```
// end hiding from old browsers -->
</SCRIPT>
<H1> Move through the windows </H1>
</HEAD>
```

6. Create the BODY section and include a form with two buttons. In the onClick event of one of the buttons call the MoveBack JavaScript function and in the onClick event of the other button call the MoveForward JavaScript function.

```
<BODY>
<FORM NAME="MoveForm">
<INPUT TYPE="button" VALUE="<< Back" onClick="MoveBack()">
<INPUT TYPE="button" VALUE=">> Forward" onClick="MoveForward()">
</FORM>
</BODY>
</HTML>
```

7. Close the file and save it as MOVE.HTM. From your browser open any Web page, the MOVE.HTM, and then some other Web page. Move back to the MOVE Web page and use the Forward and Backward buttons to move to the other Web pages.

How It Works

The History object is a property of the Document object and allows you to access the URLs the user has visited within the current session and within the current window or frame. The object has three methods: Forward(), Back(), and Go(). The first two were detailed in the code. The third function, Go() will allow you to go to a specific URL in the list or to a URL specified in the function call. The numbers are relative to the current document. For example:

```
history.go(1)
history.go(-3)
```

The first call will move to the next URL in the linked list and the second will move to the URL that is three back in the linked list.

Comments

There are several objects related to the History object. A Location object is the complete URL of the current document. A link is a hypertext object represented by an HREF tag, and the Links Array contains all the links embedded in the current document source code. Both the Location object and the Links Array are accessible in JavaScript.

CHAPTER 4
WINDOWS

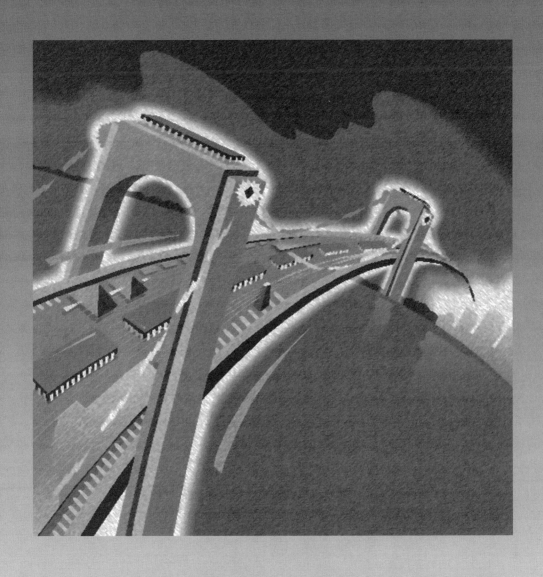

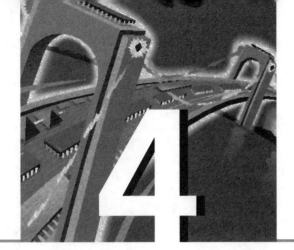

WINDOWS

How do I...

The Window object provides both the display area and navigational tools to display the Document object. As the Document object is a property of a Window object, a window is considered to be the topmost object in the hierarchy that contains document, location, and history.

The Window object itself has few properties other than synonyms such as *Top* and *Self* or *Parent,* which all basically refer to the window in one state or another, or to another associated window. In addition, it has few methods. One method is Open(), which will open a new window and display either an existing document or a new blank document. When opening the document, various aspects of the window can be changed, such as whether it has a toolbar or not, or displays a status bar, or is a specified size. Once the window is opened, objects it contains can be accessed by the calling window and certain of the properties of the new window can be read or modified.

Lastly, interactive communication with the user occurs via one of the dialogs that is opened using Window methods. These dialogs include an Alert message, a Confirmation message, and a Prompt message.

4.1 Perform background processing when a window is loaded

Some of the JavaScript objects have events that you can associate with event handlers. The Window object has the OnLoad event, which you can trap and use to perform background processing when the window is being loaded with a document.

4.2 Use a popup window

When you open a Document object using the Open method, the document will be opened into the existing window and will overwrite the document contained in the window. This How-To demonstrates how to use JavaScript to open a new window and how to write HTML commands directly to it.

4.3 Change the features of a popup window

A popup window in Netscape is technically another instance of the application. There are several options you can specify when using the Open method for the Window object, such as whether to add a toolbar or scrollbars. This How-To lists each one and demonstrates how to use them.

4.4 Write to the status bar of a popup window

Once you have opened a new window you have access to a variable containing a reference to the window. You can use this to display a message in the status bar of the new window if you have created it with one. This How-To demonstrates the technique.

4.5 Create a custom warning or error message

An interactive Web page will require that you communicate with the user. This How-To describes how to use the Alert, Confirm, and Prompt methods to do it.

4.6 Create a prompt dialog that prompts for more than one value and returns the values to the calling window

This How-To will provide a demonstration of the new Opener property. When opening a new window, the Opener property can be set to the window that opened the new window, thereby establishing two-way communication between them.

COMPLEXITY

BEGINNING/INTERMEDIATE

4.1 How do I...
Perform background processing when a window is loaded?

COMPATIBILITY: NAVIGATOR 2.X   NAVIGATOR 3.X

Problem

I want to be able to set values and do some other processing just after a Web page is loaded but before any other events can occur. How can I do processing in the background after the page is loaded but before the Web page reader has a chance to perform any action?

Technique

JavaScript has an event, onLoad, that is called just after a window is loaded. You can trap this event and perform any background processing that you need whenever the page is loaded. This event can only be trapped in the BODY tag, and can then call a JavaScript function.

Steps

Open the file TIMEDAY.HTM in your browser. This page consists of a graphic and a text field as shown in Figure 4-1. When the document first opened, it actually displayed a different graphic and then changed to one that was representative of the time of day. The image, the background color, and the message in the text field all reflect the time of day. If you open this page during different days of the week and different times of the day, you will find that the background color changes. It has one color for each day of the week, such as red for Sunday or yellow for Tuesday, and the brightness of the color decreases from morning to afternoon to night. The image shown in Figure 4-2 was captured during a Friday evening. The processing to get the time and day of the week and to set the color all occur from a function that is called from the onLoad event. To re-create this page follow the steps below.

1. Create an empty HTML file.

2. Type in the code to start the HEAD and a JavaScript section.

```
<HTML>
<HEAD><TITLE> Time of Day </TITLE>
<SCRIPT LANGUAGE="JavaScript">
<!--- hide script from old browsers
// JavaScript global variables

// JavaScript Functions
```

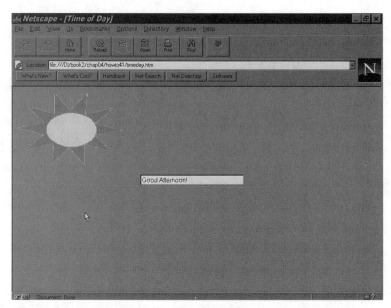

Figure 4-1 TIMEDAY when opened on a Tuesday in the afternoon

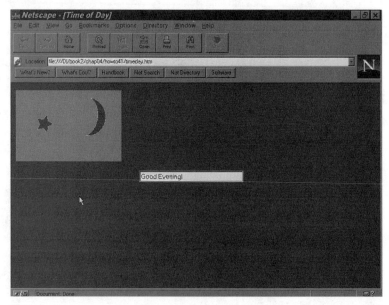

Figure 4-2 TIMEDAY when opened on a Friday in the evening

3. Create a JavaScript function that will find a color brightness based on the time of day. The time of day is a variable that was set in the function SetDayTime, defined in a later step.

```
// SetTime
// Function will find the brightness based
// on time of day
// Accepts Hours value
// Returns brightness
function SetTime(iTime) {
    var iBright = ""
    // set hue/saturation based on time of day
    if (iTime > 4 && iTime <= 11) {
        iBright = "FF"
        }
    else if (iTime > 11 && iTime <= 19) {
        iBright = "BB"
        }
    else    {
        iBright = "77"
        }
    return iBright
    }
```

4. Create the next function, ChangeImage. This function is actually called as a result of a *triggerevent* and will change the image that is in the document with the one that fits the time of day. The event must be processed after a timer to allow time for the images array to be instantiated.

```
// Called by the timer
// will check time of day and
// set appropriate image
//
// greeting based on time of day
function ChangeImage() {
    if (iTime > 4 && iTime <= 11)
        document.images[0].src="/sunrise.gif"
    else if (iTime > 11 && iTime <= 19)
        document.images[0].src="/sun.gif"
    else
      document.images[0].src="/night.gif"
    }
```

5. Create another function that will change the greeting message in the form text field and that will set up a timer event to call ChangeImage. This timer event will allow the document to fully load, including loading of image array.

```
// ChangeGreeting()
//
// function will change the message in the
// text field based on time of day
// function will then setup call to ChangeImage
```

continued on next page

continued from previous page

```
function ChangeGreeting() {
    // greeting based on time of day
    if (iTime > 4 && iTime <= 11)
      sMessage = "Good Morning!"
    else if (iTime > 11 && iTime <= 19)
      sMessage = "Good Afternoon!"
    else
      sMessage = "Good Evening!"

    document.FormTime.TimeBanner.value=sMessage
    setTimeout('ChangeImage()',100)
    }
```

6. Next, create a function, SetDay, that will generate a color value based on the day of the week, using the new color brightness value found calling the SetTime function.

```
// SetDay
// Function will build the hexidecimal
// color string
// Accepts the brightness value and day of week
// returns the color string
function SetDay(iBright, iDay)    {
    var iColor = "#"

    // set color based on day of week
    if (iDay == 0) {
       iColor = iColor + iBright + "0000"
       }
    else if (iDay == 1) {
       iColor = iColor + "0000" + iBright
       }
    else if (iDay == 2) {
       iColor = iColor + iBright + iBright + "00"
       }
    else if (iDay == 3) {
       iColor = iColor + "00" + iBright + "00"
       }
    else if (iDay == 4) {
       iColor = iColor + "00" + iBright + iBright
       }
    else if (iDay == 5) {
       iColor = iColor + iBright + "00" + iBright
       }
    else {
       iColor = iColor + iBright + iBright + iBright
       }
    return iColor
    }
```

7. Create a function, SetDayTime, which will get the day of the week and current time in hours using a Date object and will call the SetTime and SetDay function. It will then use the generated color string to set the background color of the current window document.

```
// SetDayTime
// function will change the background color
// of the document based on day of week and
// time of day
function SetDayTime() {
   var dateObj = new Date()
   var iDay = dateObj.getDay()
   var iTime = dateObj.getHours()

   // set hue and color
   var iBright = SetTime(iTime)
   var iColor = SetDay(iBright, iDay)
   document.bgColor = iColor
   }
```

8. Type in the code to close the JavaScript and HEAD sections and to create the BODY section. This section contains an image and a form with one text field. The image is set to a generic one that acts as a placeholder. Notice in the BODY tag that the onLoad event is trapped and the functions SetDayTime and ChangeGreeting are called.

```
// end hiding from old browsers -->
</SCRIPT>

</HEAD>

<BODY
  onLoad="SetDayTime(); ChangeGreeting()">

<IMG SRC="rain.gif" NAME="TimeImage" width=230 height=148>

<P>
<FORM NAME="FormTime">
<CENTER><INPUT TYPE="text" NAME="TimeBanner" size=30>
</CENTER>
</FORM>

</BODY>
</HTML>
```

9. Close and save the file as TIMEDAY.HTM. Test your code by opening the file in your browser over different days of the week and different times of the day. Or, to speed things up, hardcode the time of day and the day of the week.

How It Works

The onLoad event fires just after the window is loaded or after all frames in a FrameSet have been loaded. Trap this event by placing an event handler into the BODY tag statement. Call a JavaScript function that contains processing that you want to do every time a window is loaded. Among some of the actions that can occur are presetting variable values or instantiating objects.

The timer event is used to delay the calling of the function ChangeImage. This will give time for the document to not only finish loading but to display. This is necessary for the images array to be populated and for the ChangeImage function to work properly.

Comments

Instead of changing the image in the document, the image could be changed physically on the Web page server. However, a better approach could be to place an image reflecting the weather for the day into a generic filename such as WEATHER.GIF. This will be pulled up as the dummy image when the document is loaded. With it, you might actually want to delay the opening even longer so that the Web page reader can observe the weather image. The delay is normally to allow time for the initial image to load. Otherwise, the time of day image will not load properly.

COMPLEXITY

INTERMEDIATE

4.2 How do I...
Use a popup window?

COMPATIBILITY: NAVIGATOR 2.X   NAVIGATOR 3.X

Problem

I have several interrelated links in my Web page. I would like to open them in their own windows instead of opening them as documents in my current window. How can I open a popup window for a Web page?

Technique

The Window object has a method, Open(), that will allow you to create and open a new browser window. With this you can open an existing or blank document in a new window. With this you can have more than one document open in your workspace at a time.

Steps

Open the file OPENWIN.HTM in your browser. You have four buttons, each representing a Web page created elsewhere in the book and used here for example only. As can be seen from the Windows 95 taskbar in Figure 4-3, this is also the only browser window currently open. Click on the Open URL Example. The example will open in a separate window which will also have its own icon on the Windows 95 taskbar, as can be seen in Figure 4-4. The code to create this Web page is listed below.

1. Create an empty HTML file.

2. Type in the code to begin a HEAD and JavaScript code section.

```
<HTML>
<HEAD><TITLE> Open PopUp Window </TITLE>
<SCRIPT LANGUAGE="JavaScript">
<!--- hide script from old browsers

// JavaScript Global Variables

// JavaScript Functions
```

3. Create a function called OpenWindow that will open a new window using the document that the Web page reader has selected. The document is local to the OPENWIN.HTM file.

```
// OpenWindow
// Function will open a new window
// using URL passed to it
function OpenWindow(sURL) {
   newwindow = window.open(sURL)
   }
```

4. End the JavaScript code and HEAD sections.

```
// end hiding from old browsers -->
</SCRIPT>
</HEAD>
```

5. Create the BODY section, including a form that will contain four Radio buttons. Each button will provide an event handler for the onClick event and will call the OpenWindow function. Each button will pass the HTML filename represented by the button.

```
<BODY>
<H1> Open a new Window and display...</H1>
<FORM>
<INPUT TYPE="radio" NAME="OpenWin" VALUE="Open LastModified Example"
   onClick="OpenWindow('moddate.htm')">Open LastModified Example
<br><INPUT TYPE="radio" NAME="OpenWin" VALUE="Open URL Example"
   onClick="OpenWindow('urlloc.htm')">Open URL Example
<br><INPUT TYPE="radio" NAME="OpenWin" VALUE="Open Time/Day Example"
   onClick="OpenWindow('timeday.htm')">Open Time/Day Example
<br><INPUT TYPE="radio" NAME="OpenWin" VALUE="Open Move Example"
   onClick="OpenWindow('move.htm')">Open Move Example
</FORM>
</BODY>
</HTML>
```

6. Close the file and save it as OPENWIN.HTM. To successfully test your file you will need to copy the MODDATE.HTM, URLLOC.HTM, MOVE.HTM, and TIMEDAY.HTM files into the same subdirectory where your new document will be saved.

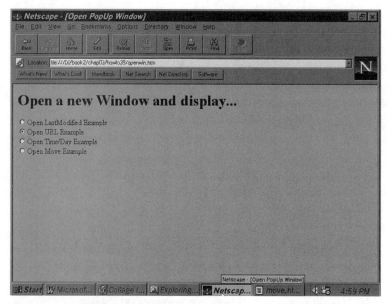

Figure 4-3 OPENWIN.HTM and Windows 95 taskbar showing only one browser window open

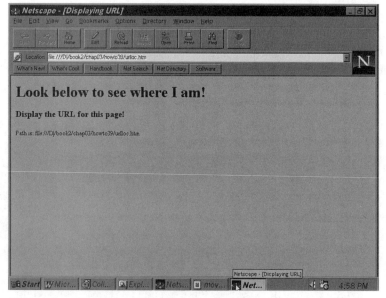

Figure 4-4 URLLOC.HTM example and Windows 95 taskbar showing two browser windows open

How It Works

The Open() Window object method will open a new browser window. This window will contain your document if you passed in the URL or will contain a blank document if you open it with an empty string as the URL (""). The complete syntax of this method is `window.open("URL", "window name", "features")`. The only required parameter is the first, and you do not have to specify either a window name or any features. By default all features will be set to True or Yes or 1, whatever the positive value is for the feature. How-To 4.3, Changing the Features of a Popup Window, will cover the features in more detail.

Comments

A word about scoping is due here. A document is contained within a window as it is a property of a window. If the Open() method had been called without preceding it with the Window object identifier, a new document would have been opened in the current window instead of a new window. This is because the Open() method of the Child object, the Document, overrides the Open() method of the Parent object, the window.

COMPLEXITY

INTERMEDIATE

4.3 How do I...
Change the features of a popup window?

COMPATIBILITY: NAVIGATOR 2.X   NAVIGATOR 3.X   EXPLORER 3.X

Problem

I want to be able to open a new browser window with a blank document and I want to write HTML tags directly to this new document. I also want to be able to scale the size of the window and I don't want to see the toolbar. How can I control the opening of a new window and how can I open it with a blank document?

Technique

The window Open() method has a third optional parameter, the *Windows Features* parameter, which allows you to specify how the window will look when it is opened. In addition, specifying an empty string as the first parameter of the Open() method, the URL parameter, will open the window with a blank document.

Steps

Open the WINCHG.HTM file in your browser. The window has a text box and a button, as shown in Figure 4-5, with the string, Hello!, already loaded into the text field. Click the button and a new window pops up that displays the text field string with a magenta background and white letters. In addition, the window is much smaller than the Parent window and does not have a toolbar as shown in Figure 4-6. Return to the original WINCHG.HTM window and type in a different message and again click the button. The same window is still displayed but the previous string has been replaced by the new one. The code to create this Web page is in the following steps.

1. Create a new HTML file.

2. Type in the code to start the HEAD and a JavaScript code section.

```
<HTML>
<HEAD><TITLE> Open PopUp Window </TITLE>
<SCRIPT LANGUAGE="JavaScript">
<!--- hide script from old browsers

// JavaScript Global Variables

// JavaScript Functions
```

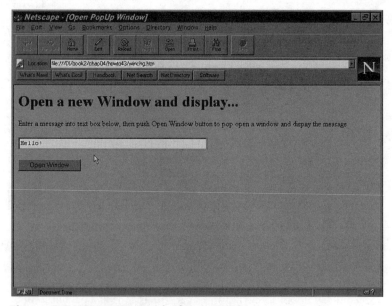

Figure 4-5 WINCHG.HTM before opening new window

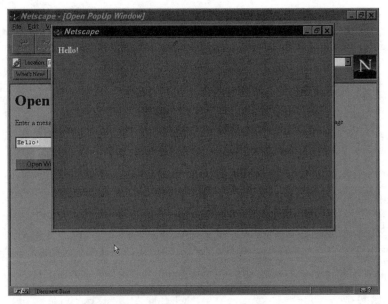

Figure 4-6 WINCHG.HTM and new window

3. Create a JavaScript function called OpenNewWindow, which will open a new browser window that contains a blank document. The window is opened with a status bar and without a toolbar or directories and with the width and height of the window specified by setting the toolbar, directories, width, and height variables as shown. When the window is opened, a document is opened in it, and its background and foreground (text) colors are set after writing out the BODY tag for the new document. Finally, the BODY tags are written and the message, found in the text field of the form, is written to the new document. The document is then closed, which forces the drawing of the document.

```
// OpenNewWindow
// Function will open a new window
// using URL passed to it
function OpenNewWindow() {
    var sMessage = document.OpenWindow.Message.value
    newwindow = window.open("","newWin",
        "toolbar=no,directories=no,width=600,height=400")
    newwindow.document.open()
    newwindow.document.writeln("<HEAD></HEAD>")
    newwindow.document.bgColor="#FF00FF"
    newwindow.document.fgColor="#FFFFFF"
    newwindow.document.writeln("<BODY><BIG>" + sMessage + "</BIG>")
    newwindow.document.writeln("</BODY>")
    newwindow.document.close()
    }
```

4. Close the JavaScript and HEAD sections.

```
// end hiding from old browsers -->
</SCRIPT>
</HEAD>
```

5. Create the BODY section. In it, include a form that contains a text field and a button. The onClick event of the button will call the OpenNewWindow() JavaScript function.

```
<BODY>
<H1> Open a new Window and display...</H1>
<p>
Enter a message into text box below, then push Open Window button to
pop open a window and dispay the message
<FORM NAME="OpenWindow">
<p><INPUT TYPE="text" NAME="Message" VALUE="Hello!" size=50>
<p><INPUT TYPE="button" NAME="OpenWin" VALUE="Open Window"
   onClick="OpenNewWindow()">
</FORM>
</BODY>
</HTML>
```

6. Close your file and name it WINCHG.HTM. Test your code by opening the file in your browser and trying different messages, clicking the button between messages.

How It Works

The Open() method has a third parameter, the Windows features parameter, where the features of the new window can be modified. When you open a new window without specifying anything in this parameter, the feature attributes are set to their default values. The default values are always true, except for width and height, which are set to the default size of the Netscape application. The features are listed in Table 4-1.

WINDOW FEATURE	PURPOSE	FALSE OR OFF VALUES	TRUE OR ON VALUES
toolbar	Browser toolbar	No or 0	Yes or 1
location	Location entry	No or 0	Yes or 1
directories	Standard directory buttons	No or 0	Yes or 1
status	Status bar	No or 0	Yes or 1
menubar	Browser menu bar	No or 0	Yes or 1
scrollbars	Horizontal or vertical	No or 0	Yes or 1
resizable	Allows user to resize	No or 0	Yes or 1

WINDOW FEATURE	PURPOSE	FALSE OR OFF VALUES	TRUE OR ON VALUES
width	Window width	N/A	Number in pixels
height	Window height	N/A	Number in pixels

Table 4-1 Window features used in open() method

COMPLEXITY
BEGINNING

4.4 How do I...
Write to the status bar of a popup window?

COMPATIBILITY:

Problem

I am using a popup window to display a second document based on the user's actions and I need to be able to display messages to the user in this window. How can I display a message in the status bar of a popup window?

Technique

One of the Window properties that can be changed after the window has been opened is the Status property. This is the value that is displayed in the status bar at the bottom of the window.

Steps

Open the file WINSTAT.HTM in your browser. This page consists of two buttons and a text field, as shown in Figure 4-7. Clicking the Open Window button will open the TIMEDAY.HTM Web page in a separate window, as shown in Figure 4-8. Type the message, Now this is a new message in the status line, in the text field and click the second button labeled Update Status. The status bar on the new window now displays your new message as shown in Figure 4-9. The steps to create this page follow.

1. Create a new HTML file.

2. Begin the document HEAD and a JavaScript code section. In the section for global variables, create a variable called *newwindow*. Set the window variable to null.

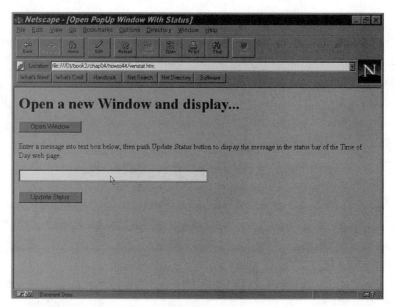

Figure 4-7 WINSTAT.HTM after opening

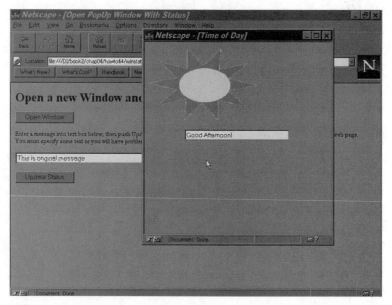

Figure 4-8 WINSTAT.HTM and TIMEDAY.HTM after clicking
Open Window button

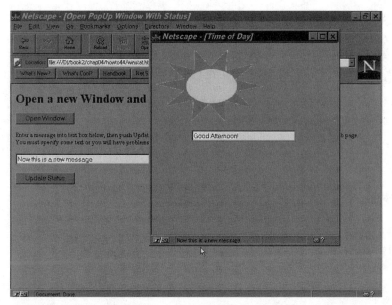

Figure 4-9 WINSTAT.HTM and TIMEDAY.HTM after entering message and clicking Update Status button

```
<HTML>
<HEAD><TITLE> Open PopUp Window With Status </TITLE>
<SCRIPT LANGUAGE="JavaScript">
<!--- hide script from old browsers

// JavaScript Global Variables
newwindow = ""
```

3. Next, create a JavaScript function section and a function called OpenNewWindow. This function will create a new window object using Open() and will load the document TIMEDAY.HTM into it. In addition, the new window will be sized, set to *resizeable*, and created with a status bar. The new window is assigned to the *newwindow* global variable to make it accessible in other functions. Note that the message variable is tested to make sure a message has been entered.

```
// OpenNewWindow
// Function will open a new window
// using URL passed to it
function OpenNewWindow() {
    var sMessage = document.OpenWindow.Message.value
    if (sMessage == null || sMessage == "") {
        alert("You must type in a message.")
        return
```

continued on next page

continued from previous page

```
        }

    newwindow = window.open("timeday.htm", "NewWindow",
    "status=yes,resizeable=yes,width=400,height=400")
    newwindow.defaultStatus=sMessage
    }
```

4. Create another function and call this one WriteStatus. This function will
take a string and display it in the status bar of the newly opened window.
Again, note the code checking that a message has been entered and that the
window variable is not null (that is, a window has been opened).

```
// WriteStatus
// Function will write to new windows status
function WriteStatus(sMessage) {

    // check if message entered
    if (sMessage == null || sMessage == "") {
        alert("You must type in a message.")
        return
        }

    // check if window opened
    if (newwindow == null) {
        alert("You must open window first.")
        return
        }

    newwindow.status=sMessage
    }
```

5. Create the BODY section. In it, create a form with two buttons and a text
field. The first button will call the OpenNewWindow function when it is
clicked, and the second will call the WriteStatus function when it is clicked.
The value passed to this function is the value of the Message text field.

```
<BODY>

<H1> Open a new Window and display...</H1>

<FORM NAME="OpenWindow"
<p><INPUT TYPE="button" NAME="OpenWin" VALUE="Open Window"
    onClick="OpenNewWindow()">

<p>Enter a message into text box below, then push Update Status
button to dispay the message in the status bar of the
Time of Day web page.
<p><INPUT TYPE="text" NAME="Message" VALUE="" size=50>
<p><INPUT TYPE="button" NAME="stat" VALUE="Update Status"
    onClick="WriteStatus(Message.value)">
</FORM>
</BODY>
```

6. Close the file and name it WINSTAT.HTM. Copy the TIMEDAY.HTM to the subdirectory where your new file is stored. Test your new page by loading it into your browser and trying different status messages.

How It Works

One of the properties of a window that can be accessed and modified after the window has been loaded is the Status property. This is the value that is currently displayed in the status bar of the window. To change this on your opened window, make sure that when you create the window you assign it to a variable that you can access later. Use this variable to access the properties and objects of the new window.

Comments

Opening a window and setting the defaultStatus property to an empty or null string can actually cause some problems with your browser. You will always want to check the value provided by the Web page reader before using it in any of your JavaScript code.

COMPLEXITY

ADVANCED

4.5   How do I...
Create a custom warning or error message?

COMPATIBILITY:  NAVIGATOR 2.X   NAVIGATOR 3.X

Problem

I don't care too much for the JavaScript Alert message style. I don't like the fact that I can't customize it with a different icon and I don't like the fact that it displays JavaScript Alert so prominently. I find this to be confusing to my Web page readers. How can I create my own Warning and Error messages?

Technique

The only real modification you make to the three message-style dialogs that come with JavaScript (Alert, Confirm, and Prompt) is to change their messages. However, you can transform a popup window, with a little bit of help from the timer, to your own Warning or Error message window.

Steps

Open the OPENWARN.HTM file in your browser. It consists of two Radio buttons, one labeled Warning Dialog and one labeled Stop Dialog as shown in Figure 4-10. Press the Warning Dialog button. A new window pops up that displays a warning icon and a text field with a not-too-friendly warning message, as shown in Figure 4-11. Press the OK button to close the window. Next, click on the Stop Dialog Radio button. As can be seen from Figure 4-12, an Error message window pops open with the traditional stop sign icon and a message that many of us would like to give when the user ignores our warnings!

The steps to create these message dialogs follow.

1. Create the Warning dialog message window first. Start with a new HTML document.

2. In the HEAD section type in the title and start the BODY section. Type in the image tag for the warning icon.

```
<HTML>
<HEAD><TITLE> Alert! </TITLE></HEAD>
<BODY>
<H1>Warning!</H1>
<p>
<IMG SRC="warn.gif" width=50 height=50>
```

3. Finish the window by creating a form, one text field, and a button. In the onClick event of the button, trap the event and close the window.

```
<p>
<FORM NAME="DiagForm">
<INPUT type="text" size=50 Name="Msg">
<p><CENTER>
<INPUT type="button" Value="      OK      ",
    onClick="window.close()">
</FORM>
</BODY>
</HTML>
```

4. Close and save the file as WARN.HTM.

5. Create the Stop dialog window by again starting with a new HTML document.

6. Create the HEAD section and start the BODY section with the stop sign icon.

```
<HTML>
<HEAD><TITLE> Stop! </TITLE></HEAD>
<BODY>
<H1>Stop It!</H1>
<p>
<IMG SRC="stop.gif" width=50 height=50>
```

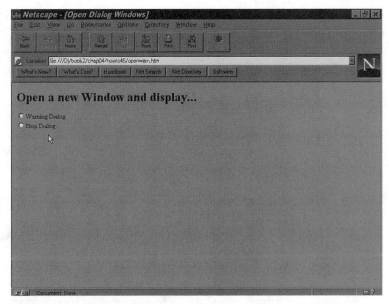

Figure 4-10 OPENWARN.HTM after opening

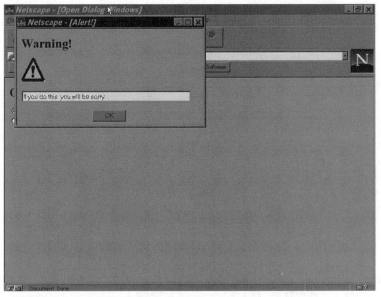

Figure 4-11 OPENWARN.HTM and Warning message

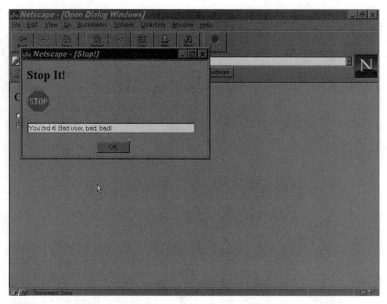

Figure 4-12 OPENWARN.HTM and Stop message

7. Finish this document with a form, a text field, and a button. The onClick event of this button will again close the window.

```
<p>
<FORM NAME="DiagForm">
<INPUT type="text" size=50 Name="Msg">
<p><CENTER>
<INPUT type="button" Value="     OK     ",
    onClick="window.close()">
</FORM>
</BODY>
</HTML>
```

8. Close and save this document as STOP.HTM.

9. Create a new HTML document.

10. Start the HEAD section and a JavaScript code section. Also create two global variables for message and for window.

```
<HTML>
<HEAD><TITLE> Open Dialog Windows </TITLE>
<SCRIPT LANGUAGE="JavaScript">
<!--- hide script from old browsers

// JavaScript Global Variables
newWindow = null
msgTime = null

// JavaScript Functions
```

11. Create a function, WriteMessage, that will set the message passed to it in its argument list, into the form text field of a document that is contained in a window referenced with your global window variable. This variable is set later in another function. The function was called by a timer event and this is cleared as a precaution.

```
// write message
function WriteMessage(sMessage) {

   newWindow.document.DiagForm.Msg.value=sMessage
   clearTimeout(msgTime)

}
```

12. Create another function, OpenAlert, that will open a window using the HTML document that fits the type called for by its first parameter. It also sets a timer event to call the WriteMessage function.

```
// OpenAlert
// Redefined alert message
//
function OpenAlert(iType, sMessage) {
   // open window based on alert type
   if (iType == 1) {
      newWindow=window.open("warn.htm","",
      "toolbar=no,directories=no,width=400,height=200")
      }

   else     {
      newWindow=window.open("stop.htm","",
      "toolbar=no,directories=no,width=400,height=200")
      }
   msgTime=setTimeout("WriteMessage('" + sMessage +"')",1000)

}
```

13. Create a third function, called OpenDialog, that will create the message and set the type based on the dialog requested. Also close out the JavaScript and HEAD sections.

```
//
// OpenDialog
// Function will open the appropriate
// dialog and print out results
function OpenDialog(sDialog) {
   if (sDialog == "Warn Dialog") {
      OpenAlert(1, "If you do this, you will be sorry...")
      }
   else     {
      OpenAlert(2,
       "You did it!  Bad user, bad, bad!")
      }
   }
// end hiding from old browsers -->
</SCRIPT>
</HEAD>
```

14. Create the BODY with a form and two Radio buttons. The onClick event of both buttons will call the OpenDialog function and pass to the function its own value as a parameter.

```
// end hiding from old browsers -->
</SCRIPT>
</HEAD>
<BODY>
<H1> Open a new Window and display...</H1>
<p>
<FORM NAME="DialogForm">
<INPUT TYPE="radio" NAME="OpenWin" VALUE="Warn Dialog"
    onClick="OpenDialog(this.value)">Warning Dialog
<br><INPUT TYPE="radio" NAME="OpenWin" VALUE="Stop Dialog"
    onClick="OpenDialog(this.value)">Stop Dialog
</FORM>
</BODY>
</HTML>
```

15. Close and save the file as OPENWARN.HTM. Test your new window by opening it in the browser and trying both message types.

How It Works

You have the ability to pop open a new window and use a predefined HTML file to define the contents of the window. Additionally, when you open the window, you can maintain a reference to the window in a variable. The key to making something like this message window work is to have a Timer event that allows the new window to fully open before setting the message, or the attempt to set the message will fail. That is the disadvantage of this technique and may be tricky to work with in an Internet environment. However, in an Intranet environment, where you have a little more control as to the speed of access to a window, this approach can be very effective.

COMPLEXITY
ADVANCED

4.6 How do I...
Create a prompt dialog that prompts for more than one value and returns the values to the calling window?

COMPATIBILITY: NAVIGATOR 3.X   EXPLORER 3.X

Problem

The Prompt() method and resulting message window is handy when I want one piece of information from the user, but it does not work well when I need several pieces of information. I don't always want to put fields for all possible values in my form. How can I create a customized, multiple-input Prompt dialog window?

Technique

You can open a new window that will contain a form with fields for the values you want. To maintain two-way connectivity between the two windows, set the Window Opener property of the new window to reference the old window. This property is available only on Netscape 3.0.

Steps

Open the document OPENDIAG.HTM in your browser. The page has two text fields and an Open Dialog button, as shown in Figure 4-13. Click on this button and a new smaller window opens up, which in turn has two text fields, an OK button and a Cancel button, as shown in Figure 4-14. Fill in the two fields and click the OK button. The new window closes and the values in the two fields are now in the original form as shown in Figure 4-15.

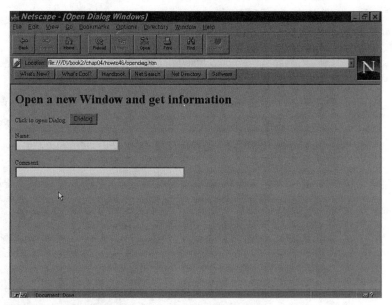

Figure 4-13 OPENDIAG.HTM after opening

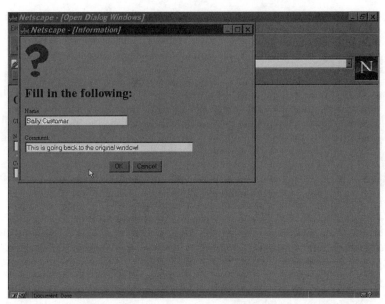

Figure 4-14 OPENDIAG.HTM and new dialog window

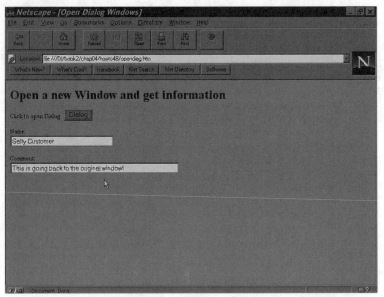

Figure 4-15 OPENDIAG.HTM after closing new dialog window

The steps to create these two windows follow.

1. Create the Dialog window first by creating a new HTML document.

2. Start a HEAD section and a JavaScript section by typing the following code.

```
<HTML>
<HEAD><TITLE> Information</TITLE>

<SCRIPT LANGUAGE="JavaScript">
<!--- hide script from old browsers

// JavaScript Global Variables
```

3. Create a function called SetInformation that will set values to the two input fields in the form of the window that called it. It will then close itself. Note that the reference to the previous window is the new Window Opener property that allows for two-way communication between windows.

```
// SetInformation
//
// function will get input values
// and set to calling window
function SetInformation() {

    opener.document.CallDiag.Name.value=
        document.DiagForm.Name.value
    opener.document.CallDiag.Comment.value=
        document.DiagForm.Comment.value

    window.close()
    }
// end hiding from old browsers -->
</SCRIPT>

</HEAD>
```

4. Create the BODY section with a question mark image and a form with two input fields and two buttons. The first button will trap the onClick event and call the SetInformation function. The second will capture the onClick event and close the window.

```
<BODY>
<IMG SRC="question.gif" width=50 height=70>

<H1>Fill in the following:</H1>
<p>
<FORM NAME="DiagForm">
Name:
<br><INPUT type="text" size=30 Name="Name">
<p>
Comment:
<br><INPUT type="text" size=50 Name="Comment">
<p><CENTER>
<INPUT type="button" Value="  OK  "
    onClick="SetInformation()">
```

continued on next page

continued from previous page

```
 
<INPUT type="button" Value="Cancel" onClick="window.close()">
</CENTER>
</FORM>

</BODY>
</HTML>
```

5. Close and save the window as DIAG.HTM.

6. Create a new HTML document.

7. Start a JavaScript and HEAD section and create two global variables, one for a timer and one for a new window.

```
<HTML>
<HEAD><TITLE> Open Dialog Windows </TITLE>
<SCRIPT LANGUAGE="JavaScript">
<!--- hide script from old browsers

// JavaScript Global Variables
newWindow = null
msgTime = null

// JavaScript Functions
```

8. Create a function called OpenDialog that will open the new Dialog window and set its Opener property to the current window.

```
// OpenDialog
// Redefined alert message
//
function OpenDialog(iType, sMessage) {
    // open window
    newWindow=window.open("diag.htm","",
        "toolbar=no,directories=no,width=500,height=300")

    if (newWindow != null && newWindow.opener == null)
        newWindow.opener = window
    }

// end hiding from old browsers -->
</SCRIPT>
</HEAD>
```

9. Create the BODY section with a new form that contains a button and two input fields. The button traps the onClick event and provides an Event Handler that will call the OpenDialog function.

```
<BODY>
<H1> Open a new Window and get information</H1>

<FORM NAME="CallDiag">
<p>Click to open Dialog  
<INPUT TYPE="button" NAME="OpenWin" VALUE="Dialog"
    onClick="OpenDialog()">
```

```
<p>
Name:
<br><INPUT type="text" size=30 Name="Name">
<p>
Comment:
<br><INPUT type="text" size=50 Name="Comment">
</FORM>
</BODY>
</HTML>
```

10. Close and save the file as OPENDIAG.HTM. Test the new documents in your browser.

How It Works

Prior to the new Window Property Opener, to maintain two-way communication between windows meant having to create a variable in the called window, which was then set by the calling window. As timing was an issue, the setting of this variable usually had to occur after a Timer Event to insure that the called window was open and the variable accessible prior to being set. The Opener property has simplified this so that using Dialog windows to access additional information is more than feasible.

CHAPTER 5
LANGUAGE SYNTAX

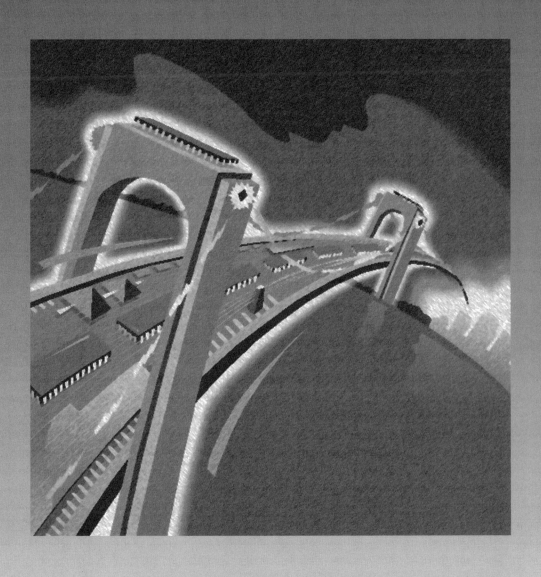

LANGUAGE SYNTAX

How do I...

As powerful as the HyperText Markup Language (HTML) is, it lacks some very basic application capabilities, such as looping through code based on a conditional value or creating a function that can be called from an event. Prior to JavaScript, anything requiring these capabilities meant that the Web page developer would need to provide server-based computing through the Common Gateway Interface (CGI) or use complicated API calls or something like Java. JavaScript provides these capabilities in a format that can be embedded directly into your HTML document and that is fairly intuitive and easy to learn. Best of all, you do not need to be a professional programmer to use them.

JavaScript gives you the ability to define functions and call them in response to user-initiated events. In addition, you can pass values to and return values from functions. You can create blocks of code that can be entered only when a condition is met or that can be looped through more than once, based on some condition. You can also define variables or groups of similar variables in arrays. Best of all, you can comment your code. Not only is this important for you to understand why you did something a specific way at a later time, it is essential if you publish your JavaScript code for others to use.

5.1   Define and call a function

The simplest way to capture a block of code and control when it is executed is by using a function. JavaScript functions are easy to create. This How-To also demonstrates how easy they are to call by tying a call to a function directly to a response from the user.

5.2   Declare global and local variables

Unless your code is performing very simple operations, you will probably make use of variables to hold the results of intermediate operations or to contain values that might change due to user or other action. This How-To discusses local and global variables and demonstrates how to define and use both.

5.3   Create and populate an array of variables

When you need to store several values, you can declare and use a variable for each, or you can declare and use an array. This How-To provides a sample of declaring and using a JavaScript array.

5.4   Use the new Array functionality to create an array

Beginning with the beta release of Netscape 3.0, code-named *Atlas Preview*, there is an alternative and simplified approach to creating an array. This How-To demonstrates using this capability.

5.5   Pass parameters to a function

Many times you will want the code in your function to operate in the same way regardless of what event or action called it, but there are times when you might want different functionality to occur, or you might want to change what the functionality works with. Parameters give you this ability. This How-To demonstrates calling a function and providing parameters for it.

5.6   Conditionally execute a block of code

You may only want a block of JavaScript code to execute under certain conditions, such as a variable or the property of a JavaScript object being set to a certain value. This How-To describes how to use the JavaScript conditional statement.

5.7   Loop through a block of code

You may want to run a block of code several times, based on a value in a variable or a JavaScript object property. Sometimes you might want to run through the code for a fixed number of iterations, and you will use the JavaScript FOR statement for this. Other times you might want to run through the loop until a condition is met, and the type of statement you will use is the WHILE statement. Sample code in this How-To demonstrates how to use both of these types of loops.

5.8   Place comments inside JavaScript code

Documentation of your code is important and is not complete if you do not use comments. This is true for JavaScript as well as other programming languages. This How-To demonstrates the use of commenting, both when you should use it and how.

COMPLEXITY

BEGINNING/INTERMEDIATE

5.1   How do I...
Define and call a function?

COMPATIBILITY: NAVIGATOR 2.X   NAVIGATOR 3.X   EXPLORER 3.X

Problem

I want to perform some processing whenever the user clicks on a button in my form. How can I create and call a function based on a user-initiated or other event?

Technique

A JavaScript function consists of two parts: the function code itself and the code to call it. Functions can be called as a response to user action, such as clicking on a button, or by being called from other code, such as another function.

Steps

Open the HTML file FUNCTION.HTM in your browser. The page consists of a heading, a text string, and three radio buttons, as shown in Figure 5-1. Click any of the radio buttons and a confirmation message will pop up, as shown in Figure 5-2. If you click the button, another message comes up confirming that you did press the button (see Figure 5-3). This window makes use of a function that is called when any one of the radio buttons is clicked, and another function that is called from the first function.

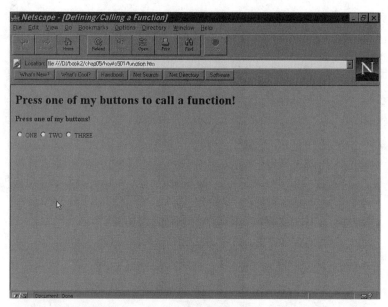

Figure 5-1 FUNCTION.HTM as it is loaded

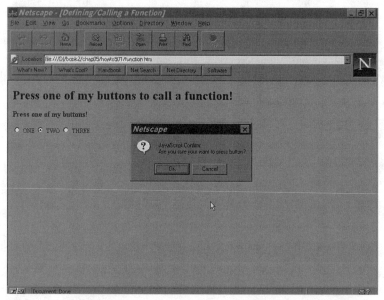

Figure 5-2 FUNCTION.HTM after clicking one of the radio buttons

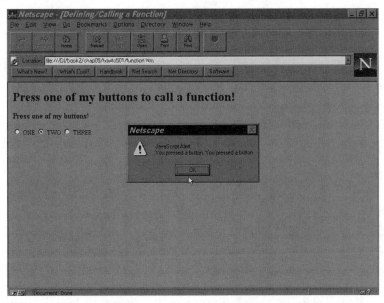

Figure 5-3 FUNCTION.HTM after clicking OK on first message

1. Create a new HTML file.

2. Type in the following code, which will create the HEAD section of the document, including the document title.

```
<HTML>
<HEAD><TITLE> Defining/Calling a Function </TITLE>
```

3. Finish the HEAD section of the document and begin the BODY section. The HEAD section will include a header, and the BODY section will include a line of text.

```
<H1> Press one of my buttons to call a function! </H1>
</HEAD>
<body>
<p><BIG><B>Press one of my buttons!</B></BIG>
```

4. Create a form that will contain three radio buttons. The buttons will trap the onClick event and provide an event handler that will call a JavaScript function called WhoPressedMe.

```
<FORM NAME="FunctionForm" >
<INPUT TYPE="radio" NAME="Pressed" VALUE="Choice One"
onClick="WhoPressedMe()"> ONE
<INPUT TYPE="radio" NAME="Pressed" VALUE="Choice Two"
onClick="WhoPressedMe()"> TWO
<INPUT TYPE="radio" NAME="Pressed" VALUE="Choice Three"
onClick="WhoPressedMe()"> THREE
</FORM>
```

5. Next, type in the YouPressedMe function that will put out a message that a button was pressed. The JavaScript function is placed in HTML comments so that non–JavaScript-compliant browsers will not be confused by the code.

```
// Reply
//
// Function will reply
function YouPressedMe() {
alert("You pressed a button. You pressed a button")
}
```

6. Create the WhoPressedMe function that will query Web page readers whether or not they really want to press that button. If the reader responds positively, the YouPressedMe function is called. If not, a rather snippy message is displayed.

```
// WhoPressedMe function
// This function will respond back with a confirmation message
// stating that a radio button has been pressed
function WhoPressedMe() {
var bResult=
confirm("Are you sure your want to press button?")

if (bResult)
YouPressedMe()
else
alert("Too late!")
}
```

7. Close out the script and the document by typing the following code.

```
// end hiding from old browsers -->
</SCRIPT>

</BODY>
</HTML>
```

8. Close the document and save it as FUNCTION.HTM. Test the document by loading it into your browser.

How It Works

A function in JavaScript is preceded by the function keyword. Any statements that are included in the function must be enclosed by curly brackets ('{', '}'). The function code will be read and loaded into memory when the document is parsed, but the code will not run until the function is invoked or called.

Functions can be called directly in JavaScript code or in response to an event in the object's event handler. This is the only instance in which JavaScript does not need to be enclosed by <SCRIPT> tags, but will need to be enclosed with quotes.

Comments

Any time you have a block of code that you want to call more than once, enclose that code in a function. The function will be loaded into memory once but can be called several times. In addition, if you have a bit of JavaScript code that you think others might want to use, create an HTML document that defines the function and place a representative call to this function in the BODY of the document. Others can then find and examine your function code easily, can see at a glance how the function is called, and can copy and embed the function code directly in their HTML documents.

COMPLEXITY
BEGINNING

5.2 How do I...
Declare global and local variables?

COMPATIBILITY:

Problem

In my JavaScript code I need to be able to store values based on the reader's actions, and I sometimes need to store intermediate results in a calculation. How do I do this with JavaScript?

Technique

Placing a value directly into the code forces that value to remain static unless it is changed programmatically. Placing a variable into the code will allow the value to change, based on reader-originated or other events. JavaScript has the capability of using variables that can be defined globally and used throughout the document, or that can be declared locally and used throughout a function. Additionally, JavaScript variables are loosely typed, and the variables are assigned types when they are used, though you can change their types just by assigning another literal value of a different type to it.

Steps

Open the file VARIABLES.HTM in your browser. The page has a header, a text field, and two buttons. Click the Add/Subtract button several times and notice how the value increases by five each time you press it. Now click the Change Operator button and then click the Add/Subtract button several times. This time the value decreases by five each time the button is pressed, as shown in Figure 5-4. The steps to create this code using variables are listed below.

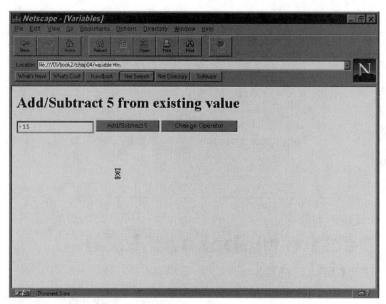

Figure 5-4 VARIABLES.HTM after changing operator and
clicking the Add/Subtract button several times

1. Create a new HTML document.

2. Type in code to begin the HEAD document section and add in the code to
start a JavaScript section. In this section you will be declaring two global
variables and setting their initial values.

```
<HTML>
<HEAD><TITLE> Variables </TITLE>
<H1> Add/Subtract 5 from existing value </H1>

<SCRIPT LANGUAGE="JavaScript">
<!--- hide script from old browsers

// Global Variables
iCurrentValue=0
bSubtract=false
```

3. Next you will create a function that will change the value of the operator
Boolean variable when the user clicks the Change Operator button.

```
// ChangeOperator
// Function will change operator
// boolean to opposite value
function ChangeOperator() {
if (bSubtract==true) {
bSubtract = false
}
else{
```

```
bSubtract = true
}
}
```

4. The next function you will create will call one of two JavaScript functions, based on the value that is currently set in the operator Boolean global variable. If the flag is true, the SubtractFive function is called; otherwise, the AddFive function is called.

```
// OperateFive
// Function will check to see if subtract flag
// is true
// If it is will call SubtractFive, else
// will call AddFive
function OperateFive() {
if (bSubtract==false) {
AddFive()
}
else{
SubtractFive()
}
}
```

5. Create the AddFive function. Notice how a bSubtract variable is used to temporarily hold a numeric value.

```
// AddFive
// Function will add 5 to current value
// and will set this to display
function AddFive() {
var bSubtract = iCurrentValue + 5
document.ValueForm.current_value.value=bSubtract
iCurrentValue = bSubtract
}
```

6. Create the SubtractFive function. Notice that in this function, a new variable is created to hold a temporary numeric result.

```
// SubtractFive
// Function will subtract 5 from current value
// and will set this to display
function SubtractFive() {
var iTempValue = iCurrentValue - 5
document.ValueForm.current_value.value=iTempValue
iCurrentValue = iTempValue
}
```

7. Finish the document by ending the JavaScript code section and the HEAD document section and creating the document BODY. The document will contain a form with a text field and two buttons.

```
// end hiding from old browsers -->
</SCRIPT>

</HEAD>
```

continued on next page

continued from previous page

```
<body>

<FORM NAME="ValueForm">
<INPUT TYPE="text" NAME="current_value" VALUE="0" SIZE=20 >
<INPUT TYPE="button" NAME="Change" VALUE="Add/Subtract 5" ⇐
OnClick="OperateFive()">
<INPUT TYPE="button" NAME="Operator" VALUE="Change Operator"
OnClick="ChangeOperator()">
</FORM>

</BODY>
</HTML>
```

8. Close and save the document as VARIABLES.HTM. Test the document by opening it in your browser, selecting both buttons, and viewing the results.

How It Works

Variables in JavaScript are loosely typed, and you will not be specifying their type when you declare them. In addition, the use of the VAR statement keyword is not used outside of a JavaScript function. The variable names start with a letter or an underscore (_) and may contain uppercase letters (A–Z), lowercase letters (a–z), digits (0–9), or the underscore character. JavaScript is case-sensitive, so be consistent or your code will not work. The scope of the variables is global if they are declared outside of a function and is local when declared with the VAR keyword and contained in a function. Notice also from the listing in Step 5 that you can use a global variable as a local one by re-declaring it. This will not have an impact on the value contained in the global variable.

JavaScript recognizes a very small set of data types: numeric, Boolean, strings, and a null value. Numeric values can have the form of 1 or 1.0 or -1. Boolean variables have values of true and false. Strings are delimited by string delimiters and look similar to "string" or 'string'. The null data type is specified as null. There is no date data type, but there is a Date JavaScript object, which can be accessed by its methods. JavaScript also allows for implicit conversion when working with differing data types. Notice from the listing in Step 7 that the value for the text field is being set by a string, but the value is being set to numeric values elsewhere in the listings. You can do such things as add a numeric and a string together, resulting in a string. There are explicit conversion functions that will be covered in detail in Chapter 7, "Converting Between Data Types."

Comment

Notice from the listing samples in this How-To that the variables are preceded by a character that for the most part reflects their data type. This is not a standard convention in JavaScript—there really are no standard conventions—but is borrowed from other languages. Using this and carefully using lowercase and uppercase type can make the code a little bit easier to read. Another good programming practice is not to re-declare global variables for use as local variables, as this can make your code difficult to read.

COMPLEXITY

INTERMEDIATE/ADVANCED

5.3 How do I...
Create and populate an array of variables?

COMPATIBILITY: NAVIGATOR 2.X   NAVIGATOR 3.X   EXPLORER 3.X

Problem

I need to store several values of the same data type, but I cannot find anything in the JavaScript documentation about creating and using arrays. How can I create and use a JavaScript array?

Technique

There is an Array object type beginning with version 3.0 of Netscape, but by using the technique outlined in the current How-To, you can create an array of virtually any object type. How-To 5.4, "How do I use the new Array functionality to create an array?" discusses the new Array object type approach.

JavaScript is an object-oriented language that is loosely typed. This gives you the ability to create an object directly in your code, using the new operator, and instantiate it later in your code. Taking this a step further, you can create an object directly in your code that has the capability of being instantiated up to a specific number of times in your code. Now that we have clearly defined what an array is, perhaps an example might be in order to ensure that you understand its use.

Steps

Open the file ARRAY.HTM in your browser. This page consists of two text fields, eight checkboxes, and one button, as shown in Figure 5-5. Check a couple of the checkboxes and then push the Calculate button. This will generate a binary string, which is placed in one of the text fields, and its decimal equivalent, which is placed in the other. Click on the checkboxes labeled Eight, Six, Four, Three, and One, and click the Calculate button. The binary string represented by the checkbox pattern is placed in the Binary text field, and its decimal equivalent is placed in the Decimal text field, as shown in Figure 5-6. In addition, the checked boxes are used to derive a new background color. The steps to create this follow.

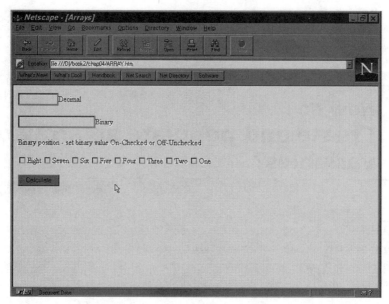

Figure 5-5 ARRAY Web page before checking boxes and pushing Calculate button

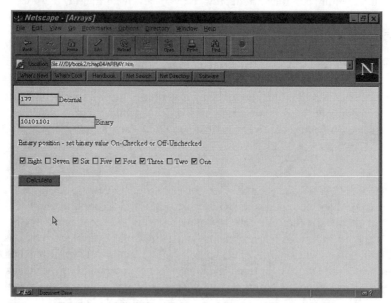

Figure 5-6 ARRAY Web page after checking boxes and pushing Calculate button

1. Create an empty HTML document file.

2. Type in the following <HEAD>, <TITLE>, and <SCRIPT> tags.

```
<HEAD> <TITLE> Arrays </TITLE>

<SCRIPT LANGUAGE="JavaScript">
<!--- hide script from old browsers

// JavaScript functions
```

3. Type in the code to create the MakeArray function. This function, developed by Netscape personnel, will allow you to generate an array that can then be used for any data type.

```
// MakeArray originated at Netscape
// and is probably include in most if not all HTML
// documents that use JavaScript
//
// MakeArray will create a generic array object with
 function MakeArray(n)
 {
        this.length = n;
        for (var i = 1; i <= n; i++)
        { this[i] = 0 }
        return this
 }
```

4. Next, you will type in the code to create an array of eight variables. Populate the array values with the decimal equivalent of the binary position as it is represented in the array. As the binary number reads from left to right, the largest value will be in the first array index, and the smallest will be in the eighth.

```
// initiate array
var colBytes = new MakeArray(8);
colBytes[1] = 132
colBytes[2] = 64
colBytes[3] = 32
colBytes[4] = 16
colBytes[5]= 8
colBytes[6]= 4
colBytes[7]= 2
colBytes[8]= 1
```

5. Create another array called colors. This array will take name/value pairs, of which a color name is used for the name value and the hexadecimal representation of the color is the value.

```
colors = new MakeArray(8)
colors[0] = "white"
colors.white="#FFFFFF"
colors[1] = "black"
colors.black="#000000"
colors[2] = "red"
```

continued on next page

continued from previous page

```
colors.red="#FF0000"
colors[3] = "blue"
colors.blue="#0000FF"
colors[4] = "green"
colors.green="#00FF00"
colors[5] = "yellow"
colors.yellow="#FFFF00"
colors[6] = "magenta"
colors.magenta="#FF00FF"
colors[7] = "cyan"
colors.cyan="#00FFFF"
colors[8] = "gold"
colors.gold = "#C0C0C0"
```

6. Create a JavaScript function called CalculateDecimal by typing the following code. This code will access each checkbox object and see if it is checked or not. If it is checked, the equivalent decimal value is accessed from the colBytes array. This is added to a variable that adds the decimal values from the checked objects. In addition, a string is built of the binary equivalent of the value. Finally, the leftmost checkbox that is checked is used to derive a new background color. If any of the checkboxes are checked, the array is accessed by using the array index, and the color is used to set the background color. If none of the boxes is checked, the color is set to gold by using the array name to access the array value.

```
// Other JavaScript functions

// CalculateDecimal
//
// function will return decimal number represented by
// binary break down
function CalculateDecimal(){
var iDecimalValue = 0
var iValue = 0
var sString = ''
var iIndex = 0

for (i = 2; i <= 9; i++) {
if (document.BinaryForm.elements[i].checked) {
iIndex = i - 1
iValue = colBytes[iIndex]
iDecimalValue = iDecimalValue + iValue
sString = sString + '1'

// reset color
if (iColor == -1) {
var iColor = i - 2
document.bgColor=colors[iColor]
}
}
else {
sString = sString + '0'
}
```

```
}

// no boxes are checked - set to gold
// use name of name/value color array
// to set background color
        if (iValue == 0)
document.bgColor=colors.gold

document.BinaryForm.Output.value=iDecimalValue
document.BinaryForm.Binary.value=sString}

// end hiding from old browsers -->
</SCRIPT>
```

7. Create the BODY section of the document by typing in the code below, which will create a form with two text fields, eight checkboxes, and a button. The OnClick event of the button will call the CalculateDecimal function.

```
</HEAD>
<BODY>
<H1> Translate Binary to Decimal </H1>
<p>
<!-- create form with 8 checkbox buttons,
each representing on or off for binary position
// display choice-->

<FORM NAME="BinaryForm">
<INPUT TYPE="text" NAME="Output" Size=10>Decimal
<p>
<INPUT TYPE="text" NAME="Binary" Sisze=20>Binary
<p>
Binary position - set binary value On-Checked or Off-Unchecked
<p>
<INPUT TYPE="checkbox" NAME="Eight" VALUE=0>Eight
<INPUT TYPE="checkbox" NAME="Seven" VALUE=0>Seven
<INPUT TYPE="checkbox" NAME="Six" VALUE=0>Six
<INPUT TYPE="checkbox" NAME="Five" VALUE=0>Five
<INPUT TYPE="checkbox" NAME="Four" VALUE=0>Four
<INPUT TYPE="checkbox" NAME="Three" VALUE=0>Three
<INPUT TYPE="checkbox" NAME="Two" VALUE=0>Two
<INPUT TYPE="checkbox" NAME="One" VALUE=0>One
<p>
<INPUT TYPE="button" NAME="calculate" VALUE="Calculate"
OnClick="CalculateDecimal()">
</FORM></BODY>
</HTML>
```

8. Close the file and save it as ARRAY.HTM. Test the code by opening the file in your browser.

How It Works

To declare an array in JavaScript using the technique demonstrated in this chapter, you must define the length of the array, which will be the number of array elements. Once this occurs you can use the array directly. Any data type could be used for the array elements.

Comments

You can further refine an array by adding key/value pairs. The key/value pair is created using the same MakeArray function. Afterwards, a key is added for each index, using the syntax: array[index] = "key". Then the key value of the array is accessed and populated: array.key = value. Accessing the values is as simple as referencing the key value with syntax such as array.key. With this you can create a meaningful alias to represent a less than meaningful value, such as the variable red in place of "#FF0000".

COMPLEXITY

INTERMEDIATE

5.4   How do I...
Use the new Array functionality to create an array?

COMPATIBILITY: NAVIGATOR 3.X   EXPLORER 3.X

Problem

How do I use the new Array object type of Netscape 3.0 to create, populate, and use an array of values?

Technique

Starting with version 3.0 of Netscape, you can create an array by using the new Array object type. With this you can create both a fixed-length and an open-ended array, or you can create it and populate it with the same statement.

Steps

Open the file NWARRRAY.HTM in your browser. This page contains two text fields, eight checkboxes, and a button, as shown in Figure 5-7. Checking several of the boxes and then clicking the Calculate button will generate both a decimal and a binary representation, based on which boxes were checked. Notice also that the background color has changed. The steps to create this Web page follow.

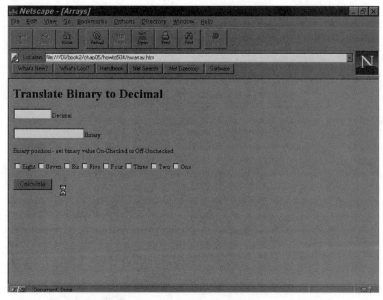

Figure 5-7 NWARRAY.HTM after opening

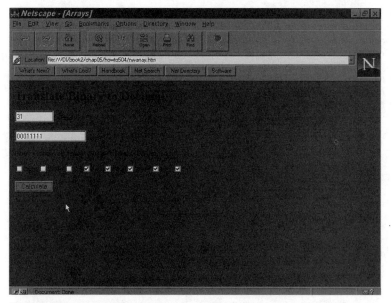

Figure 5-8 NWARRAY.HTM after checking several boxes and pressing the Calculate button

1. Create a new HTML document.

2. Start the HEAD and a JavaScript section by typing the following.

```
<HEAD> <TITLE> Arrays </TITLE>

<SCRIPT LANGUAGE="JavaScript">
<!--- hide script from old browsers

// JavaScript Variables

// JavaScript functions
```

3. Next, create two arrays using the new Array functionality. Instead of having to include the MakeArray function or an equivalent in the code and then reference it, you create the array by using the keyword new followed by the Array() function call. The first array is created and populated in the same statement. The second array is created first, and then populated. Notice, though, that the array is populated with colors and uses the hexadecimal representation for the first half of the array entries and the color text name of the colors for the second half.

```
// initiate new arrays
colBytes = new Array(132,64,32,16,8,4,2,1);

colors = new Array(8)

colors[0]="#FFFFFF"
colors[1]="#000000"
colors[2]="#FF0000"
colors[3]="#0000FF"
colors[4]="#00FF00"
colors[5] = "yellow"
colors[6] = "magenta"
colors[7] = "cyan"
```

4. Create a function called CalculateDecimal. Declare several variables and set to null or empty values.

```
// CalculateDecimal
//
// function will return decimal number represented by
// binary break down
function CalculateDecimal(){
var iDecimalValue = 0
var iValue = 0
var sString = ''
var iIndex = 0
var iColor = -1
```

5. Create a loop that will access the checked property of each of the eight checkboxes on the form. If the box is checked, the decimal value of the box in that position is added to a running decimal value. In addition, the color is set to the color represented by the array value contained in the array that you access by using the index of the checkbox item.

```
for (i = 2; i <= 9; i++) {
if (document.BinaryForm.elements[i].checked) {
iIndex = i - 2
iValue = colBytes[iIndex]
iDecimalValue = iDecimalValue + iValue
sString = sString + '1'

// reset color
if (iColor == -1) {
var iColor = i - 2
document.bgColor=colors[iColor]
}
}
else  {
sString = sString + '0'
}
}
```

6. End the function by setting the binary value and the decimal value to the two text fields on the form. Close the JavaScript and HEAD sections.

```
document.BinaryForm.Output.value=iDecimalValue
document.BinaryForm.Binary.value=sString
}

// end hiding from old browsers -->
</SCRIPT>
</HEAD>
```

7. Create the BODY section and start a form. Create two text fields in the form and call the first Output and the second Binary.

```
<BODY>
<H1> Translate Binary to Decimal </H1>
<p>
<!-- create form with 8 checkbox buttons,
each representing on or off for binary position
// display choice-->

<FORM NAME="BinaryForm">
<INPUT TYPE="text" NAME="Output" Size=10>Decimal
<p>
<INPUT TYPE="text" NAME="Binary" Sisze=20>Binary
```

8. Type in the code to create eight checkboxes.

```
<p>
Binary position - set binary value On-Checked or Off-Unchecked
<p>
<INPUT TYPE="checkbox" NAME="Eight" VALUE=0>Eight
<INPUT TYPE="checkbox" NAME="Seven" VALUE=0>Seven
<INPUT TYPE="checkbox" NAME="Six" VALUE=0>Six
<INPUT TYPE="checkbox" NAME="Five" VALUE=0>Five
<INPUT TYPE="checkbox" NAME="Four" VALUE=0>Four
<INPUT TYPE="checkbox" NAME="Three" VALUE=0>Three
<INPUT TYPE="checkbox" NAME="Two" VALUE=0>Two
<INPUT TYPE="checkbox" NAME="One" VALUE=0>One
```

9. Finally, add a button to the form. Code the event handler for the onClick event to call the CalculateDecimal function.

```
<p>
<INPUT TYPE="button" NAME="calculate" VALUE="Calculate"
OnClick="CalculateDecimal()">
</FORM>

</BODY> </HTML>
```

10. Close and save the file as NWARRAY.HTM. Test the document in your browser.

How It Works

The Array object type combined with the new operator allows you to define new array instances. With this you can create, assign, and use the array as you would any other object type.

COMPLEXITY
BEGINNING/INTERMEDIATE

5.5   How do I...
Pass parameters to a function?

COMPATIBILITY: NAVIGATOR 2.X   NAVIGATOR 3.X   EXPLORER 3.X

Problem

I am creating a JavaScript function that will process the result of the reader's actions. I want to be able to pass a parameter to a function, and I want the function to return a value. How can I do this?

Technique

JavaScript functions can accept parameters and can return values. Unlike other languages, however, parameters to a JavaScript function are passed by value only. This means that whatever changes occur to the parameter within the function will not be reflected back in the calling program.

Steps

Open the HTML document FUNCPARM.HTM. The page has a header, a text string, and three radio buttons, as shown in Figure 5-9. Press the green radio button, and the background color is changed to green, as shown in Figure 5-10. The button that was clicked was passed to the function responsible for changing the background color, and it, in turn, called a function to get the background color. The code to accomplish this follows.

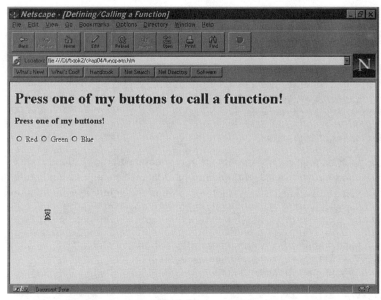

Figure 5-9 FUNCPARM.HTM when loaded

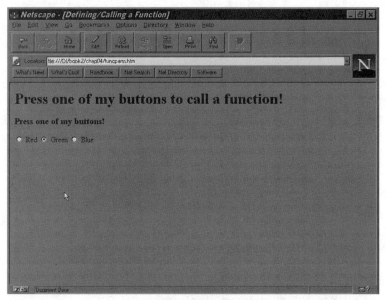

Figure 5-10 FUNCPARM.HTM after pressing the green radio button

1. Create an empty HTML document file.

2. Create the HEAD section, including the <TITLE> tag, and start a JavaScript code section.

```
<HTML>
<HEAD><TITLE> Defining/Calling a Function </TITLE>
<SCRIPT LANGUAGE="JavaScript">
<!--- hide script from old browsers

// JavaScript functions
```

3. Create a JavaScript function that takes one parameter, the button clicked, and returns a background color hexadecimal string using the statement RETURN. The background color is hardcoded into the function and will be determined by the button the Web reader has clicked. The hexadecimal value of the color will be used.

```
// ReturnBkGrndColor
// function will return a background color
// based on value passed to it
function ReturnBkGrndColor(nButton) {
var nBackground = ""
if (nButton == 'ONE') {
nBackground="#CC0000"
}
else if (nButton == 'TWO') {
nBackground="#00CC00"
}
else  {
nBackground="#0000FF"
}
return nBackground
}
```

4. Create a function called WhoPressedMe. This function is passed a string representing the button that was clicked and a second test parameter. It will, in turn, call the ReturnBkGrndColor function to get the new background color. Finally, it will change the background color of the document with this returned value. Also, type in the closing tags for the SCRIPT and HEAD sections. The second parameter will be tested to see if it is null. If it is, a message to that effect will occur.

```
// WhoPressedMe function
// This function will respond by calling a function
// to access a new background color and by setting this
// value
function WhoPressedMe(sButton, sTest) {
var nBackground = ReturnBkGrndColor(sButton)
document.bgColor=nBackground

if (sTest == null)
alert("You did not send second parameter.")
```

```
else
alert("You sent second parameter")
}

// end hiding from old browsers -->
</SCRIPT>

</HEAD>
```

5. Create the BODY section and create a form with three radio buttons. Each button is labeled with a color. Clicking any one of these buttons will trigger the onClick event, which will call WhoPressedMe. The background color of the document is changed, based on which radio button is pressed. Notice that the third button, with a value of Choice Three, passes two parameters to the function.

```
<body>
<H1> Press one of my buttons to call a function! </H1>

<p><BIG><B>Press one of my buttons!</B></BIG>
<FORM NAME="FunctionForm" >
<INPUT TYPE="radio" NAME="Pressed" VALUE="Choice One"
onClick="WhoPressedMe('ONE')"> Red
<INPUT TYPE="radio" NAME="Pressed" VALUE="Choice Two"
onClick="WhoPressedMe('TWO')"> Green
<INPUT TYPE="radio" NAME="Pressed" VALUE="Choice Three"
onClick="WhoPressedMe('THREE','test')"> Blue
</FORM>
</BODY>
</HTML>
```

6. Close and save the file as FUNCPARM.HTM and test it by bringing up the document in your browser.

How It Works

JavaScript functions will accept one or more parameters, and can return a value using the RETURN statement. Unlike many languages, parameters in JavaScript are always passed by value, which means that they can be changed in the function, but the changes will not be reflected back to the calling code.

Parameters to a function can be strings, numbers, Boolean values, and JavaScript objects such as forms. You can pass a value as a literal or as a variable. Additionally, you can define more than one parameter for a function and optionally only pass the first one or more values. If a value is not passed for a parameter, it is set to null.

COMPLEXITY
BEGINNING

5.6 How do I...
Conditionally execute a block of code?

COMPATIBILITY:

Problem

I want to perform some action only if a certain condition is met. How do I enclose a block of code so that it will not be executed without a condition being met?

Technique

As with many other programming languages, JavaScript has a statement that allows you to enclose a block of code so that it will not be executed unless a condition is met. JavaScript has the IF...ELSE statements for this type of processing. These statements are very similar to those used in C, Pascal, and other more traditional languages.

Steps

Open the file CONDIT.HTM in your browser. You will see a page that has three groupings of radio buttons, each with a two-digit hexadecimal number, as shown in Figure 5-11. The code conditionally checks the radio buttons to see which is checked and builds the background color accordingly. Colors in JavaScript are made up of three sets of hexadecimal numbers, each of which represents a different RGB (Red-Green-Blue) member. The numbers can be any number between 00, which is 0 in decimal notation, and FF, which is 255. By changing any one of these values you will be able to change the background color of the document, as shown in Figure 5-12.

1. Create a new HTML document.

2. Type in the code to start the HEAD document section and to start a JavaScript code section.

```
<HTML>
<HEAD><TITLE> Conditional Statement </TITLE>
<SCRIPT LANGUAGE="JavaScript">
<!--- hide script from old browsers

// JavaScript functions
```

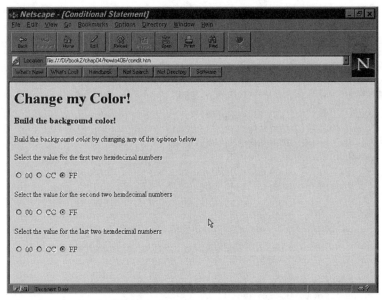

Figure 5-11 CONDIT.HTM before any radio button selected

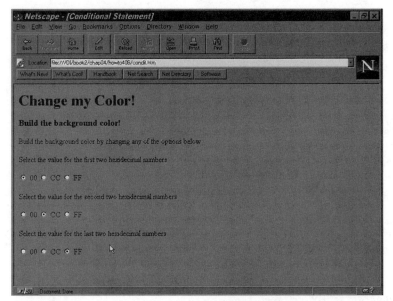

Figure 5-12 CONDIT.HTM after radio buttons have been selected

3. Create three functions that will check the radio button values of each of the three RGB groups and return the value represented by the checked radio button. The functions make use of the conditional IF...ELSE statements in order to return the correct value.

```
// GetFirstValue
// Function will find which radio button
// is clicked for 'group' and
// return its associated value
function GetFirstValue() {
if (document.forms[0].First[0].checked) {
return "00"
}
else if (document.forms[0].First[1].checked) {
return "CC"
}
else {
return "FF"
}
}

function GetSecondValue() {
if (document.forms[0].Second[0].checked) {
return "00"
}
else if (document.forms[0].Second[1].checked) {
return "CC"
}
else {
return "FF"
}
}

function GetLastValue() {
if (document.forms[0].Last[0].checked) {
return "00"
}
else if (document.forms[0].Last[1].checked) {
return "CC"
}
else {
return "FF"
}
}
```

4. Create another function called WhoPressedMe that will call each of the functions you just created and use their results to build the background color.

```
// WhoPressedMe function
// This function will respond by calling a function
// to access a new background color and by setting this
// value
function WhoPressedMe(sName) {
var sBackground = "#"
sBackground = sBackground + GetFirstValue()
```

```
sBackground = sBackground + GetSecondValue()
sBackground = sBackground + GetLastValue()
document.bgColor = sBackground
}
```

5. Type in the code to close the JavaScript code and the HEAD document section.

```
// end hiding from old browsers -->
</SCRIPT>
<H1> Change my Color! </H1>
</HEAD>
```

6. In the BODY section of the document, create three groups of radio buttons that will allow the user to fine-tune the background color. Each radio button has an event handler for the OnClick event that will call the WhoPressedMe function.

```
<BODY>
<p><BIG><B>Build the background color!</B></BIG>
<p> Build the background color by changing any of the options below

<FORM NAME="BuildForm" >
<p> Select the value for the first two hexidecimal numbers<p>
<INPUT TYPE="radio" NAME="First" VALUE="00"
onClick="WhoPressedMe()"> 00
<INPUT TYPE="radio" NAME="First" VALUE="CC"
onClick="WhoPressedMe()"> CC
<INPUT TYPE="radio" NAME="First" VALUE="FF" CHECKED
onClick="WhoPressedMe()"> FF

<p> Select the value for the second two hexidecimal numbers<p>
<INPUT TYPE="radio" NAME="Second" VALUE="00"
onClick="WhoPressedMe()"> 00
<INPUT TYPE="radio" NAME="Second" VALUE="CC"
onClick="WhoPressedMe()"> CC
<INPUT TYPE="radio" NAME="Second" VALUE="FF" CHECKED
onClick="WhoPressedMe()"> FF

<p> Select the value for the last two hexidecimal numbers<p>
<INPUT TYPE="radio" NAME="Last" VALUE="00"
onClick="WhoPressedMe()"> 00
<INPUT TYPE="radio" NAME="Last" VALUE="CC"
onClick="WhoPressedMe()"> CC
<INPUT TYPE="radio" NAME="Last" VALUE="FF" CHECKED
onClick="WhoPressedMe()"> FF

</FORM>
</BODY>
</HTML>
```

7. Close and save your document as CONDIT.HTM. Test the document by opening it from your browser, and change the background color by selecting different radio buttons.

How It Works

The conditional IF...ELSE statement supplied by JavaScript allows you to test for a condition and then execute the block of code if the condition passed. The condition must be contained within parentheses, and the block of code is usually delimited by curly brackets. If your block contains more than one statement, you must use the curly brackets. To test for equality, use the operator ==. Other operators are > and >= for greater than and greater than or equal to, and < and <= for less than and less than or equal to. Table 5-1 contains the Boolean operators you can currently use with JavaScript. In addition, you can specify a Boolean variable without an operator to test the value of the variable.

OPERATOR	MEANING	TRUE WHEN...
==	Equality	Values on both sides of operator are the same
!=	Not equal	Values on both sides of operator are different
<	Less than	Value on left side of operator is less than value on right side of operator
<=	Less than or equal	Value on left side of operator is less than or equal to value on right side of operator
>	Greater than	Value on left side of operator is greater than value on right side of operator
>=	Greater than or equal	Value on left side of operator is greater than or equal to value on right side of operator

Table 5-1 JavaScript Boolean or comparison operators

In addition to the logical operators, you can also use Boolean operators such as || for an OR join and && for AND. Use these when you want to check more than one condition, such as a variable with a value less than 15 but more than 11, or a value of 5 or 9 or 11. Combine the expressions with the same parentheses.

COMPLEXITY
BEGINNING/INTERMEDIATE

5.7 How do I...
Loop through a block of code?

COMPATIBILITY: NAVIGATOR 2.X NAVIGATOR 3.X

Problem

I want to be able to execute the same block of code again and again until a condition is met. How can I create a conditional loop in JavaScript?

Technique

JavaScript has several statements that can control the execution of a block of code. The WHILE statement will continue executing the block of code until a condition is met. The FOR statement will execute the block a set number of times. The FOR...IN statement will iterate through an object's properties, and the code will be executed for each property. In addition to these statements, the CONTINUE statement will stop the execution of the code where it occurs, reset the control flow to the condition for the WHILE statement, and update the expression for the FOR statement. The BREAK statement will suspend execution of the loop and set the control flow to the first statement following the loop.

Steps

Open the file FOR.HTM in your browser. The page consists of a header and several radio buttons. Click on any of the radio buttons and the color of the page background changes, as shown in Figure 5-13. Open the file FORIN.HTM in your browser. This Web page lists properties and their values for the Window, Document, Location, History, and Navigator JavaScript objects, as shown in Figure 5-14. Open the file WHILE.HTM in your browser. This Web page consists of a button, as shown in Figure 5-15. Clicking this button starts a process that will continuously prompt you for a new six-place hexadecimal value for the background color of the document, as shown in Figure 5-16. Typing stop into the field, as shown in Figure 5-17, will discontinue the color changing process. The steps to create these three files are listed below.

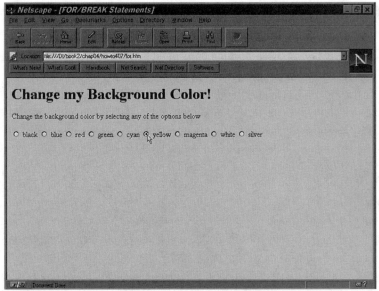

Figure 5-13 FOR.HTM after selecting the yellow radio button

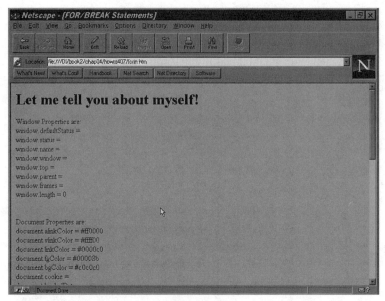

Figure 5-14 FORIN.HTM displaying the properties for several JavaScript objects

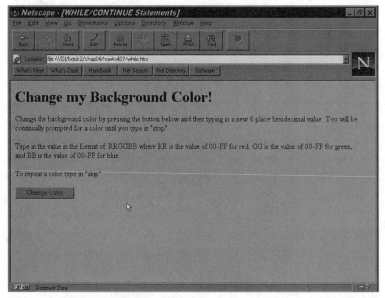

Figure 5-15 WHILE.HTM after opening

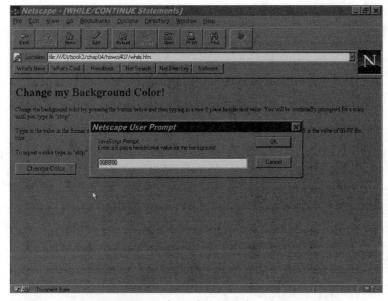

Figure 5-16 WHILE.HTM after clicking the change color button and adding the hexadecimal color value

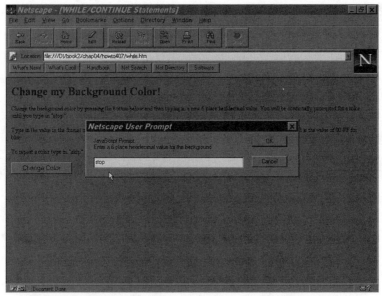

Figure 5-17 WHILE.HTM after typing in stop to discontinue the color-changing process

1. Create a new HTML file.

2. Type in the <HEAD> and <TITLE> tags and begin a JavaScript section as follows.

```
<HTML>
<HEAD><TITLE> FOR/BREAK Statements </TITLE>
<SCRIPT LANGUAGE="JavaScript">
<!--- hide script from old browsers

// JavaScript functions
```

3. Create the ChangeColor function. This function will iterate through the radio buttons on a form, checking for the one that is checked. When it finds this button, it will break out of the loop. The button's value will be accessed and used to change the document's background color. Additionally, type in the code to close both the JavaScript and the HEAD sections.

```
// ChangeColor function
// This function will respond by checked the radio buttons
// to see which was checked and changing the color accordingly
function ChangeColor(sName) {
var sBackground = "#"
for (i = 0; i < 9; i++) {
if (document.BuildForm.Color[i].checked) {
break
}
}
sBackground = document.BuildForm.Color[i].value
document.bgColor = sBackground
}


// end hiding from old browsers -->
</SCRIPT>
<H1> Change my Background Color! </H1>
</HEAD>
```

4. Type in the <BODY> tag and create a form. The form will have nine radio buttons, each with a different color hexadecimal value and each labeled with the appropriate color name. The silver color will be the beginning checked button. When you have finished creating the form, close the form and the BODY section.

```
<body bgColor="COCOCO" >
<p>Change the background color by selecting any of the options below

<FORM NAME="BuildForm" >
<INPUT TYPE="radio" NAME="Color" VALUE="000000"
onClick="ChangeColor()"> black
<INPUT TYPE="radio" NAME="Color" VALUE="0000FF"
onClick="ChangeColor()"> blue
<INPUT TYPE="radio" NAME="Color" VALUE="FF0000"
```

```
onClick="ChangeColor()"> red
<INPUT TYPE="radio" NAME="Color" VALUE="00FF00"
onClick="ChangeColor()"> green
<INPUT TYPE="radio" NAME="Color" VALUE="00FFFF"
onClick="ChangeColor()"> cyan
<INPUT TYPE="radio" NAME="Color" VALUE="FFFF00"
onClick="ChangeColor()"> yellow
<INPUT TYPE="radio" NAME="Color" VALUE="FF00FF"
onClick="ChangeColor()"> magenta
<INPUT TYPE="radio" NAME="Color" VALUE="FFFFFF"
onClick="ChangeColor()"> white
<INPUT TYPE="radio" NAME="Color" VALUE="C0C0C0" CHECKED
onClick="ChangeColor()"> silver

</FORM>
</BODY></HTML>
```

5. Close and save your document as FOR.HTM and test by opening in your browser. Try clicking several of the radio buttons and notice the color of the document.

6. For the next example, create a new empty HTML document.

7. Again, type in the code to begin the HEAD and a JavaScript section.

```
<HTML>
<HEAD><TITLE> FOR/BREAK Statements </TITLE>
<H1> Let me tell you about myself! </H1>

<SCRIPT LANGUAGE="JavaScript">
<!--- hide script from old browsers
```

8. The body of the document will be created entirely by JavaScript. Set the document's background, foreground (text), and link colors by setting the appropriate Document object properties.

```
// set document properties and start BODY
document.bgColor="#C0C0C0"
document.fgColor="#00008B"
document.linkColor="#0000C0"
document.vlinkColor="#FFFF00"
document.write('<BODY>')
```

9. Next, create a loop statement that will iterate through the properties for the Window object and type out the property name and the property value for the current Window. Note that the Window object is accessed by using the self pronoun.

```
// loop through window properties and write out
document.write('Window Properties are: <br>')
properties = ""
var obj = self
for (var i in obj) {
    properties +=  "window." + i + " = " + obj[i] + "<BR>"
    }
document.writeln(properties + '<p>')
```

10. Next, create a loop for displaying the Document object's properties.

```
// loop through document properties and write out
document.write('Document Properties are: <br>')
properties = ""
obj = document
for (var i in obj) {
    properties +=  "document." + i + " = " + obj[i] + "<BR>"
    }
document.writeln(properties + '<p>')
```

11. Create a loop for the Location object's properties.

```
// loop through location properties and write out
document.write('Location Properties are: <br>')
properties = ""
obj = location
for (var i in obj) {
    properties +=  "location." + i + " = " + obj[i] + "<BR>"
    }
document.writeln(properties + '<p>')
```

12. Create a loop for the History object's properties.

```
// loop through history properties and write out
document.write('History Properties are: <br>')
properties = ""
obj = history
for (var i in obj) {
    properties +=  "history." + i + " = " + obj[i] + "<BR>"
    }
document.writeln(properties + '<p>')
```

13. Finally, create a loop for the Navigator object's properties.

```
// loop through navigator properties and write out
document.write('Navigator Properties are: <br>')
properties = ""
var obj = navigator
for (var i in obj) {
    properties +=  "navigator." + i + " = " + obj[i] + "<BR>"
    }
document.writeln(properties)
```

14. Write out the HTML statements to close the BODY section and close the
JavaScript and HEAD sections.

```
// end hiding from old browsers -->
</SCRIPT>
</HEAD>
```

15. Close your document and save it as FORIN.HTM. Test your new code by
opening the file in your browser.

16. Create a new empty document for the final example.

17. Start the HEAD and JavaScript section by typing the following:

```
<HTML>
<HEAD><TITLE> WHILE/CONTINUE Statements </TITLE>

<SCRIPT LANGUAGE="JavaScript">
<!--- hide script from old browsers

// JavaScript functions
```

18. Create a function called Change that will continuously prompt the user to enter a hexadecimal value for the background color. This prompt will be placed in a block of code that will be processed only if the user does not type in a value of skip or stop or press the Cancel button on the Prompt dialog. If the user types in skip or clicks the Cancel button, the code is skipped, using the CONTINUE statement, which returns the control flow to the conditional statement. If the user types in stop, the CONTINUE statement returns control flow to the conditional statement, which verifies that the condition to continue the loop is no longer true. Control flow will then pass to the first statement following the loop.

```
// ChangeColor function
// This function will prompt the user to enter a
// 6 place hexidecimal value to change the background color.
// If the user types in "skip" change color skips the
// background color change but continues to prompt
// If the use types in "stop" the process will stop
function Change() {
    var sBackground = "#"
    var sValue = "COCOCO"
    while (sValue != "stop") {
        sValue=prompt("Enter a 6 place hexidecimal value for the ⇐
                    background color:",sValue)
        if (sValue == "skip" || sValue == "stop" || sValue==null) {
            continue
            }
        sBackground = "#" + sValue
        document.bgColor = sBackground
        }
    }
```

19. Close out the JavaScript and HEAD sections and type in the code for the BODY section. This code will create a form with one input control, a button. Trap the onClick event for the button and type in the code to call the Change() function.

```
// end hiding from old browsers -->
</SCRIPT>
</HEAD>
<H1> Change my Background Color! </H1>
<body bgColor="COCOCO" >
<p>Change the background color by pressing the button below and then
typing in a new 6 place hexidecimal value. You will be continually ⇐
prompted for
a color until you type in "stop".
```

continued on next page

continued from previous page

```
<p>Type in the value in the format of: RRGGBB where RR is
the value of 00-FF for red, GG is the value of 00-FF for green, and BB ⇐
is the
value of 00-FF for blue.
<p>To repeat a color type in "skip"

<FORM NAME="ChangeColor" >
<INPUT TYPE="button" NAME="Color" VALUE="Change Color"
       onClick="Change()">

</FORM>
</BODY>
</HTML>
```

20. Close your document and save it as WHILE.HTM. Test your document by opening the file in your browser.

How It Works

JavaScript supports three iteration or looping statements: the FOR, FOR...IN, and WHILE statements. The FOR loop will loop through a block of code until the variable no longer meets the condition of the loop. This usually occurs by incrementing a variable, but you can decrement the variable using the decrement (—) unary operator. The FOR...IN statement will iterate through the properties of an object. You can access the property name as well as its value using this statement. The object can be a pre-defined JavaScript object or one that you have defined using the NEW statement. The WHILE statement will iterate through a block of code as long as the result of a comparison returns the value TRUE. You can define any condition, and you can use any variable to create this condition. The block of code that will be executed for any of these statements will be contained in curly brackets ('{', '}').

In addition to the looping statements, you can also use BREAK and CONTINUE. The BREAK statement will discontinue the loop and set the control flow to the first statement following the loop. The CONTINUE statement will discontinue the execution of the code contained in the loop and will return the control flow to the conditional statement for the WHILE statement and the update expression for the FOR statement. The update expression is code similar to ++I. The loop is not discontinued.

Comments

When using the WHILE statement, pay particular attention to the conditional expression of the statement. You can easily get into a situation in which the loop will never terminate if the conditional expression is not created correctly. You will know that you have entered a non-terminating or endless loop when the processing is taking far longer than it should. As a helpful debugging aid, you could check the value of whatever you are using in the loop by using a CONFIRM or ALERT message box and displaying the value in the message.

COMPLEXITY
BEGINNING

5.8 How do I...
Place comments inside JavaScript code?

COMPATIBILITY: NAVIGATOR 2.X   NAVIGATOR 3.X   EXPLORER 3.X

Problem

I will be creating several JavaScript functions that can be used by other people. How do I document my JavaScript code?

Technique

JavaScript has two types of comments, single-line and multiple-line.

Steps

Open the file COMMENTS.HTM in your browser. This Web page consists of a brightly colored page with a title stating, "There is more to this page...then meets the eye." View the source code, using whatever technique is appropriate for your viewer, and you will see that the page does include a JavaScript code section with two types of comments, as shown in Figure 5-18. To create this page, follow the steps below.

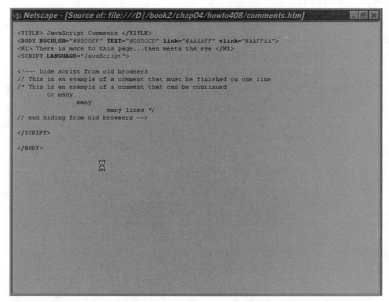

Figure 5-18 Basic Web page with JavaScript comments

1. Create an empty HTML file.

2. Use the <TITLE> tags to create the document title. Note that these do not have to be included in a HEAD section.

```
<TITLE> JavaScript Comments </TITLE>
```

3. Begin the BODY section and define the colors the document will use.

```
<BODY BGCOLOR="#BB00FF" TEXT="#0000C0" link="#AAAAFF" vlink="#AAFFAA">
```

4. Create a heading using <H1> tags, the highest level.

```
<H1> There is more to this page...then meets the eye </H1>
```

5. Start a JavaScript section. In this section, type the following comment lines. At the end, close both the JavaScript and the BODY sections.

```
<SCRIPT LANGUAGE="JavaScript">
<!--- hide script from old browsers
// This is an example of a comment that must be finished on one line
/* This is an example of a comment that can be continued
to many
many
many lines */
// end hiding from old browsers -->
</SCRIPT>
```

6. Close and save the document as COMMENTS.HTM. Test your code by running it in your browser.

How It Works

JavaScript supports the use of the double forwardslash (//) to indicate a comment that will end on the line, and the C-like begin and end comments (/*, */) to provide comments that extend over several lines. To extend comments over several lines, begin with the begin comment (/*) and type in the lines. At the end of the last line, type in the ending comment delimiter (*/). Some people prefer to use one type of commenting and make use of the double-forwardslash style or the begin/end style exclusively. Neither will have any impact on your program execution, but an inconsistent use of comments will make your code more difficult to read.

Comments

There are no rules specifying when and how to use comments in JavaScript, except for what you have learned working with other application processing tools. However, you will want to avoid over-commenting and under-commenting your code. Over-commenting can make the code so busy that the importance of what is occurring is lost, and under-commenting can leave the code reader confused about why an approach was taken or why a loop occurred.

A good rule of thumb is to define your functions, define their parameters if they have any, keep the comment brief, and define every major block of code. This, combined with meaningful variable names and keeping your blocks of code simple, should make your code readable and maintainable.

CHAPTER 6
BUILT-IN OBJECTS

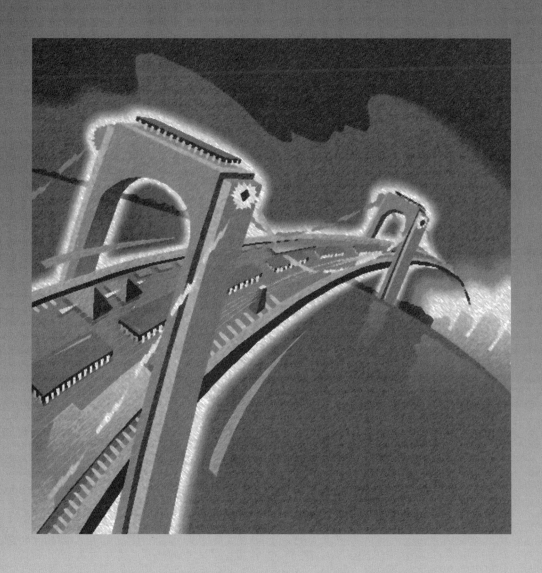

6

BUILT-IN OBJECTS

How do I...

Built-in objects represent reusable code provided as part of the JavaScript language. Until now, you have been introduced to objects such as the Navigator and Window objects, which contain information about Web-related entities. The definitions for these objects comprise the JavaScript framework. Frameworks are groups of reusable components, provided by the language designers or a third-party vendor, which reduce the time it takes to develop software. The JavaScript framework contains common objects, found in most Web-related scripts. These help reduce the burden on developers by allowing them to focus on code that is specific to the particular application. This chapter will cover three built-in objects—Math, String, and Date—common to many object-oriented languages. Unlike other JavaScript objects, which are created by the JavaScript environment, many of these objects will be instantiated by the developer.

6.1   Perform scientific numeric computations

In addition to unary and binary numeric operators, JavaScript has established a library of computational functions. These functions are members of the Math object. This How-To will introduce the Math object's computational methods by having you create an online calculator.

6.2   Generate a random number

Many things in life are left to chance. To simulate chance, the Math object also contains a random number generator. This capability is available in Navigator 2.0 for UNIX and Navigator 3.0.

6.3   Concatenate variables onto the end of a string

This How-To will demonstrate the concatenation operator, which can be used to merge several pieces of information, possibly defined as disparate data types, into a single string object.

6.4   Determine the length of a string

The String object contains a variable-length list of characters. This How-To will show you how to determine the number of characters that comprise a string.

6.5   Return the character that resides at a given position

The ability to extract individual characters from String objects is a requirement of many computer programs. Some String objects represent an aggregate of several pieces of information. Primitive data may reside at fixed positions within the string. This characteristic is associated with fixed-length, formatted strings. This How-To will teach you how to extract individual characters, based on their position, from a String object.

6.6   Locate the position of characters in a string

In addition to fixed-length, formatted strings, information may also be contained inside variable-length strings. These strings are unique in that primitive data does not reside in a given location. Their location is typically indicated by a delimiting character. Delimiters are non-standard characters, usually commas, which separate primitive date within text. This How-To will demonstrate the technique for finding delimiter characters inside a String object.

6.7   Extract substrings from within a String object

How-To 6.6 teaches the technique for locating delimiter characters inside a string. Delimiters separate individual pieces of text contained within a formatted string. This How-To will demonstrate the technique for creating a new String object based on text located between two delimiting characters. This text is commonly referred to as a *substring*.

6.8   Change the case of all characters in a string

When characters are involved, case is always an important consideration. This is because upper- and lowercase representations of the same letter contain different ASCII values. Because ASCII values are used to determine equality, for text information it is important to determine whether or not case-sensitivity is an important consideration in an application. If the application is case insensitive, this How-To will teach you how to convert all characters contained inside a String object to the same case. This technique will "level the playing field" for text comparison.

6.9   Get the current date and time from the operating system

This How-To will demonstrate the logic for getting the current date and time from the system clock.

6.10   Access a Date object's properties

In addition to the date, Date objects also contain time information. This How-To will teach you about the methods that can be used to access time and date information contained within the Date object.

6.11   Work with time zone information

The Internet is available throughout the world. This means that time zone information may be an important part of your Web site. This How-To will teach you how to determine in which time zone the users of your HTML document reside.

6.1 How do I...
Perform scientific numeric computations?

COMPATIBILITY:

Problem

The JavaScript language contains the standard set of unary and binary operators found in most programming languages. These operators provide simple numeric computation found in many business applications. My Web page requires many scientific computations that cannot be performed using the standard set of numeric operators. Does JavaScript contain library routines to perform scientific numeric computation?

Technique

The Math object contains a library of scientific constants and computational methods. Unlike other JavaScript objects, the Math object does not need to be instantiated in order to use its properties. All the Math object's properties are class properties. This means that the Math object does not have to be instantiated in order to reference its properties. In order to reference the math properties, preface the call with a reference to the Math class. This is in contrast with object properties for which each property must be tied to a specific object. Class properties are identified as static properties in other object-oriented languages, such as C++ and Java. The following code demonstrates how to invoke the Unary method sqrt in order to compute the square root of the variable *var*.

```
answer = Math.sqrt(val);
```

The value returned by sqrt is assigned to the numeric variable answer. Notice that the call to the square root function refers to the Math object type instead of referencing an object defined as an instance of the Math class. This is how you refer to class properties in JavaScript.

Table 6-1 lists all the numeric computation methods belonging to the Math object. These methods are classified as either unary or binary methods. Unary methods accept a single parameter, while binary methods take two parameters. All these methods return a floating-point number.

METHOD	TYPE	DESCRIPTION
abs	Unary	Returns the absolute value of a number
acos	Unary	Returns the arc cosine (in radians) of a number

METHOD	TYPE	DESCRIPTION
asin	Unary	Returns the arc sine (in radians) of a number
atan	Unary	Returns the arc tangent (in radians) of a number
ceil	Unary	Returns the least integer greater than or equal to a number
cos	Unary	Returns the cosine of a number
exp	Unary	Returns the Euler's constant times a number, which is the base of the natural logarithms
floor	Unary	Returns the greatest integer less than or equal to a number
log	Unary	Returns the natural logarithm (base e) of a number
max	Binary	Returns the greater of two numbers
min	Binary	Returns the lesser of two numbers
pow	Binary	Returns base to the exponent power
round	Unary	Returns the value of a number rounded to the nearest integer
sin	Unary	Returns the sine of a number
sqrt	Unary	Returns the square root of a number
tan	Unary	Returns the tangent of a number

Table 6-1 Math object methods

In addition to numeric computation functions, the Math object also contains several numeric constants. Table 6-2 lists all the numeric constants belonging to the Math object. The following code demonstrates how to reference the PI constant attribute when computing two times PI.

```
var two_pi = 2 * Math.PI;
```

CONSTANT	VALUE	DESCRIPTION
E	2.718281828	Euler's constant and the base of natural logarithms
LN2	0.693147180	The natural logarithm of 2
LN10	2.302585092	The natural logarithm of 10
LOG2E	1.442695040	The base 2 logarithm of e
LOG10E	0.434294481	The base 10 logarithm of e
PI	3.141592653	The ratio of a circumference of a circle to its diameter
SQRT1_2	0.707106781	The square root of 1/2
SQRT2	1.414213562	The square root of 2

Table 6-2 Math object constants

The With Shortcut

When all elements of a section of code reference the same object, it is often convenient to place this code inside a With container. All properties that are not tied to a particular object default to the object specified in the Web container. Any property, including both attributes and methods, without an explicit object reference will automatically be assigned to the Default object. Properties that are explicitly tied to other objects can also be included inside the With container. Any declared JavaScript object, including those automatically constructed by the browser or instantiated inside a JavaScript code fragment, can be defined as the Default object.

A With container is prefaced by a reference to the With operator and the Default object.

The container appears similar to a function call, except that the keyword, function, is omitted.

The following code represents a With container with the Math Built-in object as the Default object:

```
with(Math) {
    answer1 = sqrt(val);
    answer2 = exp(val);
}
```

If the With container were not used in this example, the code would have looked like this:

```
answer1 = Math.sqrt(val);
answer2 = Math.exp(val);
```

Although the example, which implemented the With container, contains more source code, it has some key advantages over the other example. These advantages include complexity and error reduction. In fact, if these examples contained several additional calls to Math methods, the second example would require more keystrokes than the first.

To reduce complexity, problems are broken down into small, manageable pieces. This technique allows the human mind to focus on a specific problem. This technique results in computer programs being comprised of many small, manageable pieces called *subroutines*. The most effective subroutines are distinguished by a high degree of functional cohesion, which means all source code within the routine supports a single specific purpose.

By using the With container, the first example implicitly defines a small subroutine, possibly contained within a larger routine. All the source code within the container is related because it operates on the same object. If the code in the second example were contained with a large subroutine, it would be hard to distinguish this code as supporting a single purpose.

In addition to complexity reduction, the With container can also reduce the probability of error. You will be assured that all unassigned properties will implicitly refer to the same object. This reduces the chance of referring to the wrong or an invalid object. Despite its advantages, you must decide whether or not the With container should be used for a specific problem.

Although the With container can be used with any JavaScript object, the concept can be advantageous for computationally intensive code. The With statement simplifies code that contains a lot of calls to math methods.

Steps

This example will demonstrate how to use the Math object to implement a simple scientific calculator. This calculator will allow a user to perform both simple and more sophisticated numeric computations. The calculator contains a memory location that is available to users for temporary storage for frequently used numbers.

From Navigator 2.0, load HT0601.HTM. The screen will look like Figure 6-1. Click the 5 button and notice that the number 5 appears inside the calculator's display area. This area is used to display numbers to the user. Click the 1 button and the number changes to 51. Activate the addition (+) button and the number 51 will be removed from the screen. Addition is a binary operation, requiring a second number from the user. The display area reverts back to the number 0, indicating that the user can begin entering the second operand. Click the 3 button. After the number 3 appears in the display area, click the Equals (=) button. This button executes the desired numeric computation. The answer, 54, now appears inside the display area. Click the Clear button to enter a new equation. The number 0 appears in the display area.

Now click the 9 button and notice that the number 9 appears inside the display area. Now activate the Square Root (SQRT) button. The answer, 3, is displayed on the screen. Unlike the previous example, the user has only to enter a single number. This is because the Square Root function is a unary function requiring only a single numeric parameter.

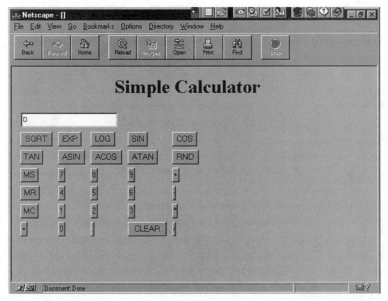

Figure 6-1 The calculator page

1. Create a new document using the following HTML code. This code specifies the layout for all input elements and supporting text needed to
construct the online calculator. The calculator is comprised of a text input
element, used to display input parameters and results of numeric computations, and a series of push buttons, representing numeric digits and
operations. An onClick event handler is defined for each push button.
This event handler calls a JavaScript function, which will be defined in a
later step. The function invoked by each button is dependent on the class
of button. Currently, there are six classes of buttons. The How It Works
section that follows gives a detailed description of each button class.

```
<HTML>
<HEAD> <TITLE> </TITLE> </HEAD>
<BODY   BGCOLOR=#D3D3D3 TEXT=#000080>
<BIG>
<CENTER> <H1> Simple Calculator </H1> </CENTER>
<FORM NAME="calculator">
<TABLE>
<TR> <TD COLSPAN=5> <INPUT TYPE="text" NAME="display" VALUE="0"> </TD>
</TR>
<TR>
<TD> <INPUT TYPE="button" NAME="S" VALUE="SQRT"
onClick="computeUnary(this.name);"> </TD>
<TD> <INPUT TYPE="button" NAME="E" VALUE="EXP"
onClick="computeUnary(this.name);">   </TD>
<TD> <INPUT TYPE="button" NAME="L" VALUE="LOG"
onClick="computeUnary(this.name);">   </TD>
<TD> <INPUT TYPE="button" NAME="I" VALUE="SIN"
onClick="computeUnary(this.name);">   </TD>
<TD> <INPUT TYPE="button" NAME="O" VALUE="COS"
onClick="computeUnary(this.name);">   </TD>
</TR>
<TR>
<TD> <INPUT TYPE="button" NAME="T" VALUE="TAN"
onClick="computeUnary(this.name);">   </TD>
<TD> <INPUT TYPE="button" NAME="N" VALUE="ASIN"
onClick="computeUnary(this.name);">   </TD>
<TD> <INPUT TYPE="button" NAME="A" VALUE="ACOS"
onClick="computeUnary(this.name);">   </TD>
<TD> <INPUT TYPE="button" NAME="G" VALUE="ATAN"
onClick="computeUnary(this.name);">   </TD>
<TD> <INPUT TYPE="button" NAME="R" VALUE="RND"
onClick="computeUnary(this.name);">   </TD>
</TR>
<TR>
<TD> <INPUT TYPE="button" NAME="save" VALUE="MS"
onClick="window.memory=parseFloat(window.document.calculator.display. ⇐
value)"> </TD>
<TD> <INPUT TYPE="button" NAME="seven" VALUE="7"
onClick="makeNum(this.value)">   </TD>
<TD> <INPUT TYPE="button" NAME="eight" VALUE="8"
onClick="makeNum(this.value)">   </TD>
<TD> <INPUT TYPE="button" NAME="nine" VALUE="9"
onClick="makeNum(this.value)">   </TD>
```

```
<TD> <INPUT TYPE="button" NAME="A" VALUE="+"
onClick="savNum(this.name)"> </TD>
</TR>
<TR>
<TD> <INPUT TYPE="button" NAME="remember" VALUE="MR"
onClick="window.document.calculator.display.value=window.memory;"> </TD>
<TD> <INPUT TYPE="button" NAME="four" VALUE="4"
onClick="makeNum(this.value)"> </TD>
<TD> <INPUT TYPE="button" NAME="five" VALUE="5"
onClick="makeNum(this.value)">  </TD>
<TD> <INPUT TYPE="button" NAME="six" VALUE="6"
onClick="makeNum(this.value)">  </TD>
<TD> <INPUT TYPE="button" NAME="S" VALUE="-"
onClick="savNum(this.name)"> </TD>
</TR>
<TR>
<TD> <INPUT TYPE="button" NAME="clear" VALUE="MC"
onClick="window.memory='';"> </TD>
<TD> <INPUT TYPE="button" NAME="one" VALUE="1"
onClick="makeNum(this.value)">  </TD>
<TD> <INPUT TYPE="button" NAME="two" VALUE="2"
onClick="makeNum(this.value)">  </TD>
<TD> <INPUT TYPE="button" NAME="three" VALUE="3"
onClick="makeNum(this.value)">  </TD>
<TD> <INPUT TYPE="button" NAME="M" VALUE="*"
onClick="savNum(this.name)"> </TD>
</TR>
<TR>
<TD> <INPUT TYPE="button" NAME="equal" VALUE="="
onClick="computeBinary()"> </TD>
<TD> <INPUT TYPE="button" NAME="one" VALUE="0"
onClick="makeNum(this.value)"> </TD>
<TD> <INPUT TYPE="button" NAME="decimal" VALUE="."
onClick="makeNum(this.value)"> </TD>
<TD> <INPUT TYPE="button" NAME="clear" VALUE="CLEAR"
onClick="window.document.calculator.display.value='0'; window.val1=0;"> ⇐
</TD>
<TD> <INPUT TYPE="button" NAME="D" VALUE="/"
onClick="savNum(this.name)"> </TD>
</TR>
</TABLE>
</FORM>
</BIG>
</BODY>
</HTML>
```

2. Inside the document's <HEAD> container, add a JavaScript <SCRIPT> container. Use the following code to begin construction of the <SCRIPT> container. This code declares three global memory variables. The *Memory* variable is used for persistence of numbers that are used repeatedly as input parameters to computational functions. The user will implement three memory buttons: Memory Remember (MR), Memory Clear (MC), and Memory Save (MS), to manage the number stored in this variable. The *val1* and *operator* variables contain information needed by Boolean functions. Boolean functions require two input parameters. Because only one number can be constructed at a time, these variables are used as temporary storage for one input parameter and the chosen binary operator while the second input parameter is being constructed.

```
<SCRIPT LANGUAGE="JavaScript">
<!-- Hide This Code From Non-JavaScript Browsers

var memory; /* Calculator's Memory */
var val1 = 0; /* Operand 1 In Binary Equation */
var operator; /* Binary Operator */
//-->
</SCRIPT>
```

3. Inside the <SCRIPT> container, use the following code to create the makeNum function. This function concatenates a numeric digit onto the end of the current number, displayed in the display text area.

```
/* ***********************************************************************
 *FUNCTION : makeNum
 *PURPOSE :This function adds the selected digit onto the calculator's
 *display text field. This allows the user to build the
 *operand
 * *********************************************************************** */

function makeNum(digit) {
if (document.calculator.display.value == '0') {
document.calculator.display.value = digit;
} else {
document.calculator.display.value += digit;
}
}
```

4. Inside the <SCRIPT> container, use the following code to create the clrNum function. This code will clear the calculator's display area.

```
/* ***********************************************************************
FUNCTION : clrNum
 PURPOSE : This function will clear the operand from the calculator's
display area
 * *********************************************************************** */

function clrNum() {
document.calculator.display.value = "0";
}
```

5. Inside the <SCRIPT> container, create a function named savNum. This function will save information needed by binary functions inside temporary storage. This allows a second number to be built inside the display area. When the second number is complete, the Equal (=) button is activated in order to perform the binary function.

```
/* **************************************************************************
 *FUNCTION :savNum
 *PURPOSE :This function saves the operand and binary operator in order
 *that the user can enter the second operand.
 * ********************************************************************* */

function savNum(op) {
val1 = parseFloat(document.calculator.display.value);
operator = op;
clrNum();
}
```

6. Inside the <SCRIPT> container, create a function named displayAnswer that can be used to display the result of numeric operations in the calculator's display area.

```
/* **************************************************************************
 *FUNCTION :displayAnswer
 *PURPOSE :This function displays an answer in the calculator's display
 * ********************************************************************* */

// This function displays the value returned by the MATH functions inside
// an alert dialog

function displayAnswer(answer) {
document.calculator.display.value = answer;
}
```

7. Inside the <SCRIPT> container, use the following code to establish the computeBinary function. This function uses the information stored in the *val1* and *operator* variables, declared in Step 2, along with the number contained inside the calculator's display area, to perform a binary numeric computation. The operator variable indicates which function should be used. The *val1* variable and the display element's value property will serve as input to the binary function.

```
/* **************************************************************************
 *FUNCTION : computeBinary
 *PURPOSE : This event handler is called when the Equals "=" button is
 *clicked. The function uses the saved operand, along with the
 *operand in the calculator's display area as input the bin. func.
 * ********************************************************************* */

function computeBinary() {
if ((val1 > 0) && (document.calculator.display.value.length > 0)) {

// Get Binary Operator And Two Operands

var val2 = parseFloat(document.calculator.display.value);

// Based On Binary Operator Selected, Perform Numeric Computation

if (operator == 'A')
            displayAnswer(val1 + val2)         // Add
```

continued on next page

continued from previous page

```
else if (operator == 'S')
            displayAnswer(val1 - val2);        // Subtract
else if (operator == 'M')
            displayAnswer(val1 * val2);        // Multiply
else if (operator == 'D')
            displayAnswer(val1 / val2);        // Divide
} else {
alert("ERROR\n\nBoth Operands Not Entered For A Binary Equation");
}

val1 = 0;
}
```

8. Inside the <SCRIPT> language, use the following code to create the computeUnary function. This function will use one of the Math object's member functions. Most of these methods are unary functions, meaning that they operate on a single input parameter. These functions will use the number visible in the calculator's display area as input. The result, returned by the unary function, will replace the input value inside the calculator's display area.

```
/* ********************************************************************
 *FUNCTION :computeUnary
 *PURPOSE :This event handler is called when one of the unary buttons
 *is clicked The function gets the value from the calculator's
 *display area, then calls the appropriate numeric function based
 *on the unary operator that was selected
 * ******************************************************************** */

function computeUnary(op) {
if (document.calculator.display.value.length > 0)  {

// Get Unary Operator And Operand

var val = parseFloat(document.calculator.display.value);

// Use The with Statement So That We Don't Have To Explicitly Say That
// The Numeric Computation Methods Belong To The Math Object

with(Math) {

// Based On Unary Operator Selected, Perform Numeric Computation

if (op == 'S') displayAnswer(sqrt(val));     // Square Root
else if (op ==  'E') displayAnswer(exp(val));    // Exponent
else if (op ==  'L') displayAnswer(log(val));    // Log
else if (op == 'I')displayAnswer(sin(val)); // Sine
else if (op == 'O') displayAnswer(cos(val));     // Cosine
else if (op == 'T')displayAnswer(tan(val)); // Tanget
else if (op == 'N')displayAnswer(asin(val));     // ASine
else if (op == 'A') displayAnswer(acos(val));     // ACosine
else if (op == 'G')displayAnswer(atan(val));     // ATanget
else if (op == 'R')displayAnswer(round(val));     // Round
}

} else {
alert("ERROR\n\nYou Must Enter A Number");
```

```
  }
}
```

9. Save your JavaScript-enabled HTML document as HT0601.HTM. Use the File/Open File menu option to load HT0601.HTM into the Navigator 2.0 browser and have fun playing with the calculator.

How It Works

The heart of the calculator is its display area. This area is the long, thin text field at the top of the document. This area is used to display input parameters and results of numeric computation functions. This area is manipulated by a series of push buttons, located beneath the display area. The calculator document contains six classes of push button. A class is distinguished by the type of functionality performed when the button is activated. Each class may be represented by more than one button on the calculator. Table 6-3 introduces the six button classes.

CLASS	EXAMPLE	DESCRIPTION
Digit buttons	1, 3, 9	These buttons are used to build a number in the calculator's display area. The selected digit is concatenated onto the end of this number. For example, let's assume that number 0 is visible inside the display area. If the five (5) button is activated, the display area will change to the number 5. Next, the user selects the one (1) button. The number 51 now displays. As you see, digit buttons are used to build a numerical operand inside the display area. This number will serve as input to the numeric computation functions represented by Unary function buttons and Binary function buttons.
Unary function buttons	SQRT, SIN	These buttons represent unary numeric functions that belong to the Math object. A unary function takes a single input parameter. This parameter is visible inside the calculator's display area when the function is selected. Each function returns a result that replaces the input parameter inside the display area.
Binary function buttons	+, *	These buttons represent binary numeric functions that are represented by JavaScript numeric operators. A binary function requires two input parameters. Because the display area can only contain a single number, each input parameter must be independently constructed. When the user clicks on a binary function button, it indicates to the calculator that the first input parameter has been specified and that the user is ready to enter the second parameter. The first parameter, along with the desired binary function, is temporarily stored while the second parameter is

continued on next page

continued from previous page

CLASS	EXAMPLE	DESCRIPTION
		constructed. The Equals button must be activated to "kick off" the numeric computation.
Equals button	=	The Equals button is used to indicate that the second input parameter is now complete and the user wishes to perform a binary function. The results of this function replace the second input parameter in the display area.
Memory buttons	MR, MC, MS	These buttons manage the single memory location that is available to users. Here users can store numbers that are used in several computations. Buttons are provided to store a number in memory, clear the number from memory, and place the number in memory inside the calculator's display area.
Clear button	C	This button clears the display area by reinitializing it to the number zero (0).

Table 6-3 Calculator button classes

Comments

In addition to numeric constants and computational functions, the Math object also contains a function that will generate a random number. How-To 6.2 will introduce this function as a means of implementing games using JavaScript.

COMPLEXITY
BEGINNING

6.2 How do I...
Generate a random number?

COMPATIBILITY: NAVIGATOR 2.X FOR UNIX NAVIGATOR 3.X

Problem

I am developing a game using JavaScript. In the game, many conditions are left to chance. How can I generate a random number to simulate chance?

Technique

In addition to the scientific number functions, introduced in How-To 6.1, the Math object also contains a method to generate random numbers. The Random() function can be used to generate a random number between 0 and 1. If the random number must be a whole number, multiply the number by 100 to create a random number between 0 and 100. If the number must be within a range of values, modulus division can be used to ensure that the number falls within this range. Modulus division returns the remainder when one number is divided by another. The remainder will fall within a certain range, determined by the denominator. The range will contain all whole numbers between 0 and the denominator, –1. The following code is an example that uses modulus division to randomly generate a whole number between 1 and 6.

```
Math.round(Math.random() * 100) % 6 + 1;
```

The Random() method is available only from a UNIX version of Navigator 2.0 or from Navigator 3.0.

Steps

This example will create an HTML document that can simulate two players rolling a single die. Each player will roll the die, and the player who rolls the highest number will be declared the winner of the game. The player will always compete against the House.

From a UNIX version of Navigator 2.0 or any version of Navigator 3.0, load the document HT0602.HTM from the CD. The document in Figure 6-2 will appear.

1. Use the following HTML code to create a new document. The document will contain a single push button with an onClick event handler. This button will be used by a player who is ready to play the game. The event handler calls the playGame() function, which will be defined in Step 2.

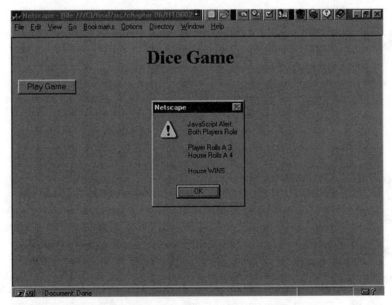

Figure 6-2 The dice game

```
<HTML>
<HEAD>
</HEAD>
<BODY>
<CENTER> <H1> Dice Game </H1> </CENTER>
<FORM>
<INPUT TYPE="button" VALUE="Play Game" onClick="playGame()">
</FORM>
</BODY>
</HTML>
```

2. Inside the <HEAD> container, create a JavaScript function based on the following code. This function will use the Math.random() method to simulate
two players rolling a single die. The function will then analyze the results of
the game and display a winner. Players will be notified of the game's outcome through an alert dialog.

```
<SCRIPT LANGUAGE="JavaScript">
function playGame() {
var player = Math.round(Math.random() * 100) % 6 + 1;
var house = Math.round(Math.random() * 100) % 6 + 1;

var winner;
if (player > house)
winner ="Player";
else if (house > player)
winner = "House";
else
winner = "Nobody";

var game = "Both Players Role\n\nPlayer Rolls A " + player + "\nHouse ⇐
Rolls A " + house + "\n\n" + winner + " WINS";
alert(game);
}
</SCRIPT>
```

3. Save the file as HT0602.HTM. In Navigator, use the File/Open File menu
option to execute the JavaScript application by loading HT0602.HTM into
the browser.

How It Works

In this example, the Math object's Random function is used to generate a number
between 0 and 1. Because the simulation requires whole numbers in the 1 to 6 range,
the random number must be manipulated to fall within this range. The manipulation process multiplies the number by 100 to convert part of the fraction to a whole
number. Modulus division is used to turn the number into a value between 1 and
6. This is accomplished by dividing the random number by 6. The remainder from
this operation will fall in the 0 to 5 range. By adding 1 to the result, the random number is successfully converted to the desired number range.

Comments

The Math section of this chapter is now complete. The next several How-To's will discuss methods belonging to the String object.

COMPLEXITY
BEGINNING

6.3 How do I...
Concatenate variables onto the end of a string?

COMPATIBILITY: NAVIGATOR 2.X   NAVIGATOR 3.X

Problem

Many JavaScript functions, such as the Alert method, accept only strings as input. Because data may not always be represented as strings, how can I display this information to the user? If the data is contained in multiple String objects, how can I concatenate several strings to form a new string?

Technique

The JavaScript language provides a concatenation operator (+) that can be used on most built-in data and object types. This operator is a binary operator, meaning that it requires two operands, or variables, as input. The output is a String object initialized to the concatenation of the two input parameters. The concatenation operator performs any data type conversion required to transform binary data to ASCII text. The concatenation operator can be chained so that multiple tokens can be concatenated in a single line of code. The following code concatenates a String object, named title, with a number variable, named edition, and two string literals to form a dynamic HTML statement.

```
var title = "JavaScript How-To";
var edition = 1.0;

document.writeln("The Book is " + title + " Edition " + edition);
```

The operator concatenates data as is, meaning that spaces are not added to separate input elements. If separation is needed, you should include a space (" ") between two input parameters. In the example above, a space is added to the end of the string literal "The Book is " to provide separation between this text and the String object title. Without this space, the concatenation of the two strings would be "The Book is JavaScript How-To".

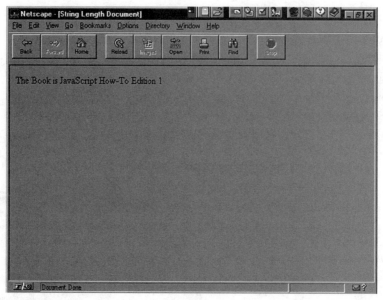

Figure 6-3 The concatenation page

Steps

This example will display an HTML document that uses the concatenation operator to merge several pieces of disparate data into a single line of text.

From Navigator 2.0, load the document HT0603.HTM from the compact disc. The document in Figure 6-3 will appear.

1. Create a new HTML document based on the following code. This code concatenates a String object, a numeric variable, and two string literals to form a dynamic HTML expression. This expression is displayed inside the body of the document.

```
<HTML>
<HEAD> <TITLE> String Length Document </TITLE> </HEAD>
<BODY>
<SCRIPT LANGUAGE="JavaScript">
<!-- Hide This Code From Non-JavaScript Browsers

// The Book Title "JavaScript How-To"
var title = "JavaScript How-To";

// The Edition Number (1.0)
var edition = 1.0;

// Concatenate The Book Title And Edition Number Onto String Literals
document.writeln("The Book is " + title + " Edition " + edition);
//-->
```

```
</SCRIPT>
</BODY>
</HTML>
```

2. Save the file as HT0603.HTM. In Navigator, use the File/Open File menu option to execute the JavaScript application by loading HT0603.HTM into the browser.

How It Works

In this example, the concatenation operator is used to build dynamic HTML text using a String object, a numeric variable, and two string literals. Because the JavaScript code is contained in the document's body, the writeln methods will display the new String object returned by the concatenation operator on the screen. The concatenation operator handles all data conversion. Notice that the number variable, named *edition*, is slightly altered when it is converted to text. The floating-point representation 1.0 will be converted to the number 1. The conversion algorithm recognizes that these values are logically equivalent.

Comments

You may notice that the concatenation operator is the same as the addition operator. The object-oriented methodology embraces a concept called *polymorphism*. This means that an entity can take on multiple forms. The actual form used is based on the specific situation. In JavaScript, the plus character is polymorphic. Depending on the situation, the JavaScript interpreter knows what function, concatenation, or addition to apply.

COMPLEXITY
BEGINNING

6.4 How do I...
Determine the length of a string?

COMPATIBILITY:

Problem

Because strings are variable-length objects, how can I determine the length of an individual String object?

Technique

The physical size of String objects varies depending on the number of characters that comprise the string. Because a string's size varies from object to object, an indicator is needed to identify the end of a string. One technique, used by the C language, is to have a terminating character indicate the end of a string. Another technique is to include a length property along with the string. Because JavaScript is an object-oriented language, it is easy to encapsulate a character array and length under a single object. JavaScript String objects possess a single public property. This property, named length, contains information about how many characters comprise a string. The following code demonstrates how to store the length of the String object title in a JavaScript variable named *len*.

```
var len = title.length;
```

Steps

This example displays a Web page that contains the title of the book you are reading and the number of characters that comprise the title.

From Navigator 2.0, pull up HT0604.HTM. The document in Figure 6-4 will appear on the screen.

1. Create a new HTML document based on the following code. This code displays the length of the string, "JavaScript How-To", inside the document's body.

```
<HTML>
<HEAD> <TITLE> String Length Document </TITLE> </HEAD>
<BODY>
<SCRIPT LANGUAGE="JavaScript">
<!-- Hide This Code From Non-JavaScript Browsers

// The Main String "JavaScript How-To"
var title = "JavaScript How-To";

// Dynamic Text Which Prints Out The Main String
document.writeln(title);

// Dynamic Text Which Prints The Length Of The Main String
document.writeln("<HR>");
document.writeln("The Length is " + title.length);

//-->
</SCRIPT>
</BODY>
</HTML>
```

2. Save the file as HT0604.HTM. In Navigator, use the File/Open File menu option to execute the JavaScript application by loading HT0604.HTM into the browser.

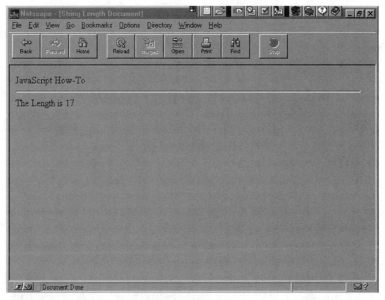

Figure 6-4 The string length page

How It Works

This example uses a JavaScript code fragment, embedded within the body of an HTML document. This enables the JavaScript code to insert dynamic HTML text into the document's body. Because the JavaScript code is not contained within the body of a function, this code is executed when the document is loaded into the browser.

The code fragment declares a single String object, named title, which is initialized with the book title, "JavaScript How-To". Unlike other JavaScript objects, a String object can be initialized without using the new operator or a String constructor method. The assignment operator implies that the string constructor should be used.

Next, the code makes three calls to the Document object's writeln method. The first call places the book title inside the document body. The last call displays the string length on the screen. The concatenation operator (+) is used to merge a string label with the length, represented as an integer.

Comments

Now that you can determine how many characters comprise a string, How-To 6.5 will teach you the technique for determining which character resides at a given position inside a string.

COMPLEXITY
BEGINNING

6.5 How do I...
Return the character that resides at a given position?

COMPATIBILITY: NAVIGATOR 2.X   NAVIGATOR 3.X

Problem

How can I return the character that resides at a given position in the string?

Technique

The String object's charAt method is used to return the character residing at a particular index. The method references the calling string to locate the character stored at the index passed to the method through a single input parameter. This parameter will accept any value ranging from 0 to the string's length property, -1. Index 0 will return the first character in the string. If the index provided is outside of this range, charAt will return an empty value. Otherwise, the character stored at the specified example will be returned. The following example shows how to use the charAt method to return the fourth character in the string variable title.

```
var ch = title.charAt(4);
```

Steps

This example displays a Web page that contains the title of the book you are reading and the character S, which resides at position four in the string.

From Navigator 2.0, pull up HT0605.HTM. The document in Figure 6-5 will appear on the screen.

1. Create a new HTML document based on the following HTML and JavaScript code. This code displays the character at position four in the title of this book.

```
<HTML>
<HEAD> <TITLE> String Length Document </TITLE> </HEAD>
<BODY>
<SCRIPT LANGUAGE="JavaScript">
<!-- Hide This Code From Non-JavaScript Browsers

// The Main String "JavaScript How To"
var title = "JavaScript How-To";

// The Desired Position (4)
var position = 4;

// Dynamic Text Which Prints Out The Main String
document.writeln(title);
```

```
// Dynamic Text Which Prints The Character At The
// Desired Location Inside The Main String

document.writeln("<HR>");
document.writeln("The Character At Position " +
position +
" is " +
title.charAt(position));
//-->
</SCRIPT>
</BODY>
</HTML>
```

2. Save the file as HT0605.HTM. In Navigator, use the File/Open File menu option to execute the JavaScript application by loading HT0605.HTM into the browser.

How It Works

This example contains a String object, named title, whose value is initialized to JavaScript How-To. The String object's charAt method is used to return the fifth character in the title string. Figure 6-6 shows the position of each character inside the title string.

The fifth character resides at position four. This is the input parameter to the charAt function. The fifth character is at position four because string index positions start with the number 0. Therefore, the first character in the string resides at position 0. In the string JavaScript How-To, the character S resides in position four.

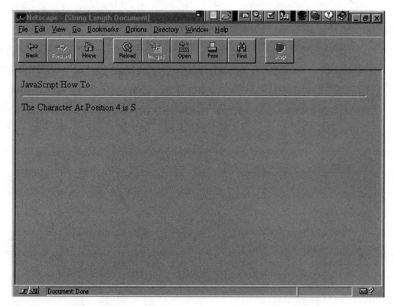

Figure 6-5 The position document

```
JavaScript How-To
01234567890123456
```

Figure 6-6 The JavaScript How-To
string

Comments

The charAt method can be used to access information contained within a formatted string. These strings contain embedded data that usually resides at a given memory location. A example of a formatted string may be a date, where the month resides in the first two positions, the date in positions 2 through 4, and the year in the last two positions.

COMPLEXITY
BEGINNING

6.6   How do I...
Locate the position of characters in a string?

COMPATIBILITY:

Problem

How can I locate the position of characters inside a string?

Technique

JavaScript's Built-in String object possesses two methods, indexOf and lastIndexOf, which can be used to locate characters inside a string. These methods search a calling string for the first occurrence of a specified search string. Both methods accept one mandatory parameter representing the character or string for which the method should search. A second optional parameter specifies the character position where a search should begin. This parameter accepts integers ranging from 0 to a string's length - 1. If this parameter is not included in method invocation, the indexOf method will start the search at the first character. The lastIndexOf method will begin the search starting from the ending character. Characters are indexed starting with the number 0 and moving left to right across the string. Therefore the last character resides at index length -1. If the search string is not located inside the calling string, both methods will return -1, indicating that the search string was not found. Both functions are case-sensitive. The following code demonstrates how to use the indexOf and lastIndexOf methods to locate the character ' ' inside a String object named title.

```
title.indexOf(' ');
title.lastIndexOf(' ');
```

Steps

This example shows a Web page that displays the string JavaScript How To along with the first and last occurrences of the letter 'a' inside this string.

From Navigator 2.0, pull up HT0606.HTM. The document in Figure 6-6 will appear on the screen. The first and last occurrences of the character ' ', inside the string, JavaScript How To, are displayed inside the document. The first occurrence of the character ' ' is at position 10, while the last occurrence is at position 14.

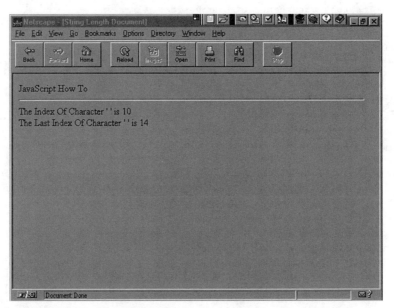

Figure 6-7 The character location document

1. Create a new HTML document based on the following code. This code searches the title string, beginning at the first character, for the first occurrence of the character ' '. The code then initiates a search, starting at the last character, for the character ' '.

```
<HTML>
<HEAD> <TITLE> String Length Document </TITLE> </HEAD>
<BODY>
<SCRIPT LANGUAGE="JavaScript">
<!-- Hide This Code From Non-JavaScript Browsers

// The Main String "JavaScript How-To"
var title = "JavaScript How-To";

// The Desired Character 'a'
var position = 'a';

// Dynamic Text Which Prints The Main String
document.writeln(title);

// Dynamic Text Which Prints The Position
// Of The First Occurrence Of The Desired
// Character Inside The Main String

document.writeln("<HR>");
document.writeln("The Index Of Character '" +
position +
"' is " +
title.indexOf(position));

// Dynamic Text Which Prints The Last Position
// Of The Last Occurrence Of The Desired
// Character Inside The Main String

document.writeln("<BR>");
document.writeln("The Last Index Of Character '" +
position +
"' is " +
title.lastIndexOf(position));
//-->
</SCRIPT>
</BODY>
</HTML>
```

2. Save the file as HT0606.HTM. In Navigator, use the File/Open File menu option to execute the JavaScript application by loading HT0606.HTM into the browser.

How It Works

The String object, named *title*, is initialized with the value "JavaScript How-To". Refer to Figure 6-6 to see the position of each character in the title string. The title string contains three tokens separated by the delimiter character ' ' . The three tokens are JavaScript, How, and To.

The indexOf method is used to locate the first occurrence of delimiter character ' ' inside this string. The search starts with the first character and ends when the desired character is located. In this example, the character ' ' resides in the 11th position inside the title string. Therefore, the value 10 is returned by this function, indicating that the character is found in position 10. Remember index numbers start at 0.

The lastIndexOf method is then used to locate the last occurrence of the delimiter character ' ' inside the string. The value 14 is returned by this function indicating that the last occurrence of the character is the 15th character in the string.

Comments

The indexOf and lastIndexOf functions are useful for finding delimiters that separate primitive data contained within a string. In this example, the title string contains three tokens separated by the character ' '. By using the indexOf function, you can locate the starting and ending position of each token inside the string. How-To 6.7 will teach you how to access embedded strings, or substrings, once you locate them inside the string.

COMPLEXITY
BEGINNING

6.7 How do I...
Extract substrings from within a String object?

COMPATIBILITY:

Problem

Now that I know how to locate the start of each token in a string, how can I access individual tokens inside the string?

Technique

How-To 6.6 demonstrated how to access single characters contained within a string. This How-To will show you the technique to create a new String object based on multiple characters contained within a main string. The String object's Substring method can be used to create a new String object based on characters contained inside another string.

For a substring to work, the member characters must all reside in a contiguous memory space. You probably have heard the term "contiguous" used in reference to the "contiguous United States." This phrase refers to the lower 48 states. These states are connected. You can travel throughout the lower 48 states without having to cross an ocean or a foreign country. Alaska and Hawaii are not included in this reference because they are separated from the rest of the country. The same concept applies in computer memory. Contiguous memory resides inside the same address space. The bits are physically located next to one another. This forms an unbreakable memory chain.

Because substrings only work on ASCII text stored in contiguous memory, the only information needed to reference this information is the starting and ending memory locations. Similar to the charAt method, these values are defined in terms of positions within a string. It is implied that all memory between these two values belongs to the substring. In JavaScript, the beginning location is included as part of the returned string. The ending character is not included inside the substring. Therefore you must specify a character index that is one greater than the last memory location that should comprise the substring. The Substring method returns a new String object initialized with the substring's characters.

Steps

This example displays a Web page that shows the string JavaScript How-To along with the middle token, How, which resides in positions 10 through 14.

From Navigator 2.0 or Navigator 3.0, open HT0607.HTM. The document in Figure 6-8 will appear on the screen.

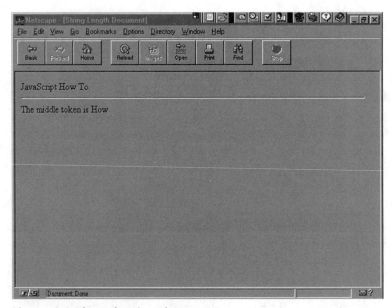

Figure 6-8 The substring document

1. Create a new HTML document based on the following code. This example will create a new String object based on the middle token inside the JavaScript How-To string. The middle token is located using the indexOf and lastIndexOf methods, introduced in How-To 6.6.

```
<HTML>
<HEAD> <TITLE> String Length Document </TITLE> </HEAD>
<BODY>
<SCRIPT LANGUAGE="JavaScript">
<!-- Hide This Code From Non-JavaScript Browsers

// The Main String "JavaScript How-To"
var title = "JavaScript How To";

// Extract The SubString "Script", Located In Position 4 Through 10
// From The Main String "JavaScript How To"
document.writeln(title);
document.writeln("<HR>");
document.writeln("The middle token is " +
title.substring(title.indexOf(' '),title.lastIndexOf(' ')));
document.writeln("<BR>");

//-->
</SCRIPT>
</BODY>
</HTML>
```

2. Save the file as HT0607.HTM. In Navigator, use the File/Open File menu option to execute the JavaScript application by loading HT0607.HTM into the browser.

How It Works

This example creates a new String object based on a substring contained with the title string JavaScript How To. Figure 6-6 shows the position of each character inside this string. The title string contains three tokens delimited by the character **' '** . The three tokens are: JavaScript, How, and To.

This example uses the technique introduced in How-To 6.6 to locate the delimiter characters inside the string. The delimiter character determines the starting and ending position of the middle token. The delimiter characters reside in positions 10 and 14. Because the token does not contain the delimiter character, the middle token resides between positions 11 and 13.

The string's Substring method is used to create a new string initialized to the middle token. The output of the indexOf method is adjusted by one position and serves as the first input parameter to the substring function. Adjustment is necessary because the first parameter indicates the first character in the middle token. The output of the lastIndexOf method is piped to the substring's second input parameter. No adjustment is necessary because the last parameter's position is not included as part of the substring.

Comments

This How-To ends the discussion about accessing characters inside a String object. How-To 6.8 will focus on the topic of the case of a character. This is an important topic because the ASCII value differs for the upper- and lowercase representation of the same character.

COMPLEXITY
BEGINNING

6.8 How do I...
Change the case of all characters in a string?

COMPATIBILITY:

Problem

I want to perform a case-insensitive comparison of two String objects. The problem is that the lower- and uppercase versions of the same character have different ASCII values. Before performing the comparison, I will convert all strings to the same case. This technique will negate differences in data entry and allow comparison to occur without taking a character's case into consideration. How can I change the case of all characters in a string?

Technique

The String object provides two methods, toLowerCase and toUpperCase, that will change the case of all characters that comprise a String object. Neither method accepts an input parameter. It is important to note that these methods do not change the value stored in the calling String object. Instead, they return a new String object initialized with the exact character sequence as the calling object. The only difference is that each character has been converted to the appropriate case representation. This means that the returned string is the same length as the calling string. The toLowerCase method returns a String object converted to lowercase. The following example converts all characters that comprise the String object, named title, to lowercase before displaying it to the screen.

```
document.writeln("The lowercase Version Is " + title.toLowerCase());
```

Despite invoking the toLowerCase method, the value stored in title remains unchanged. The toUpperCase method returns the calling string converted to uppercase. The following example converts the title object to uppercase.

```
document.writeln("The UPPERCASE Version Is " + title.toUpperCase());
```

Steps

This example will show a dynamically created HTML document that displays the upper- and lowercase representations of the string JavaScript How- To.

From Navigator 2.0, pull up HT0608.HTM. The document in Figure 6-9 will appear on the screen. The document displays the upper- and lowercase representations of the book's title.

1. Create a new HTML document based on the following code. This example changes the case of the JavaScript How-To to both the lowercase and uppercase representations of the same string.

```
<HTML>
<HEAD> <TITLE> String Length Document </TITLE> </HEAD>
<BODY>
<SCRIPT LANGUAGE="JavaScript">
<!-- Hide This Code From Non-JavaScript Browsers

// The Main String "JavaScript How-To"
var title = "JavaScript How-To";

// Dynamic Text Based On Converting The Main String
// To All Lower Case Characters
document.writeln(title);
document.writeln("<HR>");
document.writeln("The lowercase Version Is " +
title.toLowerCase());

// Dynamic Text Based On Converting The Main String
// To All Upper Case Characters
document.writeln("<BR>");
document.writeln("The UPPERCASE Version Is " +
title.toUpperCase());

//-->
</SCRIPT>
</BODY>
</HTML>
```

2. Save the file as HT0608.HTM. In Navigator, use the File/Open File menu option to execute the JavaScript application by loading HT0608.HTM into the browser.

How It Works

The toUpperCase and toLowerCase are used to return a new String object. The string is initialized with the title string "JavaScript How-To" converted to the appropriate case. Remember that these methods do not modify the calling object. Instead, they return a new String object initialized to the appropriate representation of the original string.

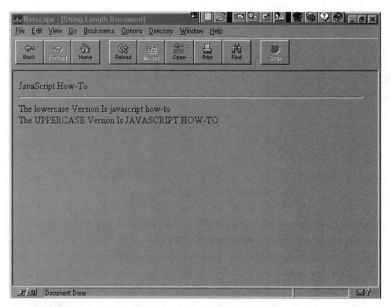

Figure 6-9 The character case document

Comments

This completes the discussion of the JavaScript String object. Next, the Date object will be introduced.

COMPLEXITY
BEGINNING

6.9 How do I...
Get the current date and time from the operating system?

COMPATIBILITY:

Problem

I would like to display the date and time a user begins interaction with my Web page. How can I get the current date and time from the operating system?

Technique

In JavaScript, new objects are instantiated by invoking the appropriate class constructor. The constructor must be prefaced by the new operator to indicate that memory must be allocated to the new object. Constructor functions are designed to initialize an object's attributes. These attributes may be initialized to either a default value or a value specified by the calling routine.

When a Date object is instantiated, the Date constructor initializes the object's attributes. These attributes contain both date (day, month, year) and time (hour, minute, second) information. If the calling function does not pass a parameter to the Date constructor, then the object is initialized with the current date and time. This information is based on the system clock in the host or client machine. The following code demonstrates how to initialize the Date object named today with the current date and time.

```
var today = new Date();
```

In addition to being called with no parameters, the Date constructor is overloaded to accept a single parameter. Overloaded functions possess the same method name but differ in the number and type of formal parameters which they accept. This difference allows the interpreter to choose which function is appropriate for a specific circumstance. The Date constructor is overloaded to accept a Date string. This string contains a textual representation of the attributes contained within the Date object. The following code initializes the Date object birthday to September 10, 1968.

```
var birthday = new Date("September 10, 1968");
```

The Date constructor also accepts another Date object as input. This is used to create and duplicate a Date object.

Steps

The following example will create a Web page that displays the current date and time to the user. The current date is synonymous with the moment when this page is loaded into the user's computer.

From Navigator 2.0, pull up HT0609.HTM. The document in Figure 6-10 will appear on the screen. The current date and time is visible inside the body of the document. The time stamp is displayed using the format: day month date hour: minute: second year.

1. Create a new HTML document based on the following code. This code uses the Document object's dynamic HTML text methods to display the current date and time inside the body of the downloaded document.

```
<HTML>
<HEAD> <TITLE> String Length Document </TITLE> </HEAD>
<BODY>
<SCRIPT LANGUAGE="JavaScript">
<!-- Hide This Code From Non-JavaScript Browsers

// Get The Current Date From The Operating System
var today = new Date();

// Create Dynamic Text Which Will Display The Current Date
```

continued on next page

continued from previous page

```
// Inside The Document's Body
document.writeln("<HR>");
document.writeln("The current date and time is " + today);
document.writeln("<BR>");

//-->
</SCRIPT>
</BODY>
</HTML>
```

2. Save the file as HT0609.HTM. In Navigator, use the File/Open File menu option to execute the JavaScript application by loading HT0609.HTM into the browser.

How It Works

This example uses a JavaScript code fragment, embedded within the body of an HTML document. This enables the JavaScript code to insert dynamic HTML text into the document's body. Because the JavaScript code is not contained within the body of a function, this code is executed when the document is loaded into a browser.

The Date constructor, which accepts no formal parameters, is used to get the system date and time from the operating system. This constructed Date object is stored inside a Date object named today. This object is declared and constructed within the same line of code.

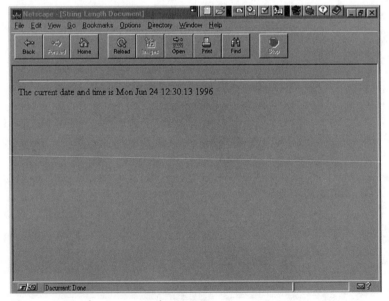

Figure 6-10 The current date page

The Document object's writeln method is used to output the date and time to the user. The example uses three calls to this method. The same functionality could have been accomplished in a single call to the writeln method. Three methods are used to make the code more readable. The second writeln call outputs the time stamp to the user. The writeln accepts a single parameter, defined as a String object. The string concatenation operator (+) is used to merge a label with the time stamp. As you may remember from How-To 6.3, this operator can be used to merge dates of disparate types into a single String object. The date is concatenated onto the string using the following format: day month date hour:minute:second year.

Comments

Now that you have seen how to create a Date object, based on the current date and time, How-To 6.10 will describe the methods required to access the attributes belonging to a Date object.

COMPLEXITY

INTERMEDIATE

6.10 How do I...
Access a Date object's properties?

COMPATIBILITY: NAVIGATOR 2.X

Problem

Now that I know how to construct a Date object, how can I access the primitive date and time attributes using the Date object's methods?

Technique

A Date object can be used to extract date and time information about a specific moment in time. Date-related information includes date, month, and year, while time-related information means hours, minutes, and seconds. The initial value for these properties is dependent on the Date constructor invoked during object creation. For example, if a Date constructor that does not accept any parameters is used, these properties are initialized to the current date and time.

After object construction, the only way to modify a Date is through the object's methods. The Date object contains get and set functions for each date and time attribute. Table 6-4 lists the public member functions that can be used to change a Date object.

METHOD	DESCRIPTION
getTime()	Returns the milliseconds since Jan 1 1970 00:00:00.
getYear()	Returns year minus 1900.

continued on next page

continued from previous page

METHOD	DESCRIPTION
getMonth()	Returns month (0=January to 11=December).
getDate()	Returns date within a month. Date range dependent on month.
getDay()	Returns day of week (0=Sunday to 6=Saturday).
getHours()	Returns hours of the day based on a 24 hour clock (0 to 23).
getMinutes()	Returns minutes within an hour (0 to 60).
getSeconds()	Returns seconds within a minute (0 to 60).
setTime(val)	Accepts the milliseconds since Jan 1 1970 00:00:00.
setYear(val)	Accepts year minus 1900.
setMonth(val)	Accepts month (0=January to 11=December).
setDate(val)	Accepts date within a month. Date range dependent on month.
setDay(val)	Accepts day of week (0=Sunday to 6=Saturday).
setHours(val)	Accepts hours of the day based on a 24 hour clock (0 to 23).
setMinutes(val)	Accepts minutes within an hour (0 to 60).
setSeconds(val)	Accepts seconds within a minute (0 to 60).

Table 6-4 Date object access methods

Each of these methods follows a standard naming convention. The first part of the name indicates the function's purpose. A get method extracts a Date attribute by returning it to the calling function. A set method should be used to change an attribute. The last part of the method name indicates the property that will be affected by the method. Possible values include: Month, Date, Day, Hours, Minutes, Seconds, and Time. The set methods each accept a single parameter which contains the new value that will be assigned to an attribute.

Several attributes store irregular value ranges to which you may not be accustomed. For example: The valid range of month values is between 0 (January) and 11 (December). Pay particular attention to these inconsistencies with normal values. If an invalid value is passed to a set attribute, no error will be returned to the calling function. This value will be assigned.

Steps

This example demonstrates a Web front end to a daily reporting tool. This front end is used to input parameters for the report. A report about the previous day's activities is run every morning. The report is run every morning about the previous day's activities. Sometimes, ad hoc reports are needed. These reports may cover from a couple of hours to an entire year. This means that the user must be able to specify the time frame of the report, identified by the start and end dates and times. Because the majority of the reports are daily reports, the user wishes to have the start and end dates initialized to the previous day. This means that the start date must be set to midnight (00:00:00) of the previous day. The end date will be set to one minute before midnight of the current day (23:59:59).

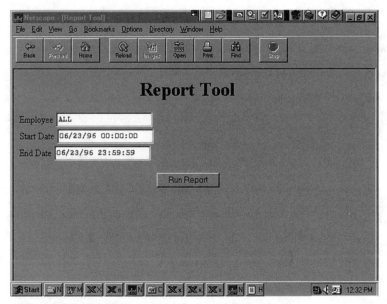

Figure 6-11 The daily report front end document

From Navigator 2.0, pull up HT0610.HTM. The document in Figure 6-11 will appear on the screen. The start and end dates are initialized to report on yesterday's activities.

1. Create a new document based on the following HTML code.

```
<HTML>
<HEAD> <TITLE> Report Tool </TITLE>
</HEAD>
<BODY>
<CENTER> <H1> Report Tool </H1> </CENTER>
<FORM>
Employee <INPUT TYPE="text" NAME="employee" VALUE="ALL">
<BR>
<CENTER> <INPUT TYPE="button" VALUE="Run Report"> </CENTER>
</FORM>
</BODY>
</HTML>
```

2. After the employee input field, add the following JavaScript container. This code establishes two input fields initialized to the previous day's date. The time element of each date is designed to provide full coverage for the entire day's activities.

```
<SCRIPT LANGUAGE="JavaScript">
<!-- Hide This Code From Non-JavaScript Browsers

var start_dt = new Date();// Create Start Date
```

continued on next page

continued from previous page

```
start_dt.setDate(start_dt.getDate()-1);// Set To Yesterday
var end_dt = new Date(start_dt);// Create End Date

// Set Start Date To 12:00:00 AM
start_dt.setHours(0);
start_dt.setMinutes(0);
start_dt.setSeconds(0);

// Set End Date To 11:59:59 PM
end_dt.setHours(23);
end_dt.setMinutes(59);
end_dt.setSeconds(59);

// Create Start Date Text Field
document.writeln("Start Date <INPUT TYPE=\"text\" NAME=\"start\" VALUE=\"" +
                 start_dt.toLocaleString() +
         "\">");

// Create End Date Text Field
document.writeln("End Date <INPUT TYPE=\text\ NAME=\"end\" VALUE=\"" +
                 end_dt.toLocaleString() +
   "\">");
//-->
</SCRIPT>
```

3. Save the file as HT0610.HTM. In Navigator, use the File/Open File menu option to execute the JavaScript application by loading HT0610.HTM into the browser.

How It Works

The Date constructor is used to get the current date and time from the operating system. This information is stored in a Date object named start_dt. The getDate and setDate methods are then used to change the date to the previous day. Next, a new Date object, named end_dt, is created. Notice that a Date constructor is used to assign the start_dt value to end_dt. If the assignment operator (=) were used, the end_dt would simply represent a reference to the start_dt object. Changes in the start_dt would also affect the end_dt. To make sure that the end_dt is a completely autonomous entity, the Date constructor is used to duplicate the start_dt's information. Date manipulation methods are used to set the start time at midnight and the end time at one minute before midnight. Because both objects are set to the same date, the time changes ensure that the time period, represented by the two objects, covers the entire day. The date information is used to initialize two input elements dynamically created in the <SCRIPT> container.

Comments

Because the Internet is a worldwide phenomenon, time zone information may be important to your Web page. After all, people from all 24 time zones can simultaneously access your site. How-To 6.10 did not cover times in its discussion of date properties. That's all right; the next How-To will provide a complete coverage of the topic.

COMPLEXITY

INTERMEDIATE

6.11 How do I...
Work with time zone information?

COMPATIBILITY: NAVIGATOR 2.X

Problem

Because Web pages can be viewed from anywhere in the world, is there any way to access the time zone where my document is being viewed?

Technique

In addition to the methods discussed in How-To 6.10, the Date object also contains two methods that deal with time zone information. The first method, getTimezoneOffset, will return the number of minutes your system differs from Greenwich Mean Time (GMT). GMT is also known as Coordinated Universal Time (UTC). In New York, getTimeZoneOffset would return -300. This means that New York time is 300 minutes earlier than GMT. By dividing the number of minutes by 60 (the number of minutes per hour), you can compute the hour offset from GMT. The accuracy of this information depends solely on the accuracy of your system clock. The following code demonstrates how you would convert the time zone information from minutes to hours.

```
var zone = window.today.getTimezoneOffset()/60
```

A second Date method related to time zone information is the toGMTString( ) method. This method converts a date to a string using the GMT convention. The return value is a formatted string that contains GMT-equivalent date and time information. A call to the toGMTString function may look like this:

```
alert(today.toGMTString());
```

The exact format returned by this method will vary between platforms. Most platforms will display the GMT string in this format:

```
Sat, 9 Sep 1967 00:23:45 GMT
```

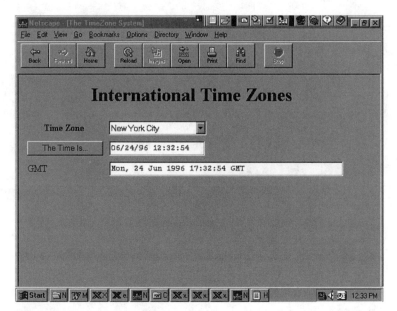

Figure 6-12 The TimeZone document

Steps

This example implements a Web page where the user can get the current date and time information for any of the world's 24 time zones. The information represents a single moment in time, meaning that this page does not implement a Web-based clock. The moment in time is defined as the second when the user activates the push button that will perform the time zone conversion.

From Navigator 2.0 or above, open the file HT0611.HTM. The document in Figure 6-12 is displayed on the screen. The Time Zone select input is set to your respective time zone. For the eastern United States, the time zone is New York. The date and time when the document was loaded into the browser displays in both locale and GMT formats. Change the time zone to Chicago and click on The Time Is... button. In the eastern United States, the time field will change to one hour before the current hour. Feel free to experiment with other time zones.

1. Use the following HTML code to create a new Web page. The page contains a menu where the user can select from a list of time zones. The current date and time for that time zone is then displayed in both locale and GMT format. The time computation has an onClick event handler that calls the newTime() function. This function will be defined in Step 3.

```
<HTML>
<HEAD> <TITLE> The TimeZone System </TITLE> </HEAD>
<BODY>
<CENTER> <H1> International Time Zones </H1> </CENTER>
```

```
<FORM NAME="time">
<TABLE>
<TR>
<TH> Time Zone </TH>
<TD>
<SELECT NAME="zone">
<OPTION VALUE="11HR"> Pacific Ocean Central
<OPTION VALUE="HNL"> Honolulu
<OPTION VALUE="ANC"> Anchoridge
<OPTION VALUE="LAX"> Los Angles
<OPTION VALUE="DEN"> Denver
<OPTION VALUE="CHI"> Chicago
<OPTION VALUE="NYC"> New York City
<OPTION VALUE="CCS"> Caribbean
<OPTION VALUE="RIO"> Rio De Janerio
<OPTION VALUE="2HR"> Atlantic Ocean East
<OPTION VALUE="1HR"> Atlantic Ocean West
<OPTION VALUE="LON"> London
<OPTION VALUE="PAR"> Paris
<OPTION VALUE="CAI"> Egypt
<OPTION VALUE="JRS"> Israel
<OPTION VALUE="JED"> Iraq
<OPTION VALUE="KBL"> Kabul
<OPTION VALUE="DEL"> Delhi
<OPTION VALUE="BKK"> Bangkok
<OPTION VALUE="HKG"> Hong Kong
<OPTION VALUE="TYO"> Tokyo
<OPTION VALUE="ADL"> Central Australia
<OPTION VALUE="SYD"> Sydney
<OPTION VALUE="SYD"> Wellington
<OPTION VALUE="WLG"> Siberia
</SELECT>
</TD>
</TR>
<TR>
<TD> <INPUT TYPE="button" VALUE="The Time Is..." onClick="newTime()"> </TD>
<TD> <INPUT TYPE="text" NAME="newt"> </TD>
</TR>
<TR>
<TD> GMT </TD>
<TD>
</TABLE>
</FORM>
</BODY>
</HTML>
```

2. Inside the <HEAD> container, use the following code to begin the construction of a <SCRIPT> container. This code contains two global variables
needed by various JavaScript code fragments in this example. The today
variable is a Date variable set to the current date and time when the document is loaded into memory. The current variable is set to the hour offset of
the current time zone from GMT.

```
<!-- Hide This Code From Non-JavaScript Browsers
var current;
var today = new Date();
</SCRIPT>
```

3. Inside the <SCRIPT> container, add a single function called newTime. The newTime function is invoked when the user clicks on the The Time Is.... button. This function gets the current date and time from the operating system. This information is then converted into the appropriate date and time for the time zone selected in the zone input.

```
/* ************************************************************************
 *FUNCTION : newTime
 *PURPOSE : Changes The Time To The Selected Time Zone. Display In Both
 *Locale And GMT Format
 * ************************************************************************ */

function newTime() {
var today = new Date();

var zn = (window.document.time.zone.selectedIndex - 12) - current;
today.setHours(today.getHours() + zn);
window.document.time.newt.value = today.toLocaleString();
window.document.time.ngmt.value = today.toGMTString();
}
```

4. Before the </TABLE> label, add a second <SCRIPT> container. This container uses the Document object's writeln method to dynamically create and initialize the GMT text input.

```
<SCRIPT LANGUAGE="JavaScript">
<!-- Hide This Code From Non-JavaScript Browsers
document.writeln("<INPUT TYPE=\"text\" NAME=\"ngmt\" SIZE=\"50\" VALUE=\"" +
today.toGMTString() + "\">");
//-->
</SCRIPT>
```

5. After the </TABLE> container, add a third <SCRIPT> container. This container will compute the time zone where the document is being viewed. This information is used to set the current time as the selected item in the zone input. The function also initializes the newt text field, the current date/time stamp display, in a locale string format. Notice that the newt and ngmt fields use a different technique for initializing the VALUE attribute.

```
<SCRIPT LANGUAGE="JavaScript">
<!-- Hide This Code From Non-JavaScript Browsers
current = Math.round(window.today.getTimezoneOffset()/60);
window.document.time.zone.selectedIndex = current + 12;
window.document.time.newt.value = today.toLocaleString();
//-->
</SCRIPT>
```

6. Save the file as HT0611.HTM. In Navigator, use the File/Open File menu option to execute the JavaScript application by loading HT0611.HTM into the browser.

How It Works

The Date object's getTimezoneOffset is used to return the number of minutes between the current time and GMT. By dividing the number of minutes by the number of minutes per hour, you have access to the GMT offset in terms of hours. The offset hours are needed to compute the time in the desired time zone. Because the current date and time are used to compute the new date and time, the current time zone will provide a reference back to GMT.

The zone select contains all time zones in chronological order. The first option has a -12 hour offset from GMT, while the last option has a +12 hour offset. Because the selectedOption for the zone select will be within the range of 0 to 24, subtract 12 from this property to achieve the GMT offset value. If the current date and time were based on the GMT time zone, the offset value could be applied to the hour property to determine the new date and time. However, the current date and time are not based on GMT time. By adding the current time zone to the desired zone, the true hour offset will be determined. Use the setHours( ) and getHours( ) to adjust the current time to the desired time.

Comments

Congratulations, you now have a truly international Web page.

CHAPTER 7

CONVERTING BETWEEN DATA TYPES

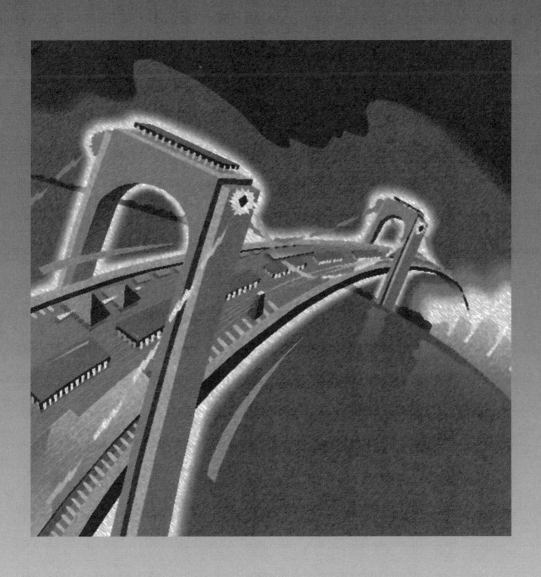

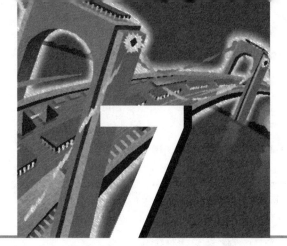

CONVERTING BETWEEN DATA TYPES

How do I...

7.1   Convert from a number to a string?

7.2   Convert from a string to a number?

**7.3   Evaluate an arithmetic expression stored as
a string?**

7.4   Convert from a date to a string?

7.5   Determine the type of the variable?

JavaScript is a loosely typed language, which means that it will, for the most part, convert simply and easily between data types. You can declare a variable and use it as an integer in one part of the code, and then assign a string value to it in another part. JavaScript handles all of the conversion for you.

There are times when you will want to use specific conversion functions in order to ensure that the result of the assignment is in the format that you want. JavaScript does provide several functions that you can call for data type conversion. The parseInt() function will accept a string and an optional numeric base and will return an integer value. The parseFloat function will accept a string containing allowable float values such as 5.6E+3 and convert the results to a float. The eval() function will, in addition to performing other actions such as implementing JavaScript statements, evaluate an arithmetic expression stored in a string and return the numeric results of the expression. Two functions, toLocaleString() and toGMTString(), will convert a date to a string in the locale format for the former and the Internet GMT (Greenwich mean time) format for the latter.

7.1   Convert from a number to a string

You can convert from a number to a string using JavaScript's capability of dynamically modifying the data type of a variable or a value in order to successfully perform an operation or an assignment. This How-To demonstrates how to convert a number to a string using concatenation and direct assignment.

7.2   Convert from a string to a number

The JavaScript function parseInt() will take a string and an optional numeric base such as "10" for base 10 and will return an integer result based on the conversion. This How-To describes how to use this function to convert a hexadecimal string to an integer.

7.3   Evaluate an arithmetic expression stored as a string

The eval() function, when used with an arithmetic expression, will return the numeric results of the expression. This How-To demonstrates using this function and also demonstrates the parseFloat() function.

7.4   Convert from a date to a string

There are two explicit date-to-string conversion functions. The first, toGMTString() will convert a date and format it using the Internet GMT conventions. The second, toLocaleString(), will convert the date and format it to use the locale conventions. This How-To demonstrates both functions.

7.5   Determine the type of the variable

There are times when you may want to know what the type of a variable or function parameter is. You might want to change how you process it or what feedback you return to the Web page reader. The new type of operator that Netscape started providing in Version 3.0 allows you to test a variable or a parameter for its data type, and this How-To demonstrates this operator.

COMPLEXITY
BEGINNING

7.1   How do I...
Convert from a number to a string?

COMPATIBILITY: NAVIGATOR 2.X   NAVIGATOR 3.X

Problem

I want to be able to print out a message showing a number. How does JavaScript handle conversion from a number to a string?

Technique

JavaScript will convert a number to a string through concatenation with another string. You can also assign a number to a string variable or property, but this object then becomes a numeric value.

Steps

Open the file CONVERT.HTM in your browser. This Web page consists of two text fields that you type numbers into: a text field for the result, and a button as shown in Figure 7-1. Type the value 6.5 into the first text field and 13.80 into the second and press the button. The first number is divided by the second and then multiplied by 100 and the result is given in the Percent text field as shown in Figure 7-2. Now, type 0 into the second input text field and press the button. A message pops up with an error, including your value of 0, stating that you must use some other value (the application will not allow you to divide by 0). The steps to create this page follow.

1. Create an empty HTML document.

2. Begin the HEAD and a JavaScript code section by typing the following code:

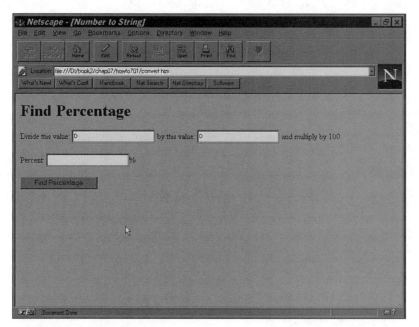

Figure 7-1 CONVERT.HTM on loading

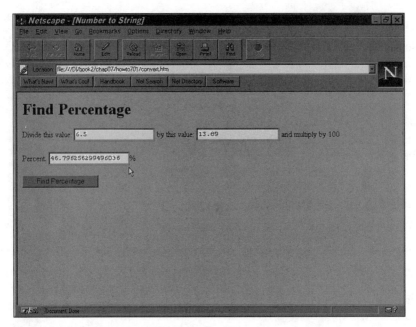

Figure 7-2 CONVERT.HTM after finding percentage

```
<HTML>
<HEAD><TITLE> Number to String </TITLE>
<H1> Find Percentage </H1>

<SCRIPT LANGUAGE="JavaScript">
<!--- hide script from old browsers

// JavaScript Global Variables

// JavaScript Functions
```

3. Next, create a JavaScript function called FindPercent. This function will get
the two values the Web page reader has input and use them to calculate the
percentage. In addition, the function will also check the divisor to ensure
that it is not 0. If it is, the value is concatenated with a string to form a message that is displayed to the reader in an alert message. Notice that the value
variables, iValue1 and iValue2, are defined to be string values if there are no
values in the input text fields, or are converted to numbers if there is a
numeric value in the input field and the variable is treated as a numeric.

```
// FindPercent
// Function will numbers and
// find percent by dividing first by second
function FindPercent() {
var sPercent = ""
var iValue1 = 0
```

```
var iValue2 = 0
var iPercent = 0

// get new value
iValue1 = document.ValueForm.first_value.value
iValue2 = document.ValueForm.second_value.value

// convert by use and by operation
if (iValue2 == "" || iValue1 == "" || iValue2 == 0 ) {
alert("You must enter a value other than " + iValue2 +
// convert by assignment to value
iPercent = iValue1 / iValue2 * 100
document.ValueForm.percent.value = iPercent
}
```

4. Close the HEAD and JavaScript function by typing in the following code.

```
// end hiding from old browsers -->
</SCRIPT>

</HEAD>
```

5. Create the BODY section with a form named ValueForm. The form will contain three text fields and a button. The onClick event handler of the button will call the newly created FindPercent function.

```
<body>

<FORM NAME="ValueForm">
Divide this value: <INPUT TYPE="text" NAME="first_value" VALUE=0 SIZE=20 >
 by this value: <INPUT TYPE="text" NAME="second_value" VALUE=0>
and multiply by 100
<p>
Percent: <INPUT TYPE="text" NAME="percent" VALUE="">%
<p>
<INPUT TYPE="button" NAME="Add" VALUE="Find Percentage"
OnClick="FindPercent()">
</FORM>

</BODY>
</HTML>
```

6. Close your file and save it as CONVERT.HTM. Test your page by loading it into your browser.

How It Works

JavaScript is a loosely typed language and will automatically convert data types where and when appropriate. In our example, the numbers that were entered into the text fields were converted into numbers when tested and when the percentage was calculated. The numeric value was converted into a string when the message was created if the divisor was 0 and implicitly converted when the percentage was displayed.

Comments

If you enter a pure string value such as "hello" into either of the input text fields, you will get an error. The function's testing checks for missing values or an incorrect numeric value, but it does not check to see that you entered a value that was not numeric (NaN). A function called isNaN() will check the value and return true if the value is numeric. Unfortunately, this function will only work on UNIX platforms. On UNIX platforms, this function is used with the parseInt() and parseFloat() functions to test their results.

There is a work-around you can use to test a value in the Windows environment. Use the parseFloat function to access the variable. If the value is not a number, the value returned will be a 0. In the case of our example code, a value of 0 in the divisor will generate error anyway and you can make a message accordingly. A value of 0 in the numerator would result in the value of 0 and you could place this in the results field. The file CONVERTS.HTM contains a safe version of the example you just created that uses this technique.

COMPLEXITY
BEGINNING

7.2 How do I...
Convert from a string to a number?

COMPATIBILITY:  NAVIGATOR 2.X   NAVIGATOR 3.X

Problem

I want to convert a string containing a hexadecimal value into a number. How can I do this in JavaScript?

Technique

JavaScript has a built-in function called parseInt() that can take a string representing a number and a radix (number base) and convert the value into the appropriate base 10 number. If parseInt cannot convert the number, it returns NaN.

Steps

Open the file CONVRTSI.HTM in your Web browser. This Web page contains two text fields and a button. Enter the hexadecimal value of FFB0CD into the first input field and press the button. The number converted into base 10 is output in the second text field as shown in Figure 7-3. The steps to create this page follow.

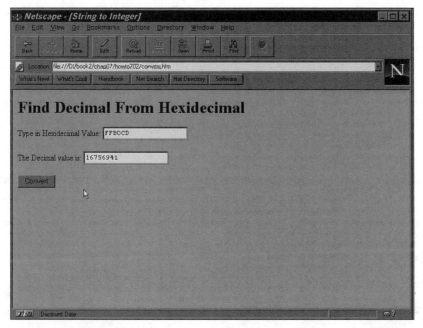

Figure 7-3 CONVRTSI.HTM after converting FFB0CD into 16756941

1. Create a new empty HTML document file.

2. Type in the following code to begin a HEAD and JavaScript code section.

```
<HTML>
<HEAD><TITLE> String to Integer </TITLE>
<H1> Find Decimal From Hexidecimal </H1>

<SCRIPT LANGUAGE="JavaScript">
<!--- hide script from old browsers

// JavaScript Global Variables

// JavaScript Functions
```

3. Create a JavaScript function called Convert that will access the string in the first input text field and use parseInt() with a radix of 16 to convert the hexadecimal value to a decimal value. Display the new value.

```
// Convert
// Function will use parseInt
// to convert a hexidecimal value to a
// decimal one
function Convert() {
// convert Decimal
var sValue = ""
```

```
sValue = document.ValueForm.dec.value
var hexVal = parseInt(sValue,16)

// output converted value
document.ValueForm.hex.value = hexVal
}
```

4. End the JavaScript and HEAD sections by typing the following.

```
// end hiding from old browsers -->
</SCRIPT>

</HEAD>
```

5. Create the BODY section and include a form called ValueForm. In the form create two text input fields and a button. Code the onClick event handler of the button to call the new Convert() JavaScript function.

```
<body>

<FORM NAME="ValueForm">
Type in Hexidecimal Value: <INPUT TYPE="text" NAME="dec" VALUE="">
<p>The Decimal value is: <INPUT TYPE="text" NAME="hex" VALUE=00>
<p>
<INPUT TYPE="button" NAME="Cnvrt" VALUE="Convert"
OnClick="Convert()">
</FORM>

</BODY>
</HTML>
```

6. Close and save the file as CONVRTSI.HTM. Test your new page by loading it into your browser.

How It Works

The parseInt() function will attempt to convert a string containing the appropriate numeric value and using the radix optionally given in the second parameter. For radix values of less than 10, the allowed values in the string will be numbers only. For radix values greater than or equal to 10, such as the hexadecimal value of 16, the string can contain alpha characters that are allowed in the base system. The hexadecimal system will allow values of 0-9 and A-F or a-f. Any other values outside of the acceptable ones will result in a NaN value.

COMPLEXITY
INTERMEDIATE

7.3 How do I...
Evaluate an arithmetic expression stored as a string?

COMPATIBILITY:

Problem

I want to be able to access an arithmetic expression stored in a string and return a numeric result. Then I want to be able to round the value and display the result. How can I do this in JavaScript?

Technique

You can use the built-in JavaScript function eval() to evaluate an arithmetic expression and return a numeric result. This result can then be modified using the various Math object methods to produce the results you want.

Steps

Open the file ARITHEVL.HTM in your browser. This document contains one input text field and two output text fields and a button labeled Evalute. Type an arithmetic expression into the input text field as shown in Figure 7-4. Press the button and the result is output to the second text field, and the rounded result is shown in the third, as displayed in Figure 7-5. To create this Web page, follow the steps below.

1. Create a new empty HTML file.

2. Type in the following code to start the HEAD and JavaScript code sections.

```
<HTML>
<HEAD><TITLE> Evaluate String Expression </TITLE>
<H1> Evaluate a Arithmetic Expression </H1>

<SCRIPT LANGUAGE="JavaScript">
<!--- hide script from old browsers

// JavaScript Global Variables

// JavaScript Functions
```

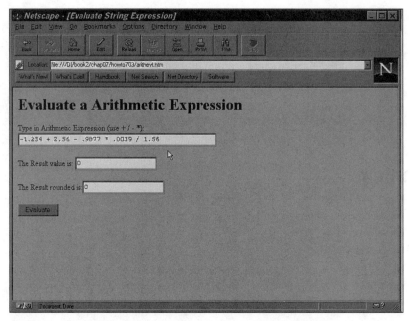

Figure 7-4 ARITHEVL.HTM with arithmetic expression

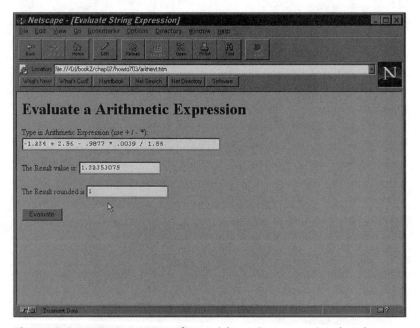

Figure 7-5 ARITHEVL.HTM after arithmetic expression has been evaluated and rounded

3. Create a function called Evaluate() that will take a string parameter and use this in an eval() function call. Eval() will evaluate an arithmetic expression and return a numeric result. This result is displayed in the second text field.

```
// Evaluate
// Function will evaluate a string expression
// and set value and then will round using math object
// Accepts string expression
function Evaluate(sExpression) {
//
var iVal = eval(sExpression)
document.ValueForm.result.value = iVal
```

4. In the function, take the results of the eval() function from the string where it is displayed and convert it to a float using the parseFloat() function. Use this with the Math object method round() to generate a value that is rounded up to a whole number value. This value is displayed in the third text field.

```
var fVal = parseFloat(document.ValueForm.result.value)
iVal = Math.round(fVal)
document.ValueForm.rndresult.value = iVal
}
```

5. End the JavaScript and HEAD section.

```
// end hiding from old browsers -->
</SCRIPT>

</HEAD>
```

6. Create a BODY section containing a form with three text inputs and one button input. In the onClick event of the button call the new JavaScript Evaluate() function and pass the value of the first input text field as an argument to this function.

```
<body>

<FORM NAME="ValueForm">
Type in Arithmetic Expression (use + / - *):<br>
    <INPUT TYPE="text" NAME="expression" VALUE="" size=50>
<p>
The Result value is:   <INPUT TYPE="text" NAME="result" VALUE=0>
<p>
The Result rounded is:<INPUT TYPE="text" NAME="rndresult" VALUE=0>
<p>
<INPUT TYPE="button" NAME="Evl" VALUE="Evaluate"
OnClick="Evaluate(ValueForm.expression.value)">
</FORM>

</BODY>
</HTML>
```

7. Close the file and save it as ARITHEVL.HTM. Test your new document by loading it into your browser and trying out different arithmetic expressions.

How It Works

The eval() built-in function will evaluate any string that contains standard JavaScript expressions or statements. As an arithmetic expression is a legal JavaScript expression, this type of command is evaluated and the results are returned. Only string values are allowed in a eval() function call.

The parseFloat function will take a string and convert it to a floating point number if the string represents a floating point number, or it will return NaN. The round() method of the Math object will round any floating-point number to its nearest whole number.

COMPLEXITY
BEGINNING

7.4 How do I...
Convert from a date to a string?

COMPATIBILITY:  NAVIGATOR 2.X   NAVIGATOR 3.X

Problem

I want to be able to display the current date in my Web page and I would like to control how it displays. How can I do this?

Technique

JavaScript has two built-in functions that will take a date and convert it into a formatted string. These functions are the toLocaleString() and the toGMTString() functions. The first function will convert the date into a format that is specific to your environment and time and the second will convert the date to an Internet GMT convention.

Steps

Open the file CONVRTDT.HTM file in your browser. It opens with the date displayed using two formats: the local date formatting and the time, and the GMT date formatting and the time, as shown in Figure 7-6. The steps to access these formatting functions follow.

1. Create a new empty HTML file.

2. Type in the statements to start a HEAD section and a JavaScript section.

```
<HTML>
<HEAD><TITLE> Date to String </TITLE>
<H1> Today's date </H1>

<SCRIPT LANGUAGE="JavaScript">
<!--- hide script from old browsers
```

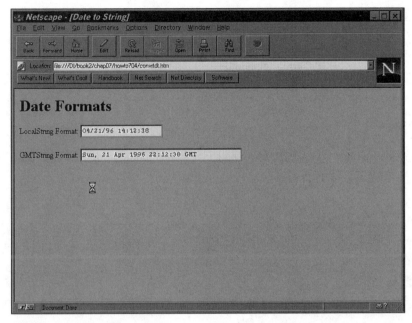

Figure 7-6 CONVRTDT.HTM displaying two different string-to-date conversion functions

```
// JavaScript Global Variables

// JavaScript Functions
```

3. Create a JavaScript function called Convert that will create a new Date object representing the current date and time. The function will then convert the date into strings using the toLocateString and toGMTString functions and display the results in two text fields.

```
// Convert
// Function will convert dates
// to string formats
function Convert() {
// convert Date
var dtObject = new Date()

// convert and display
document.ValueForm.locale.value =
dtObject.toLocaleString(dtObject)
document.ValueForm.gmt.value =
dtObject.toGMTString(dtObject)
}
```

4. Close the JavaScript and HEAD sections by typing in the following code.

```
// end hiding from old browsers -->
</SCRIPT>

</HEAD>
```

5. Create the BODY section and call the JavaScript function when the window is loaded. Create a form with two input text fields.

```
<FORM NAME="ValueForm">
LocalString Format: <INPUT TYPE="text" NAME="locale">
<p>GMTString Format: <INPUT TYPE="text" NAME="gmt" size=40>
</FORM>

</BODY>
</HTML>
```

6. Close and save the file as CONVRTDT.HTM. Test your new page by loading it into your browser.

How It Works

The toLocaleString function will generate a formatted date string using your own location's date and time. The toGMTString function will generate a formatted string using the GMT date and time. To obtain even more control of the formatting of the date you will want to access each component of the date using the applicable Date object methods and create your own string.

COMPLEXITY

INTERMEDIATE/ADVANCED

7.5   How do I...
Determine the type of the variable?

COMPATIBILITY: NAVIGATOR 3.X

Problem

I would like to create a function that receives values of different data types depending on the user's actions, but I don't want to have to create several different functions to do this. How can I determine the data type of a parameter or other variable or object?

Technique

The operator typeof will return a string representing the data type of the object on which it is applied. If the object is a JavaScript pre-defined object such as form or document, the function will return the result object.

Steps

Open the TYPEOF.HTM file. This file contains five radio buttons as shown in Figure 7-7. Pressing the Send Function button will result in a message that the parameter sent to the function was of type function as shown in Figure 7-8. Looking at Figure 7-9 you can see this working when a Boolean type is sent. The steps to create this program follow.

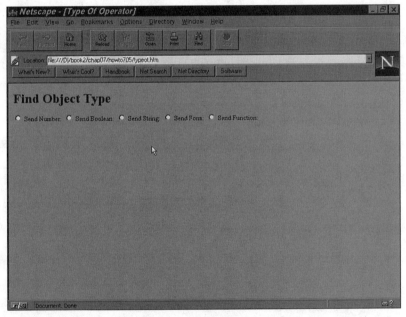

Figure 7-7 TYPEOF.HTM after opening

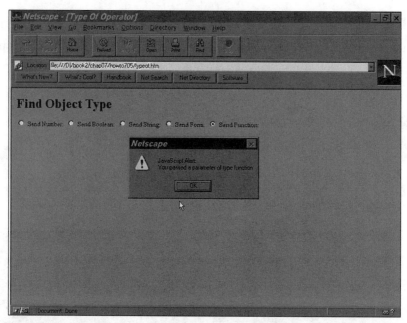

Figure 7-8 TYPEOF.HTM after pressing Send Function button

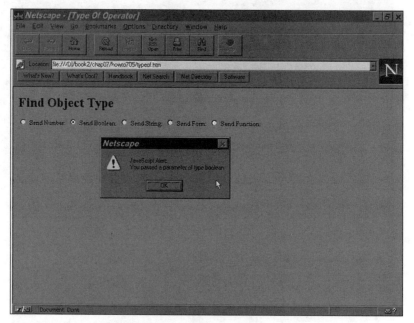

Figure 7-9 TYPEOF.HTM after pressing Send Boolean button

1. Create a new HTML document.

2. Start the HEAD and a JavaScript section by typing the following.

```
<HTML>
<HEAD><TITLE> Type Of Operator</TITLE>

<SCRIPT LANGUAGE="JavaScript">
<!--- hide script from old browsers

// JavaScript Global Variables

// JavaScript Functions
```

3. Create a function called FindTypeOf that uses the typeof operator to find the data type of the parameter. This is an operator, not a function, so make sure you do not use any parentheses. Using the operator results in an alert message.

```
// FindTypeOf
// Function will use typeof operator
// to find type of parameter
function FindTypeOf(vParameter) {

// local variables
var sTypeOf = typeof vParameter

alert("You passed a parameter of type " + sTypeOf)
}

// end hiding from old browsers -->
</SCRIPT>
</HEAD>
```

4. Create the BODY section with a form and five Radio buttons. The onClick event of each of the buttons will call the FindTypeOf function and pass the type of value that is specified in the Radio button label.

```
<body>

<H1> Find Object Type </H1>
<p>
<FORM NAME="TypeForm">
<INPUT TYPE="radio" Name="Type"
onClick="FindTypeOf(1.0)"> Send Number: 
<INPUT TYPE="radio" Name="Type"
onClick="FindTypeOf(true)"> Send Boolean: 
<INPUT TYPE="radio" Name="Type"
onClick="FindTypeOf('test')"> Send String: 
<INPUT TYPE="radio" Name="Type"
onClick="FindTypeOf(TypeForm)"> Send Form: 
<INPUT TYPE="radio" Name="Type"
onClick="FindTypeOf(FindTypeOf)"> Send Function: 
</FORM>

</BODY>
</HTML>
```

5. Close and save the document as TYPEOF.HTM. Test your new document in the browser.

How It Works

The typeof operator will return the type of any object passed to it. The types and the return values are listed in Table 7-1. With this and the loose typing of function arguments, you can create one function to process several different data types.

OBJECT	RETURN VALUE
number variable	number
string variable	string
form/form element	object
function	function
boolean	boolean
undefined	undefined

Table 7-1 Objects and their typeof values

FORM ELEMENTS

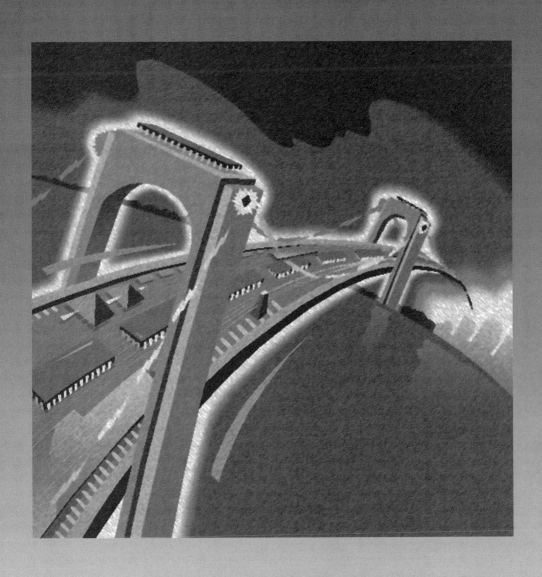

FORM ELEMENTS

How do I...

Chapters 1 through 7 discussed various methods of communicating with the user. This chapter teaches how to communicate information through the use of forms. Forms are perhaps the most widely used mechanisms for transmitting user information through the World Wide Web, and are excellent tools for creating online catalogs, opinion surveys, and order forms. This chapter focuses on how to create elements within a form and retrieve user input from the form through JavaScript. Technical aspects of form generation are stressed, while aesthetics and ergonomics are left as an exercise for the reader.

8.1   Create a form containing several types of elements

Forms contain a variety of elements for user input. This How-To provides an introduction to the various types of form elements, and depicts an example containing many of the form objects available in the JavaScript language. The concept of name/value pairs is also discussed.

8.2   Get the value the user chooses from a selection list element

Selection lists are form elements that allow the user to choose either single or multiple values from a set list of options. Both types of form objects are covered, as well as how to determine which option or options have been chosen in the selection list element.

8.3   Determine the state of a checkbox

Checkboxes are used to get true or false type inputs from the user. This How-To covers the construction of a checkbox within a form, and describes how to determine when or if it has been checked.

8.4   Determine which radio button has been selected

Radio buttons are a special form of checkboxes in which only one of the buttons in the group may be selected. This How-To discusses how to create a group of radio buttons in addition to determining which of the radio buttons in a group has been selected.

8.5   Create and use a Hidden Text object

Hidden Text objects are used to communicate information through a name/value pair without displaying the information to the screen. In this How-To the creation and use of the Hidden Text object are discussed, and an example depicts the use of this form object.

8.6   Get a password from the user without echoing the password to the screen

The Password object provides a way to hide user input when it is undesirable to display information, such as a password, on the screen. This How-To describes how to create the Password object and extract input from the object.

8.7   Access data from several elements in a form

All objects within a form may be accessed through the *elements* property of the form. This feature allows access to data in form fields from JavaScript code.

COMPLEXITY
BEGINNING

8.1   How do I ...
Create a form containing several types of elements?

COMPATIBILITY:

Problem

I want to create a form to input data using a variety of input objects, such as checkboxes, radio buttons, and text input fields. How do I do this?

Technique

Forms provide user-friendly interfaces for Web pages and require little or no training on the part of the user to operate. Assistance mechanisms are easily added to forms and increase their effectiveness. Mastering forms in JavaScript will help you to organize information and extract input from the user. For business-related Web pages, forms and their elements are essential. This section will discuss how to construct a form using several types of elements.

JavaScript resembles an object-oriented programming language in that it treats form elements as objects. In object-oriented programming languages, objects contain methods and properties. Methods are an object's encapsulated procedures. Chapter 10 provides a more complete description of accessing methods in a Form object. Properties are the equivalent of an object's data. A JavaScript program accesses data in a Form object by using the element's property. For instance the *value* property of a text field object contains the text displayed in the text field. Other properties of a Form object contain different information relating to the object's state. Accessing data for Form objects is covered more thoroughly later in this chapter.

It is not necessary to create a form in JavaScript. If the HTML page contains any forms, the Web browser will add an entry for the form to the *document.forms* object. The tags for each of the objects are the same; however, some form elements may be given additional parameters that pertain to JavaScript. Using JavaScript with forms also allows you to provide JavaScript code to be executed when certain events occur. Thus actions can occur when a user selects a checkbox or changes the focus on an input element. The code that is run when such an event occurs is called an event handler. Form objects provide event handling through parameters such as onClick, onSelect, or onFocus.

The Form Object

Forms are objects that allow users to communicate information by allowing them to input text or choose options. When a form is submitted, it passes the data as name/value pairs or standard input to a Common Gateway Interface (CGI) script or a JavaScript function. Each of the elements of a form has a name, and a user assigns the name a value by selecting or typing text in the element. Below, you'll find the syntax for constructing a form in HTML. JavaScript provides the additional onSubmit parameter, for calling user-defined JavaScript code when a submit button is pressed.

```
<FORM
NAME="formName"
TARGET="windowName"
ACTION="serverURL"
METHOD= GET | POST
ENCTYPE="encodingType"
  [onSubmit="formHandler"]>    Form Text & Elements
</FORM>
```

The NAME parameter for the <FORM> tag is used to identify the name of the form, and may be used as an object. TARGET specifies the window or frame to display the form's output. The default for TARGET is the current window. To specify a CGI script or URL to process a form's output, use the ACTION parameter. The format of the form's information is controlled by METHOD. The format specified must correspond to the method in which the server expects to receive the data. A value of GET for METHOD passes the output as name/value pairs in the environment variable QUERY_STRING. Setting METHOD to POST sends the information as name/value pairs to the standard input of the URL specified by ACTION. The value of POST for METHOD also sets the environment variable CONTENT_LENGTH to the length of standard input data. ENCTYPE specifies the MIME encoding of the form data. The parameter may be set to application/x-www-form-urlencoded, to the default, or to multipart/form-data. The value of this parameter should match what the server expects as the encoding type.

Each of these parameters is a property of the Form object. The *onSubmit* parameter specifies the JavaScript statements to be executed when the form is submitted. By providing a value for the onSubmit parameter, you are creating event handling for the submit event. The submit event can be accessed through the Submit method for the Form object. To access a form's properties and methods, use

```
formName.propertyName
formName.methodName(arguments)
```

The Forms Array

The *forms* array is a property of the document object, and contains an entry for each form in the document. The index for the forms array identifies the forms as they appear in the document, if there are more than one in a document. The index is an integer starting with zero for the first form and corresponds sequentially to each form as it appears in a document. If the form has been given a name, it can be accessed as document.forms.formName, where formName is the name specified by the NAME parameter. The following shows how to access the properties and methods of forms within a document using the forms array:

```
document.forms[index].propertyName
document.forms[index].methodName(arguments)
```

Equivalently, the code may be written using the following notation if the form has the name formName:

```
document.formName.propertyName
document.formName.methodName(arguments)
```

Checkboxes

A checkbox is an interface element used to display an element that is either selected or unselected, much like checking a box on a paper form. The syntax used to create a checkbox is as follows:

```
<INPUT
TYPE="checkbox"
NAME="checkboxElementName"
VALUE="checkboxElementValue"
 [CHECKED]
 [onClick="checkboxHandler"> Checkbox Text
```

The NAME parameter identifies the checkbox to the form. VALUE specifies the value to be returned if the checkbox is selected. The CHECKED parameter displays the checkbox as initially selected or checked on the form. Checkboxes by default are displayed as unselected if the CHECKED parameter is not specified. The onClick event handler executes the user defined code "checkboxHandler" when a user selects a checkbox.

Radio Buttons

Radio buttons are a special form of checkboxes that allow the selection of only one of the buttons in a group at a time. The format for creating a radio button is almost exactly the same as that for creating a checkbox:

```
<INPUT
TYPE="radio"
NAME="radioElementName"
VALUE="radioElementValue"
[CHECKED]
[onClick="radioHandler"> Radio Element Text
```

The NAME parameter identifies the radio group to the form. All radio buttons in the same group have the same value for NAME. VALUE specifies the value to be returned if the radio button is selected. The CHECKED parameter defaults the radio button as selected on the form. As with checkboxes, radio buttons are unselected by default if the CHECKED paramater is not specified. The onClick event handler with user-defined code is identified in the above example as the string "radioHandler".

Selection Lists

To create an element containing a list of options to choose from, use the Select object. Selection lists may have only one choice, or they may allow multiple values for selection. To construct a selection list use the following syntax:

```
<SELECT
NAME="selectElementName"
 [SIZE=integer]
 [MULTIPLE]
 [onBlur="blurHandler"]
 [onChange="changeHandler"]
 [onFocus="focusHandler"]
<OPTION
VALUE="selectOptionValue"
 [SELECTED]> Select Option Text
</SELECT>
```

As shown in the previous Form objects, the NAME parameter identifies the selection object. If MULTIPLE is used in the selection's parameter list, then more than one option may be selected from the list at the same time and the options are displayed in a scrolled list. Use SIZE to give the length of the selection list. A value of "1" for SIZE or the omission of the MULTIPLE parameter causes the Selection object to appear as a pull-down menu, with the ability to select only one option at a time. Pull-down selection lists ignore the MULTIPLE parameter. The Selection object provides three event handlers; onBlur, onFocus, and onChange. The onChange event handler executes JavaScript code when the user changes the selection state of an option. The onBlur parameter executes JavaScript code when focus shifts away from the selection list. The onFocus parameter provides event handling when the selection list is chosen for input.

The SELECTED parameter identifies which options appear selected by default. Options without the SELECTED parameter initially appear unchosen by default. To create a selection list, place the options between the <SELECT> and </SELECT> tags. An example of code for a selection list is shown below:

```
<SELECT NAME="mailing_list" SIZE=5 MULTIPLE>
<OPTION>Jackie
<OPTION>Mary Ellen
<OPTION>Sue
<OPTION>Doris
<OPTION>Kim
</SELECT>
```

Text Input

While the checkbox, radio button, and selection list elements restrict the input to only what is listed, the Text Field object allows input values of any type. The following notation constructs a text input field:

```
<INPUT
TYPE="text"
NAME="textElementName"
```

```
VALUE="textElementValue"
SIZE=integer
 [onBlur="blurHandler"]
 [onChange="changeHandler"]
 [onFocus="focusHandler"]
 [onSelect="selectHandler"]>
```

The parameters are similar to the selection list, except that SIZE denotes the length of the text field. The text object contains the additional event handler onSelect. This event handler responds to a user selecting text within the input area of the text object. What if you need to enter more than a single line of text, such as comments or an address? The Textarea object allows multiple lines to be displayed in a scrollable text field. Below you'll find the syntax for constructing the Textarea object:

```
<TEXTAREA
NAME="textareaName"
ROWS=integer
COLS=integer
 [onBlur="blurHandler"]
 [onChange="changeHandler"]
 [onFocus="focusHandler"]
 [onSelect="selectHandler"]>
</TEXTAREA>
```

The ROWS and COLS parameters specify the number of lines of text to be displayed and the maximum length of the text field, respectively. The onBlur event handler handles the shift of input focus away from the Textarea object, while the onFocus parameter provides handling for the shift of input focus to the Textarea object. The onSelect parameter executes code whenever a user selects text. A user selects text by holding down the mouse and highlighting text within the object. The onChange parameter executes code whenever a user changes the input and moves the focus to another input object.

The Submit Button

To submit a form, the Submit object is used to send the form to the specified target. You can set the button text using the VALUE parameter. The notation for the Submit object is as follows:

```
<INPUT
TYPE="submit"
NAME="submitElementName"
VALUE="submitButtonText"
 [onClick="submitElementHandler">
```

The TYPE parameter for a submit button must always be set to the string "submit". The submit button allows event handling for the *click* event through the onClick parameter. Use the VALUE parameter to set the text of the submit button. The submit button displays the default text of "submit" if the VALUE parameter is not supplied. Choose a name for the submit button by setting the NAME parameter. This name and value are passed to the server as name/value pairs when the button is pressed.

The Reset Button

To allow someone to clear a form, the Reset object is used. Selecting the reset object will reset the Form objects to their default states. As in the submit object, the text of the reset button is set using VALUE. Syntax for the Reset object is as follows:

```
<INPUT
TYPE="reset"
NAME="resetElementName"
VALUE="resetButtonText"
 [onClick="resetElementHandler">
```

The browser displays the default text of "reset" for the reset button if the VALUE parameter has not been supplied in the code. As with all buttons, the onClick parameter provides event handling for a button press event of the Reset object. The TYPE parameter must be set to the string "reset" to create a reset button.

Steps

Let's say you have a pizza takeout business and you'd like to provide your customers with the ability to order a pizza online. Using JavaScript, you can build a form combining text input and other objects such as selection lists, radio buttons, or checkboxes. The form uses many of the elements discussed in this chapter to create a form to allow someone to order a pizza through the Web. Load the program HT0801.HTM from the CD-ROM into the Netscape browser. Figure 8-1 depicts the pizza order form using checkboxes, radio buttons, selection lists, text fields, and submit and reset buttons.

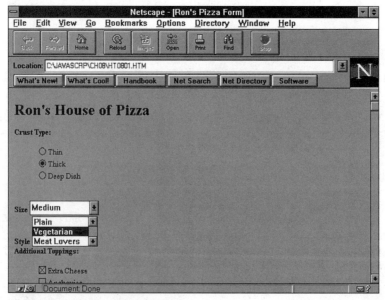

Figure 8-1 Pizza order form

1. Open an editor and create the header for the form. Set the name of the form to "pizzaOrderForm".

```
<HTML><HEAD><TITLE> Ron's Pizza Form</TITLE></HEAD>
<BODY><FORM NAME="pizzaOrderForm">
<H1>Ron's House of Pizza</H2>
```

2. Next construct a set of radio buttons for entering the crust type for the pizza. Type the following lines to create the radio buttons.

```
<B>Crust Type:</B><BR>
<MENU>
<INPUT TYPE="radio" NAME="pieCrust" VALUE="Thin">Thin<BR>
<INPUT TYPE="radio" NAME="pieCrust" VALUE="Thick">Thick<BR>
<INPUT TYPE="radio" NAME="pieCrust" VALUE="DeepDish">Deep Dish<BR>
</MENU>
```

3. For ordering the size of the pizza, construct a selection list in the form of a pull-down menu. The pull-down will offer small, medium, large, and extra-large sizes of pizza.

```
<B>Size</B>
<SELECT NAME="pieSize">
<OPTION VALUE="small">Small (8" diam)
<OPTION VALUE="medium">Medium (12" diam)
<OPTION VALUE="large">Large (16" diam)
<OPTION VALUE="square">Extra Large (3'x2' Square)
</SELECT><BR>
```

4. Now use a scrolled list to allow the selection of the style of the pizza. Add options for plain, vegetarian, meat lovers, and everything style pizzas.

```
<B>Style</B>
<SELECT NAME="pieStyle" SIZE=3  MULTIPLE>
<OPTION VALUE="Plain" SELECTED>Plain
<OPTION VALUE="Vegetarian">Vegetarian
<OPTION VALUE="Meat Lovers">Meat Lovers
<OPTION VALUE="Everything">Everything
</SELECT><P>
```

5. Because a customer may want to add to the topping offered by the "Style" selection list, create a set of checkboxes for each topping. The following adds entries for extra cheese, anchovies, pepperoni, green peppers, mushrooms, onions, olives, and sausage. Each of these entries has a corresponding checkbox and is contained within <MENU> tags.

```
<B>Additional Toppings:</B>
<MENU>
<INPUT TYPE="checkbox" NAME="" VALUE="extra_cheese">Extra Cheese<BR>
<INPUT TYPE="checkbox" NAME="" VALUE="Anchovies">Anchovies<BR>
<INPUT TYPE="checkbox" NAME="" VALUE="Pepperoni">Pepperoni<BR>
<INPUT TYPE="checkbox" NAME="" VALUE="Green Peppers">Green Peppers<BR>
<INPUT TYPE="checkbox" NAME="" VALUE="Mushrooms">Mushrooms<BR>
```

continued on next page

continued from previous page

```
<INPUT TYPE="checkbox" NAME="" VALUE="Onions">Onions<BR>
<INPUT TYPE="checkbox" NAME="" VALUE="Olives">Olives<BR>
<INPUT TYPE="checkbox" NAME="" VALUE="Sausage">Sausage
</MENU>
<P>
```

6. In this step we'll add a text entry box for the customer's name and a Textarea object for the customer's address. Set the size of the textarea to three rows by 40 characters.

```
Name
<INPUT TYPE="text" NAME="NameOfPerson" SIZE=44><BR>
Address
<TEXTAREA NAME="AddressOfPerson" ROWS=3 COLS=40>
</TEXTAREA>
<BR>
```

7. Finally, add buttons for submitting the order and clearing the form. Type in the following code for creating SUBMIT and RESET form elements. Make sure to set the text of the elements to "Order Pizza" and "Clear Order" so that a customer will understand their function.

```
<HR>
<INPUT TYPE="submit" VALUE="Order Pizza">
<INPUT TYPE="reset" VALUE="Clear Order">
</FORM>
</BODY>
</HTML>
```

8. Save the program as HT0801.HTM and load the program into the Netscape browser. Figure 8-1 depicts the pizza order form using the code constructed from Steps 1 through 7.

How It Works

In the above form the SUBMIT and RESET objects create buttons which by default perform an action with the form data. The submit button sends the form information as name/value pairs to the URL specified by the ACTION parameter for the form. The RESET button resets or clears any data that may have been entered in the form. The information submitted by the form is dependent upon user input. The form submission returns a single value for pieCrust and pieSize, while multiple values for pieStyle are possible. If a checkbox is unselected, a value of null is returned for the checkbox's name value pair.

The above form contains six different types of user input objects. JavaScript provides many additional objects not covered in this chapter.

Comments

Because JavaScript treats each form element as an object, each object may be referenced by its name. To reference an object's property, simply use the syntax *objectName.objectProperty*. An object's built-in methods also may be accessed this way, using the syntax *objectName.objectMethod()*. For example, you may wish to add event handling for when a user chooses an element of the form. If there is no more pepperoni, you could add event handling for the selection of the pepperoni checkbox. The event handler text could pop up a window stating "Sorry, we're out of pepperoni!" Event handling will be discussed in later in Chapter 9, "Event Handling."

COMPLEXITY
BEGINNING

8.2   How do I...
Get the value the user chooses from a selection list element?

COMPATIBILITY:

Problem

I want the user to choose a single option or multiple options from a fixed list of values. I also need to determine which option or options were chosen. How can I accomplish this?

Technique

How-To 8.1 introduced various form elements, one of which was the Selection List object. This How-To focuses on the Selection List object in more detail, and explains how to determine which option or options were chosen. A selection list is used when one or more choices are made from a menu or scrollable list. The selection list is very similar in function to checkboxes and radio buttons, but organizes the information in a different form. Refer to How-To 8.1 for a description of the HTML code for a Selection object.

Selection List Properties

The selection list has two properties which store the state of the object:

   selectedIndex

   options

The selectedIndex is an array of Booleans containing the selected state of the option. Options are referenced in the array using an integer starting with 0 for the first option, up to (n-1) for n options. All options in a selection list are stored in the options property for the selection object. The *options* property is an array of all the options in the selection list. The *options* array has the following properties:

- defaultSelected

- index

- selected

- text

The *defaultSelected* property stores a Boolean that indicates if the option in the selection list is chosen by default. The presence of the SELECTION attribute in the code for a selection list option sets the *defaultSelected* property to "true" for the corresponding element in the *options* array. To obtain the position of the option in the selection list, use the *index* property. The *index* property stores the position of the option as an integer beginning with 0 for the first option and ending with (n -1) for n options. The *length* property, discussed in Chapter 10, contains the number of options in the selection list. Use the *text* property of the options array to retrieve text after the <OPTION> tag. The *selected* property contains a Boolean describing whether the option was chosen; "true" if the option is selected, or "false" if unselected. Syntax for using properties of the option array is as follows:

```
selectionListName.options.length
selectionListName.options[index].property
```

Steps

The selection list will now be used to construct a software order form. Both types of selection lists are used. The first selection list contains various software packages for sale, and allows the user to select multiple choices from the list. The second scrollable list is a menu-like selection list which allows the user to choose the media desired for the software selected. The results of the user's choices are displayed in an alert message when the form is submitted. Load the program HT0801.HTM from the CD-ROM into the Netscape browser. Figure 8-2 depicts the interface for the software ordering form.

Once the form is loaded into the browser, choose the "Word Processing" and "Multi-Media Package" options from the scrollable software selection list. From the media selection menu choose the "8mm Tape" option. After pressing the submit button you should see your choices reflected in the browser, as shown in Figure 8-3.

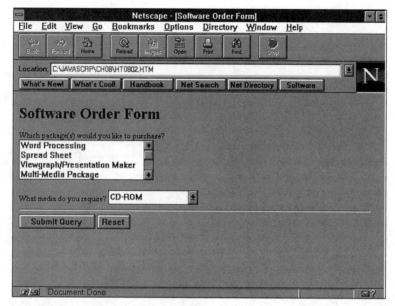

Figure 8-2 Software order form

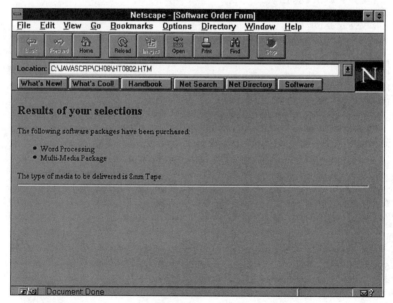

Figure 8-3 Results of the software order form

1. Construct the following program in an editor of your choice. Remember to close the <SELECT> tags, but do not close off the <OPTION> tags. Create a scrollable selection list of software packages and a selection menu for the desired media type. The scrollable list contains the options: Word Processing, Spread Sheet, Viewgraph/Presentation Maker, Multi-Media Package, Anti-Virus Package, Database Engine, CAD/Drawing Package, Electronic Mail, and OS Utilities. The media selection menu contains the options; 31/2 Floppy Disk, 8mm Tape, 1/4" Tape, and CD-ROM. For the media selection lit, set the CD-ROM option as default selected.

```
<HTML>
<HEAD>
<TITLE>Software Order Form</TITLE>
</HEAD>

<BODY>
<FORM NAME="softwareOrderForm">

<H1>Software Order Form</H1>

<P>Which package(s) would you like to purchase?
<BR>
<SELECT NAME="softwarePackage" SIZE=4 MULTIPLE>
<OPTION>Word Processing
<OPTION>Spread Sheet
<OPTION>Viewgraph/Presentation Maker
<OPTION>Multi-Media Package
<OPTION>Anti-Virus Package
<OPTION>Database Engine
<OPTION>CAD/Drawing Package
<OPTION>Electronic Mail
<OPTION>OS Utilities
</SELECT>

<P>What media do you require?
<SELECT NAME="mediaType">
<OPTION>3 1/2" Floppy Disk
<OPTION>8mm Tape
<OPTION>1/4" Tape
<OPTION SELECTED>CD-ROM
</SELECT>

<HR>
<INPUT TYPE="submit" NAME="Purchase Selections"onClick=⇐
"displaySelections()">
<INPUT TYPE="reset" NAME="Clear Selections">
</FORM>
</BODY>
</HTML>
```

2. Next add the JavaScript portion of the program after the </TITLE> tag. The JavaScript code must be surrounded by <SCRIPT> tags. Start by adding the *displaySelection* function, which prints the options chosen by the selection

list to the browser. The output of each selection list is generated by the
function constructed in Steps 3 and 4.

```
<SCRIPT LANGUAGE="JavaScript">
<!-- Hide JavaScript from older browsers
/*****************************************************************
*  Function     - displaySelection                              *
*  Parameters   - None                                          *
*  Description  - This function displays the users choices from the *
*                 software ordering form.                       *
*  Called By    - onClick event handler                         *
*                                                               *
*****************************************************************/
function displaySelections() {

    var software = getSelectedSoftware();
    var media = getSelectedMedia();

    //
    //  Print the selected software package and media type.
    //
    document.clear();
    document.writeln("<H2>Results of your selections</H2>");
    document.writeln(software);
    document.writeln(media);
    document.writeln("<HR>");
}
```

3. Create the *getSelectedSoftware* function. This function loops through each of
the options in the software selection list and determines if the option has
been chosen. If an option has been selected by the user, the text of the
option is added to a string, which prints the selected options as an HTML
list. Use the <MENU> tags to surround the chosen options, and the <LI>
tag to create a bullet for each option.

```
/*****************************************************************
*                                                               *
*  Function     - getSelectedSoftware                           *
*  Parameters   - None                                          *
*  Description  - Print the selected software packages.         *
*  Called By    - displaySelection function                     *
*                                                               *
*****************************************************************/
function getSelectedSoftware() {

    //  The software variable contains the choices selected from the
    //  software packages selection list.
    var softwareString = "<P>The following software packages have been
purchased:<MENU>";
```

continued on next page

continued from previous page

```
with (document.softwareOrderForm.softwarePackage) {
    for (i=0 ; i < options.length ; i++) {
        if (options[i].selected == true) {
            softwareString +=   "<LI>" + options[i].text;
        }
    }
}

//  End the menu of software packages selected.
softwareString += "</MENU>";

return softwareString;
}
```

4. Create another function called *getSelectedMedia* for extracting the options from the media selection menu. The function loops through each option in the *options* array for the selection list and uses the *selected* property to determine which media option has been chosen.

```
/************************************************************************
*                                                                      *
*    Function     - getSelectedMedia                                   *
*    Parameters   - None                                               *
*    Description  - Print the selected media type.                     *
*    Called By    - displaySelection function                         *
*                                                                      *
************************************************************************/
function getSelectedMedia() {

    //
    //  The media variable contains the choice selected from the
    //  mediaType selection list.
    //
    var mediaString = "<P>The type of media to be delivered is ";

    with (document.softwareOrderForm.mediaType) {
        for (j=0 ; j < options.length ; j++) {
            if (options[j].selected == true) {
                mediaString += options[j].text + ".";
            }
        }
    }

    return mediaString;
}

// end hide JavaScript -->
</SCRIPT>
```

5. Save the program as HT0802.HTM and load it into the Netscape browser. See Figure 8-2 for a picture of the software order form interface.

6. Choose the options Word Processing and Multi-Media Package from the software selection list. Also choose the 8mm Tape media type, and press the submit button marked Purchase Selections. Figure 8-3 depicts the resulting display aftter the submission of the form.

How It Works

The selection list appears as a menu or as a scrollable list based upon the inclusion of the MULTIPLE attribute. Use the scrollable selection list when it's necessary to allow multiple choices from a list, such as in the case of selecting various pieces of software. When operating a Netscape browser in a Microsoft Windows environment, you must use the CTRL button to select multiple options from a list. The menu-like selection list restricts the user to selecting only one option. The software is shipped on only one type of media, and thus the menu-like selection list is ideal for this purpose. The program retrieves the options from the selection list using the OPTIONS attribute. The options array contains the state of each of the options in the selection list, and is used by the program to construct a string containing the software packages chosen, or the type of media selected. These strings are then displayed in an alert box.

Comments

Realistic use of this program would be to store the order information in a database and to generate an automated request for the software distributor. The construction of form elements like the selection list enables the construction of online catalogs or ordering forms. Selection lists are one more way to allow the user to communicate information through a JavaScript program.

COMPLEXITY
BEGINNING

8.3 How do I...
Determine the state of a checkbox?

COMPATIBILITY: NAVIGATOR 2.X NAVIGATOR 3.X EXPLORER 3.X

Problem

I want to create a checkbox on a form and determine if the checkbox has been selected. How can I accomplish this?

Technique

A checkbox is an interface element used to display an element that is either select-ed or unselected, such as checking a box on a paper form. In How-To 8.2 a selection list was used for selecting one or more values from a list. The checkbox may be used similarly by constructing a checkbox for each option of the list. The difference between the selection list and a set of checkboxes is that each checkbox has a unique name. Thus, when a form containing checkboxes is submitted, a name/value pair is constructed for each checkbox.

Checkboxes

To construct a checkbox, set the TYPE attribute of the <INPUT> tag to "checkbox". The syntax for constructing checkboxes is as follows:

```
<INPUT
    TYPE="checkbox"
    NAME="checkboxElementName"
    VALUE="checkboxElementValue"
    [CHECKED]
    [onClick="checkboxHandler"> Checkbox Text
```

The NAME parameter identifies the checkbox to the form. VALUE specifies the value to be returned if the checkbox is selected. The CHECKED parameter displays the checkbox as selected or checked on the form. Checkboxes by default are dis-played as unselected. The onClick event handler is used to link the selection event of the checkbox with a user-defined function.

Checkbox Properties

A checkbox object has four properties which identify its state in the form.

 checked

 defaultChecked

 name

 value

The *checked* attribute contains a Boolean describing the state of the checkbox: "true" if the checkbox is selected, and "false" if it is unselected. The *defaultChecked* attribute specifies whether the checkbox is selected by default. If the defaultChecked attribute is "true," the checkbox is initially displayed as selected, and if the value of defaultChecked is "false," the browser displays the checkbox as unselected. The *name* attribute holds the string containing the name of the checkbox. Another attribute used to retrieve the state of the checkbox is VALUE . The *value* attribute for a check-box object contains the string "on" if the checkbox is selected and "off" if the checkbox has not been selected.

Steps

This section will demonstrate the use of checkboxes in a form, and will create a JavaScript function for determining whether they have been selected. The following example constructs a grocery list with several different items. Each item has a checkbox, and the submission of the form prints only the selected items. Load the program HT0803.HTM into the Netscape browser. Figure 8-4 shows the initial state of the form. You should see the checkboxes marked Milk, Dozen Eggs, and Pound of Bacon selected by default.

Select the checkbox marked Loaf of Bread and unselect the checkbox marked Pound of Bacon. After pressing the submit button marked Make List, you should see the choices appear in the browser, as shown in Figure 8-5.

1. In a text editor, create the HTML portion of the grocery list program. This form contains six checkboxes corresponding to items in a grocery list. After each checkbox, place text describing the item: Milk, Orange Juice, Dozen Eggs, Pound of Bacon, Loaf of Bread, and Box of Cereal. Choose three of these checkboxes: Milk, Dozen Eggs, and Pound of Bacon to contain the SELECTED parameter. Add reset and submit buttons to the form, and set the onClick event handler of the submit button to call the *makeGroceryList* function. This function will be constructed in Step 2.

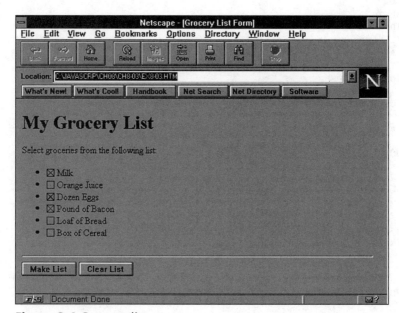

Figure 8-4 Grocery list

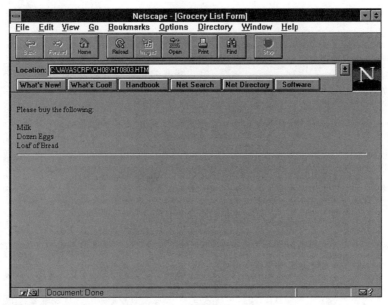

Figure 8-5 Results of the grocery list

```
<HTML>
<HEAD>
<TITLE>Grocery List Form</TITLE>
</HEAD>
<BODY>
<FORM NAME="groceryList">

<H1>My Grocery List</H1>

Select groceries from the following list:
<P>
<MENU>
<LI><INPUT TYPE="checkbox" NAME="milk" CHECKED>Milk
<LI><INPUT TYPE="checkbox" NAME="oj">Orange Juice
<LI><INPUT TYPE="checkbox" NAME="eggs" CHECKED>Dozen Eggs
<LI><INPUT TYPE="checkbox" NAME="bacon" CHECKED>Pound of Bacon
<LI><INPUT TYPE="checkbox" NAME="bread">Loaf of Bread
<LI><INPUT TYPE="checkbox" NAME="cereal">Box of Cereal
</MENU>

<HR>
<INPUT TYPE="submit" VALUE="Make List" onClick="makeGroceryList()">
<INPUT TYPE="reset" VALUE="Clear List">

</FORM></BODY>
</HTML>
```

2. Next create the JavaScript portion of the program. The code for the
JavaScript functions is contained within the <SCRIPT> tags. Add the
JavaScript code after the </TITLE> tag in the HTML program from Step 1.

This step constructs the function *makeGroceryList*. The function *makeGroceryList* constructs an HTML page displaying each of the selected grocery items. Use the Checked property of each of the form's checkboxes to determine which grocery item has been selected. The HTML page is loaded into the browser using the Writeln method of the document object.

```
<SCRIPT LANGUAGE="JavaScript">
<!-- Hide JavaScript from older browsers


/**********************************************************************
*                                                                    *
*  Function     - makeGroceryList                                    *
*  Parameters   - None                                               *
*  Description  - This function displays the users choices from the  *
*                 chekboxes in the grocery list.                     *
*  Called By    - onClick event handler                              *
*                                                                    *
**********************************************************************/
function makeGroceryList() {
   //
   //   Determine the selected groceries
   //
   var groceries = "Please buy the following:<BR>"
   if ( document.groceryList.milk.checked ) {
     groceries += "<BR>Milk";
   }
   if ( document.groceryList.oj.checked ) {
     groceries += "<BR>Orange Juice";
   }
   if ( document.groceryList.eggs.checked ) {
     groceries += "<BR>Dozen Eggs";
   }
   if ( document.groceryList.bacon.checked ) {
     groceries += "<BR>Pound of Bacon";
   }
   if ( document.groceryList.bread.checked ) {
     groceries += "<BR>Loaf of Bread";
   }
   if ( document.groceryList.cereal.checked ) {
     groceries += "<BR>Box of Cereal";
   }

   // Code needed to display the last grocery item
   groceries += "<BR>";

   document.clear();
   document.writeln(groceries);
}


// end hide JavaScript -->
</SCRIPT>
```

3. Save the program as HT0803.HTM, and open the file in the Netscape browser. Figure 8-4 depicts the browser containing the grocery list in its inital state.

4. Select a few of the items in the list and submit the form by pressing the Make List button. Figure 8-5 shows the result when the Milk, Dozen Eggs, and Loaf of Bread items are selected.

5. Clear the list by choosing the reset button marked Clear List. Each of the checkboxes returns to its inital state.

How It Works

The JavaScript program uses the CHECKED attribute of each of the checkboxes to generate the grocery list. The checked parameter contains a Boolean value of "true" or "false" depending on whether the checkbox has been selected. The checkbox appears selected when the interior of the box is filled or marked with an X, depending on your windowing system.

The results of the list are printed to the browser using the Writeln method of the Document object. The Writeln method prints the argument to the document. The Document object is a pointer to the document currently loaded in the browser. The form is cleared of the checkboxes and other objects using the Document object's Clear method. How-To 8.7 discusses a better way of accessing elements in a form, which allows a *for* loop to determine the state of each of the elements.

Comments

Checkboxes are excellent objects for multiple selection from a list. They mimic the way people generate forms. We have all at one point in our lives had to check the male/female checkboxes on some kind of form. This input object is easily recognizable, and minimizes the training needed to use a form. The next How-To introduces another kind of checkbox, called the radio button, which allows only a single selection from a group of checkboxes.

COMPLEXITY
BEGINNING

8.4 How do I ...
Determine which radio button has been selected?

COMPATIBILITY:

Problem

I want to determine which radio button has been selected from a radio group on a form. How do I do this?

Technique

How-To 8.1 introduced the radio button. This How-To deals with how to extract information from a group of radio buttons. To recap, radio buttons are a special form of checkbox that allows the selection of only one of the elements in the radio group. Thus the Radio object provides the same function as a selection menu. However, all of the options of the Radio object appear on the form, instead of only the selected option. The Radio object also allows the options in the radio group, in the form of radio buttons, to be positioned at different locations in a form.

The Radio Button Element

The format for creating a radio button appears almost exactly the same as a checkbox, and also uses the <INPUT> tag.

```
<INPUT
TYPE="radio"
NAME="radioElementName"
VALUE="radioElementValue"
[CHECKED]
[onClick="radioHandler"> Radio Element Text
```

The NAME parameter identifies the radio group to the form. All radio buttons in the same group have the same value for NAME. VALUE specifies the value to be returned if the radio element is selected. The CHECKED parameter defaults the radio button as selected on the form. As with checkboxes, radio buttons are unselected by default. The onClick event handler links the selection of a radio button with the function defined by "radioHandler". How-To 8.4 deals with this event handling for the Radio object.

Radio Object Properties

All radio buttons in a Radio object have the same Name property. Individual boxes in the radio group are accessed as an array. Each radio button has the following properties:

- checked
- defaultChecked
- index
- length
- name
- value

The CHECKED attribute contains a Boolean describing the state of the radio button: "true" if the radio button is selected, and "false" if it is unselected. As with a checkbox, the defaultChecked attribute specifies whether the radio button is selected by default. If the defaultChecked attribute is "true," the radio button is initially displayed as selected; otherwise it is unselected. The Value property also holds the user defined state of the radio group. The Value property contains the string defined for the VALUE parameter. Two properties found in the Radio object and not in the checkbox object are the Index and Length properties. The Length property gives the number of radio buttons in the radio group, and the Index property contains an integer relating to the order in which each button appears in the group. The first button in the group has an index value of 0, the second has an index of 1, and so forth. Use the following syntax to reference properties and methods of individual buttons in the Radio object:

```
document.form_name.radio_name[index].property_name
document.form_name.radio_name[index].method_name
```

See Chapter 10, How-To 10.4, for an explanation of how to use methods in a Radio object.

Steps

To get a feel for the radio group, the object will be used in a form, and upon submission of the form the JavaScript program will determine which radio button was selected. This example creates a form to survey the types of cars people would like to drive. The various models are contained in a Radio object, and the results are displayed to the browser. Load the program HT0804.HTM from the CD-ROM into the Netscape browser. Choose the Sedan/Luxury Car and Sky Blue radio buttons from the car type and car color groups of radio buttons. Figure 8-6 shows the current state of the survey form.

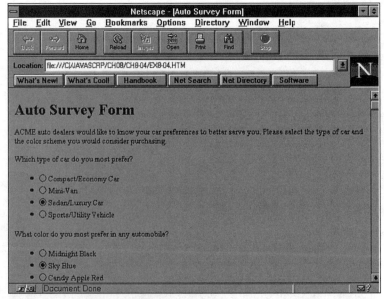

Figure 8-6 Auto survey form

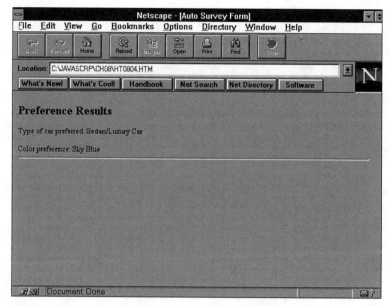

Figure 8-7 Results of the auto survey form

Notice that if you choose another option in the same radio group, the previously selected radio button becomes unselected. Press the button marked Submit Your Choices. Figure 8-7 depicts the resulting output of the program. The car model and color are displayed as HTML code in the Netscape browser.

1. Create the following program using a text editor. The survey form has two radio groups which query the color and model preferences of the user. The first radio group contains four choices for the preferred type of car; Compact/Economy Car, Mini-Van, Sedan/Luxury Car, and Sports/Utility Vehicle. In the second radio group, the user has four color choices; Midnight Black, Sky Blue, Candy Apple Red, and Teal Green. Use the onClick event handler for the submit button to run the *displayChoices* function. This JavaScript function will be constructed in Step 2.

```
<HTML><HEAD>
<TITLE>Auto Survey Form</TITLE></HEAD>
<BODY><FORM NAME="surveyForm">

<H1>Auto Survey Form</H1>

<P>ACME auto dealers would like to know your car preferences to better
serve you.  Please select the type of car and the color scheme you would
consider purchasing.

<P>Which type of car do you most prefer?<BR>
<DIR>
<LI><INPUT TYPE="radio" NAME="autoType" VALUE="compact">Compact/Economy Car
<LI><INPUT TYPE="radio" NAME="autoType" VALUE="mini-van">Mini-Van
```

continued on next page

continued from previous page

```
<LI><INPUT TYPE="radio" NAME="autoType" VALUE="sedan">Sedan/Luxury Car
<LI><INPUT TYPE="radio" NAME="autoType"
VALUE="sports/utility">Sports/Utility Vehicle
</DIR>

<P>What color do you most prefer in any automobile?<BR>
<DIR>
<LI><INPUT TYPE="radio" NAME="autoColor" VALUE="black">Midnight Black
<LI><INPUT TYPE="radio" NAME="autoColor" VALUE="blue">Sky Blue
<LI><INPUT TYPE="radio" NAME="autoColor" VALUE="red">Candy Apple Red
<LI><INPUT TYPE="radio" NAME="autoColor" VALUE="green">Teal Green
</DIR>

<HR>
<INPUT TYPE="submit" onClick="displayChoices()" VALUE="Submit Your Choices">
<INPUT TYPE="reset" VALUE="Reset Your Choices">
</FORM>
</BODY>
</HTML>
```

2. Next add the JavaScript portion of the program after the </TITLE> tag. The first function you will create displays the choices selected from the survey form. The display choices function writes the choices from the form to the browser. It calls the *getPreferences* function for each Radio object to retrieve the value of the selected radio button.

```
<SCRIPT LANGUAGE="JavaScript">
<!-- Hide JavaScript from older browsers


/**********************************************************************
*                                                                    *
*    Function     - displayChoices                                   *
*    Parameters   - None                                             *
*    Description  - This function displays the users choices from the*
*                   auto survey.                                     *
*    Called By    - onClick event handler                            *
*                                                                    *
**********************************************************************/
function displayChoices() {

    //
    //   Variables for storing the selected type and color preference.
    //
    var typeResults = "<P>Type of car preferred: ";
    var colorResults = "<P>Color preference: ";

    //
    //   Get the value of the selected radio buttons for car type and color.
    //
    typeResults += getPreference(document.surveyForm.autoType);
    colorResults += getPreference(document.surveyForm.autoColor);

    //
    // Clear the document and print the results of the survey.
    //
```

```
document.clear();
document.writeln("<H2>Preference Results</H2>");
document.writeln(typeResults);
document.writeln(colorResults);
document.writeln("<HR>");
}
```

3. Add a function to loop through each radio button in a group, and determine which one has been selected. The function returns the value of the selected radio button. Use the *checked* property of the Radio object to determine if an option has been selected, and the *length* property to determine the number of buttons in the radio group.

```
/************************************************************************
*                                                                      *
*   Function      - getPreference                                      *
*   Parameters    - radioGroup     (Object conatining the radio group) *
*   Description   - This function returns value of the selected radio  *
*                   button.                                            *
*   Called By     - displayChoices function                           *
*                                                                      *
************************************************************************/
function getPreference( radioGroup ) {
   var resultString;

   //
   //   Determine the selected radio object
   //
   for (i=0 ; i < radioGroup.length ; i++) {
      if (radioGroup[i].checked == true) {

          // set the return string to the value of the radio button
          resultString = radioGroup[i].value;

          // quit the loop
          i = radioGroup.length;
      }
   }

   // return the value of the selected radio button
   return resultString;
}

// end hide JavaScript -->
</SCRIPT>
```

4. Save the program as HT0804.HTM. Load the program into the Netscape browser and select one of the options from each radio group. When the program is initially loaded into the browser, none of the radio buttons in either group are selected. Figure 8-6 shows the form with the Sedan/Luxury Car and Sky Blue radio buttons selected.

5. Next choose the submit button marked Submit Your Choices. The program displays the results of the survey to the browser as shown in Figure 8-7.

How It Works

The program performs similarly to the checkbox example in How-To 8.3. When the form is submitted, the *displayChoices* function is called. Setting the onSubmit attribute of the Submit object enables you to connect the submission of a form to a desired JavaScript function. The program determines the chosen radio buttons by using the CHECKED attribute of the radio object. A *for* loop is used to check each radio button in the group, and determine if the checked attribute is "true". When the selected radio button is found, the value attribute of the radio button is used to create the output HTML text to be printed to the browser. The number of radio buttons in each group is deduced by using the Radio object's Length property.

Comments

Radio buttons are excellent form objects for data input. Choices are visually displayed as with the checkbox, and when a different Radio object is selected, any other choices are automatically unselected. The drawback of the Radio object is that it consumes real estate on the form. How-To 8.5 discusses an element that does not consume real estate, the hidden object.

COMPLEXITY
INTERMEDIATE

8.5 How do I ...
Create and use a Hidden Text object?

COMPATIBILITY:

Problem

I want to pass data in a form without using a displayable input object, such as a checkbox, radio button, or text field. How do I do this?

Technique

In How-To 8.1 you learned how to create a form using several different form objects. This How-To will build on that knowledge by showing you how to use the hidden text object. Remember that when a form is submitted, information is passed as name/value pairs. The "name" part of the pair is equivalent to the name of the Form object. It is similar to a variable, and the value is set by selecting or entering text into the object. Suppose there is a need to pass information without allowing the user to modify an input object? The Hidden Text object solves this problem.

The Hidden Object

Essentially the Hidden object is a text field element that does not display itself on a HTML form. Because the Hidden object is another type of form input, it uses the <INPUT> tag. To create a Hidden object, use the following syntax:

```
<INPUT
    TYPE="hidden"
    NAME="hiddenName"
    [VALUE="hiddenTextValue"]>
```

The TYPE of the input is Hidden while the NAME of the object is distinct from other form objects. To preset the Hidden Text object, set the VALUE parameter to its default string. The Hidden object, as with any form object, is accessible using the name of the object and its Value property. You may also use the elements Array for the form. JavaScript constructs an elements array for every form, and allows the objects to be accessed from the array. The array contains the elements in the order they appear in the form. Use the following syntax to access the hidden object:

```
hiddenName.propertyName
formName.elements[index].propertyName
```

A form may contain any number of Hidden Text objects. Because the Hidden object is a form of text field, it may pass any type of information that a normal text field can contain. This object allows a user to pass information of any type through the submission of a form, without the need to display the object in the browser.

Steps

This example uses the Hidden object to store the selection of a radio button and display the results in an alert dialog. The Radio object selects the crust type for a pizza, and uses the onClick event handler to store its value in the Hidden Text object. Load the program HT0805.HTM from the CD-ROM into the Netscape browser. Select the radio button marked Thick, and submit the form by pressing the Order Pizza button. The program launches an alert dialog displaying the contents of the Hidden Text object as shown in Figure 8-8.

1. Open an editor and create the header for the form. Set the name of the form to "pizzaOrder". The title of the Web page is enclosed in <TITLE> tags, and the form elements are enclosed inside the <FORM> container.

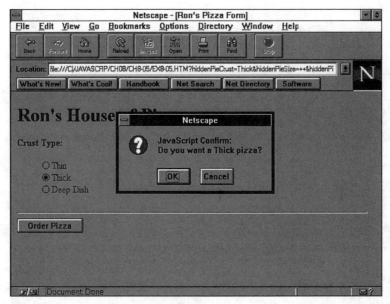

Figure 8-8 Hidden Text object example

```
<HTML>
<HEAD>
<TITLE>Ron's Pizza Form</TITLE>
</HEAD>
<BODY>
<FORM NAME="pizzaOrder">
<H1>Ron's House of Pizza</H2>
```

2. Create a Hidden Text object to store the value of the radio button. The default value for the hidden object is "untouched".

```
<INPUT TYPE="hidden" NAME="hiddenPieCrust" VALUE="untouched">
```

3. Create a radio group to select one of three types of pizza crust; "Thin", "Thick" or "Deep Dish". Add the onClick event handler to each of the radio buttons. The code for the onClick event handler sets the contents of the Hidden Text object to the value of the radio button.

```
<B>Crust Type:</B>
<BR>
<MENU>
<INPUT TYPE="radio" NAME="PieCrust" VALUE="Thin"
onclick="document.pizzaOrder.hiddenPieCrust.value=this.value">Thin<br>
<INPUT TYPE="radio" NAME="PieCrust" VALUE="Thick"
onclick="document.pizzaOrder.hiddenPieCrust.value=this.value">Thick<br>
<INPUT TYPE="radio" NAME="PieCrust" VALUE="DeepDish"
```

```
onclick="document.pizzaOrder.hiddenPieCrust.value=this.value">Deep Dish<br>
</MENU>
<HR>
```

4. Add a Submit object to the form, and set its text to "Order Pizza". Also connect the onClick event handler to an alert dialog that proclaims which crust option was chosen by the user. This dialog displays the value stored in the Hidden Text object.

```
<INPUT TYPE="submit" VALUE="Order Pizza" onClick="alert('You ordered a ' +
document.pizzaOrder.hiddenPieCrust.value + ' pizza')">

</FORM>
</BODY>
</HTML>
```

5. Save the program as HT0805.HTM and load it into the Netscape browser. Choose the "Thick" option from the radio group.

6. Press the "Order Pizza" button. Figure 8-8 displays the resulting alert dialog.

How It Works

In the above example, a hidden text object is used to store a value from a radio group. The onClick event handler was used to store the state of the form in the Hidden Text object. When the form is submitted, a confirm dialog box displays the state of the form by revealing the contents of the Hidden Text object. If the form has been modified the Hidden Text object's value has been changed to "modified". If no radio button was selected, then the contents of the Hidden Text object are equal to the default value, "untouched".

The Hidden Text object is useful for storing information such as totals for items selected by the form. It has the advantage of passing the information stored in the object when the form is submitted. A JavaScript variable could contain the items selected by the form, but it cannot pass its value to the server.

Comments

The Hidden Text object is useful when there is a need to pass information through the submission of the form, without displaying that information to the user. This ensures that the information remains unchanged. This is perhaps the most common use of the object, because CGI scripts often are reused. An interface to the script may not contain all the information needed to be passed to the CGI script. An error results if the CGI script does not receive all of the expected name/value pairs. The Hidden Text object is used to fill in the missing information for the CGI script.

A database query illustrates one example of filling in the name/value pairs to a CGI script. Generic CGI scripts are often used to query a database, and require name/value pairs for each of the columns that compose a table. If you want to search only one of the columns, it is still necessary to pass the null values for the rest of the columns. The Hidden Text object is useful because the user does not need to see these null values displayed on the form.

COMPLEXITY
BEGINNING

8.6   How do I ...
Get a password from the user without echoing the password to the screen?

COMPATIBILITY: NAVIGATOR 2.X   NAVIGATOR 3.X   EXPLORER 3.X

Problem

I want to get a password from the user without having the password echoed to the screen. How can I do this?

Technique

In many instances you will be required to create a form that has the user enter information that should not be echoed to the screen, such as a password, credit card number, or Personal Identification Number (PIN). JavaScript uses a special Form object, called the Password object, for this purpose. The Netscape browser, without the security plug-in, will pass information submitted through a form as clear text. When submitting forms through the Netscape browser without the security features enabled, a warning message appears notifying the user the information will be passed as clear text. Passing information in clear text form could allow others to view your personal information.

The Netscape browser provides the option to cancel the transaction. Passing sensitive information such as passwords or credit card numbers as clear text is undesirable, because anyone could potentially view the data coming across the Internet. Packets on the Internet are frequently passed from server to server before they reach their intended destination. Anyone at these packet-forwarding sites could easily view their contents. Using the security plug-in module, the Netscape browser encrypts any information submitted by the form. If you intend to pass any sensitive information over the Internet, it is highly recommended to download the security plug-in from Netscape's Web site. Otherwise, you run the risk of allowing anyone access to your private information.

The Password Object

A Password object appears exactly the same as a text field object. However any text typed within the Password object does not echo to the screen. A Password object is created using the following syntax:

```
<input
  TYPE="password"
  NAME="passwordName"
  [VALUE="textValue"]
  SIZE=integer>
```

Another difference between the Password object and the Text object is that JavaScript does not provide any event handling for the Password object. The lack of event handling means that the Password object cannot perform actions when focus shifts to and from the object, or when text has been selected. This event handling is true of other text input objects such as the Text Field and Textarea objects.

Steps

The following example simulates the interface for an Automated Teller Machine (ATM). The Password object handles the user's PIN. An asterisk is echoed to the screen in place of the actual numbers when the user enters the PIN. Load the program HT0806.HTM from the CD-ROM into the Netscape browser. Figure 8-9 displays the interface for the JavaScript ATM.

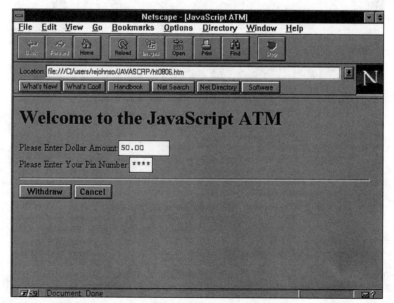

Figure 8-9 JavaScript automated teller machine

Enter the correct PIN number by typing 1234 into the password field, and withdraw money from the ATM by pressing the submit button marked Withdraw. Figure 8-10 shows the resulting message displayed by the browser which prints the contents of the password and text fields.

1. Create source code in a text editor. The JavaScript ATM form contains a Password object, Text Field, Submit and Reset objects. The Submit object sends the information entered by the user to the CGI script post-query.

```
<HTML>
<HEAD>
<TITLE>JavaScript ATM</TITLE>

<SCRIPT LANGUAGE="JavaScript">
<!-- Hide JavaScript from older browsers
/***********************************************************************
*                                                                     *
*   Function      - withdrawMoney                                     *
*   Parameters    - None                                              *
*   Description   - This function checks the PIN and displays the amount*
*                   withdrawn, or a rejection message if the PIN is    *
*                   is invalid.                                        *
*   Called By     - onClick event handler                             *
*                                                                     *
***********************************************************************/
```

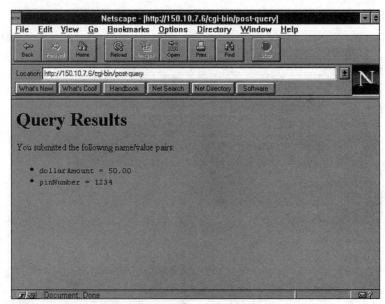

Figure 8-10 JavaScript ATM form submission

```
function withdrawMoney() {
  amount = document.javascriptATM.dollarAmount.value;
  if (document.javascriptATM.pinNumber.value == "1234") {
    document.javascriptATM.submit();
    alert("You have withdrawn $" + amount + " dollars.");
  } else {
    alert("Sorry, your PIN was rejected.");
  }
}


// end hide JavaScript -->
</SCRIPT>
</HEAD>
<BODY>
<FORM NAME="javascriptATM">

<H1>Welcome to the JavaScript ATM</H1>

Please Enter Dollar Amount:
<INPUT TYPE="text" NAME="dollarAmount" SIZE=10>
<BR>
Please Enter Your Pin Number:
<INPUT TYPE="password" NAME="pinNumber" SIZE=4>
<HR>
<INPUT TYPE="button"
       onClick="withdrawMoney()"
       VALUE="Withdraw">
<INPUT TYPE="reset" VALUE="Cancel">
</FORM>
</BODY>
</HTML>
```

2. Save the program as HT0806.HTM and load it into the Netscape browser. Enter the correct PIN (the string 1234) in the JavaScript ATM's password field. Notice that the characters appear as asterisks. This insures that a password cannot be viewed by another. Figure 8-9 depicts the resulting display.

3. Now try entering the correct PIN number by typing 1234 into the password field. Submit the form by pressing the button marked Withdraw. Figure 8-10 shows the result which prints the text entered into the password and text fields.

How It Works

This program uses the NCSA CGI script, post-query, to print the text entered in a password field. By defining the Form object's action to the URL containing the post-query CGI script, the submission of the form prints the contents of the password and text fields to the browser. The PIN entered by the user appears as asterisks, instead of the actual characters typed into the Password object. Protecting the password (PIN) is necessary for maintaining security against password theft.

Comments

This example is not secure because it sends the password as clear text. Clear text is an ASCII representation of the string. For a more secure setup, store passwords in encrypted form. When the password string is passed to the JavaScript function, encrypt the password and match it with the encrypted password in a database. Storing passwords in clear text opens the doors for intruders to view anyone's password. Encryption packages are available for storing passwords or other sensitive information. You can purchase commercial versions or obtain free software from the Internet. Some encryption technologies have export restrictions. If you are obtaining software from a country outside the United States, its very possible you will not be allowed to purchase software containing encryption technology. The next How-To uses the Password object to enter a credit card number, and shows how to access various elements in a form.

COMPLEXITY
INTERMEDIATE

8.7   How do I ...
Access data from several elements in a form?

COMPATIBILITY: NAVIGATOR 2.X   NAVIGATOR 3.X   EXPLORER 3.X

Problem

I need to access the values for several different elements in a form. I also want to be able to use the data in an event handler or a function connected to an event handler. How can I do this?

Technique

In previous chapters JavaScript programs acquired the attributes of an object by using the object's name. This requires the full name of the object to be used each time you need to access data or perform a method of the object. JavaScript forms contain the built-in property *elements*, which contain references to each of the objects in a form. Because the ELEMENTS attribute is an array, a program may use a counter-loop to access data from each of the elements in a form.

The Elements Array

The Elements array is an index of pointers to each element in the order they appear in the code. The array contains entries for all objects in a form. A form element is one of the following: Button, Checkbox, Hidden, Password, Radio, Reset,

Select, Submit, Text, or Textarea object. Use the Length property to retrieve the size of the Elements array. The size of the elements array is equal to the number of elements in the form. Another important distinction between the Elements array and the name of the Form object is that the objects in the Elements array are read-only. Any attempt to set the value of an object using the Elements array will have no effect. To reference Form objects in the Elements array use an index of "0" for the first input element to appear in the form. The second object has an index of "1", and the other objects follow the same index convention. The following is an example of the syntax for referencing properties and methods of objects in a form through the Elements array:

```
formName.elements[index].propertyName
formName.elements[index].methodName(parameters)
```

Steps

Now we'll create a JavaScript program that uses the Elements property of a form to access data from several different elements. The example constructs an order form for a fictitious beer distributor. Four different types of Form objects are accessed using the Elements array; Text Field, Textarea Field, Selection List, and Checkbox. Load the program HT0807.HTM from the CD-ROM into the Netscape browser. Figure 8-11 shows the display after entering order information into the form.

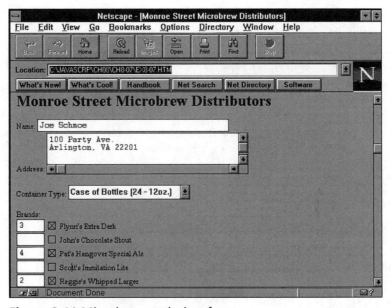

Figure 8-11 Microbrew ordering form

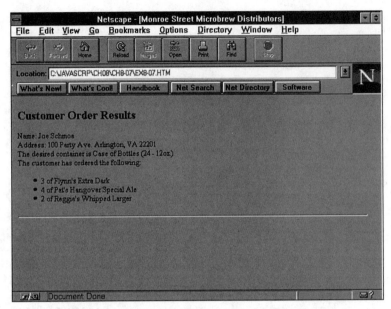

Figure 8-12 Results of the microbrew order form

Once the form has been filled, press the button marked Submit Your Order. The program displays the order information as HTML code in the browser. Figure 8-12 depicts the resulting display when the information shown in Figure 8-11 has been submitted.

1. Create the HTML portion of the program in a text editor. This form contains a text field and a textarea field for entering name and address information. The form also contains a selection list for choosing the desired type of container, checkboxes for choosing a particular brew, and corresponding text input fields for entering the quantity to be ordered. Finally, add Submit and Reset objects. Use the onClick parameter of the submit button to call the *printOrder* function constructed in step two.

```
<HTML>
<HEAD>
<TITLE>Monroe Street Microbrew Distributors</TITLE></HEAD>
<BODY><FORM NAME="microbrewOrderForm">

<H1>Monroe Street Microbrew Distributors</H1>

Name:
<INPUT TYPE="text" NAME="customerName" SIZE=40><BR>
Address:
<TEXTAREA NAME="customerAddress" ROWS=3 COLS=40>
</TEXTAREA><BR>

<P>
```

```
Container Type:
<SELECT NAME="microContainer">
<OPTION>Case of Bottles (24 - 12oz.)
<OPTION>Case of Cans (24 - 12oz.)
<OPTION>1/4 Keg
<OPTION>1/2 Keg
</SELECT><BR>
<P>
Brands:
<BR><INPUT TYPE="text" NAME="darkBeer" SIZE=5>
<INPUT TYPE="checkbox" NAME="microBrands" VALUE="Flynn's Extra Dark">
Flynn's Extra Dark
<BR><INPUT TYPE="text" NAME="amberBeer" SIZE=5>
<INPUT TYPE="checkbox" NAME="microBrands" VALUE="John's Chocolate Stout">
John's Chocolate Stout
<BR><INPUT TYPE="text" NAME="aleBeer" SIZE=5>
<INPUT TYPE="checkbox" NAME="microBrands" VALUE="Pat's Hangover Special
Ale">
Pat's Hangover Special Ale
<BR><INPUT TYPE="text" NAME="liteBeer" SIZE=5>
<INPUT TYPE="checkbox" NAME="microBrands" VALUE="Scott's Immitation Lite">
Scott's Immitation Lite
<BR><INPUT TYPE="text" NAME="largerBeer" SIZE=5>
<INPUT TYPE="checkbox" NAME="microBrands" VALUE="Reggie's Whipped Larger">
Reggie's Whipped Larger
<HR>

<INPUT TYPE="submit" onClick="printOrder()" VALUE="Submit Your Order">
<INPUT TYPE="reset" VALUE="Clear Order Form">
</FORM></BODY>
</HTML>
```

2. Next create the JavaScript portion of the program between the <SCRIPT> tags. The JavaScript program contains one function for printing the data entered in the form back to the browser. A *for* loop accesses data from each of the checkbox and text field elements. The *for* loop also checks which items have been chosen in the selection list. The printOrder function constructs a string containing the order information in HTML format and displays the order information in the browser using the Writeln method of the Document object.

```
<SCRIPT LANGUAGE="JavaScript">
<!-- Hide JavaScript from older browsers
/********************************************************************
*                                                                  *
*   Function    - printOrder                                       *
*   Parameters  - None                                             *
*   Description - This function prints the order information for the *
*                 customer.                                        *
*   Called By   - onClick event handler                            *
*                                                                  *
********************************************************************/
```

continued on next page

continued from previous page

```
function printOrder () {
   //
   //   Declare variables for the customer order information
   //
   var Name;
   var Address;
   var Type;
   var Order;

   //
   //   Retrieve the form information
   //
   with ( document.microbrewOrderForm ) {

      Name    = "Name: " + elements[0].value + "<BR>";
      Address = "Address: " + elements[1].value + "<P>";

      //
      //   Retrieve the container type from the selection list
      //
      Type = "The desired container is ";
      for (var i=0 ; i < elements[2].options.length ; i++) {
         if ( elements[2].options[i].selected == 1 )
            Type += elements[2].options[i].text + "<P>";
      }

      //
      //   Create a menu list of the orders
      //
      Order = "The customer has ordered the following:<BR><MENU>";
      for (i=3 ; i < elements.length - 2; i += 2) {
         if ( elements[i+1].checked == true)
            Order += "<li>" + elements[i].value + " of " +
                     elements[i+1].value;
      }
      Order += "</MENU>";
   }
   //
   //   Print the customer's name, address & oreder information
   //
   document.clear();
   document.writeln("<h2>Customer Order Results</h2><p>");
   document.writeln(Name);
   document.writeln(Address);
   document.writeln(Type);
   document.writeln(Order);
   document.writeln("<hr>");
}
// end Hide JavaScript -->
</SCRIPT>
```

3. Save the program as HT0807.HTM and load the code into the Netscape browser. Figure 8-11 depicts the order form after a user has typed in information.

4. Choose some of the beers using the checkboxes and enter the desired quantity. In this example the order is for three cases of Flynn's Extra Dark, four cases of Pat's Hangover Special, and two cases of Reggie's Whipped Larger.

5. Press the button marked Submit Your Order. The browser displays the order information to the browser as shown in Figure 8-12.

How It Works

The elements array references each of the elements in the form as they appear. Because the text input object appears first in the form, its index is "0". The Textarea object for the customer address appears directly after, and thus has an index of "1". The third object in the form receives the choice of container through a selection list. A *for* loop is used to check each option in the array. Instead of using the name for the selection list, the JavaScript program references the object through the elements array. The program retrieves data entered into the rest of the form with a *for* loop. When a checkbox is selected the program adds the order to the menu list to be displayed. The result, shown in Figure 8-12, summarizes the customer's order.

Comments

Chapter 8 depicts the various Form objects and how to access their data. Each of the Form objects relates to an HTML object, yet has enhanced capabilities for accessing its data. These added features allow for more flexibility in designing interfaces and retrieving input data. JavaScript also provides capabilities for accessing a user's action within a Form object. Chapter 9 discusses event handling for Form objects.

CHAPTER 9
EVENT HANDLING

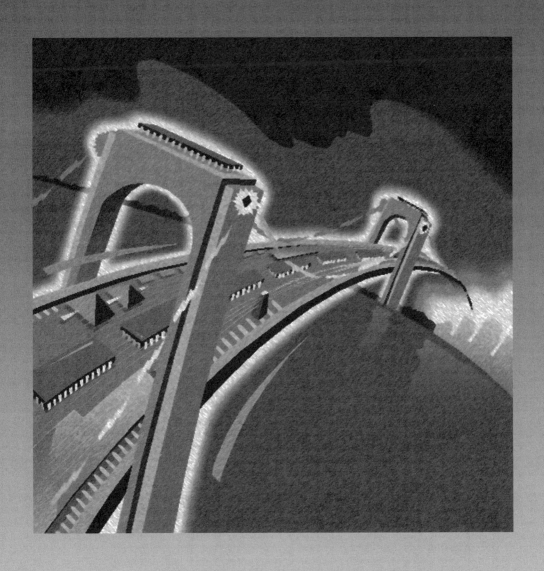

EVENT HANDLING

How do I...

9.1 **Detect when the focus has moved to a form element?**

9.2 **Detect removal of the focus from a form element?**

9.3 **Validate data entered into a text field?**

9.4 **Activate a function when a button is clicked?**

9.5 **Detect when part of a text field has been selected?**

9.6 **Get notified when the mouse is over a hyperlink?**

Chapter 8, "Form Elements," introduced the creation and purposes of various form elements. Chapter 10, "Form Methods," covers examples of events generated through a JavaScript function. This chapter deals with event handling for a form object. Events occur through the actions of a user or through methods called by a JavaScript program. Some examples of user-generated events are typing text in a text field, selecting text in a text field, moving a mouse over an anchor, clicking a button, or choosing an option in a selection list.

9.1 Detect when the focus has moved to a form element

When the user moves the focus to an object which receives text, a focus event is generated for that object. The reader will learn how to detect the focus event and perform an appropriate action.

9.2 Detect removal of the focus from a form element

Two types of event handlers, onBlur and onChange, allow you to manage the removal of focus from a Form object. The onChange event handler detects when an input object loses focus and its input has changed. The onBlur event handler simply detects when the input focus changes. This How-To explains the use of these event handlers.

9.3 Validate data entered into a text field

Modifying data and switching the focus for an input object produces a change event. This How-To explains how to validate input using the onChange event handler.

9.4 Activate a function when a button is clicked

Button objects allow users to perform a designated function within a form. This How-To explains event handling for buttons and constructs a simple JavaScript calculator.

9.5 Detect when part of a text field has been selected

Text fields offer the option of unformatted user input. This section explains how to detect when text has been selected within the object.

9.6 Get notified when the mouse is over a hyperlink

Hyperlinks, also referred to as anchor objects, can handle the mouseOver event. A mouseOver event occurs when the user moves the mouse pointer over a hyperlink. This section enables the reader to detect a mouseOver event and take appropriate action.

COMPLEXITY
BEGINNING

9.1 How do I...
Detect when the focus has moved to a form element?

COMPATIBILITY:

Problem

I want to detect when the focus has moved to an input object so that I can display a warning message. How do I do this?

Technique

Any time a user interacts with an object in a form, an event occurs. JavaScript recognizes events such as selecting text inside a text input object, choosing an item from a selection list, loading or unloading a document, clicking a button, or placing the mouse over an anchor object. JavaScript provides capabilities for handling these types of events and allows the user to add code to respond to the event. JavaScript also provides a means to artificially create the event through the use of built-in methods.

The onFocus Event Handler

A focus event occurs when the focus moves to an input object. To move the focus to an input object, tab with the keyboard or click on the object with the mouse. The *onFocus* parameter of form elements allows handling for the event by attaching a JavaScript function. The onFocus event handler provides the capability of rejecting input for the object when it is desirable to display information without allowing it to be changed. Handling for the focus event is also useful when you wish to provide an informational message about the input object. You must be careful when using this event to create dialogs however, because the dismissal of a dialog returns the focus to the input object. This will create another dialog, thus forming an endless loop. Use a conditional statement to prevent the endless loop from occurring.

Steps

In this example, you'll create a JavaScript program that mimics a self-destruct system. The program uses the focus event to create an alert box, which asks the user for confirmation before the self-destruct code can be entered. The program will also check to make sure that you've typed in the correct password. If you haven't, the self-destruct will be aborted! Load the program HT0901.HTM from the compact disc (CD) into the Netscape browser. Figure 9-1 depicts the resulting interface for the destruct system.

If you type in the password string "123" and press the button marked Initiate Auto Destruct, the program responds with a dialog stating that the destruct has been set and the time remaining. If you mistype the password string, the form pops up an alert dialog aborting the self-destruct, as shown in Figure 9-2.

1. Open up a new file in a text editor and create the HTML portion of the program. The title of this program is the "ACME Self Destruct System." This step sets up the form for the self-destruct system and creates a text input field for the self-destruct code. Set the text field's onFocus method to the *selfDestructConfirm* function. This JavaScript function will be constructed in Step 3.

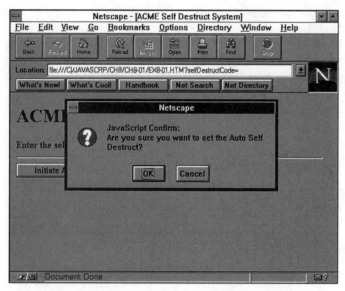

Figure 9-1 JavaScript self-destruct system with confirmation dialog

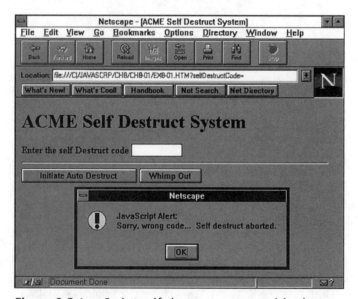

Figure 9-2 JavaScript self-destruct system with alert dialog

```
<HTML>

<HEAD><TITLE>ACME Self Destruct System</TITLE></HEAD>

<BODY><FORM NAME="acmeSelfDestruct">

<H1>ACME Self Destruct System</H1>
<P>
<B>Enter the self Destruct code</B>
<INPUT TYPE="text" NAME="selfDestructCode" SIZE=10
        onFocus="selfDestructConfirm()">
```

2. Create Submit and Reset objects for initiating the self-destruct command or clearing the form. Finally make sure to close the form, body, and document.

```
<HR>
<INPUT TYPE="submit" VALUE="Initiate Auto Destruct"
        onClick="destroyTheShip()">
<INPUT TYPE="reset" VALUE="Wimp Out">

</FORM></BODY>
</HTML>
```

3. Add the global variable *confirmState* and the function selfDestructConfirm. The selfDestructConfirm function asks the user for confirmation before typing in the password to activate the self-destruct system. Initialize the value of confirmState to "1," meaning that the user has not yet received a warning message. When the warning message is displayed, set the value confirmState to "0."

```
<SCRIPT LANGUAGE="JavaScript">
<!-- Hide from older browsers

//
//  Global containing the state of the warning message.
//
confirmState = 1;
/*********************************************************************
*                                                                   *
*   Function     - selfDestructConfirm                              *
*   Parameters   - None                                             *
*   Description  - This function creates a one-time confirm dialog when*
*                  the focus is shifted to the password input.      *
*   Called By    - onFocus event handler                            *
*                                                                   *
*********************************************************************/
function selfDestructConfirm () {
   if (confirmState) {
     confirmState = 0;
     confirm("Are you sure you want to set the Auto Self Destruct?");
   }
}
```

4. Construct the function *destroyTheShip* to check the password entered by the user. If the password is correct, issue an alert warning of the time remaining to abandon the ship. If the code is incorrect, display a confirmation dialog stating the self-destruct has been aborted.

```
/***********************************************************************
*                                                                     *
*   Function     - destroyTheShip                                     *
*   Parameters   - None                                               *
*   Description  - This function checks the password entry and warns  *
*                  the user when the auto destruct is set.            *
*   Called By    - onClick event handler                              *
*                                                                     *
***********************************************************************/
function destroyTheShip() {
   if(document.acmeSelfDestruct.selfDestructCode.value == "123") {
     alert('Self Destruct Activated: You have 60 seconds to abandon
ship!');
   } else {
     confirm('Sorry, wrong code... Self destruct aborted.');
   }
}


// end Hide script -->
</SCRIPT>
```

5. Save the program as HT0901.HTM and load the program into the Netscape browser. Figure 9-1 depicts the ACME self-destruct form.

6. Move the focus of the form to the text input by placing the mouse over the text field and pressing the mouse button. The program displays an informational message which asks if the user is sure about activating the self-destruct system. Figure 9-2 shows the resulting alert dialog.

7. Upon submitting the form, the program checks the password string "123", and displays an alert dialog warning of the time remaining to abandon ship.

How It Works

The *onFocus* parameter allows the JavaScript program to respond to the focus change to a text input field or selection list. The previous example uses the onFocus parameter of a text input to trap the focus event. When a user attempts to enter the self-destruct code, the program asks the user for confirmation before proceeding.

Comments

The onFocus event handler is useful for creating a text field that cannot be modified. The text field display for a calculator might be an example of when you would not want to allow the user to modify information in a text field. The onFocus handler could be used to switch the focus away from the calculator's display field to prevent the user from changing the result.

COMPLEXITY
BEGINNING

9.2 How do I...
Detect removal of the focus from a form element?

COMPATIBILITY:

Problem

I want to write a program that detects when the focus has been removed from an input object. How do I do this?

Technique

As discussed in the previous chapter, JavaScript provides event handling by attaching functions to the event handler of an input object. The onFocus parameter enables event handling for a focus event. This section introduces the *blur* event and discusses methods for handling the event.

The onBlur Event Handler

A blur event occurs when a selection list, text field, or textarea on a form loses focus. JavaScript provides handling for this event through the *onBlur* parameter. You can also artificially generate the blur event by using the blur method for the object, or the *focus* method for any other object in the form. Chapter 10 discusses the concept of generating events in more detail.

Steps

The following program creates a color choosing tool. The user enters the red, blue, and green content, and the tool displays the resulting color whenever the cursor leaves an input field. The onBlur parameter detects when the focus has left any of the input boxes and calls changeColor() to update the background color of the document. Each of the input boxes takes a two-digit hexadecimal number. The three numbers are concatenated to form the hexadecimal RGB triplet used to set the background color.

The bgColor Property

A document's background color resides in the document property *bgColor*. The bgColor property stores a hexadecimal RGB triplet, or a string literal of a color name. The hexadecimal RGB triplet is a hexadecimal number in the form of "RRGGBB." The first two hex characters represent the red content, the second two represent the green content, and the last two represent the blue content. The hexadecimal two-digit number ranges from "00" to "FF". The hex number "00" expresses the minimum content of the color, and "FF" represents the maximum content. Setting bgColor to the RGB triplet "FFFFFF" yields a white background, while setting bgColor to "000000" yields a black background. The same results appear by setting bgColor to the strings "white" and "black" respectively.

Load the program named HT0902.HTM from the CD into the Netscape browser. Figure 9-3 depicts the color chooser form.

Try changing the input in the green and blue content fields to the string "FF". Figure 9-4 shows the resulting browser output.

1. Create the HTML portion of the color chooser form in a text editor. The form has three input fields for the red, blue, and green content of the form's background color. The onBlur parameter for each of the fields will call the changeColor function to be added in Step 2. Set the initial value of each of the fields to the string "00".

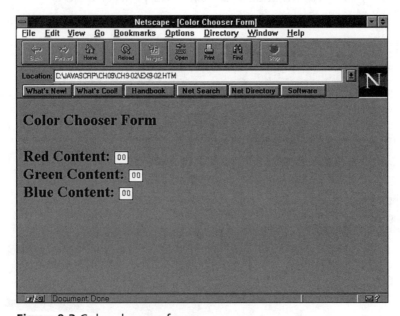

Figure 9-3 Color chooser form

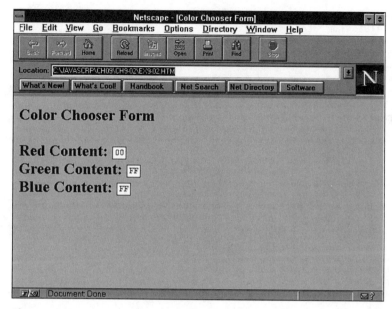

Figure 9-4 Color chooser form for the color aquamarine

```
<HTML>
<HEAD><TITLE> Color Chooser Form</TITLE></HEAD>

<BODY>
<FORM NAME="colorChooserForm">

<H1>Color Chooser Form</H1>
<P>
Red Content:
<INPUT TYPE="text" NAME="redContent" VALUE="00" SIZE=2
onBlur="changeColor()">
<BR>
Green Content:
<INPUT TYPE="text" NAME="greenContent" VALUE="00" SIZE=2
onBlur="changeColor()">
<BR>
Blue Content:
<INPUT TYPE="text" NAME="blueContent" VALUE="00" SIZE=2
onBlur="changeColor()">

</FORM></BODY>
</HTML>
```

2. Add the following JavaScript program after the <TITLE> tags. The
changeColor() function retrieves data from the three text input fields, concatenates the data, and sets the background color to the result. The onBlur
event handler for each of the fields calls the changeColor() function when
the user shifts the focus from one input field to another.

```
<SCRIPT LAGUAGE="JavaScript">
<!-- Hide from older browsers
/********************************************************************
*                                                                  *
*    Function     - ChangeColor                                    *
*    Parameters   - None                                           *
*    Description  - This function updates the background color of the  *
*                   document.                                      *
*    Called By    - onBlur event handler                           *
*                                                                  *
********************************************************************/
function changeColor() {
    //  String for storing background color.
    var hexColor;

    // Use the with statement for shorthand element names
    with (document.colorChooserForm.elements) {
        hexColor = redContent.value +
                    greenContent.value +
                    blueContent.value;
    }
    // Update the document's background color.
    document.bgColor = hexColor;
}

// end Hide script -->
</SCRIPT>
```

3. Save the program as HT0902.HTM and load it into the browser. Figure 9-3 depicts the initial state of the browser. The default background color is gray.

4. Change the input in the green and blue content fields to the string "FF". The program sets the color of the background to the string "00FFFF". This RGB triplet is the equivalent of the color aquamarine. Figure 9-4 shows the resulting form color.

How It Works

A blur event occurs when the text input or selection list loses focus by tabbing or a mouse click. Attaching a function to the blur event is accomplished by adding code to the onBlur parameter of the form object. The above example uses the blur event to change the background color of the document when the user changes the red, green, or blue content inputs and shifts the focus to another form element. The changeColor() function retrieves data from the three text input fields, concatenates the data, and sets the background color to the result. The onBlur event handler for each of the fields calls the changeColor() function when the user shifts the focus from one input field to another.

Comments

The onBlur and onChange event handlers are also useful for validating form input. This concept is explained in How-To 9.3. The example program used the bgColor property to change the background color. Similarly, the fgColor property controls the color of the document foreground text. The fgColor parameter is set using the hexadecimal RGB triplet such as "00FFFF" or a string literal such as **"aqua"**. Color is one more way to liven your Web pages using JavaScript.

COMPLEXITY
BEGINNING

9.3   How do I...
Validate data entered into a text field?

COMPATIBILITY:

Problem

I want to validate data entered into a text field and prevent the user from entering an illegal value. How do I do this?

Technique

Sometimes it is necessary to ensure that the user of a form does not enter erroneous data. For example, if the form contains a field for entering a phone number, you wouldn't want the user to be able to enter letters in the field. HTML does not possess the capacity for validating user input until after the form information is submitted. This method of validation can be very frustrating if the user has to re-enter data each time a mistake is made. This is especially true if a form contains large numbers of input objects. JavaScript, however, provides input validation through the magic of event handling. The act of moving the focus away from an input object generates a blur event. As shown in the previous How-To, the *onBlur* parameter for a text field, textarea, or selection list enables the JavaScript program to detect a blur event. Similarly, this chapter uses event handling for the change event to demonstrate input validation.

The onChange Event Handler

A change event occurs when the input to a text field, textarea, or selection list changes, and the focus leaves the input object. For each of these input objects, the onChange parameter acts as an event handler for the change event. The onChange event handler is ideal for text validation, because the event occurs only when the input changes. As shown in previous chapters, an input object may be referenced using the *this* pointer. Use the *value* method of the input object to reference the text entered by a user.

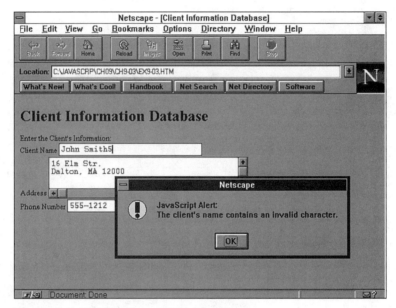

Figure 9-5 Client information database

The following is an example call to a validation function using the value method of the *this* pointer.

```
<INPUT TYPE="text" onChange="validateText(this.value)"  ...>
```

Steps

This example creates a form for entering data into a phone database. The program uses the onChange parameter to validate information entry in a text field. If a character other than a letter or space is entered into the client's name field, the program displays an alert message warning that the client's name information is invalid. If a letter or non-number character is submitted for the client's phone number, again the program warns of invalid entry.

Load the program HT0903.HTM from the CD into the Netscape browser. Figure 9-5 illustrates the interface for the client information database entry form.

1. Create the HTML portion of the program in a text editor. The program contains two text fields and one textarea field for entering the client's name, address, and phone number. The name and phone number text fields use the onChange event handler to call the validateNameEntry and validateNumberEntry functions.

```
<HTML>
<HEAD><TITLE>Client Information Database</TITLE></HEAD>
<BODY><FORM NAME="clientDatabase">
```

```
<H1>Client Information Database</H1>
Enter the Client's Information:
<BR>
Client Name
<INPUT TYPE="text" NAME="name" SIZE=30
       onChange="validateNameEntry(this.value)">
<BR>
Address
<TEXTAREA type="text" NAME="address" ROWS=3 COLS=40>
</TEXTAREA>
<BR>
Phone Number
<INPUT TYPE="text" NAME="phone" SIZE=12
       onChange="validateNumberEntry(this.value)">
</FORM></BODY>
</HTML>
```

2. Now add the JavaScript portion of the program between the <SCRIPT> tags. This step creates the validateNameEntry function which is called by the onChange event handler for the name text field This function accepts the input string entered in the name text field, and makes a call to the validateCharacter routine for each character in the string.

```
<SCRIPT LANGUAGE="JavaScript">
<!-- Hide JavaScript from older browsers
/************************************************************************
*                                                                      *
*    Function     - validateNameEntry                                  *
*    Parameters   - validString                                        *
*    Description  - This function checks if the argument string is a    *
*                   valid name, and displays an alert dialog if not.    *
*    Called By    - onChange event handler                             *
*                                                                      *
************************************************************************/
function validateNameEntry(validString) {

   //  This variable is true if the string contains all valid characters,
   //  and false otherwise.
   var isCharValid = true;

   //  Loop through each of the characters in the string argument.
   for (i=0 ; i < validString.length ; i++) {
     // check if the character is valid
     if (validateCharacter(validString.charAt(i)) == false) {
       isCharValid = false;
       i=validString.length;
     }
   }

   //  If the string contains any non-valid characters display
   //  an alert dialog.
   if (isCharValid == false) {
      alert("The client's name contains an invalid character.");
   }
}
```

3. Now add the validateCharacter function, which returns a true or false based on whether the input was a letter or a non-letter.

```
/**********************************************************************
*                                                                    *
*   Function      - validateCharacter                                *
*   Parameters    - character                                        *
*   Description   - This function validates the character argument as an*
*                   upper or lower case alphabetic character or space. *
*   Called By     - validateNameEntry Function                       *
*                                                                    *
**********************************************************************/
function validateCharacter(character) {

    //  Return true if valid, false otherwise.
    if ((character >= 'a' && character <= 'z')
        || ( character >='A' && character <='Z')
        || ( character == ' '))
      return true;
    else
      return false;
}
```

4. The next function you'll create is the validateNumberEntry function, which checks each of the characters in the argument string to make sure it is a valid phone number. The validateNumberEntry function in turn calls the *validateNumber* function, which verifies each character from the argument string.

```
/**********************************************************************
*                                                                    *
*   Function      - validateNumberEntry                              *
*   Parameters    - validString                                      *
*   Description   - This function checks if the argument string is a  *
*                   valid phone number, and displays an alert dialog  *
*                   if it is not.                                     *
*   Called By     - onChange event handler                           *
*                                                                    *
**********************************************************************/
function validateNumberEntry(validString) {

    //  This variable is true if the string contains valid numbers,
    //  and false otherwise.
    var isNumValid = true;

    //  Loop through each of the characters in the string argument.
    for (i=0 ; i < validString.length ; i++) {

      // check if the number is valid
      if (validateNumber(validString.charAt(i)) == false) {
        isNumValid = false;
        i=validString.length;
      }
    }
```

```
//
//   If the string contains any non-valid numbers,
//   display an alert dialog.
//
if (isNumValid == false) {
   alert("The client's phone number contains an invalid character.");
}
}
```

5. This step creates the validateNumber function to check if the argument is a number between "0" and "9" or a dash, and returns true or false based on the outcome.

```
/************************************************************************
*                                                                      *
*    Function     - validateNumber                                     *
*    Parameters   - character                                          *
*    Description  - This function returns a value of true if the       *
*                   character argument, is a number or dash.           *
*    Called By    - validateNumberEntry Function                       *
*                                                                      *
************************************************************************/
function validateNumber(character) {

   //   Return true if valid, false otherwise.
   if ((character >= '0' && character <= '9')
      || ( character =='-'))
     return true;
   else
     return false;
}

// end Hide JavaScript -->
</SCRIPT>
```

6. Save the program as HT0903.HTM and load the program into the Netscape browser.

7. Enter information into the form, and attempt to enter a numeral into the client's name field. When the focus is shifted to another field, the program displays an alert, as shown in Figure 9-5.

How It Works

The above example uses the change event for validating user input. When the focus shifts from one text input field to another, the onChange event handler passes the text entered into the field to a function for validation. The *validateTextEntry* function accepts the string entered into the client's name field and calls the *checkCharacter* function to verify that each character is a letter or space. If the user enters an invalid character, the function prompts the user with an alert dialog warning that the client's name contains an invalid character. The validateNumberEntry function is attached to the onChange parameter of the client's phone number. When the phone number information is changed, the *validateNumberEntry* function calls the *checkNumber* function to validate each character of the phone number. When a non-number is entered into the phone number field, an alert is also displayed warning that the phone number information is incorrect.

Comments

Data entry is crucial to the success of a database. Inaccurate information in a client's phone number or address could potentially cause you to lose the customer. More than one package or fax has been sent to the wrong person. Databases become corrupted by users entering a letter where a number is expected or the reverse. Validation at the input level provides a more user-friendly interface because the feedback is immediate. The above example could be augmented by checking the zip code against the city and state strings. A JavaScript program could also check for the correct number of digits in a phone number field. As with any computer, garbage in equals garbage out. Data input validation provides more robust interfaces and reduces the headaches of a database administrator.

COMPLEXITY
BEGINNING

9.4 How do I...
Activate a function when a button is clicked?

COMPATIBILITY: NAVIGATOR 2.X   NAVIGATOR 3.X   EXPLORER 3.X

Problem

I want to perform a function when the user presses a button or selects a checkbox or radio button. How is this done?

Technique

So far the onBlur, onChange, and onFocus event handlers have been discussed. These events are activated by the shift in focus from one input element to another. JavaScript also handles another type of event, the click event. A click event occurs whenever the mouse button is pressed while the cursor is on a button, checkbox, or radio button. The interface responds by depressing the button, toggling the checkbox, or selecting the radio button.

The onClick Event Handler

Event handling for the click event is accomplished through the onClick parameter for the object. Handling of the click event allows the object to respond to its selection by activating a function. Submit and Reset objects are examples of specialized buttons with default handling for a click event. When a submit button is pressed, the document is automatically submitted. Similarly, when a reset button is pressed, the click event causes a form's input objects to reset to their default values.

The Button Object

Buttons are created using the <INPUT> tag with the TYPE parameter set to "button". The following is an example of the syntax for a button.

```
<INPUT
TYPE="button"
NAME="buttonName"
VALUE="buttonText"
[onClick="buttonClickHandler"]>
```

The TYPE parameter is generic for all input objects and is set to the value "button". The name of the button element is identified by the text supplied to the NAME parameter. Text supplied to the VALUE parameter is displayed on the surface of the button. The onClick parameter provides optional handling for a mouse button press in the object.

Steps

This example will use JavaScript to create a simple calculator. The math operations add, subtract, multiply, and divide are attached to buttons of the calculator. The operands are entered using buttons, and the result is also displayed in a text field. A more complex calculator could be built, but this example serves to teach the concept of attaching functions to buttons. Load the program HT0904.HTM from the CD into the Netscape browser. Figure 9-6 shows the interface for the simple JavaScript calculator.

1. Begin by typing the HTML portion of the program into a text editor. Add buttons to the form for each of the arithmetic operators, a text field to display the result, a reset button for clearing the calculator, and 11 buttons for the numbers and decimal point. Set the onClick parameter for the operator buttons to call the *Operator* function. The *Operator* function will be constructed in Step 3. Each of the data keys also uses the onClick event handler to activate the *Data* function, which is constructed in Step 4.

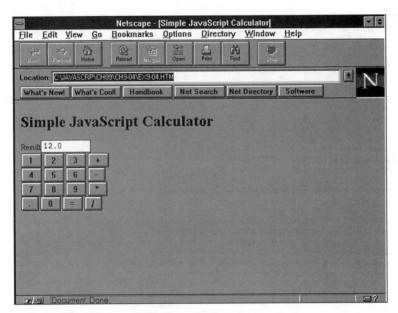

Figure 9-6 Simple JavaScript calculator

```
<HTML>
<HEAD><TITLE>Simple JavaScript Calculator</TITLE></HEAD>

<BODY><FORM NAME="javascriptCalculator">

<H1>Simple JavaScript Calculator</H1>

Result<INPUT TYPE="text" NAME="displayResult" SIZE=10>
<BR>
<INPUT TYPE="button" NAME="one" VALUE="  1  " onClick="Data('1')">
<INPUT TYPE="button" NAME="two" VALUE="  2  " onClick="Data('2')">
<INPUT TYPE="button" NAME="three" VALUE="  3  " onClick="Data('3')">
<INPUT TYPE="button" NAME="addOp" VALUE=" + "
onClick="Operator(this.value)">
<BR>
<INPUT TYPE="button" NAME="four" VALUE="  4  " onClick="Data('4')">
<INPUT TYPE="button" NAME="five" VALUE="  5  " onClick="Data('5')">
<INPUT TYPE="button" NAME="six" VALUE="  6  " onClick="Data('6')">
<INPUT TYPE="button" NAME="subOp" VALUE=" - "
onClick="Operator(this.value)">
<BR>
<INPUT TYPE="button" NAME="seven" VALUE="  7  " onClick="Data('7')">
<INPUT TYPE="button" NAME="eight" VALUE="  8  " onClick="Data('8')">
<INPUT TYPE="button" NAME="nine" VALUE="  9  " onClick="Data('9')">
<INPUT TYPE="button" NAME="mulOp" VALUE=" * "
onClick="Operator(this.value)">
<BR>
```

```
<INPUT TYPE="button" NAME="period" VALUE="  .  " onClick="Data('.')">
<INPUT TYPE="button" NAME="zero" VALUE="  0  " onClick="Data('0')">
<INPUT TYPE="button" NAME="eqOp" VALUE=" = "
onClick="Operator(this.value)">
<INPUT TYPE="button" NAME="divOp" VALUE=" / "
onClick="Operator(this.value)">
<BR>
<INPUT TYPE="reset" NAME="clear" VALUE="CLEAR">
</FORM></BODY>
</HTML>
```

2. Next add the JavaScript portion of the program between the SCRIPT tags. Create four global variables for storing the state of the calculator. The *statement* variable contains a string of the math statement, and the *displayString* contains the current display of the calculator. The Boolean variable *newDisplay* signals to the program that an operator button has been pressed and the display should form a new number when a data key is pressed. The *hasOperator* variable signals that the user has already pressed an operator, and any further operator keys should calculate intermediate results to the display.

```
<SCRIPT LANGUAGE="JavaScript">
<!-- Hide JavaScript from older browsers

var statement ="";    // Contains the math statement
var displayString;    // Contains the displayed string
var newDisplay = true; // Flag to used to signal formation of a new number
var hasOperator = false;  // Flag used to update the display for an
                          // operator
```

3. After the global variables, add the Operator function which performs the math operations for the calculator. The onClick event handler for each of the operator keys calls this function.

```
<SCRIPT LANGUAGE="JavaScript">
<!-- Hide JavaScript from older browsers

var statement ="";    // Contains the math statement
var displayString;    // Contains the displayed string
var newDisplay = true; // Flag to used to signal formation of a new number
var hasOperator = false;  // Flag used to update the display for an
                          // operator
```

4. In addition to the Operator function, add the *Data* function. The Data function handles numerical keypad entry and updates the display by concatenating the button's value to the display. Each of the number keys uses its onClick event handler to call the Data function and passes its value as its argument.

```
/*********************************************************************
*                                                                   *
*    Function     - Data                                            *
*    Parameters   - numberString                                    *
*    Description  - This function handles number or decimal key press. *
*    Called By    - onClick event handler                           *
*                                                                   *
*********************************************************************/
function Data(numberString) {

   //  If an operator has previously been pressed start with a
   //  new string, otherwise concatenate the number to the current
   //  display.
   if (newDisplay == true) {
      newDisplay = false;
      displayString = numberString;
   } else {
      displayString += numberString;
   }

   // Update the display.
   DisplayString();
}
```

5. Add the third and final function *displayString* to the JavaScript program. Both the Operator and Data functions use the displayString function to update the display of the calculator. Close off the JavaScript program using the </SCRIPT> tag.

```
/*********************************************************************
*                                                                   *
*    Function     - DisplayString                                   *
*    Parameters   - None                                            *
*    Description  - Prints the displayString global to the display. *
*    Called By    - Operator and Data functions.                    *
*                                                                   *
*********************************************************************/
function DisplayString() {
   //  Print the new display string
   document.javascriptCalculator.displayResult.value = displayString;
}

// end Hide JavaScript -->
</SCRIPT>
```

6. Once the program has been written, save it as HT0904.HTM and load the file into the Netscape browser.

7. Try multiplying 3 times 4 and displaying the result by pressing the equals key. Figure 9-6 illustrates output of the simple JavaScript calculator.

How It Works

Interaction with the calculator is performed solely by button press. Each button sends its value to either the Data or Operator function. The Operator function accepts the string representation of the operator and constructs the math statement to be evaluated by the calculator. When a user presses the equals button, the Operator function displays the evaluated math statement. The Data function accepts a number or decimal character and updates the display by concatenating this character to the current display string.

Comments

This is a simplistic version of a calculator. With a little effort you could probably construct a more complex version, with all the features available to comparable scientific characters. This chapter also introduced the *eval* function which will be covered more completely in Chapter 11, "Create New Objects," which explains how to dynamically create and evaluate JavaScript expressions.

COMPLEXITY
BEGINNING

9.5 How do I...
Detect when part of a text field has been selected?

COMPATIBILITY:

Question

I want to be notified when a user has selected part or all of the text in a text field. How can I detect when this occurs?

Technique

Whenever a user selects text in a text field or Textarea object, the act of selecting the text generates a selection event. Text is selected by positioning the mouse over text, holding the mouse button down, and dragging the cursor over the section of text to be selected. JavaScript allows for the detection of this event through the onSelect event handler. The *onSelect* attribute is available only for the Text and Textarea objects. JavaScript does not provide selection event handling for the Password object, because JavaScript has no access to password fields for security reasons.

The onSelect Event Handler

The onSelect parameter, found in both the Text object and Textarea form objects, connects a selection event to user-supplied JavaScript code. Event handling for a selection event is useful when the interface should warn against changing the selected text. As discussed in How-To 9.1, the onFocus attribute provides a similar capability. A selection event, however, occurs after the focus has shifted to the Text or Textarea objects.

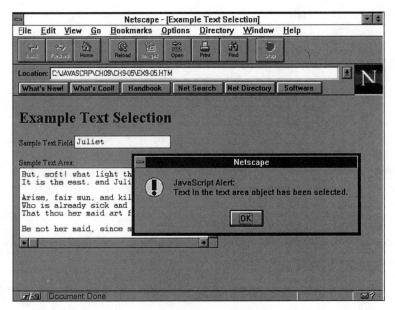

Figure 9-7 Event handling for text selection

Steps

The following example creates a Textarea object and text field and attaches notifying functions to the onSelect attributes of each object. When a user attempts to select text in either of the objects, an alert dialog is displayed notifying the user that the text has been selected. This example also introduces the status bar. When the user selects text within a text input object, the status bar explains the purpose of the object. Load the program HT0905.HTM from the CD into the Netscape browser. Figure 9-7 shows what happens when you select a portion of the text inside the textarea field.

1. Create the HTML portion of the program in a text editor. The form contains a text field and a Textarea object. Both of these objects use the onSelect event handler to activate the functions constructed in Steps 3 and 4. Add initial values to the fields so that a user may select some of the text.

```
<HTML>
<HEAD><TITLE>Example Text Selection</TITLE></HEAD>

<BODY><FORM NAME="exampleSelection">

<H1>Example Text Selection</H1>

Favorite Character:
<INPUT TYPE="text" NAME="sampleField" VALUE="Juliet"
        onSelect="textfieldSelected()">
```

```
<P>
Favorite Line:
<BR>
<TEXTAREA NAME="sampleArea" ROWS=8 COLS=40
          onFocus="textareaSelected()">
But, soft! what light through yonder window breaks?
It is the east, and Juliet is the sun!

Arise, fair sun, and kill the envious moon,
Who is already sick and pale with grief,
That thou her maid art far more fair than she:

Be not her maid, since she is envious;
Her vestal livery is but sick and green,
And none but fools do wear it; cast it off.

It is my lady; O, it is my love!
O, that she knew she were!
</TEXTAREA>

</FORM></BODY>
</HTML>
```

2. Create the JavaScript portion of the program surrounded by the <SCRIPT> tags. Two global variables are used in this example to denote whether the text in the fields has been selected or not. This prevents the *textareaSelected* and *textfieldSelected* functions from displaying multiple dialogs.

```
<SCRIPT LANGUAGE="JavaScript">
<!-- Hide JavaScript from older browsers
var textareaMessage = false; //  True if text area already selected
var textfieldMessage = false; //  True if text field already selected
```

3. Add the *textareaSelect* function for detecting when a portion of the input in the textarea field has been selected by the user. This function is called by the onSelect event handler of the textarea field.

```
/*******************************************************************
*                                                                 *
*   Function     - textareaSelected                               *
*   Parameters   - None                                           *
*   Description  - This function creates a dialog when text in the *
*                  textarea is selected, and displays a warning in the *
*                  status bar.                                     *
*   Called By    - onSelect event handler                         *
*                                                                 *
*******************************************************************/
function textareaSelected() {
self.status='The Text Area object contains a portion of text from Romeo and
Juliet.';
if ( textareaMessage == false ) {
textareaMessage = true;
alert("Text in the text area object has been selected.");
}
}
```

4. Add another function, called textfieldSelected, for creating a dialog when the input in the text field has been selected. The function also displays a message in the status bar.

```
/***********************************************************************
*                                                                     *
*   Function    - textfieldSelected                                   *
*   Parameters  - None                                                *
*   Description - This function creates a dialog when text in the text*
*                 field is selected, and displays a warning in the    *
*                 status bar.                                          *
*   Called By   - onSelect event handler                              *
*                                                                     *
***********************************************************************/
function textfieldSelected() {
self.status='Enter the name of your favorite character from Romeo and
Juliet.';
if ( textfieldMessage == false )  {
textfieldMessage = true;
alert("Text in the text field object has been selected.");
}
}

// end Hide JavaScript -->
</SCRIPT>
```

5. Save the program as HT0905.HTM and load the program into the browser. Attempt to select text from either the textarea or text field. Figure 9-7 depicts the result when a portion of text is selected from the Textarea object.

How It Works

The selection event triggers the user's defined textareaSelected or textfieldSelected functions when a portion or all of the text in the corresponding objects is selected. Selection of text is possible through clicking and dragging over text with the mouse, or by the select method. The select method, explained in Chapter 10, "Form Methods," allows a JavaScript function to perform the text selection. This function-generated selection event is also handled by the onSelect attribute.

Comments

Many text editors warn a user when a large selection of text is about to be deleted. This feature can be provided on a form, or the act of selecting text can be discouraged. One noticeable deficiency of JavaScript is that the language does not provide an attribute or method for returning the section of text selected by the user. JavaScript also cannot select only a portion of text. Selection of text and how to stop text entry in an input object are explained in more detail in Chapter 10, "Form Methods."

COMPLEXITY
BEGINNING

9.6 How do I...
Get notified when the mouse is over a hyperlink?

COMPATIBILITY:

Question

When the user moves the mouse over a hyperlink, I want to execute a JavaScript function without the user having to select the anchor. How do I do this?

Technique

When creating an HTML document, it's good programming practice to provide the user with as much information as possible about each hyperlink. This enables the user to navigate the HTML documents intelligently. JavaScript provides an added layer of information for navigating hyperlinks through the mouseOver event. A mouseOver event occurs when the mouse pointer moves on top of a hyperlink. In JavaScript a hyperlink is also referred to as a Link object. To add information to your HTML documents, the mouseOver event could be connected with popping up a window or generating a message in the status bar for displaying added information about the hyperlink.

The onMouseOver Event Handler

The mouseOver event is managed using the *onMouseOver* parameter for a Link object. In the following example, the onMouseOver event handler provides the user with information about the hyperlink in the status bar.

```
<A HREF="http://www.nasa.gov/"
   onMouseOver="window.status= 'Choose this link for Space Shuttle
pictures.'; return true;">
Nasa's Home Page
</A>
```

When the user moves the mouse over the hyperlink "Nasa's Home Page", the status bar will echo the message, "Choose this link for Space Shuttle pictures." The onMouseOver event handler may also be used to call a JavaScript function, as shown in the next section.

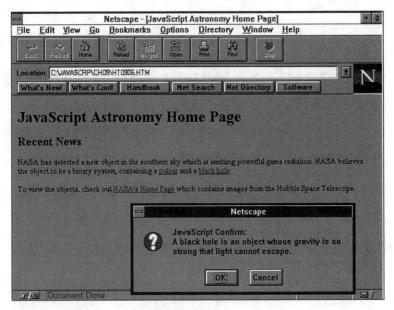

Figure 9-8 Astronomy home page

Steps

The following example illustrates the use of the onMouseOver event handler for performing an action when the mouse cursor moves on top of a hyperlink. A home page is constructed with astronomy information, intended to instruct the reader. Hyperlinks are provided to other pages to further explain information on the page or link to another site containing more information. Load the program named HT0906.HTM from the CD into the Netscape browser. Figure 9-8 displays the Astronomy home page constructed using JavaScript.

1. Enter the following program in a text editor. Construct two hyperlinks for displaying information about the black hole and pulsar link objects, and a hyperlink for connecting to the NASA home page.

```
<HTML><HEAD>
<TITLE>JavaScript Astronomy Home Page</TITLE></HEAD>

<BODY><FORM NAME="astronomyForm">

<H1>JavaScript Astronomy Home Page</H1>

<H2>Recent News</H2>
Nasa has detected a new object in the southern sky which is
emitting powerful gamma radiation. Nasa believes the object
to be a binary system, containing a
<A HREF="pulsar.htm" onMouseOver="pulsarInfo(); return true;">pulsar</A>
and a
```

```
<A HREF="blackhol.htm" onMouseOver="blackHoleInfo(); return true;">black
hole</A>.

<P>
To view the objects, check out
<A HREF="http://www.nasa.gov/"
   onMouseOver="window.status='Choose this link to download images from the
NASA web site.'; return true;">
Nasa's Home Page</A>
which contains images from the Hubble Space Telescope.

</FORM></BODY>
</HTML>
```

2. Next create the JavaScript portion of the program before the </HEAD> tag. This step creates the function *pulsarInfo* for handling the mouseOver event for the pulsar link.

```
<SCRIPT LANGUAGE="JavaScript">
<!-- Hide JavaScript from older browsers
/**********************************************************************
*                                                                    *
*    Function     - pulsarInfo                                       *
*    Parameters   - None                                            *
*    Description  - Provides information about a pulsar.             *
*    Called By    - onMouseOver event handler                       *
*                                                                    *
**********************************************************************/
function pulsarInfo() {
    confirm("A pulsar is a spinning neutron star which periodically emits
large amounts of X-rays and gamma radiation.");
}
```

3. Next create the function *blackHoleInfo* for handling the mouseOver event for the black hole hyperlink.

```
/**********************************************************************
*                                                                    *
*    Function     - blackHoleInfo                                    *
*    Parameters   - None                                            *
*    Description  - Provides information about a black hole.         *
*    Called By    - onMouseOver event handler                       *
*                                                                    *
**********************************************************************/
//
// Provide more information about a black hole.
//
function blackHoleInfo() {
    confirm("A black hole is an object who's gravity is so strong that
light cannot escape.");
}

// end Hide JavaScript -->
</SCRIPT>
```

4. Save the program as HT0906.HTM and then load it into the Netscape browser. Figure 9-8 displays the home page after a user has moved over one of the hyperlinks.

5. Move the mouse on top of the black hole hyperlink. A confirm dialog displays further information about the astronomical object.

How It Works

When the mouse moves over either of the pulsar or black hole link objects, the onMouseOver event handler calls the function *pulsarInfo* or *blackHoleInfo*, respectively. Each of these functions displays a confirm dialog containing information about the astronomical object. When a user clicks on the hyperlinks, the browser loads documents "pulsar.htm" or "blackhol.htm," depending on the link selected. The Netscape browser also displays the link object's reference in the status bar. When the mouse moves over the Nasa's Home Page hyperlink, the status bar displays the http address of the NASA home page. The onMouseOver attribute for this link updates the status bar with the message, "Choose this link to download images from the NASA Web site."

Comments

The onMouseOver event handler provides the user with the ability to link any action with moving a mouse over a hyperlink. Conceivably a mouseOver event could cause hyperlinks to change color, checkboxes to toggle, or text to be typed in text fields. This type of interaction makes a Web page unpredictable and thus should be avoided. The onMouseOver event handler should only be used to provide more information about the hyperlink. This allows for a more interactive look and feel for a Web document, and provides the user with helpful information for navigating its links.

CHAPTER 10

FORM METHODS

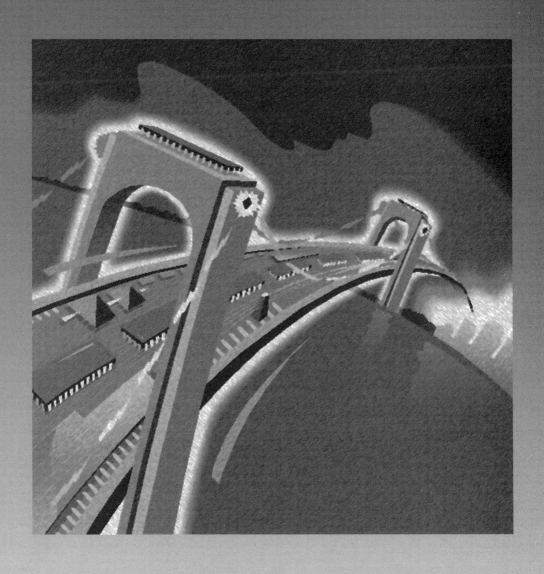

10

FORM METHODS

How do I...

10.1 Switch the focus from one element to another element?

10.2 Highlight a text field and position the cursor for user response?

10.3 Change the selected checkbox or radio box?

10.4 Change the current selected state of an option in a selection list?

Chapter 8 discussed Form Input objects, and Chapter 9 explained how to handle events generated by Input objects. This chapter discusses how to artificially create these events using the object's built-in methods. Usually events are generated by a user's interaction with an object, such as toggling a checkbox, switching the input focus, or selecting text. Methods allow a JavaScript program to simulate user interaction, and provide yet another way to spice up your Web pages. Several built-in methods for Form Input objects are discussed along with possible uses for method generated events.

10.1 Switch the focus from one element to another element

Through the focus method, a JavaScript program switches the focus from one Input object to another. These methods may be used to ensure user input in a form in mandatory input fields or prevent a user from accessing an Input object.

10.2 Highlight a text field and position the cursor for user response

This How-To explains how to use the select method to highlight text in a Text, Textarea or Password object. When input to a text field is inaccurate, the select method effectively communicates which text is undesirable.

10.3 Change the selected checkbox or radio box

Have you ever wanted to change the state of a checkbox or select a different choice in a radio group depending on a the state of another Input object? JavaScript provides the check method to allow toggling checkboxes or selecting radio buttons.

10.4 Change the current selected state of an option in a selection list

Selection lists are another form of Input objects with a distinct list of choices. Learn how to select or deselect an option in a Selection object. This How-To also explains how to dynamically add options to a selection list.

COMPLEXITY
BEGINNING

10.1 How do I...
Switch the focus from one element to another element?

COMPATIBILITY:  NAVIGATOR 2.X   NAVIGATOR 3.X   EXPLORER 3.X

Problem

I want to move the focus from one element in a form to another element, without requiring the user to tab or select the object with the mouse. How can I accomplish this?

Technique

Chapter 9 explored event handling for the movement of focus to and from objects. The onFocus, onChange, and onBlur event handlers were discussed for handling when the user moves the focus from one object to another. JavaScript provides the means to artificially move the focus through the use of an object's built-in methods. Methods are accessed using the object's name followed by a period and the method name. If the object does not contain the method, JavaScript displays an error message. JavaScript uses two built-in methods, the blur and focus methods, to position the focus in a form.

The Focus Method

The focus method changes the input focus to the specified Input object. The Password, Select, Text, and Textarea objects all have the built-in focus method. The Netscape browser displays a Method Not Found error if a program attempts to call the focus method for any other Form object. The following list gives the four possible syntaxes for using the focus method:

```
passwordName.focus()
selectName.focus()
textName.focus()
textareaName.focus()
```

The above example uses the string password Name for the name of the Password object, the selectName equates to the Selection List object, and so forth. As discussed in How-To 8.7, any of the Form objects are accessible through a built-in property of the Form object, called the elements array. Use the order in which each object appears as the index to the array. The following shows syntax for using the focus method through the Elements array:

```
document.formName.elements[indexNumber].focus()
```

The Blur Method

The blur method provides another way to move the input focus between objects. Unlike the focus method, which moves the focus to some specified object, the blur method moves the focus away from an object. Password, Select, Text, and Textarea objects all contain the blur method. When the focus is removed from one of the Input objects, the input focus moves to the next available Form object. As with the focus method, the blur method uses the same syntax:

```
passwordName.blur()
selectName.blur()
textName.blur()
textareaName.blur()
document.formName.elements[indexNumber].blur()
```

If the element referenced by the index array is not a Password, Selection list, Text field or Textarea object, the browser will return a Method Not Found error.

Steps

The following program creates a form that uses a Radio object to choose which Form object will reject input. The onFocus event handler detects when the focus arrives at the object, and the blur method removes the input focus. The switchFocus function determines if the object should reject input and displays an alert message if such an event occurs. Load the program HT1001.HTM from the compact disc (CD) into the Netscape browser. Figure 10-1 depicts the example input focus form.

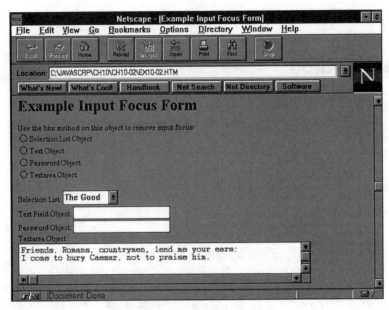

Figure 10-1 Example input focus form

Select one of the objects from the radio group. When you attempt to enter text or change the selection list corresponding to the chosen radio button, the program blurs the input focus and displays an alert dialog as shown in Figure 10-2.

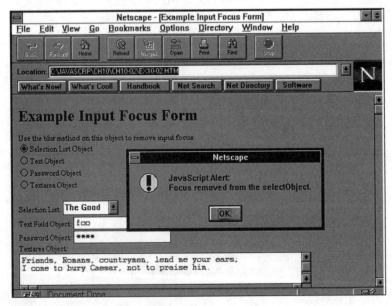

Figure 10-2 Input focus switching

1. Type the HTML portion of the program into a text editor. The form contains Selection List, Text, Textarea, and Password objects. Four radio buttons correspond to each object. The selection of a Radio object for one of the four object renders it unusable. Each time a user attempts to modify input to an object selected by its corresponding radio button, the input focus is rejected.

```
<HTML>
<HEAD>
<TITLE>Example Input Focus Form</TITLE>
</HEAD>
<BODY>
<FORM NAME="inputFocus">

<H1>Example Input Focus Form</H1>
<P>
Use the blur method on this object to remove input focus:
<BR><INPUT TYPE="radio" NAME="blurSelection"
    VALUE="Select">Selection List Object
<BR><INPUT TYPE="radio" NAME="blurSelection"
    VALUE="Text">Text Object
<BR><INPUT TYPE="radio" NAME="blurSelection"
    VALUE="Password">Password Object
<BR><INPUT TYPE="radio" NAME="blurSelection"
    VALUE="Textarea">Textarea Object

<P>
Selection List:
<SELECT NAME="selectObject"
   onFocus="switchFocus(this, inputFocus.blurSelection, 0)">
<OPTION> The Good
<OPTION> The Bad
<OPTION> The Ugly
</SELECT>
<BR>

Text Field Object:
<INPUT TYPE="text" NAME="textObject"
   onFocus="switchFocus(this, inputFocus.blurSelection, 1)">
<BR>

Password Object:
<INPUT TYPE="password" NAME="passwordObject"
   onFocus="switchFocus(this, inputFocus.blurSelection, 2)">
<BR>

Textarea Object:<BR>
<TEXTAREA NAME="textareaObject" ROWS=3 COLS=60
   onFocus="switchFocus(this, inputFocus.blurSelection, 3)">
Friends, Romans, countrymen, lend me your ears;
I come to bury Caesar, not to praise him.
</TEXTAREA>

</FORM>
</BODY>
</HTML>
```

2. Next, create the JavaScript portion of the program. Add the JavaScript code between the <SCRIPT> tags. Create the *switchFocus* function so that the function accepts a pointer to a Form object. This function checks the object's name against the corresponding button in the radio group. If the corresponding radio button has been selected, the *switchFocus* function removes the focus from the Form object.

```
<SCRIPT LANGUAGE="JavaScript">
<!-- Hide JavaScript from older browsers

/*********************************************************************
*                                                                   *
* Function   - switchFocus                                          *
* Parameters - FormObject (Pointer to the form object)              *
*         RadioObject (Pointer to a radio object)                   *
*         Index     (Index of the radio option)                    *
* Description - This function switch focus away from an input       *
*         object, if selected by its corresponding radio           *
*         button.                                                   *
* Called By  - onFocus event handler                               *
*                                                                   *
*********************************************************************/
function switchFocus(FormObject, RadioObject, Index) {
  //
  // If the object's radio button is selected, blur the input focus.
  //
  if ( RadioObject[Index].checked == true ) {
   FormObject.blur();
   alert("Focus removed from the " + FormObject.name + ".");
  }
}

// end Hide JavaScript -->
</SCRIPT>
```

3. Save the program as HT1001.HTM and load it into the Netscape browser. Figure 10-1 shows the form that contains the Input objects and a set of radio buttons used to choose one of the objects.

4. Choose one of the objects in the set of radio buttons, and attempt to modify that Input object's content. The program displays an alert dialog as shown in Figure 10-2 and moves the focus to another Input object.

How It Works

Each of the four objects passes a pointer of itself to the switchFocus function. The switchFocus function determines if the user has selected this object from the set of radio buttons. If the object has been selected, the function uses the blur method to remove the focus and the alert method to display which object rejected the input focus.

Comments

A practical example of switching the input focus is a modification to the JavaScript calculator program in How-To 9.4. The calculator could be modified to use the blur method to switch the input focus away from its display. This forces the user to enter input through the buttons and makes the program act more like a real calculator. The next How-To demonstrates another use for shifting the input focus. The example program in How-To 10.2 uses the focus method to move the input focus for positioning the cursor to a desired text field.

COMPLEXITY
INTERMEDIATE

10.2 How do I...

Highlight a text field and position the cursor for user response?

COMPATIBILITY: NAVIGATOR 2.X NAVIGATOR 3.X EXPLORER 3.X

Problem

I want to highlight text entered into a text field and position the cursor so that the user can change the text. How do I do this?

Technique

How-To 9.3 demonstrated how to validate user input to a text field. If the input was not a valid entry, the JavaScript program displayed an error message. Selecting the offending text improves the program, because it simplifies the process for the user to change the entry. This How-To will demonstrate the use of the select method to accomplish this feat.

Using the Select Method

The Text, Textarea, and Password objects all contain the select method. The select method combined with the focus method highlights text within a field and positions the cursor so that the user can re-enter the text. As shown in How-To 10.1, the focus method switches the focus to a Text, Textarea, or Password object. When the desired object acquires input focus, the select method highlights all text within the object. The select method does not require any parameters. Syntax for calling the select method from an object follows:

```
passwordName.select()
textName.select()
textareaName.select()
```

Steps

Because highlighting text provides effective feedback for an input form, this example builds from the example constructed in How-To 9.3. Expand the client information database form to include a password field, and add the select and focus methods to each validation function. Two functions validate the input; one validates the client's name, and a second validates number entry. The data validation functions are modularized, except on the two functions, by passing the object's pointer as an argument. Both the Password object and a text field use the validate number entry. Load the program HT1002.HTM into the Netscape browser. Type a string containing a non-letter. Figure 10-3 shows what happens when the client's name string contains the number 5. The program displays an alert dialog and selects the client's name text field.

If a non-number is entered into the client's phone number text field, the program displays an alert dialog and selects the text field as shown in Figure 10-4.

1. Create the HTML portion of the example program in an editor. The form contains a text field for the client's name and phone number, a textarea field for the client's address, and a password field for the client's credit card number. Use the onChange event handler for the client's name and phone number text fields to call the functions, validateNameEntry and validateNumberEntry. These functions validate the input for the client's name and phone number text fields respectively.

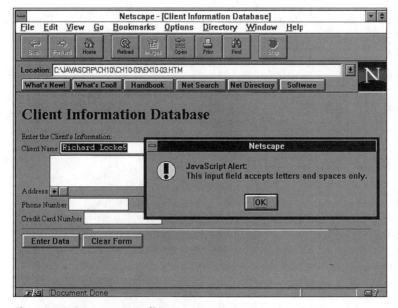

Figure 10-3 Improper client name entry

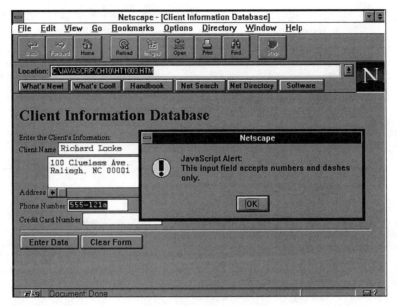

Figure 10-4 Improper phone number entry

```
<HTML>
<HEAD>
<TITLE>Client Information Database</TITLE>
</HEAD>
<BODY>
<FORM NAME="clientDatabase">

<H1>Client Information Database</H1>
Enter the Client's Information:<BR>

Client Name
<INPUT TYPE="text" NAME="clientName" size=30
    onChange="validateNameEntry(this)"><BR>

Address
<textarea type="text" NAME="clientAddress" ROWS=3 COLS=40>
</TEXTAREA><BR>

Phone Number
<INPUT TYPE="text" NAME="clientPhone" size=12
    onChange="validateNumberEntry(this)"><BR>
Credit Card Number
<INPUT TYPE="password" NAME="creditCardNum" size=16>

<HR>
<INPUT TYPE="submit" NAME="submitData" VALUE="Enter Data">
<INPUT TYPE="reset" NAME="clearForm" VALUE="Clear Form">
</FORM>
</BODY>
</HTML>
```

2. Next add the JavaScript portion of the program after the </TITLE> tag. Create the validateNameEntry function to check the client's name input. If the name information contains characters other than letters or spaces, the function switches the focus back to the text field and highlights the input for user response. The validateNameEntry function loops through each of the characters in the input string and uses the validateCharacter function to check each one.

```
<SCRIPT LANGUAGE="JavaScript">
<!-- Hide JavaScript from older browsers

/**********************************************************************
*                                                                    *
* Function   - validateNameEntry                                     *
* Parameters - Field  (Text field containing the string)             *
* Description - This function validates a string typed into the      *
*          client's name text field.                                 *
* Called By  - onChange event handler                                *
*                                                                    *
**********************************************************************/
function validateNameEntry(Field) {
  var pos; // Position in the character string
  var isCharValid = true; // True if the string is valid
  var String = Field.value; // Get the string to be evaluated

  // Loop through each of the characters in the string to search
  // for a character other than a letter or space.
  for (pos=0 ; pos < String.length ; pos++) {
   if (validateCharacter(String.charAt(pos)) == false) {
    isCharValid = false;
    pos = String.length;
   }
  }

  //
  // If there is an invalid character in the string
  // display an error message, and select the text for re-entry.
  //
  if (isCharValid == false) {
   Field.focus();
   Field.select();
   alert("This input field accepts letters and spaces only.");
  }
}
```

3. Add the validateCharacter function to check a character in the client's name string. If the character passed to the function is not a letter or a space, the function returns a value of false.

```
/******************************************************************
*                                                                *
* Function   - validateCharacter                                 *
* Parameters - character  (Character to be validated)            *
* Description - This function checks if the character is a letter or *
*         space, and returns a boolean reflecting the outcome.   *
* Called By  - validateNameEntry function                        *
*                                                                *
******************************************************************/
function validateCharacter(character) {
  if ((character >= 'a' && character <= 'z')
    || ( character >='A' && character <='Z')
    || ( character == ' '))
  return true;
  else
  return false;
}
```

4. For handling the change event generated by input to the phone number
text field or credit card password field, construct the validateNumberEntry
function. This function highlights the phone number or credit card number
fields if the input string contains characters other than numbers or dashes.

```
/******************************************************************
*                                                                *
* Function   - validateNumberEntry                               *
* Parameters - Field  (Text field containing the string)         *
* Description - This function validates a phone number entry in a *
*         text field.                                            *
* Called By  - onChange event handler                            *
*                                                                *
******************************************************************/
function validateNumberEntry(Field) {
  var pos; // Position in the character string
  var isNumValid = true; // True if the number is valid
  var String = Field.value; // Get the string to be evaluated

  //
  // Loop through each of the characters in the string to search
  // for a character other than a letter or space.
  //
  for (pos=0 ; pos < String.length ; pos++) {
   if (validateNumber(String.charAt(pos)) == false) {
    isNumValid = false;
    pos = String.length;
   }
  }

  //
  // If there is an invalid character in the number
  // display an error message, and select the text for re-entry.
  //
```

continued on next page

continued from previous page

```
   if (isNumValid == false) {
   Field.focus();
   Field.select();
   alert("This input field accepts numbers and dashes only.");
   }
}
```

5. Add the validateNumber function to check if the argument is a number or a dash character. If the input is not a dash or number, the function will return a value of false. This function is called by the validateNumberEntry function with each of the characters in the input string.

```
/*********************************************************************
*                                                                   *
* Function   - validateNumber                                       *
* Parameters - character  (Character to be validated)               *
* Description - This function checks if the chcracter is a number or *
*          dash, and returns a boolean reflecting the outcome.       *
* Called By  - validateNumberEntry function                         *
*                                                                   *
*********************************************************************/
function validateNumber(character) {
   if ((character >= '0' && character <= '9')
     || ( character =='-'))
   return true;
   else
   return false;
}


// end Hide JavaScript -->
</SCRIPT>
```

6. Save the program as HT1002.HTM and load it into the Netscape browser. Enter a string that includes an invalid character into the client's name field and move the focus to another input element. Figure 10-3 depicts the resulting alert dialog. Notice that focus has shifted back to the text field for the client's name and that the string containing an invalid character has been selected.

7. Now try entering an invalid number string in either of the phone or credit card number fields. The program displays another alert dialog as shown in Figure 10-4. As with the client's name, focus is shifted back to the text field and the offending string is selected.

How It Works

The validateNameEntry and validateNumberEntry functions perform event handling for the change event. The act of changing an entry in a text field and moving the focus to another input object generates a change event. In the case of the client's name field, the pointer to the field is passed to the validateNameEntry function. From the text field's pointer the function obtains the string entered by the user and calls the validateCharacter function. Each character from the user's input string is fed to the validateCharacter string. If the argument is other than letter or space, the function returns a value of "false." When an invalid character appears in the string, the validateNameEntry function displays an alert dialog warning of the invalid entry. Focus switches back to the client's name field, and the function highlights the text field's contents and positions the cursor for user response. The focus and select methods for the Text Field object moves the focus and highlights the input text.

The validateNumberEntry function performs similarly. In the event the input string contains a character other than a number or dash, the function displays an alert, moves focus back to the input field, and highlights the text.

Comments

Returning the focus and selecting invalid input visually cue the user as to which text field contains the offending input. Without selecting the invalid text, the program can only provide an ambiguous error message. The select method gives indisputable direction as to which input field caused the problem. The select method is also useful for showing which field the user should modify. One example is modifying information contained within a database. The program could retrieve the information and populate a form with fields from the database. The field to be modified should be automatically highlighted to assist the user in updating the information. The next How-To shows yet another way to interact with form elements. How-To 10.3 discusses how to change the state of checkboxes and Radio objects.

COMPLEXITY
INTERMEDIATE

10.3 How do I...
Change the selected checkbox or radio box?

COMPATIBILITY:

Problem

I have a form containing checkboxes and radio groups. Through a JavaScript function, I would like to change the selected radio box in a radio group or toggle the state of a checkbox. How is this done?

Technique

Checkboxes and radio buttons contain a built-in function called the click method. The click method simulates a button press. Use of the click method on radio buttons and checkboxes produces slightly different results. The click method toggles the checkbox and chooses one of the radio buttons in a radio group. To access the click method for a particular radio button, choose the corresponding radio button's index. The following provides an example of syntax for using the click method in radio buttons and checkboxes:

```
checkboxName.click()
radioGroupName[index].click()
```

The Checked and defaultChecked Property

Both the Checkbox and Radio object contain the defaultChecked property. You can use this property to determine the default setting for a Checkbox or Radio object. Setting the defaultChecked property changes the default settings, but does not change the current settings. The default settings for checkboxes and radio buttons are important. Whenever the browser loads a form or a user presses the Reset object, a form displays the default settings for an object. Default settings for an object increase the usefulness of a form.

Chapter 8 explained how to determine the state of a checkbox or radio button through the checked property. Setting the value of this property for a checkbox or radio button produces the same effect as calling the click method. This property cannot be changed using the Elements property of a form. The Elements array only allows a user to view the values of properties. You cannot call methods or change the values for properties using the Elements array. Instead, the object's full name must be used to change its properties or call the object's methods.

Steps

This example builds off of the pizza form program introduced in Chapter 8. The Selection List object, which chooses the types of pizza, sets default responses for the form. For example, when the user selects a Meat Lover's style pizza, the event sets the corresponding topping and crust style. Thus an event in a Selection List object toggles checkboxes and selects radio buttons. Load the program HT1003.HTM from the CD into the Netscape browser. Figure 10-5 shows the pizza form interface, which changes the state of radio button and checkbox form events generated by a selection list.

1. Create the HTML portion of the program in a text editor. Add a function for choosing the correct checkboxes and radio buttons based on the style of pizza chosen. The Vegetarian style pizza chooses all of the vegetable toppings on the thin crust pizza. The Meat Lover's option sets the Thick crust radio button and all of the checkboxes containing meat toppings. When the user selects the Everything option, the program toggles all checkboxes and selects the Deep Dish style crust.

```
<HTML>
<HEAD>
<TITLE>Joe's Pizza</TITLE>
</HEAD>
<BODY>
<FORM NAME="pizzaOrder">

<H1>Joe's Pizza</H1>
```

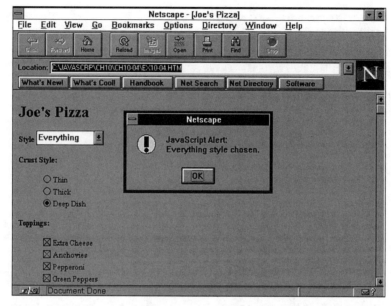

Figure 10-5 Pizza form using interactive selection list

```
<B>Style</B>
<SELECT NAME="PieStyle"
    onChange="choosePizza(this)">
<option VALUE="Plain" SELECTED>Plain
<option VALUE="Vegetarian">Vegetarian
<option VALUE="Meat Lovers">Meat Lovers
<option VALUE="Everything">Everything
</SELECT>

<P>
<B>Crust Style:</B>
<MENU>
<INPUT TYPE="radio" NAME="pieCrust" VALUE="Thin">Thin<BR>
<INPUT TYPE="radio" NAME="pieCrust" VALUE="Thick">Thick<BR>
<INPUT TYPE="radio" NAME="pieCrust" VALUE="Deep Dish">Deep Dish<BR>
</MENU>

<B>Toppings:</B>
<MENU>
<INPUT TYPE="checkbox" NAME="extraCheese"
    VALUE="extra_cheese">Extra Cheese<BR>
<INPUT TYPE="checkbox" NAME="anchovies"
    VALUE="Anchovies">Anchovies<BR>
<INPUT TYPE="checkbox" NAME="pepperoni"
    VALUE="Pepperoni">Pepperoni<BR>
<INPUT TYPE="checkbox" NAME="greenPeppers"
    VALUE="Green Peppers">Green Peppers<BR>
<INPUT TYPE="checkbox" NAME="mushrooms"
    VALUE="Mushrooms">Mushrooms<BR>
```

continued on next page

continued from previous page

```
<INPUT TYPE="checkbox" NAME="onions"
    VALUE="Onions">Onions<BR>
<INPUT TYPE="checkbox" NAME="olives"
    VALUE="Olives">Olives<BR>
<INPUT TYPE="checkbox" NAME="sausage"
    VALUE="Sausage">Sausage
</MENU>

<HR>
<INPUT TYPE="submit" VALUE="Place Order">
<INPUT TYPE="reset" VALUE="Clear Order">
</FORM>
</BODY>
</HTML>
```

2. Next add the JavaScript portion of the program. Create the function choosePizza to modify the radio buttons and checkboxes based on an option chosen from a selection list. The choosePizza function uses the pointer to the selection list to determine which option has been selected, and then changes the state of each of the radio buttons and checkboxes to match the style of pizza chosen.

```
<SCRIPT LANGUAGE="JavaScript">
<!-- Hide JavaScript from older browsers

/************************************************************************
*                                                                      *
* Function   - choosePizza                                             *
* Parameters - SelectObject (Pointer to the selection list object)     *
* Description - This function chooses toppings and pizza crust based    *
*         on the selection list object.                                *
* Called By  - onChange event handler of the select object             *
*                                                                      *
************************************************************************/
function choosePizza(SelectObject) {
  var Option;
  var index;

  for ( index=0 ; index < SelectObject.options.length ; index++ ) {
    if ( SelectObject.options[index].selected == true ) {
    Option = SelectObject.options[index].text;
    index = SelectObject.options.length;
    }
  }

  if ( Option == "Vegetarian" ) {

    document.pizzaOrder.pieCrust[0].checked = true;
    document.pizzaOrder.anchovies.checked = false;
    document.pizzaOrder.pepperoni.checked = false;
    document.pizzaOrder.sausage.checked = false;
    document.pizzaOrder.extraCheese.cheked = false;
    document.pizzaOrder.greenPeppers.checked = true;
    document.pizzaOrder.mushrooms.checked = true;
```

```
      document.pizzaOrder.onions.checked = true;
      document.pizzaOrder.olives.checked = true;

  }

  if ( Option == "Meat Lovers" ) {

      document.pizzaOrder.pieCrust[1].checked = true;
      document.pizzaOrder.anchovies.checked = false;
      document.pizzaOrder.pepperoni.checked = true;
      document.pizzaOrder.sausage.checked = true;
      document.pizzaOrder.extraCheese.cheked = true;
      document.pizzaOrder.greenPeppers.checked = false;
      document.pizzaOrder.mushrooms.checked = false;
      document.pizzaOrder.onions.checked = false;
      document.pizzaOrder.olives.checked = false;

  }

  if ( Option == "Everything" ) {

      document.pizzaOrder.pieCrust[2].checked = true;
      document.pizzaOrder.anchovies.checked = true;
      document.pizzaOrder.pepperoni.checked = true;
      document.pizzaOrder.sausage.checked = true;
      document.pizzaOrder.extraCheese.cheked = true;
      document.pizzaOrder.greenPeppers.checked = true;
      document.pizzaOrder.mushrooms.checked = true;
      document.pizzaOrder.onions.checked = true;
      document.pizzaOrder.olives.checked = true;

  }

  alert(Option + " style chosen.");
}

// end Hide JavaScript -->
</SCRIPT>
```

3. Save the program as HT1003.HTM and load it into the browser. Choose one of the topping styles. Figure 10-5 depicts the result when a user chooses the Everything style of pizza from the Selection List object.

How It Works

The Selection List object chooses a style of pizza through the onChange event handler. When a new option is selected and the focus moves to another object, the onChange event handler calls the choosePizza function. This function checks which option has been selected and toggles the appropriate checkboxes and radio buttons. A call to the choosePizza function passes the Selection List object's pointer, so that the selected option may be determined. The choosePizza function sets the checked attribute to a value of true or false depending on the desired state of the checkbox or radio button. For example, the "Everything" select option sets the checked attributes of all of the checkboxes to true. Figure 10-5 shows the resulting state of the Radio and Checkbox objects.

Comments

The above example shows how to build an interactive form. By pre-selecting options from the form, the program increases the user-friendliness of the interface. A customer need only select a pre-defined style of pizza, rather than checking each individual checkbox or radio button on the form. So far you have learned how to set the state of Button, Text, Textarea, Password, Radio, and Checkbox objects. How-To 10.4 demonstrates how to manipulate the Selection List object.

COMPLEXITY
BEGINNING

10.4 How do I...
Change the current selected state of an option in a selection list?

COMPATIBILITY:

Problem

I want to change which option or options have been chosen in a Selection List object. How do I do this?

Technique

The Selection List object provides a compact way for organizing options in a Form object. The scrollable version of a Selection List object performs the same functionality as a list of checkboxes. It offers a set of Boolean choices. The menu version of a Selection List object corresponds to a radio group. Only one option in either object is selectable at any one time.

The defaultChecked and Checked Properties

JavaScript does not provide a method for changing selected options. Instead, you must use the checked property. The checked property contains the current selection state of an option. Setting the checked property to true chooses the option. Setting an option's checked property to false deselects an option. The defaultChecked property operates in the same manner and contains the state of whether the option is by default chosen. This property may also be dynamically set so that when a form is reset or reloaded, different options are chosen by default. To reference an option's checked or defaultChecked property, use the following syntax:

```
selectObjectName[index].checked
selectObjectName[index].defaultChecked
```

Steps

The following program demonstrates how to change selection list options from input to a checkbox or radio box. The form is used to construct an ice cream sundae. Selection List objects are used to query the user's choice of ice cream and toppings for the sundae. Identical choices are displayed in checkboxes and radio buttons. When a user selects a radio button for an ice cream flavor, the corresponding option is selected for the flavor selection list. Similarly, the selection of a topping through a checkbox object causes the identical option in the toppings selection list to become selected. Load the program HT1004.HTM from the CD into the Netscape browser. After selecting the Chocolate radio button, you should see the selection list change to the same options shown in Figure 10-6.

The selection list for the toppings also changes when you select any of the checkboxes. Figure 10-7 shows the change to the selection list when the Cherry and Whipped Cream checkboxes are toggled.

1. Type the HTML portion of the program into a text editor. Add a selection list and a matching set of radio buttons to select ice cream flavors for the sundae. Use the onClick event handler of the radio buttons to call the changeFlavor function, which will be constructed in Step 3.

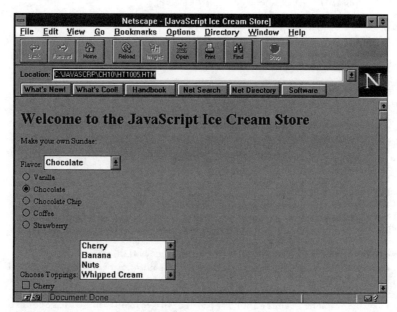

Figure 10-6 JavaScript ice cream form

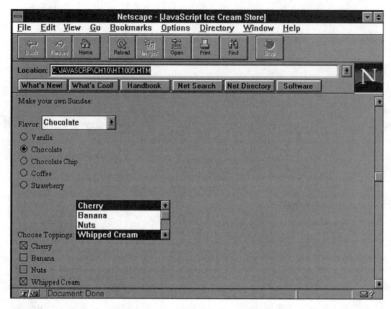

Figure 10-7 Selected ice cream sundae toppings

```
<HTML>
<HEAD>
<TITLE>JavaScript Ice Cream Store</TITLE>
</HEAD>
<BODY>
<FORM NAME="icecreamOrder">

<H1>Welcome to the JavaScript Ice Cream Store</H1>

<P>
Make your own Sundae:
<P>
Flavor:
<SELECT NAME="selectFlavor"
        onChange="changeFlavor(document.icecreamOrder.radioFlavor, this);">
<option SELECTED>Vanilla
<OPTION>Chocolate
<OPTION>Chocolate Chip
<OPTION>Coffee
<OPTION>Strawberry
</SELECT>

<BR><INPUT TYPE="radio" NAME="radioFlavor" VALUE="vanilla"
onClick=" document.icecreamOrder.selectFlavor.options[0].selected = true;">
Vanilla
<BR><INPUT TYPE="radio" NAME="radioFlavor" VALUE="chocolate"
onClick=" document.icecreamOrder.selectFlavor.options[1].selected = true;">
Chocolate
<BR><INPUT TYPE="radio" NAME="radioFlavor" VALUE="chocolatechip"
onClick=" document.icecreamOrder.selectFlavor.options[2].selected = true;">
```

```
Chocolate Chip
<BR><INPUT TYPE="radio" NAME="radioFlavor" VALUE="coffee"
onClick=" document.icecreamOrder.selectFlavor.options[3].selected = true;">
Coffee
<BR><INPUT TYPE="radio" NAME="radioFlavor" VALUE="strawberry"
onClick=" document.icecreamOrder.selectFlavor.options[4].selected = true;">
Strawberry
```

2. Add a selection list and a group of checkboxes to select the toppings for the sundae. Use the onClick event handler for the checkboxes to call the changeToppings function, which modifies the state of the selection list. The changeToppings function modifies the selection list to match the selection state of the corresponding checkbox.

```
<P>
Choose Toppings:
<SELECT NAME="selectToppings" MULTIPLE size=4
        onChange="changeToppings(this, document.icecreamOrder);">
<OPTION>Cherry
<OPTION>Banana
<OPTION>Nuts
<OPTION>Whipped Cream
<OPTION>Chocolate Sprinkles
<OPTION>Jimmies
<OPTION>Hot Fudge
</SELECT>

<BR><INPUT TYPE="checkbox" NAME="cherry"
onClick=" document.icecreamOrder.selectToppings.options[0].selected =
this.checked;">
Cherry
<BR><INPUT TYPE="checkbox" NAME="banana"
onClick=" document.icecreamOrder.selectToppings.options[1].selected =
this.checked;">
Bannana
<BR><INPUT TYPE="checkbox" NAME="nuts"
onClick=" document.icecreamOrder.selectToppings.options[2].selected =
this.checked;">
Nuts
<BR><INPUT TYPE="checkbox" NAME="whippedcream"
onClick=" document.icecreamOrder.selectToppings.options[3].selected =
this.checked;">
Whipped Cream
<BR><INPUT TYPE="checkbox" NAME="chocolatesprinkles"
onClick=" document.icecreamOrder.selectToppings.options[4].selected =
this.checked;">
Chocolate Sprinkles
<BR><INPUT TYPE="checkbox" NAME="jimmies"
onClick=" document.icecreamOrder.selectToppings.options[5].selected =
this.checked;">
Jimmies
<BR><INPUT TYPE="checkbox" NAME="hotfudge"
onClick=" document.icecreamOrder.selectToppings.options[6].selected =
this.checked;">
Hot Fudge
```

continued on next page

continued from previous page

```
</FORM>
</BODY>
</HTML>
```

3. Next create the JavaScript portion of the program after the </TITLE> tag. The first function you'll add changes the selection list for the ice cream flavor to reflect a change in the corresponding radio group. The function's name is changeFlavor, and it uses the pointer of the selection list to change its value.

```
<SCRIPT LANGUAGE="JavaScript">
<!-- Hide JavaScript from older browsers

/***********************************************************************
*                                                                     *
* Function   - changeFlavor                                           *
* Parameters - RadioObject (Pointer to the radio group object)        *
*              SelectObject (Pointer to the selection list object)    *
* Description - This function changes the state of the flavor         *
*               selection list.                                       *
* Called By   - onClick event handler of the radio group             *
*                                                                     *
***********************************************************************/
function changeFlavor(RadioObject, SelectObject) {
  var index;

  // Loop through each option in the radio group
  for ( index=0 ; index < SelectObject.options.length ; index++ ) {

   // If the radio button is selected change the selection
   // list to match.
   if ( SelectObject.options[index].selected == true ) {
     RadioObject[index].checked = true;
     index = SelectObject.options.length;
   }
  }
}
```

4. This step constructs the changeToppings function, which changes the state of the sundae toppings selection list. The function has three arguments that accept pointers to the Checkbox and Selection List objects, and a string containing the text of the option corresponding to the Checkbox object.

```
/***********************************************************************
*                                                                     *
* Function   - changeToppings                                         *
* Parameters - Form           (Pointer to the icecream order form)    *
*              SelectObject (Pointer to the selection list object)    *
* Description - This function changes the state of the toppings       *
*               selection list.                                       *
* Called By   - onClick event handler of the checkbox object         *
*                                                                     *
***********************************************************************/
```

```
function changeToppings(SelectObject, Form) {
    //  Set each checkbox to the state of the corresponding
    //  selection list item.
    Form.Cherry.checked               = SelectObject.options[0].selected;
    Form.Banana.checked               = SelectObject.options[1].selected;
    Form.Nuts.checked                 = SelectObject.options[2].selected;
    Form.WhippedCream.checked         = SelectObject.options[3].selected;
    Form.ChocolateSprinkles.checked = SelectObject.options[4].selected;
    Form.Jimmies.checked              = SelectObject.options[5].selected;
    Form.HotFudge.checked             = SelectObject.options[6].selected;
}

// end Hide JavaScript -->
</SCRIPT>
```

5. Save the program as HT1004.HTM and load it into the Netscape browser. Try choosing a flavor from one of the radio buttons. Figure 10-6 shows the result when a user chooses the radio button for the flavor chocolate. Immediately after the Chocolate radio button is selected, the Chocolate option from the selection list becomes selected.

6. Now choose some of the checkboxes from the toppings section of the form. When a user chooses any of the checkboxes, the program selects the corresponding option in the scrollable selection list. Selecting the toppings Cherry and Whipped Cream from the checkbox list produces the output shown in Figure 10-7.

How It Works

The program uses the *onClick* event handler to call functions that change the selected state of options in the flavor and toppings Selection List objects. The radio buttons, when selected, pass a pointer to themselves and the flavor selection list. Because the flavor selection list allows only a single option to be selected, it acts like a Radio object. The changeFlavor function uses the pointer to the radio button to determine which option has been chosen. The function uses the pointer argument of the flavor selection list to modify the chosen option.

Similar interaction occurs between the checkboxes and the scrollable selection list for the toppings section. Three parameters are required to pass information to the changeTopping function. The function accepts as arguments the checkbox object pointer, a string denoting the option, and a pointer to the selection list. When a user toggles a checkbox, the function searched for the corresponding option in the toppings selection list. The changeTopping function then sets the state of the option in the selection list to the state of the corresponding checkbox. Thus the form keeps the option chosen through Checkbox objects in sync with those displayed through the selection list.

Comments

You can make an improvement to the ice cream form by having the Selection List objects set the corresponding Radio and Checkbox objects. This provides two ways of entering the same information that are linked by the user's actions. This kind of input is wasteful, but clearly demonstrates how to change the chosen options in a selection list. Now that built-in methods for Form objects have been covered, it's time to discuss how to make your own methods and objects. Chapter 11 shows how to create new objects and provides examples of how to access their properties and methods.

CREATE NEW OBJECTS

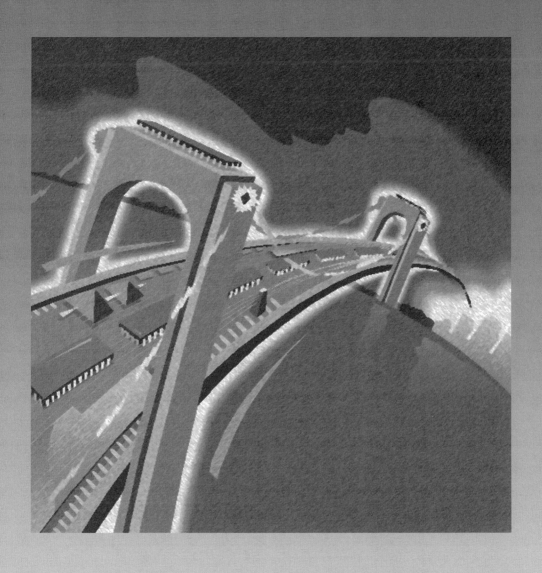

11

CREATE NEW OBJECTS

How do I...

JavaScript uses a simple object-oriented paradigm. The object-oriented paradigm considers both data and actions of equal importance. An object is a unified software component that incorporates both the data for the object and actions that operate on the data. When using the object-oriented paradigm, it is important to understand object-oriented terminology. The object-oriented paradigm uses the word "method" to indicate an object's action. As shown in Chapter 10, many form element objects contain built-in methods. Data that may be referenced from outside of an object is referred to as a "property" or "attribute." The object type itself is called a "class" of the object. In this chapter you will learn how to define object classes and create properties and methods within the objects.

A well-designed object operates as an independent unit, and contains all of the methods necessary to operate on its data. Well-designed objects operate independently of each other, and model everything in their corresponding real-world objects. This independence is sometimes called encapsulation. Objects hide their implementation details, and provide a standard interface for accessing data within the object. This concept is known as information hiding. This chapter demonstrates these concepts, and teaches how to properly implement the object-oriented paradigm in the JavaScript language.

11.1 Define a new object type by writing a function

This How-To explains how to create an object class using the "function" statement. This How-To will discuss how to define cohesive and modular objects, and how to use them.

11.2 Create an instance of an object using the new operator

The new style operator allows a user to create another instance of an object. This How-To builds off the knowledge gained from How-To 11.1, and demonstrates the new operator in action.

11.3 Access the properties of an object

Learn how to access data within an object, or hide an object's data from the outside world. This How-To teaches the concepts of information hiding and encapsulation.

11.4 Define an object as a property of another object

Objects themselves may be properties, or data, of other objects. This How-To explains how to define an object as a property of another object, and interact with both objects.

11.5 Add a method to an object type

Methods are functions or actions within an object. Learn how to create and use methods of an object, and how to link these methods to the object using the *this* pointer.

11.6 Create and populate an array of objects

Learn how to create arrays using JavaScript, and how to create array of objects. This How-To also explains how to initialize and populate the objects inside an array.

COMPLEXITY
INTERMEDIATE

11.1 How do I...
Define a new object type by writing a function?

COMPATIBILITY:

Problem

I want to define an object type and use it to create an object in a program. How is this done?

Technique

This chapter introduces the *object-oriented* paradigm, and explains how to create an object type using the JavaScript language. The subsection on object-oriented techniques provides terminology for many of the various object-oriented concepts. If you're already familiar with the object-oriented paradigm, you may want to skip this section and get right into the JavaScript object model.

The Object-Oriented Paradigm

Unless you've been living under a rock, by now you have probably heard the term object-oriented. The object-oriented paradigm is a way of modeling a system as objects that contain both data structure and behavior. Object-oriented methodology applies this model to software development by organizing the system into a collection of objects.

There are several benefits of using the object-oriented paradigm in developing software. Object modeling offers better understood models that closely reflect real-world systems and operations. Object-oriented techniques encourage code reuse and improve overall productivity. Finally, object models easily handle changes, because a change in one object should not have an impact on another.

Properties

An object's properties define its structural attributes. You can think of a property as an entity within an object that takes on a single value. For example, if this book were modeled as an object, it would have properties such as title, authors, publisher, copyright, and number of pages. Each of these properties acquires a single value. For this book, the properties take on values shown in Table 11-1.

PROPERTIES:	PROPERTY VALUES:
Title	JavaScript: How-To
Authors	George Pickering, Shelley Powers and Ron Johnson
Publisher	Waite Group Press
Copyright	1996
Number of Pages	600

Table 11-1 Property names and values for a book object

Methods

The behavior of an object is defined by its methods. Methods perform operations within an object, and are specific implementations of an operation. For example, you can drive a boat, car, or plane. Each of these objects contains the drive method, yet specific implementations of the drive method are very different from one object to another.

Even though two objects contain the same type of method, they sometimes require different implementations to operate on different objects. Remember that a method is a specific implementation of an operation. When a method behaves differently on different classes, that is, requires more than one method, the method exhibits the property of polymorphism. Because changes to the methods of one class do not affect another class, polymorphism enables the reuse of a method across multiple classes.

Classes

Objects of similar type and function are grouped together in a class. More specifically, objects within the same class must have identical structure and methods. A class contains one or more objects. For example, a pickup truck, a bus, and a sports car are all objects that belong to the automobile class. Properties for the automobile class may include make, model, and year. The automobile class also contains operations such as start, stop, turn, and back-up. The pickup truck is a particular instance of a class. Each object of a class is called an instance. Every instance of a class has the same methods, but not necessarily the same properties.

Superclasses and Subclasses

Classes are usually organized into hierarchical relationships. A class above another class in the hierarchy is called a superclass. The subordinate class, a class below a superclass, inherits properties and methods from the superclass. Superclasses are created using the process of generalization. Generalization factors out all of the common attributes and operations within a set of classes. Assigning these properties and methods to a broader class constructs a superclass. For example the classes *plane*, *train*, *car*, and *boat* all share common properties and methods. A vehicle superclass could have the properties Speed, Passengers, Make, Model, and Weight. Common methods for the vehicle superclass might include Accelerate, Stop, Start, Turn, and Reverse.

The reverse of generalization is specialization. Specialization refines classes into smaller classes called subclasses. A subclass inherits the attributes of the superclass. For instance, the superclass vehicle could be split into three subclasses: airborne vehicle, land vehicle, and waterborne vehicle. The subclass adds additional properties and methods to the superclass. For example, the land vehicle subclass could have the added property, Wheels, and the added method, Signal Turn.

The JavaScript Object Model

JavaScript is based on a simple object-oriented approach. Objects are created using the function statement. Properties may be variables or other objects defined within the object. Methods are defined externally through the function statement and linked to the object by the *this* pointer. How-To 11.5 discusses how to create methods in JavaScript and use them within an object. Functions provide the fundamental building blocks for creating objects using the JavaScript language.

Why Create Objects?

Previously this How-To explained the benefits of object-oriented programming. Even if you are designing a small-scale system, it is important to follow sound object-oriented practices. Creating objects within JavaScript allows these objects to be reused by other components of the program, or other programs. Object types or classes also allow the dynamic creation of objects. For example the form input from a user could be stored in an object for use by other functions.

Creating New Object Types

JavaScript and LiveWire, Netscape's serverside version of JavaScript, contain a number of predefined objects. Each of these objects provides methods and properties for accessing data and performing operations on the object. For example the Radio object contains properties such as Name or Value and methods such as Click.

In addition to these objects, JavaScript allows the creation of new object types. When creating your own object you must perform two steps:

 Define the object class

 Create an instance of the object

JavaScript accomplishes the first step by using the function statement to create a new object type, or class. The function variables are the equivalent of a class's properties. You must design the function so that it initializes the variables through arguments to the function. By allowing the properties to be initialized, a user can instantiate the object. The following code shows how to create the *dog* class:

```
function dog(theName, theBreed, theAge, theColor) {
    this.name   = theName;
```

continued on next page

continued from previous page

```
    this.breed = theBreed;
    this.age   = theAge;
    this.color = theColor;
}
```

The function accepts the arguments *theName*, *theBreed*, *theAge*, and *theColor* to define and instantiate the properties Name, Breed, Age, and Color.

Steps

In this section you will construct an object using the *function* statement and print its properties. Load program HT1101.HTM from the CD-ROM into the Navigator 2.0 browser. Figure 11-1 depicts the JavaScript program as displayed by the browser.

First press the button marked Create an Object. This button creates and instantiates an object. Next press the button marked Print the Object. This button makes a call to a function to print the object's properties to the browser, as shown in Figure 11-2.

If you try to print the object before it is created, no properties are printed for the object. Try reloading HT1101.HTM in the browser and pressing the Print the Object button first. Figure 11-3 displays the result.

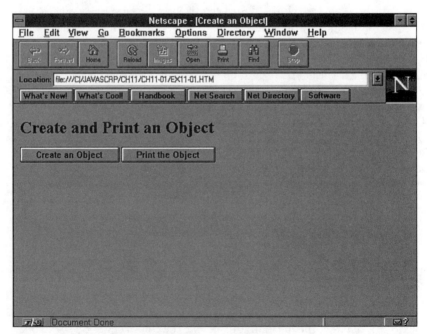

Figure 11-1 Creating and printing an object

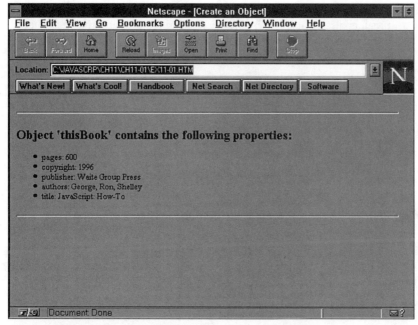

Figure 11-2 Printing the properties of an object

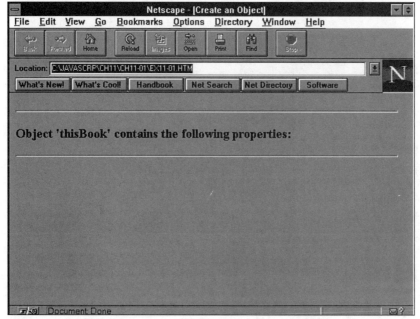

Figure 11-3 Printout of the object before instantiation

1. First create the HTML portion of the program in a text editor. The following program also creates two buttons, Create an Object and Print the Object. Each of these buttons performs the creation and printout of the object and its properties.

```
<HTML><HEAD>
<TITLE>Create an Object</TITLE></HEAD>
<BODY><FORM NAME="createObject">
<H1>Create and Print an Object</H1>
<INPUT TYPE="button" onClick="thisBook = instantiateObject()"
       VALUE="Create the Object">
<INPUT TYPE="button" onClick="printObject(thisBook, 'thisBook')"
       VALUE="Print the Object">
</FORM></BODY>
</HTML>
```

2. The JavaScript portion of the program contains three functions. The first function, Book, defines the object. The global variable, thisBook, contains the object instantiated by the instantiateObject function.

```
<SCRIPT LANGUAGE="JavaScript">
<!-- Hide JavaScript from older browsers

var thisBook;

/*********************************************************************
*                                                                   *
*   Function    - Book                                              *
*   Parameters  - title        (Title of the book)                  *
*                 authors      (String containing the list of authors) *
*                 publisher    (Publisher of the book)              *
*                 copyright    (Date string of copyright)           *
*                 pages        (Integer number of pages)            *
*   Description - This function defines the Book object type.       *
*   Called By   - instantiateObject function                       *
*                                                                   *
*********************************************************************/
function Book(title, authors, publisher, copyright, pages) {

    //
    //  Add properties to the object.
    //
    this.title     = title;
    this.authors   = authors;
    this.publisher = publisher;
    this.copyright = copyright;
    this.pages     = pages;
}
```

3. Create a function to instantiate the Book object. Give the Book object properties of JavaScript: How-To for the title, George, Ron, Shelley for the authors, Waite Group Press for the publisher, 1996 for the copyright, and 600 for the page count. The function returns the newly created object.

```
/**********************************************************************
*                                                                    *
*    Function      - instantiateObject                               *
*    Parameters    - None                                            *
*    Description   - This function instantiates and returns the Book *
*                    object.                                         *
*    Called By     - onClick event handler                          *
*                                                                    *
**********************************************************************/
function instantiateObject() {
  var newBook = new Book("JavaScript: How-To",
                         "George, Ron, Shelley",
                         "Waite Group Press",
                         1996,
                         600);

  return newBook;
}
```

4. Add a third and final JavaScript function to print the Book object's properties. Use the *for* statement to loop through each of the properties of the
Book object, and print them to the browser.

```
/**********************************************************************
*                                                                    *
*    Function      - printObject                                     *
*    Parameters    - object          (Object to be printed)         *
*                    objectName   (Name of the object to be printed) *
*    Description   - Print the argument object to the browser.       *
*    Called By     - onClick Event Handler                          *
*                                                                    *
**********************************************************************/
function printObject(object, objectName) {
    //
    //   Clear the document and create the header.
    //
    document.writeln("<HR>");
    document.writeln("<H2>Object '" + objectName +
                     "' contains the following properties:</H2>");

    //
    //   Create a menu list of the object's property names & values.
    //
    document.writeln("<P><MENU>");
    for (property in object) {
       document.writeln("<LI>" + property + ": " + object[property]);
    }
    document.writeln("</MENU><P><HR>");
}


// end Hide JavaScript -->
</SCRIPT>
```

5. Save the program as HT1101.HTM and then load it into Navigator browser.
Figure 11-1 shows the form created by the above program.

6. Press the button marked Create the Object and then the button marked Print the Object. The first properties of the Book object are displayed in the browser as shown in Figure 11-2.

7. Reload the program and attempt to print the object before its creation. Figure 11-3 depicts the screen displayed by the browser. No properties are printed for the Book object, because it has not been instantiated.

How It Works

The function instantiateObject creates the Book class, which defines an object using a function. The buttons use the onClick event handler to call the instantiateObject and printObject functions when either button is pressed. Clicking the Create an Object button calls the instantiateObject function, which in turn instantiates Book. The onClick handler sets the global variable, thisBook, to the newly created object. When the Print the Object button detects the click event, its handler text calls the printObject function with thisBook as an argument. The printObject function loops through each of the properties in the object argument and prints each in a menu list to the browser. Figure 11-2 depicts the resulting printout.

Comments

This chapter introduced several object-oriented concepts. Care should be taken to implement these concepts in your programming. Objects are independent of each other and are thus easily reused and modified. Objects make your code more readable and closely model the real world. The overall benefit of creating objects with JavaScript is more maintainable code. In the rapidly changing environment of the Web, you must design your Web pages with maintainability in mind, otherwise you will spend more time maintaining your pages than creating them.

COMPLEXITY
INTERMEDIATE

11.2 How do I...
Create an instance of an object using the new operator?

COMPATIBILITY:

Problem

I want to create multiple instances of an object class. How is this done without writing a function for each of the objects?

Technique

Object-oriented programming uses classes to define a template for an object. By giving values to the properties of a class, you instantiate the class as an object. Until now, you have created functions to define objects, and then set the properties of the object through the function's parameters. Each new object required you to define a new function. What if you wanted to create two objects with the same structure? JavaScript provides a way for you to create copies of objects and instantiate them through the new operator. Reusability is an important part of object-oriented programming and provides an effective method for replicating data structures and procedures.

The New Operator

The *new* operator creates a replica of an object. The parameters to the function instantiate the object. JavaScript provides some predefined objects such as the Date object. The new operator allows you to create a new instance of the Date object. By initializing a variable with the New object, you now have a brand new copy of the object. The notation for using new to create a new Date object is as follows:

```
var todaysDate = new Date();
```

The variable todaysDate now contains a replica of the Date object. You can now access or modify its attributes and methods using the variable name. For instance, suppose you want to get a string containing your locale's current date and time. As discussed in How-To 6.7, you can use the *toLocaleString* method of the Date object to retrieve the date and time string from the object. The following shows the notation for accessing the newly created object's date string:

```
dateString = todaysDate.toLocaleString();
```

Be sure to include the parentheses on the end of the method. Without them, JavaScript will treat the method name as a property.

Extending Objects

After objects have been instantiated with the new operator, you can extend the objects by adding new properties and methods to the object. To extend an object's definition simply add a new property or method to the existing object. The following example adds the property *newProperty* and the method *newMethod*:

```
objectName.newProperty = 'some value';
objectName.newMethod   = newMethodName;
```

To create a new property you must initialize it with a value. Similarly, the method function must be defined before you can add the method to the object. Note that other objects of the same type as *objectName* remain unaffected. JavaScript 2.0 does not provide a way to extend object types after the objects have been instantiated.

> **NOTE**
>
> The prototype property is exclusively a JavaScript 3.0 feature.
> Previous versions of JavaScript do not allow you to extend object
> types.

JavaScript 3.0 provides a way to extend an object's definition after the object has been instantiated. Using an object's *prototype* attribute, you can define new properties that are shared by all of the objects of the specified type. This includes predefined objects in JavaScript such as string and date. To extend the object's class through the prototype property, use the following notation:

```
objectClassName.prototype.propertyName
```

In this example the name of the object type is *objectClassName*, and *propertyName* is the name of the new property which extends the object type.

Steps

In this section you will build a JavaScript application that allows a potential car buyer to surf the literature of an automobile dealer. The program uses the new operator to make instances of objects that contain data on each of the cars offered through the online catalog. The interface for the catalog should contain buttons for selecting each model, and text fields for displaying the car's statistics. Load the program HT1102.HTM from the CD into your Netscape browser. Figure 11-4 shows how the online catalog will look when a user selects one of the buttons.

The information displayed by the catalog changes each time a user selects one of the buttons. Figure 11-5 displays information for a different car selection.

A user may also choose to view an image of the automobile by selecting another button to load the image in a separate window, as shown in Figure 11-6.

1. First create the HTML portion of the program that constructs a form to display sales information for each car model in the automobile catalog. The Web page contains four buttons that are used to select the desired sales information. Add text fields to display the car's type, make, model, color, price, and image. Also add a button to create a separate window to display the picture of the selected car.

```
<HTML>
<HEAD>
<TITLE>Dewey, Cheetam & Howe's Auto Dealership</TITLE>
</HEAD>
<BODY>
<FORM NAME="autoCatalog">
<H1 ALIGN=center>Dewey, Cheetam & Howe's Auto Dealership</H1>
<H3 ALIGN=center>Welcome to our online auto catalog!</h3>
Choose one of the following categories for pricing info:<BR>
```

```
<INPUT TYPE="button" VALUE="Sports/Utility"
       onClick="displayCar(SportsUtility)">
<INPUT TYPE="button" VALUE="Sedan/Luxury"
       onClick="displayCar(SedanLuxury)">
<INPUT TYPE="button" VALUE="Mini-Van"
       onClick="displayCar(MiniVan)">
<INPUT TYPE="button" VALUE="Compact/Economy"
       onClick="displayCar(CompactEconomy)">
<BR><HR><P>

Name:  <INPUT TYPE="text" NAME="carName"   onFocus="this.blur()"><BR>
Model: <INPUT TYPE="text" NAME="carModel"  onFocus="this.blur()"><BR>
Make:  <INPUT TYPE="text" NAME="carMake"   onFocus="this.blur()"><BR>
Color: <INPUT TYPE="text" NAME="carColor"  onFocus="this.blur()"><BR>
Price: <INPUT TYPE="text" NAME="carPrice"  onFocus="this.blur()"><BR>
Image: <INPUT TYPE="text" NAME="carImage"  onFocus="this.blur()">
<INPUT TYPE="button" NAME="displayImage" VALUE="Display Car"
       onClick="displayImage(carImage.value, carName.value)"><BR>

</FORM></BODY>
</HTML>
```

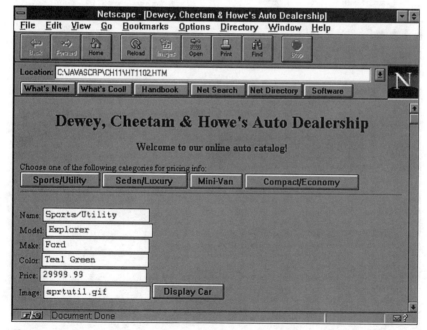

Figure 11-4 JavaScript online automobile catalog

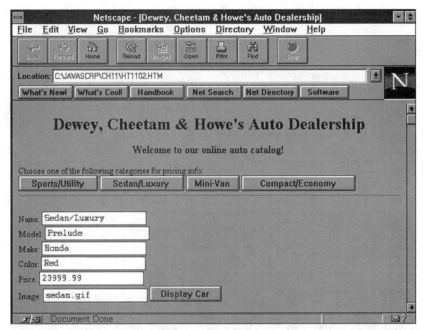

Figure 11-5 Online automobile catalog displaying new information

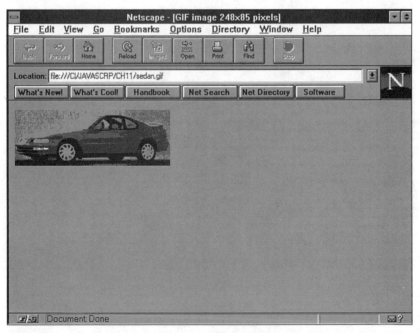

Figure 11-6 Online automobile catalog displaying the car's image

2. Next add the JavaScript portion of the program after the </TITLE> tag. The JavaScript program is contained within the <SCRIPT> tags. Add a function to define the Car object that contains a car's sales information. The Car object has the property's name, model, make, color, price, and image.

```
<SCRIPT LANGUAGE="JavaScript">
<!-- Hide JavaScript from older browsers

/*********************************************************************
*                                                                   *
*    Function      - carObject                                      *
*    Parameters    - name    (Name of the type of car)             *
*                    model   (Model of the car)                    *
*                    make    (Manufacturer of the car)             *
*                    color   (Car's color)                         *
*                    price   (Car's price tag)                     *
*                    image   (Name of file containing car's image) *
*    Description   - This function defines the car object's properties *
*                    and methods.                                  *
*    Called By     - onClick event handler                         *
*                                                                   *
*********************************************************************/
function carObject(name, model, make, color, price, image) {
  this.name  = name;
  this.model = model;
  this.make  = make;
  this.color = color;
  this.price = price;
  this.image = image;
}
```

3. Next add global variables for each of the four car models: sports/utility, sedan/luxury, mini-van, and compact/economy. Use the new operator to initialize each of these variables with instantiated Car objects.

```
//
//   Global variables containing the four car objects.
//
var SportsUtility =
     new carObject('Sports/Utility', 'Explorer', 'Ford',
                   'Teal Green', '29999.99', 'sprtutil.gif');
var SedanLuxury =
     new carObject('Sedan/Luxury', 'Prelude', 'Honda',
                   'Red', '23999.99', 'sedan.gif');
var MiniVan =
     new carObject('MiniVan', 'AeroStar', 'Ford',
                   'Blue', '18999.99', 'minivan.gif');
var CompactEconomy =
     new carObject('Compact/Economy', 'CRX', 'Honda',
                   'White', '12999.99', 'compact.gif');
```

4. Add the function *displayCar* to print a Car object's information to the browser. Set the *value* property of each of the text fields to the corresponding property of the Argument object.

```
/***********************************************************************
*                                                                     *
*    Function    - displayCar                                         *
*    Parameters  - car    (Object containing car's information)       *
*    Description - This function prints the cars information to the   *
*                  browser.                                           *
*    Called By   - onClick event handler                             *
*                                                                     *
***********************************************************************/
function displayCar(car) {
    //
    //  Display each property in the appropriate text field.
    //
    with ( document.autoCatalog ) {
        carName.value  = car.name;
        carModel.value = car.model;
        carMake.value  = car.make;
        carColor.value = car.color;
        carPrice.value = car.price;
        carImage.value = car.image;
    }
}
```

5. Finally add the function displayImage to display the car's image in a separate window. This function uses the Open method of the Window object to create a new browser window, which displays the image.

```
/***********************************************************************
*                                                                     *
*    Function    - displayImage                                       *
*    Parameters  - image    (File name of the image to display)       *
*                  name     (Name of the car to be displayed)         *
*    Description - Function to display the image of the selected car. *
*    Called By   - onClick event handler                             *
*                                                                     *
***********************************************************************/
function displayImage(image, name) {
    //
    //  Open a window with the image.
    //
    window.open(image, name);
}

// end Hide JavaScript -->
</SCRIPT>
```

6. Save the program as HT1102.HTM and load the program into the Netscape browser. Select one of the car types by pressing one of the four buttons. Pressing a button causes the car's information to be displayed in the text fields as shown in Figure 11-4.

7. After choosing a car type, try choosing another car. The information in each of the fields should change as shown in Figure 11-5.

8. Finally, view the image of the car by pressing the button marked Display Car. Figure 11-6 shows the newly created window displaying the image of the car.

How It Works

The new operator creates instances of each of the four car models using only one function to define the Car object class. The carObject function defines the properties associated with the car class. The four global variables *SportsUtility*, *SedanLuxury*, *MiniVan*, and *CompactEconomy* are used to store the four instantiated Car objects. When a user presses one of the buttons, the displayCar function uses the object instance to print the sales information to the text fields on the form. Each of the text fields uses the onFocus event handler to detect when a user attempts to change information in the field. The application prevents the user from changing the information by using the Blur method to remove the focus from the text field.

Comments

The new operator allows you to create new instances of built-in or user-defined objects. After an object has been instantiated, you can extend the object's properties and methods. This allows you to reuse objects without having to create new functions for similar object types. The next How-To demonstrates how to create and include methods within an object, and builds on the auto catalog program.

COMPLEXITY
INTERMEDIATE

11.3 How do I...
Access the properties of an object?

COMPATIBILITY: NAVIGATOR 2.X NAVIGATOR 3.X EXPLORER 3.X

Problem

I want create an object, define its properties, and access them using JavaScript. How do I do this?

Technique

Because objects are created using functions, the data variables within the functions are the equivalent of properties within a class. The act of instantiating an object gives an object values for its properties. Thus proper construction of object classes in JavaScript requires that the function accept the values of the properties as objects. Instantiating a JavaScript object is the equivalent of passing data to the function, which in turn is used by the function to initialize its variables.

Objects and Properties

JavaScript already provides several built-in objects. Many of JavaScript's built-in objects contain properties. Properties of these objects are accessed using the following notation:

```
objectName.propertyName
```

Both the object name and property names are case sensitive. A period separates the object name and property name and denotes that the property belongs to the object. Properties are defined by assigning them a value. For example to assign properties to the object myDog, use the following notation:

```
myDog.name  = "Zeke";
myDog.breed = "German Shepherd";
myDog.age   = 5;
myDog.color = 'brown';
```

Objects as Arrays

Arrays provide a way to store a list of items. Each element of an array contains a single item. Properties and arrays are closely related in JavaScript and are treated the same way. In fact, properties are accessible using the same notation for arrays:

```
myDog["name"]  = "Zeke";
myDog["breed"] = "German Shepherd";
myDog["age"]   = 5;
myDog["color"] = 'brown';
```

This type of array is known as an associative array, because each index element is associated with a string value. Each of the properties of this object may also be accessed using an index number. The objects are assigned index numbers, starting with 0, according to the order they were assigned in the object. Thus for the myDog object, the name property has an index of 0, the breed property has an index of 1, etc. Index numbers for the properties of myDog are as follows:

```
myDog[0] = "Zeke";
myDog[1] = "German Shepherd";
myDog[2] = 5;
myDog[3] = 'brown';
```

The For Statement

JavaScript programs may also access an object's properties using the *for* statement. In the following example, the *for* statement iterates the value of the variable *varName* through each property in the object *objName*. For each property the *for* statement executes the statements enclosed in brackets:

```
for (varName in objName) {
    statements
}
```

This statement can be used to print the names and values of the properties of an object, without having previous knowledge of the names or types of the object's properties.

The following example uses the *for* statement to cycle through each of the object's properties. The function *printProperties* accepts a pointer to the object. This pointer is passed to the function through the *objectPointer* argument, and the string name of the object is passed through the *objectName* argument. The function uses the *for* statement to loop through each property in the objectPointer object. The *for* loop constructs a string containing each of the property names and their values. Upon finishing the loop, the function returns the final string containing all of the objects' properties and their values. The following code shows how to implement this function:

```
function printProperties(objectPointer, objectName) {
    // Printout of the properties of the object
    var resultString = "";
    var index;

    // Loop through each property in the object
    for (index in objectPointer) {
        resultString += objectName + "." + index + " = " +
                        objectPointer[index] + "\n";
    }

    // Return the print out of the object's properties
    return resultString;
}
```

Using the This Pointer in Referencing an Object

The keyword *this* contains a pointer that references the object in which it appears. An object's properties may be created and assigned using *this* as shown:

```
this.newProperty = propValue;
```

When used inside a form, the *this* pointer references the Form object in which it is used. For instance, if a Checkbox object passes a *this* pointer to a function, the pointer to the checkbox is actually passed to the function. The following code prints the checkbox's value to the browser when it is toggled:

```
<INPUT TYPE="checkbox" NAME="checkMe"
    onClick="document.writeln(this.value)">
```

Chapters 8, 9, and 10 provide numerous examples of how to use the *this* pointer to refer to JavaScript's built-in objects, properties, and methods.

Objects and Inheritance

Classes in a hierarchy share features with those below them. Thus a subclass inherits the properties of its superclass. The subclass can also take on new methods and properties that are different from the superclass. Inheritance allows sharing of methods and properties among classes realized by generalization. How-To 11.2 explains in detail how to add methods and properties to objects after they have been created.

Steps

Using the Dog object example explained previously in this How-To, you will construct a form to implement a canine tracking system. This example takes information about a particular dog and stores the data as properties in an object. The object contains such properties as name, breed, and age. When a user submits the form, the object's properties are displayed to the browser. This gives the user a record of what information was entered, and demonstrates how to change and retrieve properties in an object. The object's properties are updated whenever data changes in the property's corresponding text field. Load the program HT1103.HTM from the CD into the Navigator browser. Figure 11-7 depicts the interface upon loading the program.

After filling out the form and submitting the information, the properties of the object are printed to the browser. Figure 11-8 shows information entered through the Canine Tracking System form for a dog named Friday. Each of the object's properties are displayed to the browser.

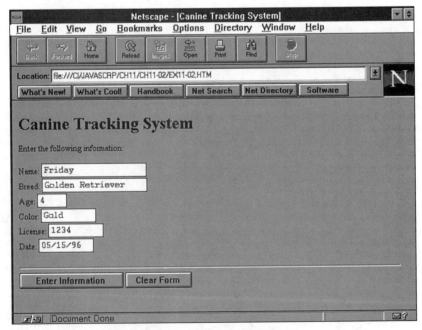

Figure 11-7 Canine Tracking System interface

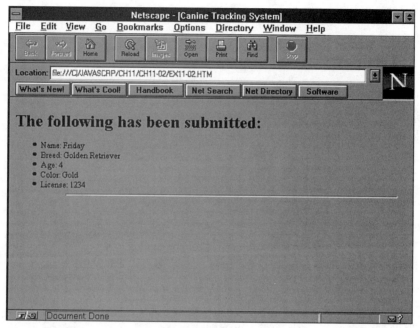

Figure 11-8 The Dog object's properties

1. Create the HTML portion of the program in a text editor. Set the onLoad event handler for the <BODY> tag to call the initDog function, which initializes the object and form information. Create text fields in the form that correspond to each of the properties of the object: name, breed, age, color, license, and date. Set the *onChange* parameter of each of these text fields to update the corresponding property of the thisDog object. The code supplied to the onChange parameter uses the Value property of the this pointer for the text field to extract the user input.

```
<HTML>
<HEAD><TITLE>Canine Tracking System</TITLE></HEAD>

<BODY onLoad="initDog()">
<FORM NAME="canineTracker">

<H1>Canine Tracking System</H1>

Enter the following information:
<P>
Name:
<INPUT TYPE="text" NAME="dogsName" SIZE=30
       onChange="thisDog.name = this.value" ><BR>
Breed:
<INPUT TYPE="text" NAME="dogsBreed" SIZE=30
       onChange="thisDog.breed = this.value" ><BR>
Age:
```

continued on next page

continued from previous page

```
<INPUT TYPE="text" NAME="dogsAge" SIZE=5
       onChange="thisDog.age = this.value" ><BR>
Color:
<INPUT TYPE="text" NAME="dogsColor" SIZE=20
       onChange="thisDog.color = this.value" ><BR>
License:
<INPUT TYPE="text" NAME="dogsLicense" SIZE=20
       onChange="thisDog.license = this.value" ><BR>
Date:
<INPUT TYPE="text" NAME="dogsDate" SIZE=20
       onChange="thisDog.date = this.value" ><BR>
<P>
<HR>
<INPUT TYPE="submit" VALUE="Enter Information"
       onClick="printDogInfo(thisDog)">
<INPUT TYPE="reset" VALUE="Clear Form">

</FORM></BODY>
</HTML>
```

2. Next create the JavaScript portion of the program by adding the <SCRIPT> tag after the </TITLE> tag. Add the global variable *thisDog* to hold the Dog object, and add the function newDog to define the newDog object.

```
<SCRIPT LANGUAGE="JavaScript">
<!-- Hide JavaScript from older browsers

//
//  Global variable containing the dog object.
//
var thisDog;

/*****************************************************************
*                                                               *
*    Function      - newDog                                     *
*    Parameters    - name      (Name of the Dog)                *
*                    breed     (Dog's breed type)               *
*                    age       (Integer of the dog's age in years) *
*                    color     (Dog's primary color)            *
*                    license   (License Number of the dog's tags) *
*                    date      (Date of the license)            *
*    Description   - This object contains the form's information on a *
*                    particular dog                             *
*    Called By     - initDog function                           *
*                                                               *
*****************************************************************/
function newDog(name, breed, age, color, license, date) {

    //
    //  Add properties to the object.
    //
    this.name    = name;
    this.breed   = breed;
    this.age     = age;
    this.color   = color;
    this.license = license;
    this.date    = date;
}
```

3. Create the function printDogInfo to print the properties of the object passed as its argument. This function expects the object to be of the newDog type, and prints the property names and values to the browser.

```
/**********************************************************************
*                                                                    *
*    Function    - printDogInfo                                      *
*    Parameters  - objectName                                        *
*    Description - This function prints the dog's information to the  *
*                  browser.                                          *
*    Called By   - onClick event handler                            *
*                                                                    *
**********************************************************************/
function printDogInfo(objectName) {
    document.clear();
    document.writeln("<H1>The following has been submitted:</H1><P><MENU>");
    document.writeln("<LI> Name: " + objectName.name);
    document.writeln("<LI> Breed: " + objectName.breed);
    document.writeln("<LI> Age: " + objectName.age);
    document.writeln("<LI> Color: " + objectName.color);
    document.writeln("<LI> License: " + objectName.license);
    document.writeln("<MENU><HR>");
}
```

4. Finally add the initDog function, which initializes the *thisDog* global variable. The *thisDog* variable will contain default values of none for each property of the newDog object.

```
/**********************************************************************
*                                                                    *
*    Function    - initDog                                           *
*    Parameters  - None                                              *
*    Description - This function initializes the newDog object.      *
*    Called By   - onLoad event handler                             *
*                                                                    *
**********************************************************************/
function initDog() {
  //
  //   Get Today's Date
  //
  var todaysDate = new Date();

  //   Set up the newDog object.
 thisDog = new newDog('none', 'none', 'none', 'none', 'none',
todaysDate.toLocaleString());

  //
  //   Print the date string to the form.
  //
  document.canineTracker.dogsDate.value = thisDog.date;
}

// end Hide JavaScript -->
</SCRIPT>
```

5. Save the program as HT1103.HTM and load it into the Navigator browser. Figure 11-7 depicts the interface for the Canine Tracking System.

6. Fill out the information fields in the form. In this instance, the form is submitted with information for a golden retriever named Friday. Submit the form information by pressing the Enter Information button. Figure 11-8 illustrates the information printed to the browser by the application.

How It Works

The newDog function defines the object type or class used by the Canine Tracking System. Upon loading, the onLoad event handler calls the initDog function. This function instantiates the thisDog object with default values for properties of the newDog class. The built-in Date object is used to store the current date, and is added as a property of the thisDog object. When a user moves the cursor between fields, the thisDog object is called to store the form's current information. When the Enter Information button is pressed, the onClick event handler for the button calls the printDogInfo function with the thisDog object as an argument. This function first clears the current document from the browser, and then prints the properties of the object.

Comments

If the user does not provide information for one or more text fields the corresponding property will be printed out as none. The initObject function creates an instance of the newDog object with values of none for all of the object's properties except the date. The thisDog global variable contains the newly created object and is updated whenever form information is changed by the user. If the user does not enter data in a text field the corresponding property's value remains none.

Objects are excellent ways to store data entered through a form. An improvement to this example would be to include a method within the object to print its properties. Also, there may be other objects associated, such as the owner of the dog. This object could contain the dog object as a property. How-To 11.4 shows how to define an object as the property of another object.

COMPLEXITY

INTERMEDIATE

11.4 How do I...
Define an object as a property of another object?

COMPATIBILITY: NAVIGATOR 2.X NAVIGATOR 3.X EXPLORER 3.X

Problem

I want to create an object and then include it in another object as a property. I also want to be able to reference the properties of either object. How is this accomplished?

Technique

Previously you learned how to define objects through the style function method, and how to access their properties. This How-To builds on that knowledge by defining an object as the property of another object. Including objects within other objects is an integral part of the object-oriented paradigm. Most real-world objects include other objects. For instance, a car object contains several objects, such as a body, an engine, and four wheels. Each of these objects could contain other objects. A car engine contains pistons, valves, and other parts. Whenever you model a real-world system, you must include one or more objects within another object. This type of structure is called an *object hierarchy*. Object hierarchies define how objects interact with one another, and provide the basis for an object model of a system. JavaScript allows the creation of object hierarchies by allowing you to define an object as the property of another object.

To create an object that includes another object as its property, you perform the same steps as assigning a property to an object. For the purposes of this discussion, the object that contains another object is the parent. The object contained within an object is the child. In the Parent object, add a property and set its value to the name of the Child object. The following shows the function definition for the Parent object. The first function, Wheel, defines the Wheel object with the properties of Rim, Tire, and Pressure. The statement following the wheel function instantiates the Wheel object with the values Alloy, All Weather, and 28.

```
function parentObject(prop1, prop2, object) {
   this.prop1 = prop1;
   this.prop2 = prop2;

   // Add the object as you would a normal property.
   this.childObject = object;
}
```

The instantiation of the Parent object requires that the Child object already be instantiated. The following section of code creates a Wheel object and instantiates the Wheel object.

```
function wheel(rim, size, pressure) {
   this.rim      = rim;
   this.tread    = tread;
   this.pressure = pressure;   // Pressure in PSI
}

// Instantiate the wheel object.
newTire = new wheel("Alloy", "All Weather", 28);
```

The next section of code creates a Car object and includes the Wheel object as a property of the Car object. The car function defines the Car object with the properties wheels, doors, and wheelObject. The statement after the function instantiates the Car object with the Wheel object as the *newTire* property.

```
function car(wheels, doors, wheelobject) {
   this.wheels      = wheels;
   this.doors       = doors;
   this.wheelObject = wheelObject;
}

// Instantiate the car object.
newCar = new car(4, 2, newTire);
```

The Child object may be a predefined object, such as Date or String, as well as a user-defined object. Properties of the Child object are still accessible through the Parent object. Use the following notation to access the Child object's properties:

```
parentObject.childObject.childProperty
```

Similar notation may be used to access the Child object's methods. You can also define new properties for the Child object using the same notation. For instance, to add an additional property, age, use the statement

```
parentObject.childObject.age = 21;
```

This statement creates a new property, *age*, for the *childObject*.

Navigator Object Hierarchy

The Netscape browser itself demonstrates the concept of including objects as properties of other objects. Each of the objects in Navigator forms a hierarchy, which represents the structure of the browser. The Navigator and Window objects are the top objects in the hierarchy and contain other objects such as documents. These objects in turn contain still more objects. Thus the Navigator itself follows the object-oriented paradigm. Navigator objects are, in fact, instances, because they have predefined properties and methods. Thus the Navigator's structure could be called an instance hierarchy because all of the objects in the hierarchy have been instantiated. For example, a Document object may contain the Form object as a property. However, the Form object may also contain other objects such as text fields or Radio buttons.

Steps

The following program improves the Canine Tracking System to add owner information to the system. The application stores the data on the owner of a dog in an object, and information on the dog in a separate object. The Canine Tracking System defines the Dog object as a property of the Owner object. Try loading the HT1104.HTM program from the CD into the Netscape browser. Figure 11-9 shows the new version of the Canine Tracking System's interface.

When a user adds information to the form, the program uses the Owner object to reference properties of the Dog object. Figure 11-10 displays the resulting printout of both the Owner and Dog objects when a user submits the form.

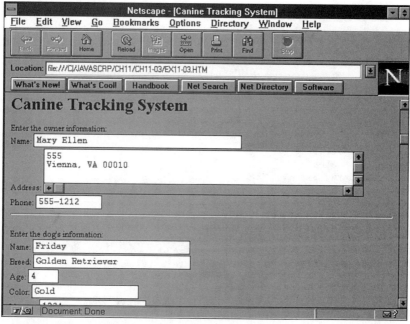

Figure 11-9 Improved Canine Tracking System

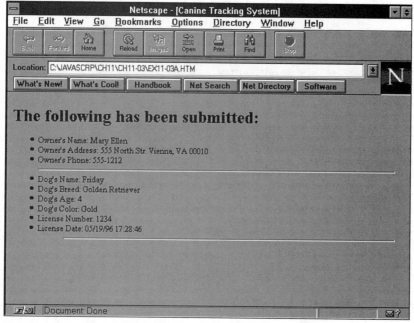

Figure 11-10 Properties of the Owner and Dog objects

1. First create the HTML portion of the program in a text editor. This form differs from the one constructed in How-To 11.3 as it includes fields for the owner. As with text fields for the dog information, use the onChange event handler to update properties in the Owner and Dog objects. The fields for the dog information use the Owner object as the reference point for changing the Dog object properties.

```html
<HTML><HEAD>
<TITLE>Canine Tracking System</TITLE></HEAD>

<BODY onLoad="initInfo()">
<FORM NAME="canineTracker">
<H1>Canine Tracking System</H2>

Enter the owner information:<BR>
Name: <INPUT TYPE="text" NAME="ownerName" SIZE=40
            onChange="thisOwner.name = this.value"><BR>
Address:
<TEXTAREA NAME="ownerAddress" ROWS=3 COLS=60
          onChange="thisOwner.address = this.value">
</TEXTAREA><BR>
Phone: <INPUT TYPE="text" NAME="ownerPhone" SIZE=12
            onChange="thisOwner.phone = this.value"><BR>

<HR>
<P>
Enter the dog's information:<BR>
Name:
<INPUT TYPE="text" NAME="dogsName" SIZE=30
        onChange="thisOwner.dog.name = this.value" ><BR>
Breed:
<INPUT TYPE="text" NAME="dogsBreed" SIZE=30
        onChange="thisOwner.dog.breed = this.value" ><BR>
Age:
<INPUT TYPE="text" NAME="dogsAge" SIZE=5
        onChange="thisOwner.dog.age = this.value" ><BR>
Color:
<INPUT TYPE="text" NAME="dogsColor" SIZE=20
        onChange="thisOwner.dog.color = this.value" ><BR>
License:
<INPUT TYPE="text" NAME="dogsLicense" SIZE=20
        onChange="thisOwner.dog.license = this.value" ><BR>
Date:
<INPUT TYPE="text" NAME="dogsDate" SIZE=20
        onChange="thisOwner.dog.date = this.value" ><BR>

<P>
<HR>
<INPUT TYPE="submit" VALUE="Enter Information"
        onClick="printInfo(thisOwner)">
<INPUT TYPE="reset" VALUE="Clear Form">

</FORM></BODY>
</HTML>
```

2. Next, create the JavaScript portion of the program. You must add a function to define the Owner object. When you create the Owner object, define the Dog object as a property of the Owner object. A single global variable, *thisOwner*, holds information on the owner and its properties and member objects.

```
<SCRIPT LANGUAGE="JavaScript">
<!-- Hide JavaScript from older browsers

//
//   Global variable containing the owner object.
//
var thisOwner;

/*********************************************************************
*                                                                   *
*   Function     - newOwner                                         *
*   Parameters   - name      (Name of the dog's owner)              *
*                  address (Owner's address)                        *
*                  phone   (Owner's phone number)                   *
*                  dog     (Pointer to the dog object)              *
*   Description - This object contains the form's information on the *
*                 dog's owner.                                      *
*   Called By   - initDog function                                 *
*                                                                   *
*********************************************************************/
function newOwner(name, address, phone, dog) {
   this.name    = name;
   this.address = address;
   this.phone   = phone;

   // Property containing the dog object.
   this.dog     = dog;
}
```

3. Now create a function to define the Dog object with the properties of Name, Breed, Age, Color, License, and Date. This object is exactly the same as the one in How-To 11.3, and contains pertinent information about the dog.

```
/*********************************************************************
*                                                                   *
*   Function     - newDog                                           *
*   Parameters   - name      (Name of the Dog)                      *
*                  breed   (Dog's breed type)                       *
*                  age     (Integer of the dog's age in years)      *
*                  color   (Dog's primary color)                    *
*                  license (License Number of the dog's tags)       *
*                  date    (Date of the license)                    *
*   Description - This object contains the form's information on a  *
*                 particular dog                                    *
*   Called By   - initInfo function                                *
*                                                                   *
*********************************************************************/
```

```
function newDog(name, breed, age, color, license, date) {

    //
    //   Add properties to the object.
    //
    this.name    = name;
    this.breed   = breed;
    this.age     = age;
    this.color   = color;
    this.license = license;
    this.date    = date;
}
```

4. Create the function printInfo to print the Owner and Dog object properties
to the browser. This function capitalizes on the fact that the Dog object is a
property of the Owner object and thus requires only the Owner object as an
argument. Use the Clear and Writeln methods of the Document object to
print the information to the browser.

```
/**********************************************************************
*                                                                    *
*    Function     - printInfo                                        *
*    Parameters   - None                                             *
*    Description  - This function prints the dog's and owner's        *
*                   information to the browser.                       *
*    Called By    - onClick event handler                            *
*                                                                    *
**********************************************************************/
function printInfo(owner) {
    document.clear();
    document.writeln("<H1>The following has been submitted:</H1><P><MENU>");
    document.writeln("<LI> Owner's Name: " + owner.name);
    document.writeln("<LI> Owner's Address: " + owner.address);
    document.writeln("<LI> Owner's Phone: " + owner.phone);
    document.writeln("<HR>");
    document.writeln("<LI> Dog's Name: " + owner.dog.name);
    document.writeln("<LI> Dog's Breed: " + owner.dog.breed);
    document.writeln("<LI> Dog's Age: " + owner.dog.age);
    document.writeln("<LI> Dog's Color: " + owner.dog.color);
    document.writeln("<LI> License Number: " + owner.dog.license);
    document.writeln("<LI> License Date: " + owner.dog.date);
    document.writeln("<MENU><HR>");
}
```

5. Finally, add a function to instantiate the Dog and Owner objects and initialize the value of the thisOwner global variable. The *initInfo* function sets the
properties of both the Dog and Owner objects to none, and includes the
Dog object as a property of the Owner object.

```
/**********************************************************************
*                                                                    *
*    Function     - initInfo                                         *
*    Parameters   - None                                             *
*    Description  - Instantiate the Dog and Owner objects.            *
*    Called By    - onLoad event handler                             *
*                                                                    *
**********************************************************************/
```

```
function initInfo() {
  //  Get Today's Date
  var todaysDate = new Date();

  //  Instantiate the Dog object.
  var thisDog = new newDog('none', 'none', 'none', 'none', 'none',
                           todaysDate.toLocaleString());

  //  Instantiate the Owner object.
  thisOwner = new newOwner('none', 'none', 'none', thisDog);

  //  Print the date string to the form.
  document.canineTracker.dogsDate.value = thisOwner.dog.date;
}

// end Hide JavaScript -->
</SCRIPT>
```

6. Save the program as HT1104.HTM and load the program into the browser. Try typing information into fields on the form. Figure 11-9 shows how the form should appear.

7. Submit the form by pressing the button marked Enter Information. This action prints the information to the browser as shown in Figure 11-10.

How It Works

When a user enters text in any of the text fields, the onChange event handler for that field updates the corresponding attribute of the Dog or Owner objects. The application uses the *this* pointer to retrieve input from the text field. Because the Dog object is a property of the Owner object, the dog attributes are accessed using the notation:

```
ownerObject.dogObject.propertyName
```

When a user submits the form, the onClick event handler for the submit button calls the *printInfo* function to display the Dog and Owner object properties to the browser. The printInfo function accepts the Owner object as an argument and prints all of the properties of the Owner and Dog objects. The preceding notation is used to retrieve the properties of the Dog object.

Comments

By including the Dog object as a property of the Owner object, the application reduces the number of arguments needed to pass information to a function. In the next How-To you will learn how to incorporate methods into objects, which further increase the capabilities of objects.

Object hierarchies allow you to model real-world systems by incorporating objects within objects. When designing a JavaScript program, or when using an object-oriented programming language, you should first map out your objects and organize them into hierarchies. This helps define your objects and helps you decide where methods and objects may be reused. Forms are excellent examples of object hierarchies, because they contain multiple elements. A good object model allows independence between objects, yet forms a cohesive structure that performs its intended function. Learning sound object-oriented techniques will help you to create reusable JavaScript applications. JavaScript will soon allow you to create JavaScript libraries that may be referenced by any HTML document. Creating effective reusable components allows you to reuse objects between applications. By taking advantage of objects, you can save yourself time and money when developing JavaScript applications.

COMPLEXITY
INTERMEDIATE

11.5 How do I...
Add a method to an object type?

COMPATIBILITY:

Problem

I wish to add methods to an object, and access the methods from another object. How is this accomplished using JavaScript?

Technique

An object encapsulates related properties and methods. Methods define an object's behavior, and provide a mechanism to pass information between objects. You can think of a method as a function or procedure contained within an object, which operates on the object's data. As discussed in How-To 11.1, objects can contain similar methods. This How-To will show how to define a method and incorporate it as part of an object. JavaScript allows methods to be reused among objects. Thus a method used to print an object may be added to another object without having to duplicate code.

The Function Statement

Functions provide the building blocks for creating objects and methods in JavaScript. The function statement encapsulates a set of data and statements that perform a specific task. A function may be called anywhere in your application, by any other object or function.

A function definition consists of the following parts:

- The *function* keyword

- The name of the function

- A list of arguments to the function

- A list of statements to be performed by the function

Names for a function must begin with a letter and cannot match any of the reserved words. Arguments must also conform to the same naming convention. In addition, values passed through the arguments of a function are not limited to numbers and strings. How-To 11.3 demonstrated how to pass whole objects in a function's parameter list.

You can also have a function call another function. JavaScript provides a number of built-in functions, such as *eval*, for use in statements of user-defined functions. Functions may also perform recursion. In other words, a function may make a call to itself in its statement list. This function uses recursion to compute a factorial:

```
function factorial(number) {
    if (number <= 1)
        return 1;
    else
        return (number * factorial(number - 1));
}
```

The above function subtracts one from the argument and passes the result to itself. The return from the function is the argument times the call to itself. This function keeps calling itself until the argument is less than or equal to one.

When designing a recursive function keep in mind two simple guidelines: there must be an ending point to the recursion, and the recursion should make the problem simpler. While recursive functions add powerful capabilities to your document, care must be taken in their construction. An out-of-control recursive function could potentially lock the browser.

Functions as Methods

Methods are functions encapsulated by an object. You can define methods in JavaScript exactly the same way you would define a function. To add the method to an object, use the following syntax:

```
objectName.methodName = functionName;
```

In this example *objectName* is the name of the object, and the object must already exist in the application. Use *methodName* to assign the name of the object's method. The object's method name need not be the same as the name of the function. To call an object's method, use the following notation:

```
objectName.methodName(parameters);
```

When a function accesses its object's properties, it may use the *this* pointer to reference an object's properties or methods. For example, if you have the following object,

```
function car(wheels, doors, seats) {
    this.wheels = wheels;
    this.doors  = doors;
    this.seats  = seats;
}
```

you can write a method for this object that prints the number of wheels. Notice that the following function uses the *this* pointer to access the object's wheel property.

```
function printWheels() {
    document.writeln("The car has " + this.wheels + " wheels.");
}
```

To add the method to the object, you can either redefine the object,

```
function car(wheels, doors, seats) {
    this.wheels = wheels;
    this.doors  = doors;
    this.seats  = seats;
    this.printWheels = printWheels;
}
```

or you can add or extend the object after it has been instantiated:

```
mycar = new car(4, 2, 4);
mycar.printWheels = printWheels;
```

By adding the method to an object instance, you only give the method to that object. Defining an object class with a method insures that all other objects instantiated with that class contain the method. In How-To 11.2 you learned how to change the object type after its objects have been instantiated with the *prototype* keyword. This also applies to adding methods to an object. To extend all objects instantiated from the car class, use the following notation:

```
car.prototype.printWheels = printWheels
```

This statement will add the *printWheels* method to all objects instantiated with the Car object.

Steps

In this example you will create an improved version of the online automobile catalog. The improvement derives from incorporating the displayCar and displayImage functions as methods to the car object. Load the HT1105.HTM file from the CD into the Netscape browser. Figure 11-11 shows the interface for the online catalog.

When a user presses one of the buttons, the application displays information in the text fields, similar to the example program in How-To 11.2. This application differs by using a method of the Car object to print its data to the Web page. When a user attempts to display the car's image, the application uses a different method in the Car object to display the car's picture. Figure 11-12 illustrates the auto catalog displaying a car's image in a separate window.

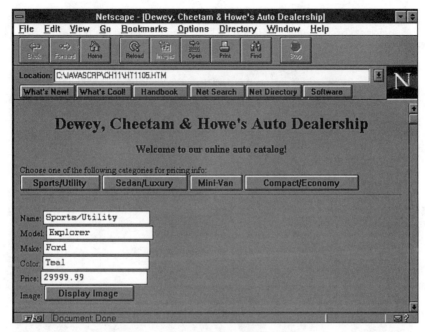

Figure 11-11 Improved auto catalog application

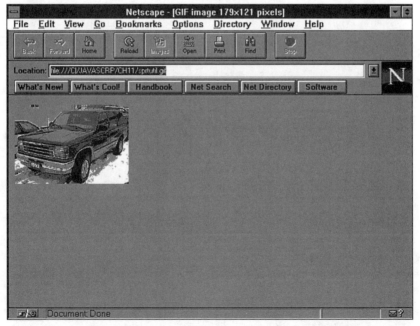

Figure 11-12 Improved auto catalog application displaying an image

1. Create the HTML portion of the program in a text editor. Add the same text fields as those created in How-To 11.2. The one important difference here is that the calls for displaying the car's information or image use methods are added to the Car object. For instance, to display the information on the sports/utility vehicle, use the notation, "SportsUtility.displayCar()". These methods are created in later steps. Link the calls for displaying information to onClick event handlers of the four buttons at the top of the form.

```
<TITLE>Dewey, Cheetam & Howe's Auto Dealership</TITLE></HEAD>
<BODY>
<FORM NAME="autoCatalog">
<H1 ALIGN=center>Dewey, Cheetam & Howe's Auto Dealership</H1>
<H3 ALIGN=center>Welcome to our online auto catalog!</H3>
Choose one of the following categories for pricing info:<BR>
<INPUT TYPE="button" VALUE="Sports/Utility"
        onClick="SportsUtility.displayCar()">
<INPUT TYPE="button" VALUE="Sedan/Luxury"
        onClick="SedanLuxury.displayCar()">
<INPUT TYPE="button" VALUE="Mini-Van"
        onClick="MiniVan.displayCar()">
<INPUT TYPE="button" VALUE="Compact/Economy"
        onClick="CompactEconomy.displayCar()">
<BR><HR><P>

Name:  <INPUT TYPE="text" NAME="carName"  onFocus="this.blur()"><BR>
Model: <INPUT TYPE="text" NAME="carModel" onFocus="this.blur()"><BR>
Make:  <INPUT TYPE="text" NAME="carMake"  onFocus="this.blur()"><BR>
Color: <INPUT TYPE="text" NAME="carColor" onFocus="this.blur()"><BR>
Price: <INPUT TYPE="text" NAME="carPrice" onFocus="this.blur()"><BR>
Image:
<INPUT TYPE="button" NAME="displayImage" VALUE="Display Image"
        onClick="car.displayImage()"><BR>

</FORM></BODY>
</HTML>
```

2. Now add the JavaScript function inside the <SCRIPT> tags after the </TITLE> tag. Define the Car object to contain the properties name, model, make, color, price, and image. In addition to these properties, include two methods, *displayCar* and *displayImage*, for displaying the car's information and opening a window with its image. The displayCar and displayImage functions are defined in Steps 4 and 5.

```
<HTML><HEAD>
<SCRIPT LANGUAGE="JavaScript">
<!-- Hide JavaScript from older browsers

/*********************************************************************
*                                                                   *
*   Function    - carObject                                         *
*   Parameters  - name    (Name of the type of car)                *
*                 model   (Model of the car)                        *
*                 make    (Manufacturer of the car)                *
```

```
*               color   (Car's color)                        *
*   price   (Car's price tag)                                *
*                   image   (Name of file containing car's image)  *
*   Description - This function defines the car object's properties  *
*                   and methods.                             *
*   Called By    - onClick event handler                     *
*                                                            *
**********************************************************************/
function carObject(name, model, make, color, price, image) {

    //
    // Add properties to the car object.
    //
    this.name  = name;
    this.model = model;
    this.make  = make;
    this.color = color;
    this.price = price;
    this.image = image;

    //
    //  Add the displayCar and displayImage methods.
    //
    this.displayCar = displayCar;
    this.displayImage = displayImage;
}
```

3. Next add global variables for each of the four car models: sports/utility, sedan/luxury, mini-van, and compact/economy. Use the new operator to initialize each of these variables with instantiated Car objects. Add the global variable car to point to the current Car object to be displayed by the browser. This variable is used to call the displayCar and displayImage methods of the object.

```
//
//  Global variables containing the four car objects.
//
var SportsUtility =
     new carObject('Sports/Utility', 'Explorer', 'Ford',
                    'Teal Green', '29999.99', 'sprtutil.gif');
var SedanLuxury =
     new carObject('Sedan/Luxury', 'Prelude', 'Honda',
                    'Red', '23999.99', 'sedan.gif');
var MiniVan =
     new carObject('MiniVan', 'AeroStar', 'Ford',
                    'Blue', '18999.99', 'minivan.gif');
var CompactEconomy =
     new carObject('Compact/Economy', 'CRX', 'Honda',
                    'White', '12999.99', 'compact.gif');

//
// Global to contain the current car object.
//
var car;
```

4. Add the function displayCar to print a Car object's information to the browser. Set the Value property of each of the text fields to the corresponding property of the argument object. Add a statement to update the global variable *car*, which contains the current Car object displayed by the browser.

```
/**********************************************************************
*                                                                    *
*    Function    - displayCar                                        *
*    Parameters  - None                                              *
*    Description - This function prints the car's information to the  *
*                  browser.                                          *
*    Called By   - onClick event handler                             *
*                                                                    *
**********************************************************************/
function displayCar() {
    //
    //   Display each property in the appropriate text field.
    //
    with ( document.autoCatalog ) {
        carName.value  = this.name;
        carModel.value = this.model;
        carMake.value  = this.make;
        carColor.value = this.color;
        carPrice.value = this.price;
        carImage.value = this.image;
    }


    //
    //   Set the global variable "car" to the current object.
    //
    car = this;
}
```

5. Finally, add the function displayImage to display the car's image in a separate window. This function uses the *this* pointer to display the image in a new window, and thus may be used as a method for the Car object.

```
/**********************************************************************
*                                                                    *
*    Function    - displayImage                                      *
*    Parameters  - None                                              *
*    Description - Function to display the image of the selected car. *
*    Called By   - method of carObject object                        *
*                                                                    *
**********************************************************************/
function displayImage() {
    //
    //   Open a window with the image.
    //
    window.open(this.image, this.name);
}

// end Hide JavaScript -->
</SCRIPT>
```

6. Save the program as HT1105.HTM and load it into the Netscape browser. When the Sports/Utility button is pressed, you should see the interface shown in Figure 11-11. Try to change the information in one of the forms fields. The browser should reject any attempts to move the focus to the text field.

7. Select a car type, and then click the button marked Display Image. This button should cause a window to appear with the car image depicted in Figure 11-12.

How It Works

When the user presses a button, the onClick event handler for that button calls its object's displayCar method. The displayCar method performs similarly to the displayCar function found in How-To 11.2, yet its implementation is very different. Instead of requiring the car object as an argument to display its properties on the Web page, the displayCar method uses the this pointer to access properties of the Car object. The same is true for the displayImage method. The method uses the *this* pointer to access the car's image and name properties to create a window displaying the car.

Comments

Objects are collections of related properties and methods. Methods implement the operations for an object. Adding methods to objects allows you to keep the procedures and the data on which they operate in the same package. The auto catalog program provides a good example of adding a method to an object, because the methods added to the Car object relate directly to its data. In fact the displayCar and displayImage methods display the object's data for the user. Objects become more independent, and thus more reusable, when you add methods to allow the object to print itself.

Methods can also change the properties of an object, or call other methods. Defining an object's methods is an important part of object-oriented design. Care should be taken to make sure that an object's method actually relates to the object. Adding methods to an object without any purpose wastes memory when the object is instantiated several times. Also try to keep methods generic so that they may be reused among objects of similar classes.

11.6 How do I...
Create and populate an array of objects?

COMPATIBILITY: NAVIGATOR 2.X   NAVIGATOR 3.X   EXPLORER 3.X

Problem

I want to define an object type, and then create and populate an array with instances of this object. How is this done?

Technique

Arrays are data structures that store and index a list of items. Each element of an array contains a unique item, and the index to an array gives the item's location. In languages such as Java you cannot store items of different types in the same array. Because JavaScript uses loose type-casting for variables, however, it allows an array to hold elements of multiple types.

Creating Arrays

JavaScript 2.0 does not contain an explicit array type. However the close relationship of object properties and arrays makes it easy to create an array. The following demonstrates how to write a section of code that creates and initializes an array of *num* elements:

```
function createArray(num) {
  // set array length
  this.length = num;

  // initialize each element
  for (var index=1 ; index <= num ; index++) {
    this[index] = 0;
  }

  // return the newly created array
  return this;
}
```

The length property in this case determines the size of the array. It's not necessary to include this property, but it is good programming practice.

> **NOTE**
>
> JavaScript 3.0 now includes a built-in object type for defining arrays, called *Array*. This next section applies only to JavaScript version 3.0 and later.

The Array type in JavaScript 3.0 provides a built-in class for creating and instantiating new Array objects. To construct an instance of an array, use the new operator. After you have the array instance, you can assign values to any of its elements. For example, the following statements create an array of ten elements:

```
var arrayInstance = new Array();
arrayInstance[9] = null;
```

By passing a number as the Array object's parameter, you can define the size of the array and its *length* property. The following expression creates the equivalent array by passing the length as an argument to the constructor of the Array object.

```
var arrayInstance = new Array(10);
```

A constructor of an object is a method, which is performed upon the object's instantiation. In the above expression, the constructor for the Array object sets the object's length property to the argument. The previous example for constructing an array implicitly sets the length of the array by defining an element's index. The length of the array is equal to the largest index value plus one.

A third method is available for defining arrays. You can pass multiple values to the array. The Array object's constructor method defines sequential elements for each of the arguments. For instance, if you want to define an array of five elements, use the following notation:

```
var arrayInstance = new Array("one", "two", "three", 4.0, false);
```

The newly created *arrayInstance* object has a length of 5 and the elements; "one", "two", "three", "4", and "false". The Array object's constructor method creates sequential index values for the elements, starting with "0", for the first object, and ending with "4" for the last object. As with arrays defined in JavaScript 2.0, the Array object may store element values of different types.

Populating an Array with Objects

Follow the same notation for assigning objects to arrays. First create the object, then assign an index value to the object. For instance, to assign the Date object to the third element of an array, use the statement

```
someArray[3] = new Date();
```

Objects must be instantiated before you assign them to an array. You can also populate arrays with your own objects. For example, the next set of statements create a Dog object and then populate an array with instances of the object:

```
function dog(name, breed, color) {
    this.name  = name;
    this.breed = breed;
    this.color = color;
}

myDogs = new Array(3);
myDogs[1] = new dog("Friday", "Golden Retriever", "Gold");
myDogs[2] = new dog("Spot", "Dalmation", "Black & White");
myDogs[3] = new dog("Snoopy", "Beagle", "Black & White");
```

The array now contains three Dog objects. To access properties or methods of objects in an array, use the following notation:

```
objectName[index].propertyName
objectName[index].methodName
```

Thus to set the name of the Dog object in the third element of the myDogs array, use the statement

```
myDogs[3].name = "Snoopy";
```

Steps

The following example constructs a database to store information about a customer's order in an array of objects. Load the program, HT1106.HTM from the CD. You should see a Web page similar to the one shown in Figure 11-13.

Once the Web page is loaded, try creating some customer order by typing information into each of the text fields and pressing the Create an Order button. Once you've typed in a few orders, print them out using the Print All Orders button. Figure 11-14 shows the resulting information printed to the browser.

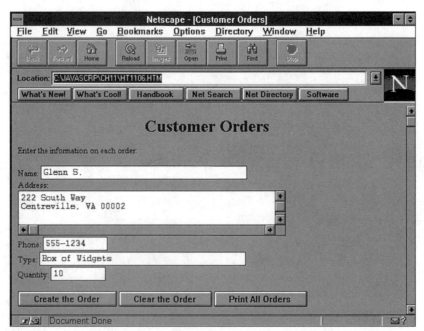

Figure 11-13 Customer order database using an array of objects

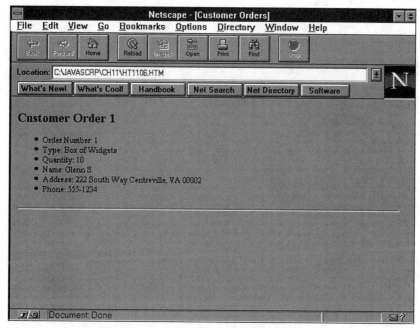

Figure 11-14 Customer order database printout

1. Create the HTML portion of the program in a text editor. This step creates
the form that will take the order information. Add a text field for the name,
phone number, order type, and quantity. Also add a textarea field for the
customer's address information. At the bottom of the form construct three
buttons which, when pressed, store the order in a global array, clear the
form, and print all orders stored in the global array. Use the onClick event
handler for the Create the Order and Print the Order buttons to call the
createOrder and printOrder functions, respectively.

```
<HTML>
<HEAD>
<TITLE>Customer Orders</TITLE></HEAD>
<BODY>
<FORM NAME="orderForm">
<H1 ALIGN=center>Customer Orders</H1>

Enter the information on each order:<P>

Name: <INPUT TYPE="text" NAME="orderName" SIZE=40><BR>
Address:<BR>
<TEXTAREA NAME="orderAddress" ROWS=3 COLS=50>
</TEXTAREA><BR>
Phone: <INPUT TYPE="text" NAME="orderPhone" SIZE=12><BR>
Type: <INPUT TYPE="text" NAME="orderType" SIZE=40><BR>
Quantity: <INPUT TYPE="text" NAME="orderQuantity" SIZE=10><BR>
<P>
```

continued on next page

continued from previous page

```
<INPUT TYPE="button" VALUE="Create the Order" onClick="createOrder()">
<INPUT TYPE="reset" VALUE="Clear the Order">
<INPUT TYPE="button" VALUE="Print All Orders" onClick="printArray()">

</FORM></BODY>
</HTML>
```

2. Next add the JavaScript portion of the program after the </TITLE> tag. You must create a global variable Orders for storing the array, and the orderCount variable for keeping track of the current order count. The global array will be populated with the objects containing the order information.

```
<SCRIPT LANGUAGE="JavaScript">
<!-- Hide JavaScript from older browsers

//
// Global to contain the array of customer orders.
//
var Orders = new MakeArray(10);
var orderCount = 0;
```

3. Create the *MakeArray* function to initialize an array of elements. The size of the array is determined by the argument to the function.

```
/******************************************************************
*                                                                *
*    Function     - MakeArray                                    *
*    Parameters   - elements (Number of elements in the array)   *
*    Description  - This function creates an array of "num" elements. *
*    Called By    - onLoad event handler                         *
*                                                                *
******************************************************************/
function MakeArray(size) {
    this.length = size;
    for (var i=1 ; i <= size ; i++) {
        this[i] = 0;
    }
    return this;
}
```

4. The object is defined by the orderObject function as shown below, and has the properties order, name address, phone, type, and quantity.

```
/******************************************************************
*                                                                *
*    Function     - orderObject                                  *
*    Parameters   - order    (Order tracking number)             *
*                   name     (Customer's name)                   *
*                   address  (Customer's address)                *
*                   phone    (Customer's phone number)           *
*                   type     (Type of product ordered)           *
*                   quantity (Quantity of product ordered)       *
*    Description  - This function defines an order object.       *
*    Called By    - createOrder function                         *
*                                                                *
******************************************************************/
```

```
function orderObject(order, name, address, phone, type, quantity) {

   //
   // Add properties to the order object.
   //
/* Change this line */
   this.order    = order+1;
   this.name     = name;
   this.address  = address;
   this.phone    = phone;
   this.type     = type;
   this.quantity = quantity;

   //
   //  Add the printOrder method.
   //
   this.printOrder = printOrder;
}
```

5. Create a function to be used as a method for the orderObject object. Use the *this* pointer to print the values of the properties of the object. This function does not use a *for* statement to loop through the properties of the orderObject, because printOrder is a method of orderObject. Thus a *for* loop would also attempt to print the printOrder method (which would probably display the code for the method).

```
/*********************************************************************
*                                                                   *
*   Function     - printOrder                                       *
*   Parameters   - None                                             *
*   Description  - This function prints the order object to the     *
*                  browser.                                         *
*   Called By    - onClick event handler                            *
*                                                                   *
*********************************************************************/
//
//   This function prints the order object to the browser.
//
function printOrder() {

   msgWindow.document.writeln("<H2>Customer Order " + this.order +
"</H2>");

   //
   //   Display each property in the object.
   //
   msgWindow.document.writeln("<MENU>");
   msgWindow.document.writeln("<LI>Order Number: " + this.order);
   msgWindow.document.writeln("<LI>Type: " + this.type);
   msgWindow.document.writeln("<LI>Quantity: " + this.quantity);
   msgWindow.document.writeln("<LI>Name: " + this.name);
   msgWindow.document.writeln("<LI>Address: " + this.address);
   msgWindow.document.writeln("<LI>Phone: " + this.phone);
   msgWindow.document.writeln("</MENU><HR>");
}
```

6. Add the createOrder function to make a new orderObject object and add it to the global array. Update the orderCount global variable each time a new object is added. The properties from the new object are instantiated with values from the input form.

```
/*******************************************************************
*                                                                 *
*   Function     - createOrder                                    *
*   Parameters   - None                                           *
*   Description  - Create an order from information contained in the *
*                  order form, and update the Orders array.       *
*   Called By    - onClick event handler                          *
*                                                                 *
*******************************************************************/
function createOrder() {

   var name     = document.orderForm.orderName.value;
   var address  = document.orderForm.orderAddress.value;
   var phone    = document.orderForm.orderPhone.value;
   var type     = document.orderForm.orderType.value;
   var quantity = document.orderForm.orderQuantity.value;

   Orders[orderCount] =
       new orderObject(orderCount, name, address, phone, type, quantity);

/* Moved this line */
   orderCount += 1;
}
```

7. Finally, create the printArray function for looping through the global array and calling the printOrder methods of each of the objects contained within the array. This function is called by the onClick event handler for the Print All Orders button.

```
/*******************************************************************
*                                                                 *
*   Function     - printArray                                     *
*   Parameters   - None                                           *
*   Description  - Print each object in the array using its printOrder *
*                  method.                                        *
*   Called By    - onClick event handler                          *
*                                                                 *
*******************************************************************/
function printArray() {
/* Changed this line */

msgWindow=window.open("","displayWindow","toolbar=no,width=375,height=480,⇐
directories=no,status=no,scrollbars=yes,resize=yes,menubar=no")
   for (var index=0 ; index < orderCount ; index++) {
       top.Orders[index].printOrder();
   }
   msgWindow.document.close()
}

// end Hide JavaScript -->
</SCRIPT>
```

8. Save the program as HT1106.HTM and load the program into the Netscape browser. Try entering information into each of the fields as shown in Figure 11-13. Press the button marked Create the Order and then add another order using the same process.

9. Print the orders by pressing the button marked Print All Orders. You should see all of the orders printed to the browser as shown in Figure 11-14.

How It Works

The createOrder function instantiates an Order object with customer information obtained from the form's text fields. The global variable, Orders, contains the array of customer information objects. When the Print All Orders button is pressed, the onClick event handler for the button calls the printArray function. The printArray function loops through each element in the Orders array and calls the printOrder method of each object in the array. This method prints each of the Order object's properties to the browser using the document object's writeln method.

Comments

The program does not use the built-in Array object, because you may be using older browsers. However, if you have Netscape 3.0 or higher, try modifying the program to define the Orders array using the Array object.

Arrays provide a handy way to store and access information sequentially. Because the JavaScript Object model treats objects as associative arrays, you can use this feature to loop through each property in an object as if it were an element in an array. This provides an excellent mechanism for displaying or modifying all the object's properties.

FRAMES

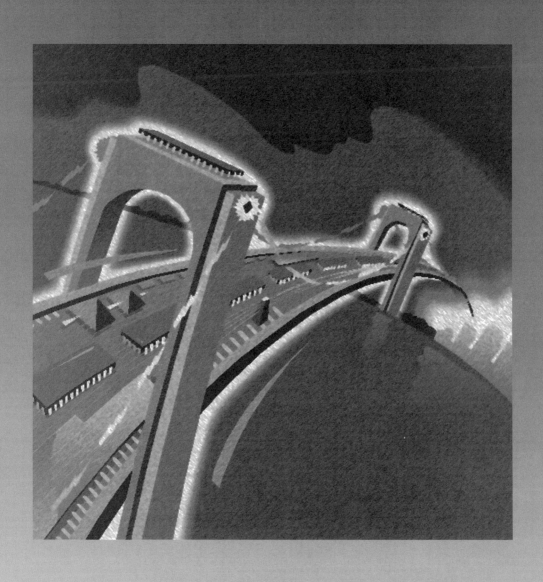

12

FRAMES

How do I...

The concept of frames is a new feature introduced in Navigator 2.0. Traditionally, browsers are restricted to displaying a single HTML document. Through frames, this restriction is removed, allowing the browser to simultaneously display multiple HTML documents. Each frame is assigned a URL, which identifies the document, image, or CGI program associated with the frame. Frames allow Web developers to create persistent pages, such as a title page, toolbar, or an employee list, that will remain visible to the users throughout their interactions with a site.

All frames are members of a frameset. Framesets divide the screen into multiple, scrollable regions. The frameset's attributes determine the initial physical size of each frame. Initial sizes can be represented as percentages, fixed-length, or relative values. Once the frameset is displayed on the screen, the user can adjust a frame's size by moving a frame's edge or by adjusting the browser's window size. Thus, users can tailor the frame composition to meet their real-time needs for viewing information.

12.1 Concurrently display multiple HTML documents using frames

Readers will learn how to use percentage-based frames to concurrently display multiple HTML documents. Percentage-based frames have their initial sizes specified as a percentage of the overall screen area. You will learn how to establish a header and footer document that will be visible throughout the user's interaction with a site.

12.2 Establish an event handler that is triggered by the loading and unloading of documents inside frames

Learn how to set up event handlers that are triggered when a frame document is loaded and unloaded into the browser.

12.3 Specify whether or not scrolling should occur in a frame

This How-To demonstrates how to specify whether or not a frame should be displayed with a scroll bar. Scroll bars are needed when a referenced document exceeds the dimensions, either horizontally or vertically, of the host frame. If no preference is specified, then the decision is left up to the browser.

12.4 Define fixed- and relative-length frames

When frame sizes are specified as a percentage of the overall screen area, window resize events will alter a frame's dimensions. This may affect the user's ability to view all content within a header or footer document. To minimize the effects of window resizing, frame dimensions should be defined in terms of fixed pixel values. This will ensure that the frame is the same size, regardless of the browser's dimensions.

Framesets that contain fixed-size frames require at least one relative-size frame. Relative-size frames absorb any extra area not allocated to the fixed-size frames. This How-To will show you how to create fixed- and relative-size frames.

12.5   Prevent users from resizing a frame

By default, the user has the ability to resize a frame. This How-To will show you how to deny users this ability. This technique is primarily applicable to fixed-length frames which are designed for a specific screen size that should not be modified by the user.

12.6   Change a frame's height and width margins

To minimize the amount of unused real estate on the screen, you may want to override a frame's default height and width margins. This How-To will show you how to explicitly define a frame's height and width margins.

12.7   Set up alternative content that will be viewed in non-frame-capable browsers

Because not all browsers support frames, this How-To will show you how to establish alternative content, in the form of an HTML document, that will be visible within non-frame-friendly browsers.

12.8   Embed a frame within a frame

This How-To will show you how to create embedded framesets, known as subframes. Embedded framesets partition individual frames into multiple regions. Through embedded frames, the screen can be partitioned in an irregular pattern.

12.9   Set up variables accessible by multiple frames

Learn how to define global variables in the parent or frame document that are accessible from documents displayed in child frames. A child frame is any frame that belongs to a particular frameset.

12.10   Access properties belonging to another frame

This How-To will show you how to access information stored inside sibling frames. Sibling frames belong to the same frameset as the current document.

COMPLEXITY
BEGINNING

12.1   How do I...
Concurrently display multiple HTML documents using frames?

COMPATIBILITY:

Question

Many HTML documents contain a title, located at the top of the document, and contact information, which resides at the bottom of the document. When the document's body is longer than the browser's viewing area, the title and contact information may not remain visible to the user. I would like to create separate documents, for the title and contact information, that will be visible throughout the user's interaction with my site. How can I use frames to concurrently display multiple HTML documents?

Technique

Frame creation involves two steps: screen partitioning, which defines a frame's dimensions, and URL assignment, which links a frame with a server object (typically an HTML document). Frames are created inside a new type of document called a frame document. The structure of a frame document is similar to that of a normal HTML document, except that the document <BODY> is replaced by a <FRAMESET>. The proper syntax for a <FRAMESET> container is

```
<FRAMESET
    ROWS="rowHeightList"
    COLS="columnWidthList"
    [onLoad="handlerCode"]
    [onUnload="handlerCode"]>
</FRAMESET>
```

If a frame document contains a <BODY> tag, the browser will ignore the <FRAMESET> tag. The browser considers the document a regular HTML document instead of a frame document. Frame documents and regular HTML documents are mutually exclusive. A document can only operate as one, not both. Each document type contains a unique set of tags. The only valid tags found in a frame document are <HEAD>, <FRAMESET>, <FRAME>, and <NOFRAMES>. If tags common to both types of documents are detected by the browser, the browser assumes the document is a regular HTML document. The <FRAMESET> tag is also ignored if the document contains any extraneous text or labels not associated with frames.

Screen Partitioning

A frameset defines how the screen will be partitioned into individual frames. Framesets contain two attributes, ROWS and COLS, which determine the dimensions of each frame. The ROWS attribute is used to create horizontal partitions, running from left to right across the screen, that divide the viewer's vertical (or Y) axis into multiple pieces. The ROWS attribute will determine the height of each frame. Screen partitions break up the opposite axis, as you can see in Figure 12-1. Therefore, the COLS attribute, which creates vertical partitions running top to bottom on the screen, will break up the viewer's horizontal (or X) axis into multiple parts. This attribute defines the width of each frame. Both attributes accept a quoted string containing a set of comma-delimited size indicators. Size indicators can be in the form of percentages (50%), fixed-length values (20), or relative sizes (2*). Fixed and relative-size indicators are discussed in How-To 12.4. The following code would establish a single horizontal partition that will divide the viewer into two regions.

```
<FRAMESET ROWS="30%,70%">
```

The first region would occupy the upper 30 percent of the screen, while the second region occupies the bottom 70 percent. In this example, frame-size is defined as a

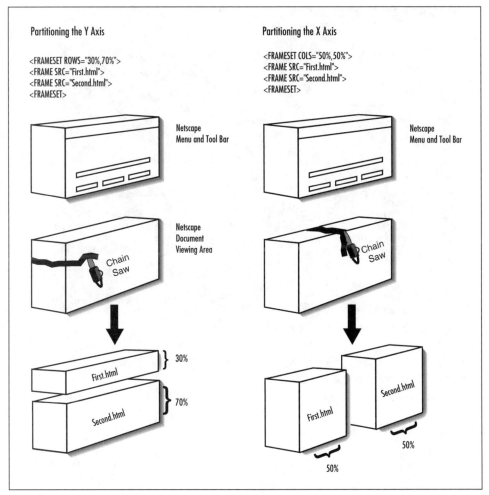

Figure 12-1 Partitioning the document viewing area

percentage of the browser's height. Percentages are logical values whose physical values are determined at runtime by the screen's dimensions. If the browser's window is resized, the physical dimensions of the two regions would change. Figure 12-2 is a visual representation of how the screen is partitioned by the example.

Adjusting Percentages

In the example above, the percentages total 100 percent. Therefore, the browser does not need to adjust the percentages when determining frame sizes. Had the percentages not totaled 100 percent, Navigator would have scaled the percentages to equal 100 percent. The scaling process is based on a frame's proportional size in relation to the

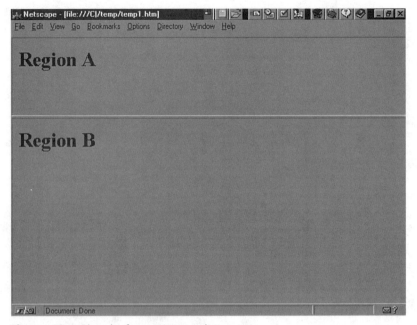

Figure 12-2 Simple frame example

other frames on the screen. In the following example, the percentages total 50 percent. Therefore, Navigator will scale values by doubling each percentage. This will ensure that the entire screen (100%) is covered. Therefore, this <FRAMESET> definition,

```
<FRAMESET ROWS="15%,35%">
```

would be implicitly converted to this <FRAMESET> definition:

```
<FRAMESET ROWS="30%,70%">
```

Computing the Number of Frames

The number of screen regions established by a <FRAMESET> can be computed by multiplying the number of horizontal partitions, established by the ROWS attribute, by the number of vertical partitions, defined by the COLS attribute. If one of the attributes is not defined, then use the multiplier of one to represent the entire screen. Undefined attributes are implied with a single size indicator equal to 100 percent. Because an attribute does not establish any screen partitions, the entire screen axis remains intact. Therefore the <FRAMESET> definition,

```
<FRAMESET ROWS="30%,70%">
```

is really the same as

```
<FRAMESET ROWS="30%,70%" COLS="100%">
```

URL Assignment

Each screen region established by viewer partitioning should have a corresponding <FRAME> tag located inside the <FRAMESET> container. The <FRAME> tag is used to represent a single frame. The format for the <FRAME> tag is

```
<FRAME SRC="location" NAME="name">
```

The SRC attribute is used to assign an HTML document to a frame. The document is represented by its URL, which is assigned as a quoted string to the SRC attribute. In addition to HTML documents, frames can point to other server objects, including executable programs and images. The following example demonstrates how to relate the document "title.htm" to a frame:

```
<FRAME SRC="title.htm">
```

If the SRC attribute is left uninitialized or is set with a malformed URL string, the frame will display a blank space on the screen. Figure 12-3 shows a <FRAMESET> that contains a frame assigned to a nonexistent document.

Nested Frames and Infinite Recursion

A <FRAME> object can be tied to a document that contains an internal <FRAMESET>. This situation is known as a nested frame. The document viewing area has already been partitioned, with a certain region assigned to the nested frame's

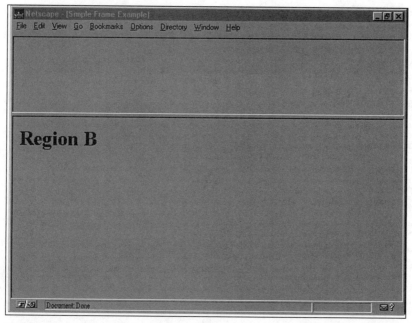

Figure 12-3 A frame assigned to display a nonexistent document

parent. The nested frameset specifies how the parent's region will be carved up. This is similar to the way embedded frames are handled (discussed in How-To 12.8).

If a frame can be used to view a frame document, which contains a <FRAMESET> container, then the possibility arises that the frame could point to its own frame document. This state would give rise to an infinite loop, caused by the recursive nature of the frameset containers. Eventually, the system would run out of memory from repeatedly loading the same document in order to divide the screen into steadily smaller regions. To prevent infinite recursion, the Navigator browser handles problem frames, whose SRC attributes are assigned the URL of an ancestor document, as blank documents. This preventive measure will stop an infinite loop from occurring.

Assigning Frames to Viewer Partitions

The <FRAMESET> tag defines how the screen is partitioned, but it does not explicitly state which frames are assigned to each screen region. Frames are assigned to regions in the order that their <FRAME> label appears in the <FRAMESET> container. The topmost frame will be assigned to the upper left partition. Assignment proceeds sequentially through the list of child frames. The browser assigns regions based on a top-down, left-right algorithm. If there are more regions than frames, those regions left unassigned will appear as blank spaces, as in Figure 12-3. If there are more frames than regions, then those frames at the bottom of the list will remain unassigned. An example of how Navigator assigns regions to frames using the <FRAMESET> specification is shown below:

```
<HTML>
<FRAMESET ROWS="30%,70%" COLS="60%, 40%">
   <!-- Frame 1 -->
   <FRAME SRC="HT0101.htm">
   <!-- Frame 2 -->
   <FRAME SRC="HT0103.htm">
   <!-- Frame 3 -->
   <FRAME SRC="HT0104.htm">
</FRAMESET>
</HTML>
```

The <FRAMESET> in this example establishes four screen regions. Table 12-1 shows how frames are assigned to each region.

REGION	HEIGHT	WIDTH	FRAME
1	30%	60%	Assigned To Frame 1
2	30%	40%	Assigned To Frame 2
3	70%	60%	Assigned To Frame 3
4	70%	40%	Unassigned

Table 12-1 Frame assignment to screen regions

Steps

This example builds a frame-based order form for the Waite Group Press. The page has a persistent header and footer document that is continuously visible to the user. The header document displays the corporate name. The footer document is a menu bar, represented as a client-side image map.

From Navigator 2.0+ or Explorer 3.0+, use the File/Open menu option to load the document HT1201.HTM into memory. The page displayed in Figure 12-4 is displayed on the screen. Once the frame document is loaded, Navigator will make additional requests to the server for individual HTML documents belonging to each frame.

Move your cursor on top of one of the frame edges. Notice that the cursor will change from a pointer to the resize icon when it is on top of the edge. When the cursor is removed from the edge, it reverts to the pointer icon. Once again, move the cursor over the frame edge. When the icon changes, depress the left mouse key and start dragging the edge (make sure the mouse key remains depressed while you are repositioning the edge). You will notice the original edge remains constant, but an edge reposition indicator now tracks your mouse movement. Once you have the location to which the edge should be moved, release the mouse key. The edge is repositioned at the location where the mouse key was released, and the Navigator browser performs some minor adjustments on the documents affected by the change.

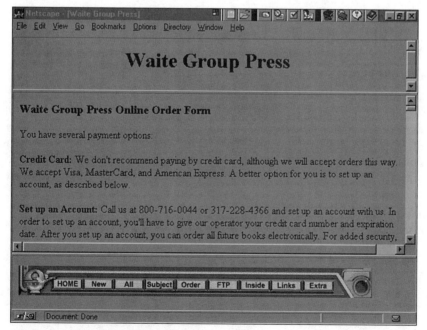

Figure 12-4 The frame document

1. Open your favorite editor and create a new frame document based on the following HTML code.

2. Define a <FRAMESET> container that partitions the document viewing area's vertical axis into three parts. This is accomplished by assigning to the ROWS attribute a quote string with three space indicator values. Viewer partitioning will be defined as a percentage of the overall space assigned to the viewing area's Y axis. The percentages assigned to the frameset's ROWS attribute are 20 percent, 60 percent, and 20 percent.

3. Add three frames to the <FRAMESET> container. Note that the SRC attribute for each frame points to a document on the *JavaScript How-To* CD.

4. Copy the files to your local work area or change the SRC attribute to point to these documents on the CD.

5. Save the frame document under the file name HT1201.HTM.

```
<HTML>
<HEAD>
<TITLE> Waite Group Press </TITLE>
</HEAD>
<FRAMESET ROWS="20%,60%,20%">
    <FRAME SRC="whead.htm">
    <FRAME SRC="worder.htm">
    <FRAME SRC="wtool.htm">
</FRAMESET>
</HTML>
```

How It Works

Three screen regions are created by the <FRAMESET> container in HT1201.HTM. The number of regions can be computed by multiplying the number of tokens assigned to the ROWS attribute by the number of tokens assigned to the COLS attribute. Remember that the COLS attribute is assumed to have a single partition representing the entire document viewing area. This example assigns three percentage values to the ROWS attribute and none to the COLS attribute. Therefore, this example will establish three screen regions.

Based on the top-down, left-right frame assignment algorithm used by the Navigator browser, the frames are then assigned to the three regions. The assignment results in this configuration:

REGION	HEIGHT	WIDTH	FRAME
1	20%	100%	Displays whead.htm
2	60%	100%	Displays worder.htm
3	20%	100%	Displays wtool.htm

Table 12-2 Frame assignment to screen regions

Comments

Frames will do for HTML documents (and the Web) what Windows has done for applications. Windows allow users to concurrently view multiple applications. Frames allow users to simultaneously view multiple HTML documents. The ability to concurrently view multiple Web pages can be a very powerful and flexible addition to your site. By allowing users to change frame sizes, your site can be configured by users to meet their individual tastes and desires. However, there is a point of diminishing return. Do not overburden the user with too many frames. Large numbers of frames, each with a specific HTML document, could cause information overload and result in people shying away from your site.

COMPLEXITY
BEGINNING

12.2 How do I...
Establish an event handler that is triggered by the loading and unloading of documents inside frames?

COMPATIBILITY:

Question

Can I set up event handlers that fires when a document is loaded and unloaded into a frame?

Technique

JavaScript provides two event handlers tied to the loading and unloading of documents inside a window or frame. The onLoad handler is fired when a document is displayed on the screen, while the onUnload handler is activated after the document is removed from view. The onLoad and onUnload event handlers belong to the Window object, but they are specifically established inside the <FRAMESET> tag. These event handlers can also be established inside the <BODY> of normal HTML documents.

Because framesets are used to concurrently display multiple HTML documents, there is the strong possibility that multiple onUnload event handlers may be fired by a single Unload event. For example, an onUnload handler may be fired for a <FRAMESET> and inside the <BODY> of a document displayed inside one of the child frames. The firing sequence of these handlers results in a document <BODY> handler being executed before a <FRAMESET> handler. When multiple document handlers are present, the browser fires them off according to their host frame's position in the frameset container. You can look at the <FRAMESET> definition to determine a frame's position within a frameset.

Steps

This example establishes several representative event handlers for framesets and documents displayed inside the child frames. The purpose of this exercise is to analyze the firing sequence of multiple onUnload events.

From Navigator 2.0+ or Explorer 3.0, use the File/Open menu option to load HT1202.HTM into memory. After all the documents have finished loading, click on the Home key to move to another page. Notice that an alert displays with the message Unload Event In Document 2. Acknowledge this alert by clicking the OK button. A second alert appears with the message Unload Event In Document 3. Acknowledge the alert that says Unload Event In Document 4, followed by the alert in Figure 12-5. Notice that the document event handlers fire before the frameset's handler fires. You also see that the document event handlers fire based on their frame's position in the <FRAMESET> container.

1. Open an editor and use the following HTML code to create a new frame document.

2. In the <FRAMESET> tag, add an onUnload event handler. This handler will be executed when the user makes a request for another document while the frame document is visible on the screen.

3. Save the frame document under the file name HT1202.HTM.

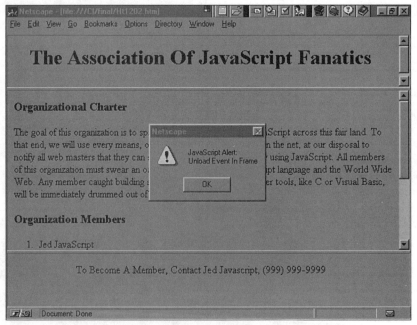

Figure 12-5 The frameset's alert dialog

```
<HTML>
<FRAMESET ROWS="20%,60%,20%" onUnload="alert('Unload Event In Frame')">
<FRAME SRC="js_head.htm">
<FRAME SRC="js_chart.htm">
<FRAME SRC="js_foot.htm">
</FRAMESET>
</HTML>
```

How It Works

The frameset's onUnload event handler is executed when the frame document is replaced on the screen by another document. This event is known as the Unload event. Any onUnload handlers specified for documents hosted in any child frame will be executed before the frameset's handler is fired.

Comments

In JavaScript, the rule of thumb is that sequence is determined by an object's definition inside the HTML document. This rule will explain the behavior of the onUnload event handlers in this example. The firing sequence of the document handlers is based on their host frame's position inside the <FRAMESET>.

COMPLEXITY
BEGINNING

12.3 How do I...
Specify whether or not scrolling should occur in a frame?

COMPATIBILITY:

Question

I have noticed that, for certain documents, the entire content is visible within the frame. However, the frame still displays a scroll bar. How can I specify that a frame be displayed without a scroll bar?

Technique

In order to shut off scrolling in a frame, you must assign a No value to the frame's SCROLLING attribute. This attribute may be assigned one of three values: Yes, No, and Auto. A Yes value indicates that scrolling should always occur. If the entire document is visible, the scroll bar is still displayed. A No value prevents a scroll bar from displaying, even in circumstances when the entire document is not visible on the screen. Auto leaves the decision up to the browser. If the SCROLLING attribute is not defined, the frame will use auto scrolling. An example of how to define a frame that should not display a scroll bar is

```
<FRAME SRC="Main.htm" SCROLLING="no">
```

Steps

This example uses the Waite Group Press order form, created in How-To 12.1. The frames containing the header and footer documents will have their scrolling capabilities turned off. This is because the content of these documents is completely visible to the user.

From Navigator 2.0+ or Explorer 3.0, use the File/Open menu option to load HT1203.HTM into memory. The document in Figure 12-6 will appear on the screen.

1. Add three frames to the <FRAMESET> container.

2. To prevent users from scrolling through the "whead.htm" file, the first frame should have its SCROLLING attribute set to no.

3. The last frame will also have its SCROLLING attribute set to no.

4. The middle frame retains the default SCROLLING value ("auto") which leaves the scrolling decision up to the browser.

5. Save the modified document to disk.

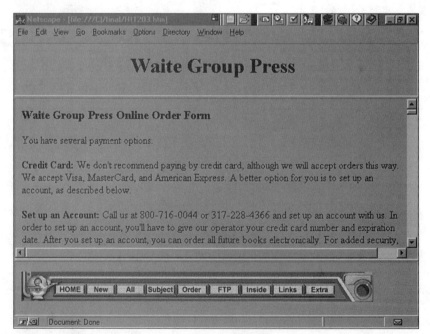

Figure 12-6 The frame document, with scrolling shut off for the title and contact frame

```
<HTML>
<FRAMESET ROWS="20%,60%,20%">
    <FRAME SRC="whead.htm" SCROLLING="no">
    <FRAME SRC="worder.htm">
    <FRAME SRC="wtool.htm" SCROLLING="no">
</FRAMESET>
</HTML>
```

How It Works

If you viewed HT1201.HTM on a 640×480 screen, you probably noticed that the title and content frames were displayed with scroll bars, even though the contents of both documents were visible on the screen. HT1203.HTM assigns a value of "no" to the SCROLLING attribute for both frames, indicating that they should be displayed without the unnecessary scroll bar. When you load HT1203.HTM into Navigator, you will notice that the scroll bars are not present.

Comments

You should only override the default SCROLLING attribute in special circumstances. Window resize events could affect how much of a document is visible on the screen. If scrolling is shut off, the user may be able to see the entire document only when the browser's window has been maximized.

COMPLEXITY
INTERMEDIATE

12.4　How do I...
Define fixed- and relative-length frames?

COMPATIBILITY:　NAVIGATOR 2.X　NAVIGATOR 3.X　EXPLORER 3.X

Question

If I display an HTML document in a percentage-based frame, browser resize events may result in the document's content being wholly or partially obscured from the user. How can I define a fixed-length frame to ensure the document content will be displayed? How can I set up a relative-length frame to reside in the remaining part of the viewer?

Technique

In How-To 12.1 you learned how to specify a frame's height and width—in other words, dimension—by assigning a comma-delimited string of percentages to the frameset's ROWS and COLS attributes. This technique constructs percentage-based frames whose size is dependent on the physical dimensions of the screen. In addi-

THIS IS NOT USED

tion to percentage-based frames, the Navigator browser also supports fixed- and relative-size frames.

To specify fixed-length frames, the COLS string should contain numeric values, instead of percentages. These values specify the number of pixels that the browser should use to represent the frame. Because pixels are physically represented on the screen, the ability to define a frame's size in pixels means that the frame's size will be static. Unlike percentage-based frames, window resize events will not affect the frame's size. With percentages, the viewer size is needed to convert logical percentages into physical pixels.

Specifying every frame's size in terms of pixels may sometimes lead to undesired results. Problems arise when the total number of pixels assigned to each frame exceeds the number of pixels that comprise the screen. Problems include frames that are not completely visible to the user and frame pages that take up only part of the total screen area. To avoid these problems, you should intermix fixed and relative values assigned to the ROWS and COLS attributes.

Relative-size frames are designed to absorb any remaining space assigned to a document. As you may remember from How-To 12.1, framesets define the height and width of each child frame. Height is related to the screen's vertical dimension while width is tied to the horizontal dimension. A screen terminal has a specified setting in each dimension. For example, a 640×480 screen contains 640 pixels across the horizontal axis and 480 pixels down the vertical axis. Because the COLS attribute partitions the horizontal axis, a fixed frame assigned this attribute will use some of the 640 available pixels. If the fixed frame has a size of 200, 440 pixels remain unallocated. By also assigning a relative-size frame to the COLS attribute, this extra space will be assigned to another frame.

The wildcard (*) token represents a relative-size frame. By including a relative-size frame along with a fixed-size frame, any remaining space will be assigned to the relative-size frame. Remaining space refers to any pixels left over after space is assigned to the fixed-length frames. The amount of additional space for each dimension is determined by subtracting the amount of fixed space already assigned to frames from the total amount of space assigned to the browser's document viewing area. The following example demonstrates the use of a relative-size frame with two fixed-size frames.

```
<!-- Total Height Of Browser's Viewing Area = 400 Pixels -->

<FRAMESET ROWS="100,*,100">
<FRAME SRC="Main1.htm"> <!-- Height == 100 Pixels -->
<FRAME SRC="Main2.htm"> <!-- Height == 200 Pixels -->
<FRAME SRC="Main3.htm"> <!-- Height == 100 Pixels -->
</FRAMESET>
```

If the window is resized, the relative frame is adjusted accordingly.

```
<!-- Browser's Viewing Area Resized To = 300 Pixels -->

<FRAMESET ROWS="100,*,100">
<FRAME SRC="Main1.htm"> <!-- Height == 100 Pixels -->
<FRAME SRC="Main2.htm"> <!-- Height == 100 Pixels -->
<FRAME SRC="Main3.htm"> <!-- Height == 100 Pixels -->
</FRAMESET>
```

Notice how the height of the second frame, assigned to the document "Main2.htm", is the only frame affected by the change in the browser's dimensions. This frame is the only relative frame defined in the frameset. Any remaining spaces are assigned to this frame. When the viewing area had a height of 400 pixels, 200 pixels were assigned to this frame. As the viewing area was resized to 300 pixels, only 100 pixels remained unassigned to the other two frames. The size of the top and bottom frames remains constant because they were specified to have a fixed length of 100 pixels.

Multiple Relative-Size Frames

Navigator does not place a restriction on the number of relative-size frames. If more than one relative-size frame is specified, then the remaining free space, after allocating the desired number of pixels to fixed-length frames, will be evenly distributed to the remaining relative-size frames. To specify a second relative-size frame in the previous example, simply add a second relative-size indicator (*) to the ROWS string:

```
<!-- Total Height Of Browser's Viewing Area = 400 Pixels -->

<FRAMESET ROWS="100,*,*,100">
<FRAME SRC="Main1.htm">          <!-- Height == 100 Pixels -->
<FRAME SRC="Main2-2.htm">    <!-- Height == 100 Pixels -->
<FRAME SRC="Main2-1.htm">    <!-- Height == 100 Pixels -->
<FRAME SRC="Main3.htm">          <!-- Height == 100 Pixels -->
</FRAMESET>
```

The addition of the second relative-size frame will result in the 200 remaining pixels, which are left over after distribution to fixed-size frames, being evenly allocated to both frames.

If you did want an even allocation of remaining pixels, then you can specify a proportion the browser should use when assigning free space to multiple relative-size documents. By specifying a number before the relative-size (*) indicator, proportional distribution will be used. The method of specifying a proportion in the context of a relative-size document is very similar to that for proportional-size documents. The one exception is that the proportion is based on space left after assignment to the fixed-length frames. By adding a 3 before the first relative-size (*) indicator in the example above, the browser will assign three pixels to this frame for every pixel assigned to the second relative-size frame.

```
<!-- Total Height Of Browser's Viewing Area = 400 Pixels -->

<FRAMESET ROWS="100,3*,*,100">
<FRAME SRC="Main1.htm">          <!-- Height == 100 Pixels -->
<FRAME SRC="Main2-2.htm"> <!-- Height == 150 Pixels -->
<FRAME SRC="Main2-1.htm"> <!-- Height == 50 Pixels -->
<FRAME SRC="Main3.htm">          <!-- Height == 100 Pixels -->
</FRAMESET>
```

To determine how relative-space allocation is performed by the browser, add up all the numbers before each relative-size indicator. For an indicator without any number, assume a default size of one. The total represents the numerator of the proportional fraction. The denominator is based on the specific proportion for each individual frame. For this example, the total number is four and the frames are given proportional fractions of 3/4 and 1/4.

Steps

This example will modify the Waite Group Press order form created in How-To 12.1. Instead of using percentage-based frames, we need to use a combination of fixed and relative frames. Fixed frames are needed to ensure that the header document will always be completely visible to the user. With percentage-based frames, the content was partially obscured when the window was not maximized.

From Navigator 2.0+ or Explorer 3.0+, use the File/Open menu option to load the document HT1204.HTM into memory. The document in Figure 12-7 will appear on the screen. Resize the browser to reduce the dimensions of the document viewing area. The frames will change to look like those in Figure 12-8. Notice that the upper frame remains the same. The real estate lost as a result of the resize is removed from the middle and bottom frames. Notice that these frames keep their proportional size in comparison with each other.

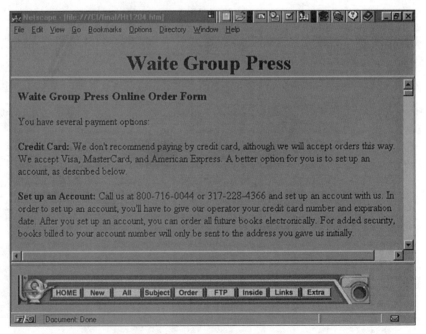

Figure 12-7 A maximized frame document

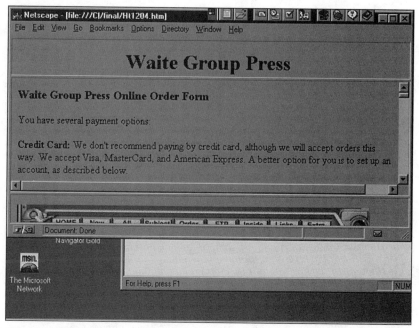

Figure 12-8 Resizing effects on relative-size frames

1. Open HT1201.HTM into an editor.

2. Change the <FRAMESETS> ROWS attribute to a combination of fixed and relative-size indicators. The top region will now have a fixed height of 60 pixels. Because the middle and bottom partitions use relative sizes, any remaining space in the viewing area's vertical axis is divided between these two regions. Remaining space is allocated based on the ratio 4.5-to-1.

3. Save the modified frame document to disk.

```
<HTML>
<FRAMESET ROWS="60,4.5*,1*">
    <FRAME SRC="whead.htm" SCROLLING="no">
    <FRAME SRC="worder.htm">
    <FRAME SRC="wtool.htm" SCROLLING="no">
</FRAMESET>
</HTML>
```

How It Works

The new value assigned to the ROWS attribute changes the size of each individual child frame. The topmost frame, which houses "whead.htm", becomes a fixed-length frame. This frame takes up 60 pixels on the screen. The remaining pixels in the screen's vertical axis are allocated to the two bottom frames. Because the middle frame has a 4.5 multiplier, 4.5 pixels are allocated to this frame for every pixel assigned to the bottom frame.

Comments

Set up a QA (Quality Assurance) process that checks all <FRAMESET> definitions for the existence of fixed-length frames. This process should verify that a relative-size frame has been included to absorb any remaining space. Otherwise your site will look funny on different screen resolutions.

COMPLEXITY
BEGINNING

12.5 How do I...
Prevent users from resizing a frame?

COMPATIBILITY:  NAVIGATOR 2.X   NAVIGATOR 3.X   EXPLORER 3.X

Question

For certain types of documents, I may wish to prevent users from having the ability to alter the size of a frame. How can I accomplish this?

Technique

In How-To 12.1, you learned how to use a <FRAME> tag's SRC attribute to tie a Web page to a frame. Another <FRAME> attribute, the NORESIZE flag, determines whether or not the user can resize a frame. Users resize frames by selecting a frame's edge and dragging that edge to a new location. The NORESIZE flag defaults to false, which means that the user can resize a frame. In order to prevent users from resizing frames, the NORESIZE flag must be set.

```
<FRAME SRC="main.htm" NORESIZE>
```

Notice that the NORESIZE flag does not have a value assigned to it. Merely by placing the label <NORESIZE> inside the <FRAME> tag, you have specified that this frame should remain static.

Side Effects on Neighbor Frames

One important side effect of setting a frame's NORESIZE flag is that all neighbor frames lose their resize capability in the shared plane. For example, in the frame specification below, Frame 1 has its NORESIZE flag set to true.

```
<HTML>
<FRAMESET ROWS="20%,70%,10%">
    <!-- Frame 1 -->
    <FRAME SRC="HT0101.htm NORESIZE">
    <!-- Frame 2 -->
    <FRAME SRC="HT0103.htm">
    <!-- Frame 3 -->
    <FRAME SRC="HT0104.htm">
```

```
</FRAMESET>
</HTML>
```

Frame 2 shares a border with Frame 1. Its upper edge is Frame 1's lower edge. Because Frame 1 cannot be resized, Frame 2's upper edge must remain static. Therefore, the action of setting Frame 1's NORESIZE flag makes Frame 2's top edge unresizable. The user can still resize Frame 2, but using only its bottom border.

Steps

This example will modify the Waite Group Press order form. Because the top frame is now a fixed-length frame, we do not want users to be able to resize this frame. In this example, the ability to resize the top frame will be removed from the site.

From Navigator 2.0+ or Explorer 3.0+, use the File/Open menu option to load the document HT1205.HTM into memory. Position the cursor over the top frame's bottom edge. Notice that the cursor does not change from the pointer to the resize cursor. Depress the left mouse key in an attempt to grab the edge. The user is prohibited from resizing this frame. The bottom frame can still be resized because its NORESIZE flag default is set to false.

1. Open HT1201.HTM into your favorite editor.

2. Modify the string assigned to the ROWS attribute so that the bottom frame has a fixed length of 40 pixels. The old specification, which used multiple relative-size frames, was used to demonstrate a concept. For practicality, the bottom frame should be a fixed-length frame.

3. Turn on the top frame's NORESIZE flag.

4. Save the modified frame document to disk.

```
<HTML>
<FRAMESET ROWS="60,*,40">
   <FRAME SRC="whead.htm" SCROLLING="no" NORESIZE>
   <FRAME SRC="worder.htm">
   <FRAME SRC="wtool.htm" SCROLLING="no">
</FRAMESET>
</HTML>
```

How It Works

The NORESIZE flag is set for the topmost frame. This flag informs Navigator that window resize events are not allowed on this frame. The user cannot use the mouse to grab the top frame's edge. When the mouse is moved on top of the frame's edge, the resize icon will not be displayed.

Comments

Although this example contained two fixed-length frames, only one of the frames defined was made unresizable. If the bottom frame had its NORESIZE flag set, the middle frame would be implied to have the NORESIZE flag set. This is due to the fact that this frame borders two unresizable frames. Because the common edges cannot be resized, the middle frame is also unresizable.

COMPLEXITY
BEGINNING

12.6 How do I...
Change a frame's height and width margins?

COMPATIBILITY:

Question

I have noticed in the previous examples that there is wasted space above and below the title and contact information. Is there any way to redefine the margins to move the text closer to the edge of a frame?

Technique

By assigning a value to a frame's MARGINWIDTH and MARGINHEIGHT attributes, you can override the browser's ability to decide on the appropriate margin length. MARGINHEIGHT controls the upper and lower margins by indicating how far the document's content should be from the frame's top edge. MARGINWIDTH affects the left and right margins by specifying how far the text is from the left edge. Both attributes are specified in terms of number of pixels away from the appropriate frame edge. Margins must be greater than or equal to one. A value less than one would result in the text touching the frame's edge.

Steps

This example will modify the Waite Group Press order form. In order to effectively utilize screen real estate, the heights of frames will be reduced.

From Navigator 2.0+ or Explorer 3.0+, use the File/Open menu option to load the document HT1206.HTM into memory. The document in Figure 12-9 will appear on the screen. Notice that the title and contact information are closer to the frame's upper edge than in previous examples. This is because the frame's top-to-bottom margin has been set to a single pixel. Because there is less wasted real estate, the frame's height can be reduced. The height of frame one is reduced from 60 to 40 pixels, while frame two is reduced from 40 to 25 pixels.

1. Using an editor, pull up HT1201.HTM.

2. Modify the <FRAMESET> specification so that the string "40,*,25" is assigned the ROWS attribute. The top frame will have a height of 40 pixels and the bottom partition will have a height of 25 pixels.

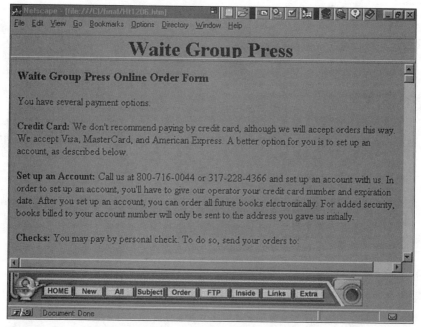

Figure 12-9 The frame document with reduced margins for the title and contact frame

3. Because the middle partition is defined as relative, any remaining space in the viewing area's Y axis is assigned to this region.

4. For the top and bottom frames, explicitly define the MARGINHEIGHT attribute as one pixel. This means that the document's content is displayed next to the upper edge of the frame.

```
<HTML>
<FRAMESET ROWS="40,*,25">
   <FRAME SRC="whead.htm" MARGINHEIGHT="1" SCROLLING="no" NORESIZE>
   <FRAME SRC="worder.htm">
   <FRAME SRC="wtool.htm" MARGINHEIGHT="1" SCROLLING="no">
</FRAMESET>
</HTML>
```

How It Works

In an attempt not to waste screen space, the top and bottom frames will have their MARGINHEIGHT explicitly set to one pixel. This means that the content inside these screens will be displayed near the top edge of the frame. Setting the child frame's MARGINHEIGHT attribute means that the ROWS attribute can be redefined. Because the middle frame is a relative frame, any extra space freed by this example will be included in the dimensions of this frame.

Comments

Use the MARGINWIDTH and MARGINHEIGHT attributes to better manage unused real estate. A 640×480 screen does not have a lot of room, and Web pages should use any extra space so that the maximum content possible will be displayed on the screen.

COMPLEXITY
BEGINNING

12.7 How do I...
Set up alternative content that will be viewed in non-frame-capable browsers?

COMPATIBILITY:

Question

Because Navigator 2.0, Navigator 3.0, and Explorer 3.0 are the only browsers that support frames, how will my frame documents appear when viewed by other browsers? Can I set up alternative content that will be displayed when a frame document is viewed in a browser that does not support frames?

Technique

The <NOFRAMES> container should be used as an alternative HTML document that will be displayed when the frame-based document is viewed from browsers other than Navigator. The example demonstrates using <NOFRAMES> to display a simple message, notifying users that they cannot see the document's contents because the frame document is being viewed with a browser other than Navigator.

```
<NOFRAMES>
Sorry, This Document Uses Frames.
</NOFRAMES>
```

Navigator was designed to ignore any text enclosed within the <NOFRAMES> container. Within the container, you can use any combination of text and HTML tags. Other browsers treat the <NOFRAMES> tag as if it were a second <HTML> tag to mark the beginning of the document. The <NOFRAMES> container is optional. If it is unused, a user will simply see an empty screen when viewing the frame document in a non-frame-compatible browser. If the <NOFRAMES> container is used, it must be enclosed within the <FRAMESET> container. Where it is located within the container is unimportant. It can be placed before, after, or in the middle of the <FRAME> specifications.

Steps

> **NOTE**
>
> For this example, you will need a Web browser that does not support frames. If you do not have access to an older browser, NCSA Mosaic can be downloaded for free on the Internet at http://www.ncsa.uiuc.edu.

This example will set up alternative content that will be displayed when the Waite Group Press order form is viewed inside a browser that does not support frames.

1. With a browser that does not support frames, open the file HT1207.HTM. The alternative content in Figure 12-10 will be displayed on the screen.

2. Start up Navigator 2.0 or higher and load HT1207.HTM. The frame document still appears on the screen.

3. Define a <NOFRAMES> container to hold alternative content that will be visible from non-frame-friendly browsers.

4. Save the frame document under the file name HT1207.HTM.

```
<HTML>
<FRAMESET ROWS="40,*,25">

<NOFRAMES>
<H1> LAME BROWSER ALERT </H1>
<P> Warning!!! Warning!!! Warning!!! Warning!!! Warning!!! </P>
<P>I'm sorry this document utilizes frames and you are using a web browser
which does not support frames. </P>
<P> Warning!!! Warning!!! Warning!!! Warning!!! Warning!!! </P>
</NOFRAMES>


        <FRAME SRC="whead.htm" MARGINHEIGHT="1" SCROLLING="no" NORESIZE>
        <FRAME SRC="worder.htm">
        <FRAME SRC="wtool.htm" MARGINHEIGHT="1" SCROLLING="no">
</FRAMESET>
</HTML>
```

How It Works

When the HT1207.HTM file is viewed using a non-frame-compatible browser, the HTML document within the <NOFRAMES> container will be displayed on the screen. Because this text contains embedded HTML tags, such as those for boldface text, the browser will honor the NOFRAMES document formatting specifications. The browser will ignore the <FRAMESET> tag, which attempts to partition the screen into three regions, and the <FRAMES> tags, which tie frames to documents and screen regions.

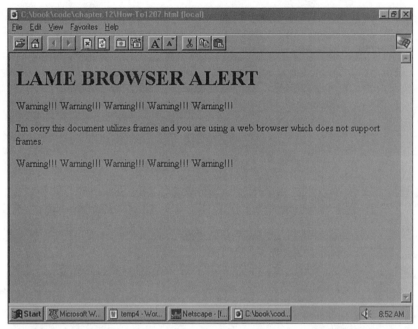

Figure 12-10 Alternative content for the frame document when viewed from Microsoft Explorer

Comments

As How-To 1.5 in Chapter 1 pointed out, portability is becoming a key issue in Web page development. Because only three browsers support frames, you should always set up alternative content, using the <NOFRAMES> container to notify users that the document they are viewing requires a frame-friendly browser. Without it, confused users will be frustrated when they reference a frame document that displays an empty screen when the document has finished loading.

COMPLEXITY
INTERMEDIATE

12.8   How do I...
Embed a frame within a frame?

COMPATIBILITY:

Question

Frames split a region of the screen into multiple parts. I have learned how to use frames to divide the browser's viewing area into several pieces. Now I wish to divide a frame into two parts to create nonsymmetric frames. How can I use an embedded frame to partition an existing frame into multiple parts?

Technique

In How-To 12.1, we learned that a frameset container was used to store a list of frame objects. The frames were assigned to screen regions, created using the frameset's ROWS and COLS attribute in sequential order based on a top-down, left-right assignment algorithm.

In addition to frames, a frameset container may also contain embedded frameset objects. When a frameset object is encountered in a frame document, it notifies the browser how to divide the document viewing area into multiple regions where frames will be displayed. In the same manner, an embedded frameset defines how an existing region should be partitioned. The primary difference between normal and embedded framesets is scope. Up to this point, all frameset objects have partitioned the document viewing area. Embedded frames partition screen regions. This code demonstrates how to use embedded frames to partition the bottom frame, represented in Figure 12-11:

```
<HTML>
<FRAMESET COLS="30%,70%">
    <FRAME SRC="First.htm" NAME="FRAME1">
    <FRAMESET ROWS="50%, 50%">
        <FRAME SRC="Third.htm" NAME="SUBFRAME3">
    </FRAMESET>
</FRAMESET>
</HTML>
```

The first frameset container splits the viewing area into two equal-size partitions. One partition is on the left side of the viewer, while the other partition occupies the right side of the viewer. Based on the top-down, left-right frame assignment algorithm used by the browser, the left partition is assigned to FRAME1. The second frameset container results in the right partition being split into two additional partitions. The first occupies the viewer's upper right corner, while the second resides in the bottom right corner. The result is that the browser's document viewing area has been divided into three parts.

You will notice that the user cannot tell that two frameset containers were used to divide the viewer into multiple regions. The two regions, created by the second frameset container, are indistinguishable from the left side region. The browser uses the same frame assignment region when assigning subframes to regions. SUBFRAME2 is assigned the upper right section of the screen and SUBFRAME3 is displayed in the lower right partition.

Steps

The following example will create a frame document that contains an embedded frameset. The document is for a club called The JavaScript Society. This society solicits donations from its membership during a semi-annual fund drive. To keep track of

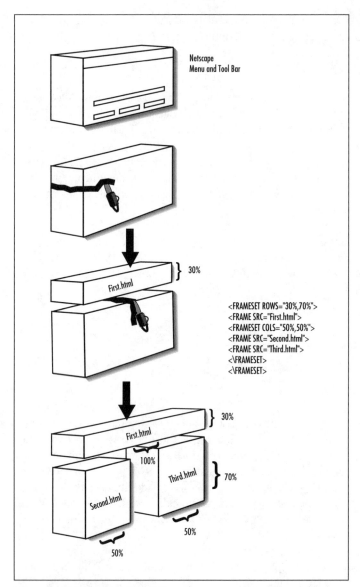

Netscape
Menu and Tool Bar

30%

First.html

```
<FRAMESET ROWS="30%,70%">
<FRAME SRC="First.html">
<FRAMESET COLS="50%,50%">
<FRAME SRC="Second.html">
<FRAME SRC="Third.html">
</FRAMESET>
</FRAMESET>
```

30%

First.html

100%

Third.html

70%

Second.html

50%

50%

Figure 12-11 Embedded frames example

member pledges, the Society has created a relational database. A JavaScript-enhanced HTML document will serve as the front-end to this database. Because of the enormous amount of information that must be displayed to volunteers, embedded framesets are used to maximize the amount of information displayed on the screen.

1. From Navigator 2.0+ or Explorer 3.0+, use the File/Open File menu option to load HT1208.HTM into memory. The document in Figure 12-12 will appear on the screen.

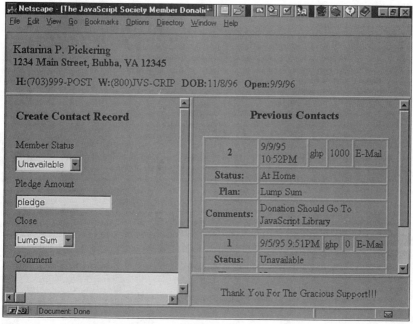

Figure 12-12 The subframe document

2. Use the following HTML code to create a new frame document. The document will contain an embedded frameset that partitions the screen into an irregular pattern.

```
<FRAMESET ROWS="100,*">
   <FRAME SRC="part1.htm" SCROLLING="no" NORESIZE>
   <FRAMESET COLS="300,*">
      <FRAME SRC="part2.htm">
      <FRAMESET ROWS="*,50">
         <FRAME SRC="part3.htm">
         <FRAME SRC="part4.htm" SCROLLING="no">
      </FRAMESET>
   </FRAMESET>
</FRAMESET>
```

How It Works

The frame document HT1208.HTM contains three framesets. The top-level frameset partitions the screen into two parts. The upper part, representing the top 100 pixels in the document viewing area, displays the "part1.htm" document. This document contains customer-specific information. In previous frame documents, you have seen the bottom portion of the screen assigned to a second HTML document. This example is different in that the bottom part is assigned to another frameset.

Similar to the topmost frameset, the embedded frameset partitions the screen into multiple pieces. The difference is that this frameset is not displayed using the entire screen. Instead, the frameset is displayed inside the frame belonging to a parent frameset. The embedded frameset will vertically partition the frame into two pieces. The left-most 300 pixels are used to display the "part2.htm" document. The remainder of the frame is assigned to a third, embedded frameset. The parent for this third frameset is not the topmost frameset. The parent is the middle frameset, which specified that this frameset should be displayed inside one of its child frames.

The parent is different because this frameset is at a new nesting level. Embedded framesets implicitly contain an attribute known as the nesting level. The nesting level indicates how far away a frameset is from the topmost frameset. You may be familiar with the concept of nesting in structured programming. Every time a frameset is embedded inside another frameset, the nesting level will increase by one. The topmost frame has a nesting level of zero. The level is zero because this frameset is not embedded inside any other frameset. The middle frameset has a nesting level of one. This indicates that the middle frameset is embedded inside a frameset. The bottom frameset is embedded inside two framesets. Therefore this frameset has a nesting level of two. The bottom frameset is embedded inside the middle frameset, which in turn is contained within the top frameset. Hence, the nesting level equals the number of sets between a frameset and the topmost frameset. The following description indicates the nesting level for each frameset that comprises this example.

```
Nesting Level 0Top-Most Frameset
Nesting Level 1Middle Frameset
Nesting Level 2Bottom Frameset
```

Comments

Now that you know about frames, let's see how JavaScript can be used to manipulate documents contained inside a frame.

COMPLEXITY
INTERMEDIATE

12.9 How do I...
Set up variables accessible by multiple frames?

COMPATIBILITY: NAVIGATOR 2.X NAVIGATOR 3.X EXPLORER 3.X

Question

Because I may need to pass data between frames, is there any way of setting up a global variable that is accessible from all child frames?

Technique

The JavaScript language has defined a Frame object, which is used to hold information about child frames. Child frames are created by a <FRAME> tag appearing inside a <FRAMESET> container. Figure 12-13 shows the properties (attributes, methods, and event handlers) of the JavaScript Frame object.

The parent property of a frame object can be used to access methods and properties of the frame's parent window. The parent window is the window or frame that displays the document containing the frame's <FRAMESET> container. The parent property references other frames in the case of an embedded frame. Remember that frames are considered to be a special type of window. Through the parent property, a child frame has access to the parent window's attributes. This includes any properties, methods, or global variables belonging to the Parent object. This JavaScript expression uses the parent property to set the status bar message to This is a test:

```
parent.status = "This is a test";
```

Because all child frames have access to the parent window, this object can serve as a place where data sharing will occur between multiple frames.

Steps

This example will begin creation of a frame document that acts like a slide projector. This example will be finished in How-To 12.10. Starting with Slide 1, the user will be able to advance sequentially through all of the slides belonging to a presentation. The bottom frame contains presentation control buttons that allow the user to move to the next slide or back to the previous slide.

Frame		
PROPERTIES	METHODS	EVENT HANDLERS
frames	setTimeout	NONE
name	clearTimeout	
length		
parent		
self		
window		

Figure 12-13 The Frame object

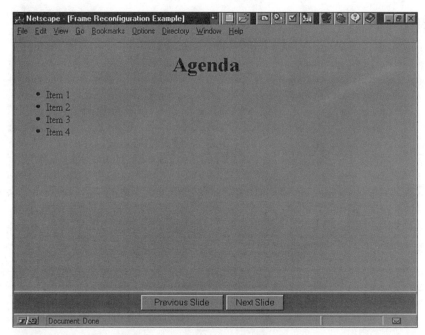

Figure 12-14 The slide projector document

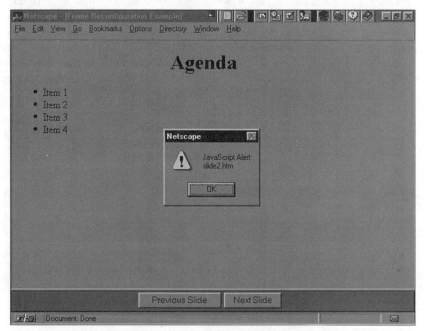

Figure 12-15 What happens when the next slide button is activated

From Navigator 2.0+ or Explorer 3.0+, use the File/Open File menu option to load HT1209.HTM into memory. The document in Figure 12-14 will appear on the screen. Click on the Next Slide button and watch the alert dialog in Figure 12-15 appear on the screen. This indicates the filename of the slide to display on the screen. How-To 12.10 will actually display this file in the viewer frame. You can use the Next Slide and Previous Slide to sequence through the presentation. These buttons will notify the user when the beginning or ending slide is reached.

1. Use the following HTML code to start the shell of a frame document.

```
<HTML>
<HEAD>
<TITLE> Frame Reconfiguration Example </TITLE>
</HEAD>
<FRAMESET ROWS="*,36">
   <FRAME SRC="slide1.htm" NAME="viewer">
   <FRAME SRC="HT1209A.htm" SCROLLING="no" NORESIZE MARGINHEIGHT="1">
</FRAMESET>
</HTML>
```

2. Before the </HEAD> tag, add the following JavaScript code block. This code will establish three properties belonging to the parent window. These attributes are accessible from the child frames through the Parent object. The three attributes represent the beginning and ending slide numbers. The SLIDE attribute indicates the current slide, which will display inside the top frame. This attribute is manipulated by the slide control document, in order to change the current slide, displayed in the viewer frame. Save the file as HT1209.HTM.

```
<SCRIPT LANGUAGE="JavaScript">
var slide = 1;
var min = 1;
var max = 5;
</SCRIPT>
```

3. Use the following HTML to begin construction of an HTML document. This document contains the slide control buttons. These buttons contain onClick event handlers that call functions defined in later steps.

```
<HTML>
<HEAD><TITLE>Tool Bar</TITLE>
</HEAD>
<BODY BGCOLOR="#708090">
<FORM NAME="toolbar">
<CENTER>
<INPUT TYPE="button" VALUE="Previous Slide" onClick="move_prev();">
<INPUT TYPE="button" VALUE="Next Slide" onClick="move_next();">
</FORM>
</BODY>
</HTML>
```

4. Inside the <HEAD> container, use the following JavaScript code to create a <SCRIPT> container. The <SCRIPT> container contains a function reload_window, which displays the name of the slide document that should be displayed inside the viewer frame. This function will be enhanced in How-To 12.10.

```
<SCRIPT LANGUAGE="JavaScript">

function reload_window(value) {
alert("slide" + parent.slide + ".htm");
}
</SCRIPT>
```

5. Inside the <SCRIPT> container developed in Step 4, add the JavaScript function move_next(). This function is called by the Next Slide button's onClick event handler. The function will perform a boundary check to ensure that the ending slide is not displayed. If the check succeeds, the function will increment the current slide index variable slide. Finally, the reload_window function is called to display the new slide.

```
function move_next() {
        if (parent.slide < parent.max) {
                parent.slide++;
                reload_window();
        } else {
                alert("\nERROR\n\nYou Are On The Last How To");
        }
}
```

6. Inside the <SCRIPT> container developed in Step 4, add a JavaScript function move_prev. This function is similar to the move_next() function except that the slide attribute is decremented instead of incremented. Save this document as HT1209A.HTM.

```
function move_prev() {
        if (parent.slide > parent.min) {
                reload_window();
        } else {
                alert("\nERROR\n\nYou Are On The First How To");
        }
}
```

7. From Navigator, use the File/Open File menu option to display the HT1209.HTM document.

How It Works

The frame document contains three pieces of information that are accessible to any child frame. The three attributes equate to the minimum, maximum, and current slides. These attributes are accessible to the Child object through the parent property. This property belongs to the window used to host the child document. Because this window represents a frame, the parent attribute can be used to reference the parent frameset document. The slide control buttons, in HT1209A.HTM, use the parent property to manipulate the current slide. The maximum and minimum slides serve as reference points to ensure that only valid slides are displayed.

Comments

Let's finish the Slide Projector document by learning how to access properties belonging to another frame.

COMPLEXITY
INTERMEDIATE

12.10 How do I...
Access properties belonging to another frame?

COMPATIBILITY: NAVIGATOR 2.X NAVIGATOR 3.X EXPLORER 3.X

Question

If I can access information belonging to the parent window, is there any way to access information belonging to another child frame?

Technique

In How-To 12.9, you were introduced to the parent property. This property can be used by child documents to access common information that relates to multiple documents displayed inside the same frame document. The parent property can also be used to access information stored in documents contained in sibling child frames. The Window object contains a frames property that holds references to each child frame. This property is represented as an array. All child frames specified in the frame document are represented inside this array. The following code demonstrates how to set the document specified in another child frame.

```
parent.frames[0].location.href = parent.frames[0].location.href;
```

In addition to the frames array, the frame name can also be used to reference another frame. Frame names are established by assigning a quoted string the <FRAME> tag's NAME attribute. Chapter 13 provides an in-depth discussion of how to assign names to individual frames. The following code uses the frame name, viewer to reference a sibling frame.

```
parent.viewer.location.href = "slide" + parent.slide + ".htm";
```

Steps

This example will modify the documents started in How-To 12.9. The next slide and previous slide functions will be modified to change the current slide displayed inside the viewer frame. Previously, this functionality simply displayed an alert dialog indicating the file name of the current slide. In addition, a new frame will be added. This frame will display the index of the current slide.

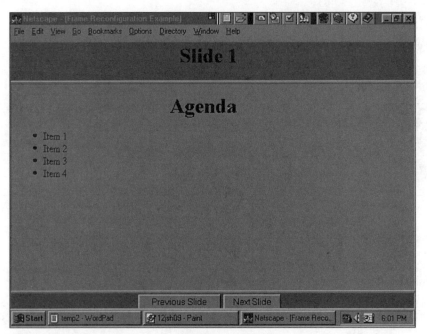

Figure 12-16 The slide projector document

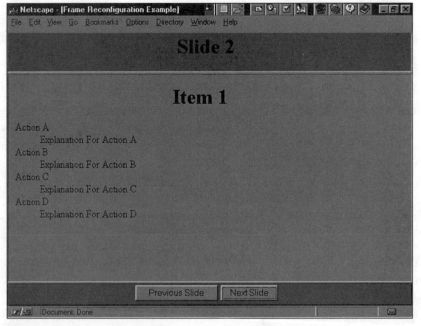

Figure 12-17 The next slide

From Navigator 2.0+ or Explorer 3.0+, use the File/Open File menu option to load HT1210.HTM into memory. The document in Figure 12-16 will appear on the screen. Click on the Next Slide button and watch the slide in Figure 12-17 appear on the screen. Use the Previous Slide and Next Slide buttons to sequence through the presentation.

1. Modify the frameset in the HT1209A.HTM document to display a third frame. This frame will reside in the upper 66 pixels of the screen. The frame will display the HT1210B.HTM document. Save the document as HT1210.HTM.

```
<FRAMESET ROWS="66,*,36">
   <FRAME SRC="HT1210B.htm" SCROLLING="no" NORESIZE MARGINHEIGHT="1">
   <FRAME SRC="slide1.htm" NAME="viewer">
   <FRAME SRC="HT1210A.htm" SCROLLING="no" NORESIZE MARGINHEIGHT="1">
</FRAMESET>
```

2. In HT1209A.HTM, modify the reload_window() function to change the slide in the viewer frame. The parent property is used to reference the viewer frame. This frame's location property is changed to represent the newly selected slide. When the location's href is set, the document displayed inside the viewer changes to the new slide. Similarly, the top frame is assigned to itself. This frame will display a document that used dynamic HTML to display the current slide number to the user. This technique, setting a frame to display the same document it already displays, forces the document to be reloaded from the server. This will result in the document updating to indicate the new frame's index.

```
function reload_window(value) {
parent.viewer.location.href = "slide" + parent.slide + ".htm";
parent.frames[0].location.href = parent.frames[0].location.href;
}
```

3. Use the following HTML code to create a new document. Save this document as HT1210B.HTM. This document uses dynamic HTML to display the current document index to the user. The parent property is used to reference the current index, which belongs to an attribute of the parent window.

```
<HTML>
<HEAD>
</HEAD>
<BODY BGCOLOR="#708090">
<SCRIPT LANGUAGE="JavaScript">
document.write("<CENTER> <H1> Slide " + parent.slide + " </H1> </CENTER>");
</SCRIPT>
</BODY>
</HTML>
```

How It Works

The reload_window() function was modified to set the hypertext reference displayed inside the viewer frame. The viewer frame is referenced through the parent property, which provides a link back to the frame document. Because both the viewer and the host frame belong to the same frameset, both have the same parent window. The frame name viewer is used to reference the middle frame. Each window contains a location attribute that can be used to set the document that is visible inside the window. The reload_window() function uses this property to sequence through the frames. In addition, the frames array is used to reload the document in the top frame. A reload is required before HT1310B.HTM, which uses dynamic HTML, will display the current slide's index. HT1310B.HTM, like HT1310A.HTM, uses the parent property to reference the index of the current slide. This index is stored in the parent's slide property.

Comments

This concludes the introduction to frames. Chapter 13, "Targeting Windows," discusses how hypertext links can be manipulated to target other frames and windows. This will allow persistent documents to be developed with referenced documents concurrently displaying inside another visible frame.

CHAPTER 13
TARGETING WINDOWS

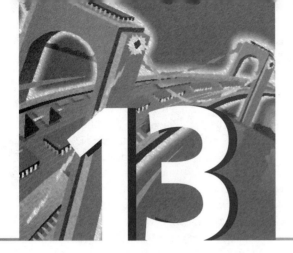

13

TARGETING WINDOWS

How do I...

When a user clicks on a hypertext link, the document tied to that link is downloaded from the Web server and replaces the calling document, which contained the activated link, on the screen. This interactive style is consistent with standard HTML, in which only one document is presented to the user at any moment. The introduction of frames in Netscape Navigator 2.0 allows multiple documents to be concurrently presented to the user. To complement the frame environment, Navigator 2.0 supports the concept of targeting windows. This feature allows Web developers to specify which frame or window will be used to display a document. Targeting windows can be used to create Web sites where a parent or main document remains persistent on the screen. When the user activates a link in the parent document, the downloaded document is displayed in one of the other frames on the screen.

13.1 Change the frame where an HTML document will be viewed

This How-To will demonstrate how to specify a target frame for a single hypertext link. When the user clicks on the link, the referenced document will be downloaded from the server and displayed inside the target frame. A frame name is used by the hypertext link to target a specific frame. Frame names distinguish individual frames within a multiple frame environment. How-To 13.1 will teach you how to set up a frame name.

13.2 Define a default target frame for all links in a document

If all hypertext links in a document target to the same frame, specifying a target frame for each individual link may be tedious. This How-To will show you how to define a default target frame. This frame applies to all hypertext links contained within a document. A default target frame will reduce the possibility of error, because links can be added to the document without the possibility of the developer forgetting to specify the target frame.

13.3 Override a document's default target frame

If all links in a document do not target the same frame, a Web developer is not precluded from establishing a default target frame. This How-To will demonstrate how individual hypertext links can override the default target frame. Within the context of this discussion, you will learn how to target the current or self frame. This frame displays the calling document.

13.4 Display a referenced document in the frameset's window when a link is clicked

All frames must belong to a frameset. As you may remember from Chapter 12, a frameset defines the physical or logical size of each member frame. A frameset's window—the parent window—represents the aggregate space needed to display all member frames. The size of this window varies because a frameset can be viewed using the entire screen or within a frame belonging to another frameset. How-To 13.4 will demonstrate how to target the parent window from an individual hypertext link.

13.5 Display a referenced document in the topmost window when a link is clicked

Because framesets can be embedded inside other framesets, the parent window may not represent the entire screen. This How-To will demonstrate how to target the entire screen to display a downloaded document.

13.6 Display a referenced document in a new window when a link is clicked

This How-To will teach you how to create new named and unnamed windows that can serve as targets for downloaded documents.

13.7 Set the target frame when a link is clicked

HTML documents can be designed to operate both inside and outside the frame environment. If a link, which targets another frame, is activated outside the frame environment, the referenced document will be displayed inside a new window. The browser uses a new window to display downloaded documents when a target frame is not visible on the screen.

This interactive style is counter to normal hypertext links, which use the current window to host downloaded documents. This How-To will demonstrate how to create documents that operate properly in both environments. The technique introduced in this chapter can also be used to create a document that can be viewed within multiple frame configurations.

13.8 Redirect documents returned by a form submission

When a form is submitted to the server, a document is returned to the client. This document is normally displayed inside the calling document's host frame. By setting a form's target window, the returned document can be redirected to another frame or window.

13.9 Set the target frame when a form is submitted to the server

How-To 13.7 taught you how to dynamically set a hypertext link's target frame. This How-To will demonstrate how to dynamically set a form's target frame.

13.10   Define a target frame for client-side image map links

Client-side image maps represent another mechanism for creating hypertext links. Learn how to establish a target frame for links contained within a client- side image map.

COMPLEXITY
BEGINNING

13.1   How do I...
Change the frame where an HTML document will be viewed?

COMPATIBILITY: NAVIGATOR 2.X   NAVIGATOR 3.X   EXPLORER 3.X

Problem

I have created a frame document that partitions the screen into two frames. When the user activates a hypertext link, the downloaded document replaces the calling document inside the host frame. The current document contains several pieces of key information that I would like to remain visible to the user. Because the frame environment supports concurrent display of multiple documents, I would like the current document to remain visible when a link is activated. This means that the downloaded document will be displayed inside the remaining frame. How can I change the frame where a downloaded document will be viewed?

Technique

Redirecting a document to another frame, known as targeting a window, is accomplished through a two-step process. First, you must assign a name to the frame that will be used to display the downloaded document. This name serves as the frame's identifier. Without this identifier, there would be no way to discriminate individual frames within a multi-frame environment. The next step is to set a link's target window. This tells the browser to display referenced documents inside the target window. Figure 13-1 displays a visual representation of the target window concept. Links in the Menu frame target the middle-right or Viewer frame. This means that the document, specified in the link's HREF attribute, will be displayed inside the Viewer frame. With the target window, this document would have been displayed in the Menu frame.

Frame names are established by assigning a quoted string to the <FRAME> tag's NAME attribute. The NAME attribute is optional. Only frames that serve as target windows require a frame name. Frames created without a NAME attribute remain nameless and therefore cannot be targeted. The following example demonstrates how to use the NAME attribute to assign the name viewer to a frame which references the welcome.htm document.

```
<FRAME NAME="viewer" SRC="welcome.htm">
```

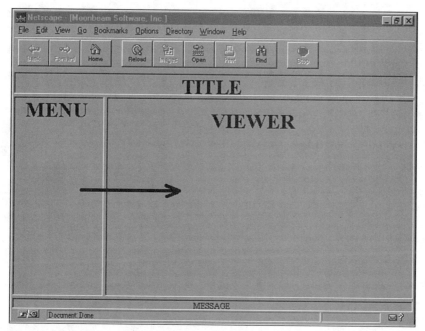

Figure 13-1 The target window concept

Valid frame names begin with an alphanumeric character. Invalid frame names are ignored by the browser. Navigator does not prevent two frames within the same frameset or document from possessing the same name. If two visible frames are assigned the same name, Navigator will select one of the frames as the target. A frame that shares the same parent as the document that targeted it will be chosen over a frame outside the current frameset. For example, in the following frame specification, two frames are named "viewer". If a link inside the HT1302A.HTM document targets the "viewer" frame, the downloaded document will be displayed inside frame 2. Navigator selected frame 2 over frame 1 because it belongs to the same frameset as the calling document's host frame ("menu").

```
<FRAMESET ROWS="50,*">
1     <FRAME NAME="viewer" SRC="comp_nm.htm" MARGINWIDTH="1">
      <FRAMESET COLS="150,*">
         <FRAME NAME="menu" SRC="HT1301A.htm" MARGINWIDTH="1">
2        <FRAME NAME="viewer" SRC="welcome.htm">
      </FRAMESET>
</FRAMESET>
```

NOTE

Even though the frame's NAME attribute is initialized, the frame name is only active if the frame's SRC attribute is also initialized.

Most hypertext links are specified using the anchor <A> tag. For a link to be active, it must define an HREF attribute. This attribute specifies the HTML document that will be downloaded from the Web server when the link is activated. In standard HTML, the downloaded document is displayed inside the host frame, which displays the calling document. The second step in establishing a target window is to assign a frame name, as a quoted string, to an individual link's TARGET attribute. This results in the downloaded document being redirected to the target frame. The following code demonstrates how to target a frame named "viewer", to display the document "welcome.htm", when the President's Welcome link is activated.

```
<A HREF="welcome.htm" TARGET="viewer"> President's Welcome </A>
```

Downloaded documents can be redirected to any visible frame. Even frames contained in parent and nested framesets can be used as target frames. If a document is redirected to a target frame, the calling document will remain visible inside the host frame. The persistence of the calling document gives users an additional point of reference not available in standard HTML. Parent documents often contain important information pertaining to the child document that is lost when a child document is displayed.

Steps

This example will begin construction of a frame-based home page for a startup software company named Moonbeam Software, Inc. The design of the home page uses four frames. The topmost frame hosts a persistent title page that displays the corporate name. The bottom page displays the document's copyright notice. Placing the corporate name and copyright notice inside separate HTML documents makes this information visible to users throughout their interactions with a site.

The middle, left frame contains a menu document implemented as an unordered list of hypertext links. The menu document is used to select the type of information users wish to view. It is important to note that the menu document should remain visible throughout a user's interaction with the site. Standard HTML look and feel dictates that when one of the links is activated, the referenced document will displace the calling document inside the host or "menu" frame. This style contrasts with the need for a persistent main menu. Because a frame name has been assigned to the middle-right frame, this window can be targeted by the menu's links. By redirecting documents to this frame, the menu document will remain on the screen.

From Netscape Navigator Version 2.0 or higher, load the file HT1301.HTM off the CD. The page shown in Figure 13-2 will appear. Click on the Corporate History link and the page shown in Figure 13-3 will appear. By activating this link, the "Corporate History" document replaces the President's Welcome document inside the middle-right frame. This happens because the Corporate History link targets the this frame. In fact, all links in the Menu document target the middle-right frame. This means that if you activate any link in the Menu document, the downloaded document will appear inside this window. Note that throughout your interaction with the site the corporation name and copyright notice remain visible to the user.

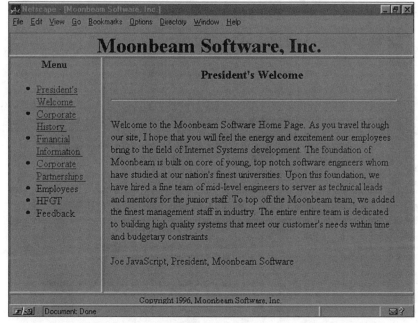

Figure 13-2 Moonbeam Software page with President's Welcome document visible in viewer frame

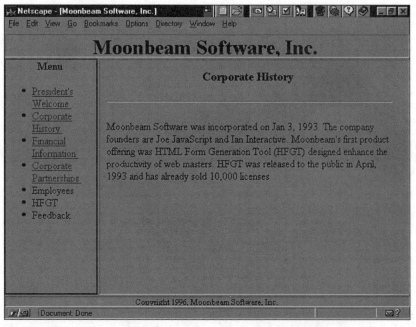

Figure 13-3 Moonbeam Software page with Corporate History document visible in viewer frame

1. Create a new frame document that will partition the screen into four regions. The top frame has a fixed height of 40 pixels and displays to the comp_nm.htm document. The bottom frame has a fixed height of 20 pixels and hosts the cright.htm document. The middle left frame has a fixed width of 150 pixels and hosts the HT1301A.HTM document. The middle-right frame is defined as a relative-size frame. This frame displays the welcome.htm document. This frame is assigned the name viewer. Hypertext links in the HT1301A.HTM document will use this name to target the viewer frame. Save the frame document as HT1301.HTM.

```
<HTML>
<HEAD>
<TITLE> Moonbeam Software, Inc. </TITLE>
</HEAD>
<FRAMESET ROWS="40,*,20">
    <FRAME NAME="title" SRC="comp_nm.htm" MARGINWIDTH="1" SCROLLING="no">
    <FRAMESET COLS="150,*">
        <FRAME NAME="menu" SRC="HT1301A.htm" MARGINWIDTH="1" SCROLLING="no">
        <FRAME NAME="viewer" SRC="welcome.htm">
    </FRAMESET>
    <FRAME NAME="msg" SRC="cright.htm" MARGINWIDTH="1" SCROLLING="no">
</FRAMESET>
</HTML>
```

2. Create a new HTML document that will contain an unordered list of hypertext links. This document represents a menu of links that will allow the user to view important information about a hypothetical startup software company named Moonbeam Software, Inc. The TARGET attribute of each link points to the viewer frame created in Step 1. When any of these links are activated, the referenced document, specified by the HREF attribute, will be displayed inside the viewer frame. Save the HTML document as HT1301A.HTM.

```
<HTML>
<HEAD>
<TITLE> Moonbeam Software, Inc. </TITLE>
</HEAD>
<BODY>
<CENTER> <B> Menu </B> </CENTER>
<UL>
<LI> <A HREF="welcome.htm" TARGET="viewer"> President's Welcome </A>
<LI> <A HREF="org_his.htm" TARGET="viewer"> Corporate History </A>
<LI> <A HREF="finance.htm" TARGET="viewer"> Financial Information </A>
<LI> <A HREF="partner.htm" TARGET="viewer"> Corporate Partnerships </A>
<LI> Employees
<LI> HFGT
<LI> Feedback
</UL>
</BODY>
</HTML>
```

3. In Navigator, use the File/Open File menu option to execute the JavaScript application by loading HT1301.HTM into the browser.

How It Works

Normally, downloaded documents replace the calling document inside the host frame. Because the Corporate History link has its TARGET attribute pointed to the viewer frame, the org_his.htm document will be displayed inside this frame. The viewer frame is established by assigning this name, as a quoted string, to the third frame defined in HT1301.HTM. This frame is assigned to the middle-right region of the screen. The frame name viewer serves to distinguish this frame from the two other frames visible on the screen. In addition to the Corporate History link, all links in HT1301A.HTM target the viewer frame.

Comments

Consistency is an important characteristic of an effective user interface. Although a document's links can be redirected to several target frames, you should try to design a frame-based page that contains a single target frame. This design approach will limit the amount of confusion relating to documents popping up all over a page. In order to achieve consistency, a default target frame can be established for an HTML document. How-To 13.2 will demonstrate the technique required to set up a default target frame.

COMPLEXITY
BEGINNING

13.2   How do I...
Define a default target frame for all links in a document?

COMPATIBILITY:

Problem

If I want all links in a document to target a specific frame, I could set the TARGET attribute of each link to the desired frame. Is there an easier way to define a target frame that applies to all links contained within a document?

Technique

The <BASE> tag can be used to set up a default target frame. In standard HTML, the <BASE> tag is used to establish an absolute URL base that will pertain to any relative URL links in a document. The syntax for the <BASE> tag is:

```
<BASE HREF="..." TARGET="...">
```

By assigning a frame name to the <BASE> tag's TARGET attribute, this frame will become the default target for all links that follow this tag. If the <BASE> tag precedes the topmost hypertext link, the default target frame will apply to all links contained within an HTML document. This tag is a shortcut that replaces the need to set the

TARGET attribute for all hypertext links in a document. As with hypertext links, the frame name is used to identify the target frame that will display downloaded documents. The following example shows how to use the <BASE> tag to make the "viewer" frame the default target frame for all preceding links.

```
<BASE TARGET="viewer">
```

When an HTML document is loaded into Navigator, the browser analyzes, or lays out, the document sequentially from top to bottom. The browser's algorithm for laying out the document dictates why the <BASE> tag must proceed the topmost link for it to apply to the entire document. If the browser encounters a link before the <BASE> tag, it is unaware of the default target specification. This link will be viewed inside the active frame.

A <BASE> tag acts like a pseudo-container object. This means that all links encountered after the <BASE> tag inherit the default target from this tag. Unlike normal HTML container tags, the <BASE> tag does not require a closing </BASE> tag. The container is closed by the end of a document or when a second <BASE> tag is encountered. Any subsequent links following the second <BASE> tag will have their documents displayed in the second <BASE> tag's target frame. The following example contains two <BASE> tags. In this example, the first two links will be redirected to the viewer frame, while the bottom two links will be displayed inside the name frame.

```
<BASE TARGET="viewer">
<LI> <A HREF="jj.htm"> Joe JavaScript </A>
<LI> <A HREF="ii.htm"> Ian Interactive </A>
<BASE TARGET="name">
<LI> <A HREF="nn.htm"> Neve Netscape </A>
<LI> <A HREF="ww.htm"> William Web </A>
```

Steps

The steps in this example will add an additional link to Moonbeam Software's menu page. This link will establish an Employee submenu which will be displayed inside host or menu frame. The menu links, created in How-To 13.1, reference regular HTML documents. These documents contain important information about Moonbeam Software. The Employee link is unique in that its document contains a submenu of employees. Similar to the main menu, this document is implemented as an unordered list of hypertext links. Each link corresponds to an employee name and references that employee's resume.

From Netscape Navigator Version 2.0 or higher, use the File/Open File menu option to load the HT1302.HTM document off the CD. The page shown in Figure 13-2 is displayed on the screen. Click on the Employees link. The document containing the list of employees replaces the main menu inside the host frame. In the Employees submenu, Click on the Joe JavaScript link. The screen, similar to Figure 13-4, will appear. In the middle-right or viewer frame, the resume of Joe JavaScript is displayed. Click on Ian Interactive's link. The screen shown in Figure 13-5 will appear. Ian Interactive's resume replaces Joe JavaScript's resume inside the viewer frame. Click on another employee and a new resume will appear in the viewer frame.

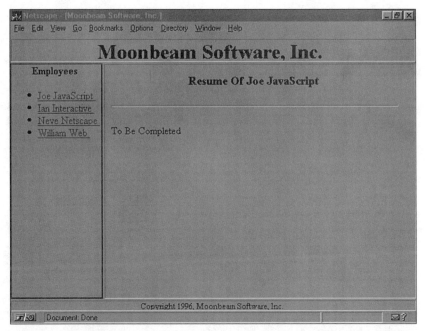

Figure 13-4 Moonbeam Software page with Joe JavaScript's resume visible in viewer frame

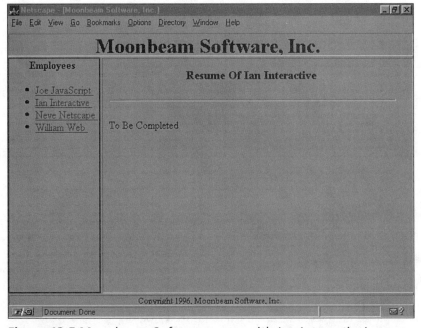

Figure 13-5 Moonbeam Software page with Ian Interactive's resume visible in viewer frame

1. This example will add to the site started in How-To 13.1. This example will use the frame document HT1301.HTM as is and will make modifications to the HT1301A.HTM document.

2. Use the following HTML code to create the Employees document. This document contains an unordered list of employee names. Each employee name is a hypertext link that will display the employee's resume when activated. Add a <BASE> tag before the first hypertext link. The <BASE> tag's TARGET attribute will point to the middle-right or viewer frame. The viewer frame is established inside HT1301.HTM. Save the document as HT1302B.HTM.

```
<HTML>
<HEAD>
<TITLE> Moonbeam Software, Inc. </TITLE>
</HEAD>
<BODY>
<CENTER> <B> Employees </B> </CENTER>
<UL>
<BASE TARGET="viewer">
<LI> <A HREF="jj.htm"> Joe JavaScript </A>
<LI> <A HREF="ii.htm"> Ian Interactive </A>
<LI> <A HREF="nn.htm"> Neve Netscape </A>
<LI> <A HREF="ww.htm"> William Web </A>
</UL>
</BODY>
</HTML>
```

3. In HT1301A.HTM, enclose the Employee list item inside an anchor container. This container will be implemented as a hypertext link that references the HT1302B.HTM document, created in Step 1. Because this link does not initialize the TARGET attribute, and HT1301A.HTM does not establish a default target frame, this document will replace the calling document inside the middle left or menu frame. Save the modified document to disk.

```
<A HREF="HT1302B.htm"> Employees </A>
```

4. In Navigator, use the File/Open File menu option to execute the JavaScript application by loading HT1301.HTM into the browser.

How It Works

In HT1302B.HTM, the <BASE> tag is used to establish the middle-right frame or viewer as the default target frame for this document. The viewer frame is established inside the frame document HT1301.HTM. By including the <BASE> tag before any hypertext link, all employee resumes will be displayed inside the default target frame. All hypertext links inherit the document's default target frame. The <BASE> tag's results in employee resumes being displayed inside the viewer frame.

Comments

If your goal is to have all links in a document target the same frame, you should use the <BASE> tag instead of setting the TARGET attribute of each link in the document. The <BASE> tag gives you a single point where a default target specification can be defined. A default target frame will reduce the possibility of error when creating or modifying the document. Errors may be caused by forgetting to establish a target frame for an individual hypertext link. Because new links automatically inherit the target frame from the <BASE> tag, the possibility for error will be minimized.

Even if one or two links do not target the default target frame, the <BASE> tag can still be used. How-To 13.3 will demonstrate how individual hypertext links can override the default target frame.

COMPLEXITY
INTERMEDIATE

13.3 How do I...
Override a document's default target frame?

COMPATIBILITY:

Problem

The <BASE> tag is an easy way to set the target frame for all hypertext links in a document. How can I exclude hypertext links from inheriting the document's default target frame set in the <BASE> tag?

Technique

The <BASE> tag can be used to establish a target frame for all links inside an HTML document. The document's default target frame can be overridden by specifying the TARGET attribute for one of the links in the document. The scope rules for target frame definition result in a link's TARGET definition taking precedence over a TARGET definition established inside a <BASE> tag.

In previous examples, frame names are used to explicitly identify an individual frame. HTML contains a set of magic target names that implicitly identify a frame. Magic names are logical names that serve as place holders for a specific frame. The specific frame, pointed to by the magic name, is determined at runtime when a document is loaded into the browser. The term "magic target name" is proper terminology when referring to these logical frame names. Magic names are distinguished from regular frame names by the fact that they begin with the underscore character. According to proper HTML syntax, normal frame names must begin with an alphanumeric character.

The magic name _self is used to represent the host frame. When this magic name is used, the link will load the downloaded document into the same frame which contained the calling document. The following is an example of a link assigned to the _self target.

```
<A HREF="HT1302B.htm" TARGET="_self"> Employees </A>
```

This _self magic name is useful when overriding a default target name. A <BASE> tag may be used to target another frame. The _self magic name can be used for individual links that want to use the current frame. An example is a menu document that contains one link tied to a submenu document. While other menu options target another frame, the submenu link could bring up its document in the same frame that hosted the main menu document.

Steps

This example will modify HT1301A.HTM, created in How-To 13.1. The target frame for the first four menu items will be replaced with a default target frame for the entire HT1301A.HTM document. The Employees link, which previously did not have a target frame, will override the default target frame by separately targeting the _self frame. After these modifications are completed, the site will remain unchanged from How-To 13.2. The purpose of this example is to demonstrate an alternative approach that you could use when creating the Menu document.

From Netscape Navigator Version 2.0 or higher, use the File/Open File menu option to load the HT1303.HTM document off the CD. The screen in Figure 13-2 will be displayed. Click on the Corporate History link and the screen, similar to Figure 13-3, will appear. Activate the Employees link and the screen will be similar to Figure 13-4.

1. This example will modify the Moonbeam Software site. This example will use, as is, the frame document HT1301.HTM and will make modifications to the HT1301A.HTM document.

2. Inside your favorite editor, open up the HT1301A.HTM document. Add a <BASE> tag directly below the <BODY> tag. The <BASE> tag's TARGET attribute should point to the viewer frame. This frame is defined inside the frame document.

```
<BASE TARGET="viewer">
```

3. Move down to the unordered menu list. Remove the TARGET attribute from the first four links. These links now inherit the default target frame, established in Step 2.

```
<LI> <A HREF="welcome.htm"> President's Welcome </A>
<LI> <A HREF="org_his.htm"> Corporate History </A>
<LI> <A HREF="finance.htm"> Financial Information </A>
<LI> <A HREF="partner.htm"> Corporate Partnerships </A>
```

4. To override the default target frame, define the TARGET attribute for the Employees link. The TARGET attribute will be set to the _self magic target name. The _self magic name indicates that HT1302B.HTM will be displayed inside the same window or frame used to host the calling document. Save the modified document to disk.

```
<A HREF="HT1302B.htm" TARGET="_self"> Employees </A>
```

5. In Navigator, use the File/Open File menu option to execute the JavaScript application by loading HT1301.HTM into the browser.

How It Works

The <BASE> tag is added to HT1301A.HTM for the purpose of establishing a default target frame for this document. The viewer frame will be established as the default target frame. By including the <BASE> tag before the first hypertext link, most links in this document will inherit the default frame. Links which define their own target frame will not inherit the default target frame. Because the Employees link assigns the magic name _self to its <TARGET> attribute, this link will override the default target.

The _self magic name indicates that the current frame should be used to display the referenced document. The _self magic name is synonymous with the menu frame name. The menu frame is the middle left frame, which hosts the main Menu document. The menu frame name could replace the _self magic name, as the target for the Employees link, with no effect on the page's look and feel. When the Employees link is activated, the list of employees will replace the main menu inside the host frame.

Comments

How-To 13.2 and How To 13.3 use different techniques to accomplish the same goal. Both examples assign a target frame to the first four links in the HT1301A.HTM document. The Employees link remains tied to the frame containing the calling document. This means that Web developers have a choice when setting up a target frame for most of the links in a document.

One technique is to set the TARGET attribute of the links you wish to redirect to another frame. Any frames without a TARGET attribute will default to the host frame. The second technique is to use the <BASE> tag to establish a target frame for an entire document. To override the document's target frame, set an individual link's TARGET attribute. Because there is no objective measure to discriminate between the two methods, method preference will be determined by personal taste.

COMPLEXITY
INTERMEDIATE

13.4 How do I...
Display a referenced document in the frameset's window when a link is clicked?

COMPATIBILITY: NAVIGATOR 2.X   NAVIGATOR 3.X   EXPLORER 3.X

Problem

Instead of having a downloaded document display inside another frame, I would like to have it display inside the window assigned to the parent frameset. How can I target the frameset's window?

Technique

How-To 13.3 introduced the _self magic name, which implicitly refers to the current frame. Another magic target name, called _parent, represents the area of the screen assigned to a frame's parent window. The parent window is the region of the screen used to display all the frames belonging to the same frameset as the current frame.

Frames are organized into groups of frames, called framesets. Each frame document contains a single frameset. Even if the document contains nested or embedded framesets, all frames belong to the document's main frameset. The dimension of the parent window is dependent on the context in which the frame document is viewed. If the frame document is viewed inside a frame, then the parent window has the same dimensions as the host frame. When the frame document is viewed as a standalone document, the parent window is synonymous with the browser's document viewing area. Figure 13-6 shows where the document viewing area is located inside the browser's main window.

By assigning the _parent magic name to the base or anchor tag's TARGET attribute, the Web developer indicates that the downloaded document should be displayed inside the parent window. Because the parent window cannot be assigned a name, the _parent magic name is the only way to reference this area of the screen. The following code indicates that "hfgt.htm" should be displayed inside the parent window.

```
<A HREF="hfgt.htm" TARGET="_parent"> HFGT </A>
```

Steps

This example will add a new hypertext link to the Moonbeam Software menu document. Moonbeam Software has a flagship product named Hypertext Form Generation Tool (HFGT). The marketing page for this product will be available from

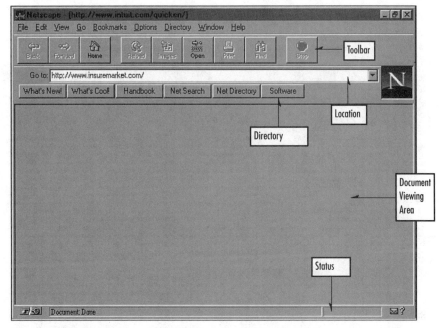

Figure 13-6 The browser's document viewing area

the main menu. To emphasize the importance of HFGT, Moonbeam Software wants the marketing page to take up the majority of the screen. This means that HFGT marketing page will occupy the space assigned to the frameset or parent window.

From Netscape Navigator Version 2.0 or higher, use the File/Open File menu option to load the HT1304.HTM document off the CD. The screen will look like Figure 13-2. Activate the HFGT link in the menu frame. The screen will change to Figure 13-7. Notice the Hypertext Form Generation Tool document replace the middle two frames on the screen. Only the top and bottom frames remain unchanged.

From Netscape Navigator Version 2.0 or higher, load HT1304A.HTM. In the previous example, this HT1304A.HTM was viewed within the context of another frame document. Now this document is being viewed as a standalone document. Activate the HFGT link in the menu frame. The screen will look like Figure 13-8. Notice that the parent window now represents the entire document viewing area.

1. This example will add to Moonbeam Software's site. This example will modify the frame document HT1301.HTM and HTML document HT1301A.HTM document.

2. Start up your favorite editor and open the file HT1301.HTM. Break the HT1301.HTM into two frame documents. Use the following code as a basis for the two documents. The nested frameset will be moved to the newly created frame document. In its place, a new <FRAME> tag, pointing to the new document, will be added. The original document is broken into two frame documents to differentiate the parent and the top window. Save the original frame document under the file name HT1304.HTM.

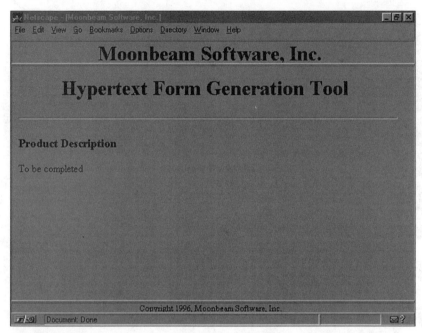

Figure 13-7 After clicking the HFGT link within a frame environment

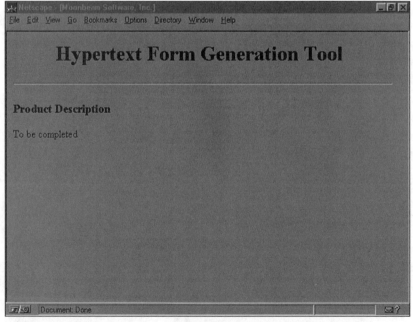

Figure 13-8 After clicking the HFGT link within a standalone environment

```
<HTML>
<HEAD>
<TITLE> Moonbeam Software, Inc. </TITLE>
</HEAD>
<FRAMESET ROWS="50,*">
    <FRAME NAME="name" SRC="comp_nm.htm" MARGINWIDTH="1" SCROLLING="no">
    <FRAME NAME="top" SRC="HT1304A.htm">
</FRAMESET>
</HTML>
```

Save the newly created frame document as HT1304A.HTM.

```
<HTML>
<HEAD>
<TITLE> Moonbeam Software, Inc. </TITLE>
</HEAD>
<FRAMESET COLS="150,*">
    <FRAME NAME="menu" SRC="HT1304B.htm" MARGINWIDTH="1" SCROLLING="no">
    <FRAME NAME="viewer" SRC="welcome.htm">
</FRAMESET>
</HTML>
```

3. Now load HT1301A.HTM, into the editor. Turn the HFGT list item into a hypertext link. This link targets the parent frame to display hfgt.htm. Save the file as HT1304B.HTM.

```
<A HREF="hfgt.htm" TARGET="_parent"> HFGT </A>
```

4. In Navigator, use the File/Open File menu option to execute the JavaScript application by loading HT1304.HTM into the browser.

How It Works

With a single frame document, as seen in previous examples, the parent window would be synonymous with the browser's document viewing area. This is due to the fact that the parent window corresponds to the screen dimensions needed to display all frames contained within the frame document. By breaking the original frame document into two separate frame documents, HT1304.HTM and HT1304A.HTM, two distinct parent windows are created. The parent window for HT1304A.HTM is the two middle frames.

The HFGT link uses the _parent magic name to target the frameset's parent window. For the HFGT link, the parent window encompasses the middle part of the screen. This is the area of the screen used to display the menu and viewer frames. The HFGT link is contained within the HT1304B.HTM document, which is displayed inside the menu frame.

When the HT1304A.HTM is viewed as a standalone document, meaning not within one of the frames belonging to HT1304.HTM, the parent window now represents the entire viewing area. For the HFGT link, the parent window changes because the frameset, defined in HT1304.HTM, has been removed from the picture.

Comments

Because links can target any visible frame, the name of the frame used to display the HT1304A.HTM can also be used to target the parent window. In the example, this frame is assigned the name "top" in Step 2. The TARGET attribute of the HFGT link can be set to "top" without changing the example. Therefore the following anchor declaration would have the same effect as the HTML code in Step 3.

```
<A HREF="hfgt.htm" TARGET="top"> HFGT </A>
```

COMPLEXITY
INTERMEDIATE

13.5   How do I...

Display a referenced document in the topmost window when a link is clicked?

COMPATIBILITY:

Problem

When a frame document is displayed by itself, the _parent magic name implicitly references the entire document viewing area. However, when the frame document is viewed within another frame, the _parent window only references a portion of the screen. I want a downloaded document to display inside the document viewing area, regardless of whether or not the frame document is viewed as a standalone document. Is there a magic name that will implicitly reference the topmost window whose dimensions are the same as the browser's document viewing area?

Technique

The magic name _top is used to represent the topmost window. The top window is synonymous with the browser's document viewing area. Figure 13-6 represents the browser's document viewing area. By assigning the magic name, as a quoted string, to a base or anchor tag's TARGET attribute, the referenced document will be displayed using the topmost window. The following example demonstrates the HTML code required to have hfgt.htm display inside the topmost window.

```
<A HREF="hfgt.htm" TARGET="_top"> HFGT </A>
```

The _top magic name is useful for breaking out of an arbitrarily deep nesting of framesets. As discussed in How-To 13.4, the dynamics of the _parent magic name may cause it to reference only a portion of the viewing area. When you want to use the entire screen to host a downloaded document, use the _top magic name instead of the _parent magic name. The topmost window never changes. It is always synonymous with the document viewing area.

Steps

This example will modify the HFGT link, added in How-To 13.4. Because of the importance of the HFGT product to the firm's business plan, Moonbeam Software wants to use the entire screen when displaying the HFGT marketing page. By using the top window, the user's attention can be focused exclusively on the information contained within the marketing page.

From Navigator 2.0 or higher, use the File/Open File menu option to load the document HT1305.HTM off the CD. The screen will look like Figure 13-2. Activate the HFGT link in the left or menu frame. The screen shown in Figure 13-9 will appear. Notice that the Hypertext Form Generation Tool document replaces the frame document inside the browser's document viewing area. When the topmost window should be targeted, the _top magic name was used to break out of an embedded frameset. This breakout cannot be accomplished by using the _parent magic name.

From Netscape Navigator Version 2.0 or higher, use the File/Open File menu option to load the HT1305A.HTM document off the CD. Notice that the frame document is being viewed as a standalone document. Click on the HFGT link. Once again, the screen shown in Figure 13-9 will appear. Although the frame environment has changed, the Hypertext Form Generation Tool document is still displayed using the topmost window. Unlike the _parent magic name, where the frame layout of the document influenced which window was referenced, the _top magic name always references the same window.

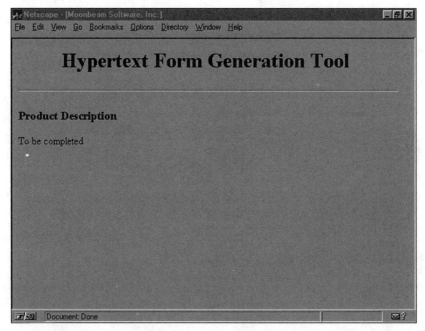

Figure 13-9 The hypertext form generation tool marketing page within the topmost window

1. This example will modify Moonbeam Software's site by modifying the HTML document HT1304B.HTM.

2. Use an editor to open up HT13.04B.HTM. Modify the TARGET attribute of the HFGT link to target the topmost window. Save the changes to disk.

```
<A HREF="hfgt.htm" TARGET="_top"> HFGT </A>
```

How It Works

The _top magic name implicitly references the entire document viewing area. Because this window is not assigned a name, the magic name is the only way to reference the browser's document viewing area. By assigning the _top magic name to a link's TARGET attribute, the referenced document is displayed using the entire frame. The _top magic name even works if the document is displayed inside the child frame belonging to an embedded frameset.

Comments

Be careful when choosing between the _parent and _top magic names! If you want to target the topmost window, then ALWAYS use the _top magic name.

COMPLEXITY
INTERMEDIATE

13.6   How do I...
Display a referenced document in a new window when a link is clicked?

Problem

Instead of having a downloaded document display inside another frame or the document viewing area, I would like to have it display inside a new blank window. How can I display a downloaded document inside a new window? Can I also use the new window as the target for other links?

Technique

There are two ways to display a downloaded document in a new window. One method uses the _blank magic name to display the referenced document in a new, unnamed window. Because this window is unnamed, other links can not target this window.

The following example will display the hfgt.htm document inside a new, blank window.

```
<A HREF="hfgt.htm" TARGET="_blank"> HFGT </A>
```

New windows resemble a second instance of the Navigator's main window. Like the main Navigator window, the new window contains a menu, toolbar, and document viewing area. Currently, there is no way to specify the characteristics of the new window.

As you may remember, a window or frame must be named before hypertext links can target it. The exception to this rule are magic names that serve as logical place-holders for specific windows. For example, the _blank magic name is used to display a new, unnamed window. However, once the new window is created, the _blank magic name cannot be used to reference the same window. If the user clicks a second time on a link targeted to a _blank window, a second new window will be displayed on the screen. Therefore, the _blank magic name cannot be used to create a new window that can be targeted from multiple links.

A new window must be named before multiple links can target it. In How-To 13.1 you learned that frames could be named by assigning a quoted string to a frame's NAME attribute. Another technique for naming windows involves hypertext links that target a window not visible on the screen. When the link is activated, the browser creates a new window whose name matches the TARGET attribute. Because the new window is assigned a name, other links can target this window. If multiple links target the same unused name, the first link activated by the user will display the new window. The <BASE> tag should be used to ensure that all links point to the same window.

Steps

This example will modify the HFGT link, added in How-To 13.4. Instead of displaying the Hypertext Form Generation Tool marketing page in the browser's document viewing area, Moonbeam Software wishes to display it inside a new, blank window.

From Navigator 2.0 or higher, use the File/Open File menu option to load the HT1306.HTM document. Activate the HFGT link in the left or menu frame. The document in Figure 13-10 will appear on the screen. This figure shows a new instance of the Navigator main window. The Hypertext Form Generation Tool document is displayed inside the new window. The _blank magic name was used to create and target the new window.

From Netscape Navigator, load the HT1306A.HTM document into the document viewing area. This document is designed to be viewed inside a frame environment. A <BASE> tag is used to target another frame named viewer. Now that this document is being viewed outside of the frame environment, the target window does not exist. Therefore, when one of the links is activated, a new window will be created. As other links are activated, their documents will be displayed inside the new window. The <BASE> tag ensures that many of the downloaded documents are viewed in the same window.

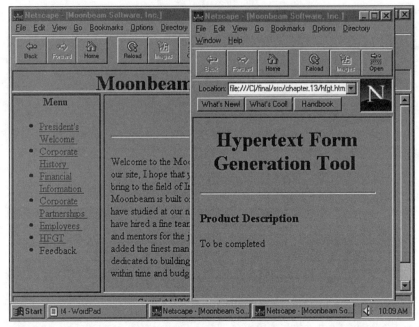

Figure 13-10 The Hypertext Form Generation Tool marketing page within a new window

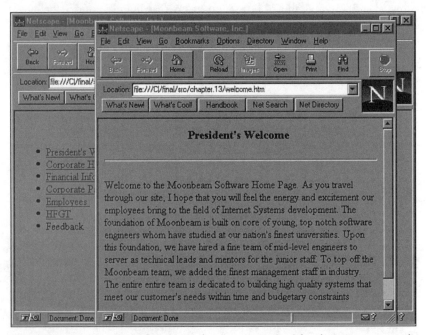

Figure 13-11 The President's Welcome page inside the new named window

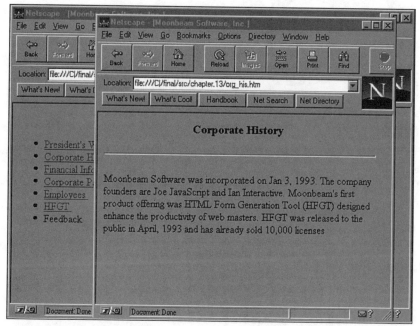

Figure 13-12 Multiple links targeting the new window

In the Menu document, click on the President's Welcome link. The document in Figure 13-11 will be visible on the screen. The new window contains the President's Welcome document. From the system menu, select Restore so that both windows can be viewed at the same time. Click on the Corporate History link and watch the referenced document display inside the new window. The screen now appears as in Figure 13-12. Because an unused frame name created the window, the new window is named. Other links can reference the window through its assigned name.

1. This example will modify Moonbeam Software's main menu document, used in previous examples.

2. In HT1304B.HTM, modify the TARGET attribute of the HFGT link to point to a new blank window. Save the document to disk.

```
<A HREF="hfgt.htm" TARGET="_blank"> HFGT </A>
```

3. In Navigator, use the File/Open File menu option to execute the JavaScript application by loading HT1304.HTM into the browser.

How It Works

The _blank magic name represents a new window. By assigning the _blank magic name to a hypertext link's TARGET attribute, the Web developer is indicating that the browser should use a new window to host the referenced document. The new window is unnamed, which means that other links cannot target this window.

Named windows are created when a link that targets an inactive frame name is activated. Inactive frame names refer to frames that are not currently visible on the screen. Because the target window does not exist, the browser will create a new window to host the downloaded document. The new window will be assigned the inactive frame name. Because the frame name is now active, multiple links can target the new window.

Comments

The use of new windows to host documents should be limited to special circumstances because the practice can get out of hand and result in numerous windows being opened. The addition of new windows will add confusion about which document is displayed inside each window.

COMPLEXITY
ADVANCED

13.7 How do I...
Set the target frame when a link is clicked?

COMPATIBILITY:  NAVIGATOR 2.X NAVIGATOR 3.X EXPLORER 3.X

Problem

HTML documents should be designed so that they can be viewed both inside and outside the frame environment. When the document is viewed as a standalone document, hypertext links should target the current or _self window. When the document is viewed within the frame environment, the links should target another frame. How can I create hypertext links where the target window is based on the environmental conditions?

Technique

There are three steps to creating a dynamic hypertext link whose target window is based on the type of environment in which the document is being viewed. The first step is to set up an event handler that will be invoked when the link is activated. This allows the target window to be in realtime right before the document is requested from the server. The second step is to identify whether or not the document is being displayed as a standalone document or inside a host frame. Finally, the link's target attribute must be set to the appropriate target frame.

The Link object's onClick event handler is invoked when a hypertext link is activated. Figure 13-13 shows all the properties belonging to the Link object. Using this event handler will allow the target frame to be established at the moment when the user makes a request for a particular document. Because the handler finishes executing before the document is requested from the Web server, any changes made

Link

PROPERTIES	METHODS	EVENT HANDLERS
hash	NONE	onClick
host		onMouseOver
hostname		
href		
pathname		
port		
protocol		
search		
target		

Figure 13-13 The Link object

will affect where a document is viewed. The following example demonstrates how to establish an onClick event handler for a hypertext link. The event handler calls a function named dynTarget.

```
<LI> <A HREF="org_his.htm" onClick="dynTarget(this)"> Corporate History </A>
```

The onClick event handler must determine whether or not a document is being viewed inside the frame environment. The document's current window can be used to determine this information. If the document is being viewed inside a frame, the window's parent property will not equal the self property. Instead, the parent property will reference the window containing the frame document. Standalone documents do not have a parent window, so this property equals the self property. The following code demonstrates a predicate statement that will test for standalone documents.

```
if (parent == self) {
   // Standalone Document
} else {
   // Inside A Frame
}
```

Once the environment is established, the Link object can be used to set the target window. A reference to this object is achieved by referencing the *this* variable inside the onClick handler. The this variable points to the corresponding Link object that represents the activated link. Link objects possess a target property, which mirrors the hypertext link's TARGET attribute. By assigning a frame or magic name to the target property, the hypertext link will target this window. The onClick event handler can be used to set a link's target at run-time. If the document is displayed as a standalone document, the _self magic name can be used to target the current frame. In the frame environment, a frame name can be used to target another window. The following code changes a link's target window.

```
link.target = "viewer";
```

Steps

This example will modify Moonbeam Software's menu document. In previous examples, most of the links in this document targeted the viewer frame. Because some employees at Moonbeam still have 640x480 screens, there is not enough real estate on the screen to effectively support the frame environment. For these employees, Moonbeam wants to establish another site that does not implement frames. Instead of recreating each HTML document in the original site, Moonbeam wants to use JavaScript to establish a dynamic Web page. Moonbeam Software wants the menu document to operate properly both inside and outside the frame environment. This means that downloaded documents will only target another window when the document is visible inside the frame environment.

From Netscape Navigator Version 2.0 or higher, use the File/Open File menu option to load the HT1307.HTM document from the CD. The HTML document in Figure 13-2 will appear on the screen. Activate the Corporate History link in the middle, left or menu frame. The document in Figure 13-3 will appear on the screen.

From Netscape Navigator 2.0 or higher, use the File/Open File menu option to load the HT1307A.HTM document off the CD. This document in Figure 13-14 is displayed on the screen. Click on the Corporate History link, and the screen will change to Figure 13-15.

1. This example will modify Moonbeam Software's main menu document so that it can be displayed inside as a standalone document without displaying referenced documents inside new windows.

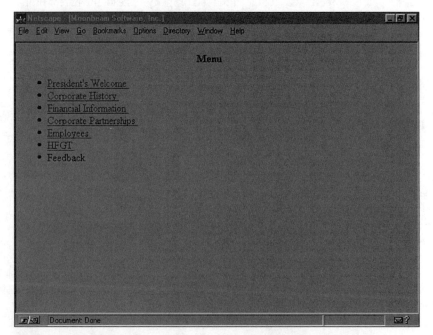

Figure 13-14 Menu document as a standalone document

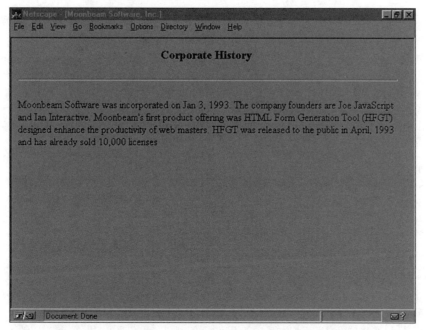

Figure 13-15 Menu document overrides the target frame

2. In HT1304B.HTM, use the following code to create a <SCRIPT> container inside the document's header. The <SCRIPT> container contains a JavaScript function named dynTarget. This function will be invoked within a link's onClick event handler. The dynTarget function dynamically sets the link's target frame based on whether or not the document is being displayed inside a frame.

```
<SCRIPT LANGUAGE="JavaScript">
<!-- Hide JavaScript Code From Older Browsers
function dynTarget(link) {
    if (parent == self) {
        link.target = "_self";
    } else {
        link.target = "viewer";
    }
}
//-->
</SCRIPT>
```

3. Inside the document <BODY>, remove the <BASE> tag. This means that the document no longer contains a default target frame. Add an onClick event handler to each hypertext link. This handler will invoke the dynTarget function, created in Step 2. Save the modifications to disk.

```
<A HREF="welcome.htm" onClick="dynTarget(this)"> President's Welcome </A>
<A HREF="org_his.htm" onClick="dynTarget(this)"> Corporate History </A>
<A HREF="finance.htm" onClick="dynTarget(this)"> Financial Information </A>
<A HREF="partner.htm" onClick="dynTarget(this)"> Corporate Partnerships </A>
```

How It Works

The Link object's onClick event handler is used to invoke the dynTarget function. This function accepts a single input parameter, which is a reference to the current Link object. Within the dynTarget, a conditional is used to assign one of two target frame names to the current link's target attribute. The conditional's predicate is based on whether or not the window's parent document is equal to the self document. This condition is true if the document is being viewed outside the frame environment.

If this is the case, then the _self magic name is specified as the target frame. This means that referenced documents are displayed inside the host frame, which displayed the current document. If the document is viewed within a frame, the target is assigned the frame name viewer. This frame is established inside the parent frame document. Because the target frame is established before the server call is made, the downloaded document will be displayed inside the specified frame.

Comments

This How-To demonstrates some of the powerful features of the JavaScript language. If this capability did not exist, a duplicate HTML document would have to be created. One document would be used inside the frame environment, while the other document would be used as a standalone document. Duplicate documents mean twice the effort is needed to make a change to the document. This is because both documents will have to be changed. By using the JavaScript language, the maintenance headache caused by this situation is eliminated.

COMPLEXITY
INTERMEDIATE

13.8 How do I...
Redirect documents returned by a form submission?

COMPATIBILITY: NAVIGATOR 2.X NAVIGATOR 3.X EXPLORER 3.X

Problem

When a form is submitted to the server, an HTML document is returned to the client. In the previous examples, we learned how to redirect documents returned when a hypertext link is activated to any frame on the screen. Can I also set up a target frame for documents returned by a form submission?

Technique

Target frames can be established from documents returned by a form submission. Like the Link object, forms also contain a TARGET attribute. This attribute can be set to any valid frame or magic names. These names have the same effect on a form submission as they do on a link activation. For example, the _top magic name can be used to reference the topmost window. Target frames, not visible on the screen, will cause the browser to create a new, named window. The TARGET attribute is optional, with the host frame serving as the target for forms without explicit target frames.

Steps

In this example, you will create a feedback for the Moonbeam Software site. The final option in the main menu is titled Feedback. This option will be converted to a hypertext link. The link will display a form, inside the viewer frame, designed to elicit user reaction to the company, its products, and the site. After the user has filled out the survey, Moonbeam Software wants to display a Thank You message to the user. This message will express the company's gratitude to the individual for taking time to respond to the survey. Moonbeam wants the Thank You message to replace the Copyright message at the bottom of the page.

From Netscape Navigator 2.0 or above, use the File/Open File menu option to load the HT1308.HTM document off the CD. In the main menu, activate the Feedback link. The screen now appears similar to Figure 13-16. Complete the form

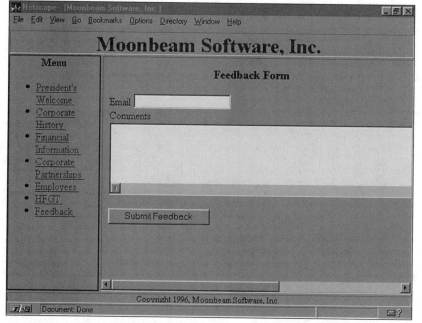

Figure 13-16 The feedback form

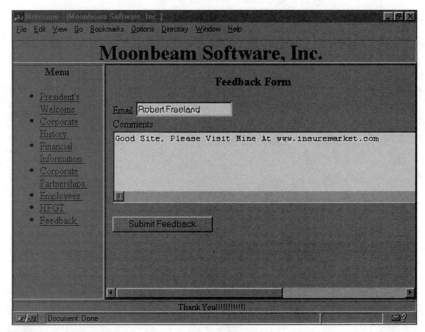

Figure 13-17 Redirected Thank You document replaces copyright page

by providing an e-mail message and comment. Click on the Submit Feedback button. The Thank You message shown in Figure 13-17 replaces the Copyright message inside the bottom frame.

1. This example will modify the menu document, HT1304B.HTM, used throughout this chapter. The final menu option will be changed to a hypertext link that pulls up a comment card.

2. Use the following code to create an HTML form. This form represents a comment card where users can provide information about the site. The <FORM> tag's TARGET attribute references the bottom, or "msg", frame (see HT1304A.HTM). Returned documents will be displayed inside this frame. Save the document as HT1309B.HTM.

```
<HTML>
<HEAD> <TITLE> Feedback Form </TITLE> </HEAD>
<BODY>
<CENTER> <H3> Feedback Form </H3> </CENTER>
<FORM ACTION="tyou.htm" TARGET="msg">
Email <INPUT TYPE="text" NAME="email" LENGTH=100> <BR>
Comments <BR>
<TEXTAREA NAME="comment" ROWS=5 COLS=100>
</TEXTAREA> <BR>
<INPUT TYPE="submit" VALUE="Submit Feedback">
</TABLE>
```

```
</FORM>
</BODY>
</HTML>
```

3. Modify HT1304B.HTM so that the Feedback list item is changed to a hypertext link. This link references the form document HT1308B.HTM, created in Step 2. Instead of defining an explicit TARGET frame, this link uses the dynTarget function, which dynamically sets the target frame.

```
<LI> <A HREF="HT1308B.htm" onClick="dynTarget(this)"> Feedback </A>
```

How It Works

When this Feedback link is activated, a feedback form is displayed inside the viewer frame. This TARGET frame for this form has been set to the bottom, or "msg", frame. This frame name is established inside the frame document HT1304.HTM. When this form is submitted to the server, the returned document is redirected to the "msg" frame. The Thank You message replaces the Copyright message inside this frame.

Comments

Because this book does not come with an HTTP server, this example does not actually submit information to a server. Instead, a canned Thank You document has been scripted. Because this document is referenced by the form's action property, it acts like a returned document. Normally the action property is tied to an executable process on the server. However, like most URL-based references, the action can point to almost anything. The only problem is that canned documents cannot handle the submitted data. So the user's feedback will be lost forever. If this example did invoke a server process, the target frame would behave no differently from this example. (Well, you may have to wait a few seconds communicating with the server.)

COMPLEXITY
ADVANCED

13.9 How do I...
Set the target frame when a form is submitted to the server?

COMPATIBILITY: | NAVIGATOR 2.X | NAVIGATOR 3.X | EXPLORER 3.X |

Problem

A link's target frame can be established on environmental conditions that exist at runtime. Can forms also contain dynamic frames?

Technique

The JavaScript environment creates a Form object for every <FORM> container located in a document. The Form object contains a target attribute which mirrors the <FORM> tag's TARGET attribute. By setting this attribute before a form submission event, a developer can change which window is used to display the returned document. Form submissions typically occur as the result of the user clicking a submit element. JavaScript allows developers to trap a submit's onClick event.

Inside the event handler, the JavaScript code must determine whether or not frames are being used. As you may remember from How-To 13.7, the window's Parent property will not equal the Self property if the document is viewed inside a frame. The parent will equal the Self property in a standalone document. Therefore the following predicate will return true in a standalone document:

```
if (parent == self) {
   // Standalone Document
} else {
   // Inside A Frame
}
```

Once the environment is known, the form's target attribute can be referenced to establish a target frame. Valid frame names and magic names can be assigned to this attribute. The following code demonstrates how to establish the "_self" window as the target frame for a form variable.

```
form.target = "_self";
```

Steps

Moonbeam wants to use the Feedback Form in several places on its site. When the form is viewed as a standalone document, the company does not want a new window to host the Thank You message. By explicitly defining a target frame, new windows will be used when the target frame is not visible on the screen. You must create a dynamic target frame for the Feedback Form in order to properly support this requirement.

From Netscape Navigator 2.0 or above, use the File/Open File menu option to load the HT1309.HTM document off the CD. Inside the main menu, activate the Feedback link. The screen now appears similar to Figure 13-16. Complete the form by providing an e-mail message and comment. Click on the Submit Feedback button. The Thank You message that appears in Figure 13-17 replaces the Copyright message inside the bottom frame.

From Netscape Navigator 2.0 or above, use the File/Open File menu option to load the HT1308B.HTM document off the CD. The form in Figure 13-18 now appears. Complete the form by providing an e-mail message and comment. Click on the Submit Feedback button. The Thank You message, in Figure 13-19, replaces the form inside the host window.

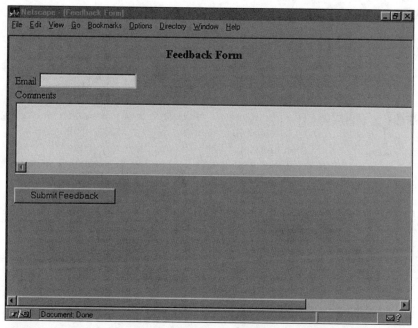

Figure 13-18 The feedback form as a standalone document

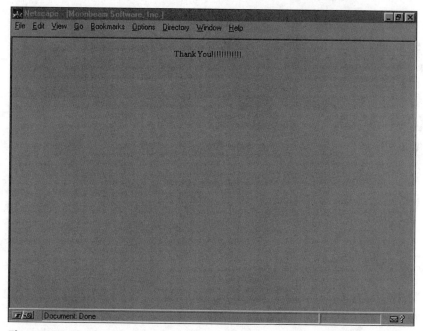

Figure 13-19 The Thank You document displayed inside the host frame

1. This example will modify the feedback form, HT1308B.HTM, created in How-To 13.8. How-To 13.7 introduced you to the concept of dynamic targets. A dynamic target changes depending on the host environment. When frames are used, the target redirects documents to another frame. If the document is viewed as a standalone document, the host frame is targeted. This example will teach you how to set up dynamic targets for frames.

2. Open HT1308B.HTM from your favorite editor. Inside the document header, add a JavaScript container based on the following code. This code creates the dynTarget function, which sets the form's target frame based on whether or not the document is being displayed inside a frame.

```
<SCRIPT LANGUAGE="JavaScript">
<!-- Hide JavaScript Code From Older Browsers
function dynTarget(form) {
    if (parent == self) {
        form.target = "_self";
    } else {
        form.target = "msg";
    }
}
//-->
</SCRIPT>
```

3. Replace the submit button's TARGET attribute with an onClick event handler. This handler calls the dynTarget function, created in Step 2. The event handler is needed to execute JavaScript code right before the form is submitted to the server. This will allow the code to detect the display environment at runtime.

```
<INPUT TYPE="submit" VALUE="Submit Feedback"
 onClick="dynTarget(this.form)">
```

How It Works

When the user submits the form, the onClick handler is fired. This handler calls the dynTarget, defined in Step 2. A reference to the current form is passed to this function. This allows the function to more easily access form members. The current window's parent and self properties are used to determine if the document is being displayed inside a frame. If the parent does not equal the child, indicating frame usage, the target frame msg is established. This frame is located at the bottom of the screen. If the form is in standalone mode, the return document is redirected to the host frame. This is the same frame that would be used had no target frame been explicitly defined.

Comments

Besides links and forms, client-side image maps can also result in a document being downloaded from the server. How-To 13.10 will wrap up the target window discussion by focusing on client-side image maps.

COMPLEXITY
INTERMEDIATE

13.10 How do I...
Define a target frame for client-side image map links?

COMPATIBILITY: NAVIGATOR 2.X   NAVIGATOR 3.X   EXPLORER 3.X

Problem

Many of the hypertext links in my HTML documents are contained inside client-side image maps. Can I define a target frame for hypertext links embedded within client-side image maps?

Technique

With client-side image maps, hypertext links are defined inside the <AREA> tag. This tag defines a sensitive region of the image. When the user clicks inside this region, the downloaded document, specified in the <AREA> tag's HREF attribute, will replace the calling document inside the host frame. If the <AREA> tag's TARGET attribute is set to a target frame, the downloaded document is displayed inside this frame. The following example demonstrates how to set up a target frame for an image area.

```
<AREA SHAPE="RECT" COORDS="0,181,113,213" HREF="help.htm" TARGET="viewer">
```

Hypertext links inside a client-side image map act just like links specified within an anchor. This means that the <BASE> tag can be used to set up a default target frame for each link in an image. Magic target names can also be assigned to an image region's TARGET attribute. The following code shows you how to target the active frame for an image map link.

```
<AREA SHAPE="RECT" COORDS="0,3,113,36" HREF="index.htm" TARGET="_self">
```

Steps

From the Navigator browser, pull up the HT1310.HTM document. The page in Figure 13-20 will appear on the screen. A client-side image map now resides inside the frame that contained the text-based menus throughout this chapter. Click on the Quotes region. Notice the screen in Figure 13-21 appear on the screen. The target frame for the Quotes region is the result of the <BASE> tag established in Step 3. Click on the Home link and watch the Index Screen page replace the calling document in the active frame. The _self magic name was used in Step 4 to override the default target for this link.

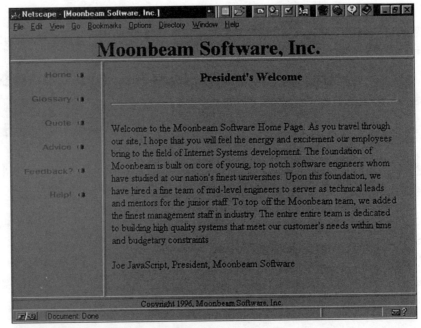

Figure 13-20 Client-side image map

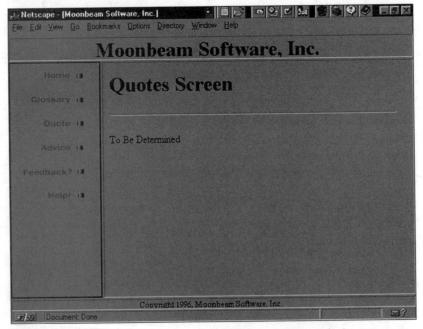

Figure 13-21 A redirected document from a client-side image map

1. In HT1301.HTM, modify the SRC attribute of the second frame to point to HT1308A.HTM. Save the modified frame document as HT1308.HTM.

```
<HTML>
<HEAD>
<TITLE> Hypertext Form Generation Tool Information </TITLE>
</HEAD>
<FRAMESET ROWS="50,*">
    <FRAME NAME="name" SRC="prod_nm.htm" MARGINWIDTH="1" SCROLLING="no">
    <FRAMESET COLS="150,*">
        <FRAME NAME="menu" SRC="HT1308A.htm" MARGINWIDTH="1" SCROLLING="no">
        <FRAME NAME="viewer" SRC="welcome.htm">
    </FRAMESET>
</FRAMESET>
</HTML>
```

2. Create an HTML document that contains the image "toolbar.gif". This image represents an image map that will be used instead of a text-based main menu. Use the <MAP> container to establish a client-side image map. The <MAP> container holds an <AREA> tag, which specifies the sensitive regions of the image map. This tag ties an HTML document to a specific area of the image. All areas in this example are rectangles defined using the minimum and maximum X and Y coordinate values. Use the <BASE> tag's TARGET attribute to establish a default document target frame. The <BASE> tag can be used to establish a default TARGET for hypertext links contained within an image map. Use the <AREA> tag's TARGET attribute to override the default target frame for the Home region. Use the _self magic target name to indicate that the "index.htm" document should be displayed inside the host frame of the calling document. Save the document as HT1308A.HTM.

```
<HTML>
<HEAD>
<TITLE> Hypertext Form Generation Tool </TITLE>
</HEAD>
<BODY>
<BASE TARGET="viewer">

<CENTER>
<IMG SRC="toolbar.gif" USEMAP="#TOOL" BORDER=0>
</CENTER>

<MAP NAME="TOOL">
<AREA SHAPE="RECT" COORDS="0,181,113,213" HREF="help.htm">
<AREA SHAPE="RECT" COORDS="0,145,113,180" HREF="feedback.htm">
<AREA SHAPE="RECT" COORDS="0,110,113,144" HREF="advice.htm">
<AREA SHAPE="RECT" COORDS="0,74,113,109" HREF="quotes.htm">
<AREA SHAPE="RECT" COORDS="0,37,113,74" HREF="glossary.htm">
<AREA SHAPE="RECT" COORDS="0,3,113,36" HREF="index.htm" TARGET="_self">
</MAP>

</BODY>
</HTML>
```

How It Works

The USEMAP attribute will link an image with a <MAP> container. The <MAP> container defines the sensitive screen regions. When the mouse is clicked inside one of these regions, a call to the HTTP server will ensue. When the user clicks on an image, the X and Y coordinates returned by the mouse click event are used to determine which region was activated. Screen regions were established in Step 2.

The <AREA> tag defines a screen region. Currently, only rectangular shape regions are possible. The <AREA> tag's COORDS attribute defines the minimum and maximum X and Y values. These values can be mixed and matched to form the rectangle's four corner points. Each image region is assigned a URL. This is done through the <AREA>'s HREF attribute.

Through the <BASE> tag, a default target frame has been established for this document. As you see, default target frames apply to links, forms, and image maps. This frame results in the downloaded document being displayed inside the middle-right or viewer frame.

Comments

Did you realize that you can simultaneously use server and client-side image maps? If the browser understands client-side maps, this method will be chosen. Otherwise, the server map will be referenced.

CHAPTER 14
DYNAMIC HTML DOCUMENTS

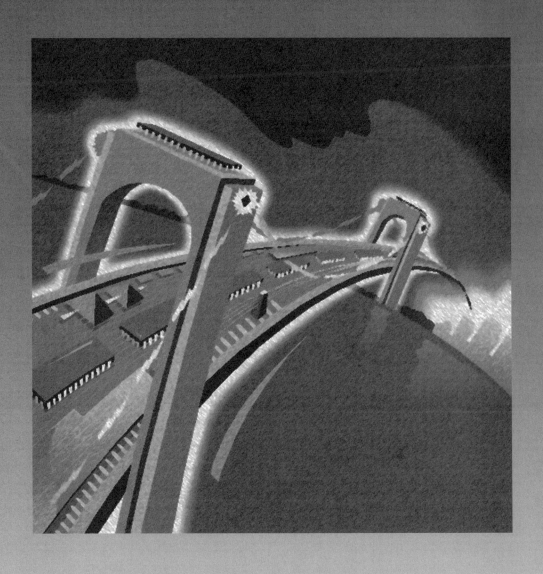

DYNAMIC HTML DOCUMENTS

How do I...

In the past, server processes were required to create dynamic HTML documents. With the advent of the JavaScript language, dependence on the server to create dynamic documents is removed. JavaScript provides methods that can be used to insert dynamic text into the document's layout stream. Dynamic documents are distinguished from regular static documents by the fact that their structure is not known in advance. Conditions that exist when the document is laid out by the browser will affect the way the document appears on the screen. The dynamic aspect of a document could range from a single HTML expression to the layout of the entire document.

14.1   Insert dynamic HTML expressions into a document

This How-To will demonstrate how to include a dynamic HTML expression in the body of an HTML document. Dynamic HTML expressions can be used to display information (the time the user downloaded the document, document's last modified date, and so on) about a user's interaction with a site. Because this information may change from one interactive session to another, the information cannot be included in the document as static text.

14.2   Set the layout of a document at runtime

This How-To demonstrates how to change the structure or layout of an HTML document. JavaScript conditionals are used to display situation-specific blocks of text and format tags. This capability allows developers to create "personalized" pages that display different text or input fields based on environmental factors. In this example, the layout of the document is dynamic.

14.3   Specify a format for a dynamic HTML expression

JavaScript's String object contains several text formatting methods that can be invoked to output dynamic HTML expressions contained within a set of standard HTML format tags. The How-To will also demonstrate how multiple text format methods can be chained together to apply multiple formats and styles to a single expression.

14.4   Dynamically create an HTML anchor

Anchors serve as placeholders that can be used by hypertext links to bring users to related text contained within a document. This How-To will show you how to dynamically create HTML anchors.

14.5   Dynamically create a hypertext link

This How-To will demonstrate how to dynamically create hypertext links that can reference either a related anchor or document.

14.6   Display a dynamically created HTML document

This How-To will dynamically demonstrate how to replace the current document with a new, dynamically created HTML document. The new document will be created when an event occurs inside the current document.

14.7 Display a dynamically created HTML document inside a new window

Learn how to use a new window to display a dynamic document. By using a new window, the user has access to both the new and calling documents.

14.8 Store persistent information in an HTTP cookie

HTTP cookies are used to store persistent information on the client machine. When a server request is issued,Common Gateway Interface (CGI) or Netscape API program, the cookie information is passed to the servers inside the HTTP header. This How-To will demonstrate how to set up an HTTP cookie for a dynamic document. Cookies that expire at some future point in time will also be discussed.

14.9 Access persistent information stored in an HTTP cookie

Because cookies are primarily used to pass data between documents, this How-To will cover the string methods that can be used to extract a value contained within an HTTP cookie.

COMPLEXITY
INTERMEDIATE

14.1 How do I...
Insert dynamic HTML expressions into a document?

COMPATIBILITY:  NAVIGATOR 2.X NAVIGATOR 3.X EXPLORER 3.X

Problem

In the past, documents were composed of static HTML expressions. Through JavaScript, I now have access to a wide array of information pertaining to the Web environment. How can I display this information to the user inside a dynamic HTML expression?

Technique

The Document object's write and writeln methods are used to insert one or more dynamic expressions into an HTML document. These methods accept multiple parameters, which will in turn accept any JavaScript expression, including numeric, string, and literals. The difference between the two methods is that the writeln method places a newline character into the document layout stream immediately following the last expression. The following example uses the writeln method to insert the expression "Prices Effective As Of MM/DD/YY" into the current document.

```
document.writeln("Prices Effective As Of " + (eff_dt.getMonth() + 1) + ⇐
"/" +
                 eff_dt.getDate() + "/" +
                 eff_dt.getYear());
```

The dynamic aspect of this expression is the effective date, which is stored inside a date variable named eff_dt. Based on the value stored in this memory location, the HTML expression output from the writeln method will not be determined until the browser lays out the document.

Placement of the dynamic expression within the document is determined by its position in the document's body. Only write and writeln methods that reference the current document contained within the <BODY> tags will be laid out by the browser at runtime. When a document is loaded in Navigator, the document is laid out on the screen. A layout stream is used to hold the text, in sequence, that will be displayed on the screen. The layout algorithm starts at the top of the document and proceeds sequentially down the document until the end of the file is reached. When Navigator encounters a section of JavaScript code, any calls to write or writeln are pushed onto the layout stream in the sequence in which they are encountered. It is important to note that write and writeln methods not contained within the document body will not affect how a document is laid out.

Steps

This following example represents the beginning of a home page for a small tie importer named Tie Die, Incorporated. Tie Die's home page will eventually show a list of available ties that may be purchased over the Internet. At the bottom of the page, Tie Die wishes to show the effective date of its tie prices. This date is the same day the home page document was last modified. Because JavaScript gives the Web developer access to the document's lastModified property, the Web developer has decided to reference this property inside a dynamic HTML expression versus "hard coding" the property into the document. By using a dynamic HTML expression, tie prices can be changed without having to modify the price effective date at the bottom of the page. Tie Die can be sure that the effective date will always represent the date when prices were changed.

From Navigator 2.0+ or Explorer, use the File/Open menu option to load the HT1401.HTM document into memory. The document shown in Figure 14-1 will appear inside the browser's document viewing area. The effective date of tie prices is displayed at the bottom of the page. The effective date is the same as the date the HT1401.HTM document was last modified. To verify this fact, make a change to the document. When you redisplay the document, this expression will change so that the effective date is the same as the day you modified the document.

1. Use the following HTML code to create a shell for Tie Die's home page. Because this page will be modified throughout this chapter, display an "under construction" image to indicate to any site visitor that this page is a work-in-progress.

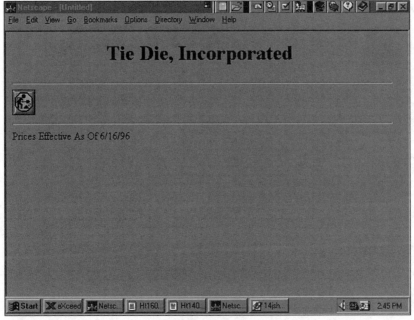

Figure 14-1 Tie Die home page with dynamic HTML expression showing the effective date of tie prices

```
<HTML>
<HEAD> <TITLE> </TITLE> </HEAD>
<BODY>
<CENTER> <H1> Tie Die, Incorporated </H1> </CENTER>
<HR>
<IMG SRC="Atwork.gif">
<HR>
</BODY>
</HTML>
```

2. Create the dynamic HTML expression by entering the following JavaScript code between the <HR> and </BODY> tags. This code uses the current document's lastModified property as the effective date of tie prices. The lastModified property includes both the date and time the document was changed. The lastModified time is irrelevant and should be ignored when showing the effective date. To extract the date information from the property, the Date object's getDate, getTime, and getYear methods will be used. Because the lastModified property is a string, this value must be converted to a date before these methods can be used. The Document object's writeln method is used to display the effective date dynamic HTML expression. The string concatenation operand (+) is used to merge the message and date properties into an HTML expression. Save the document as HT1401.HTM.

```
<SCRIPT LANGUAGE="JavaScript">

// The Effective Date For Tie Prices Is The Date This Document Was
// Was Last Modified. Since The Document's lastModified Property Is
// A String, Convert It To A Date In Order To Extract The Date, Month,
// And Year This Document Was Last Modified

var eff_dt = new Date(document.lastModified);

// Create A Dynamic HTML Expression Which Displays The Effective Date
// For Tie Prices

document.writeln("Prices Effective As Of " + (eff_dt.getMonth() + 1) + ⇐
"/" +
                eff_dt.getDate() + "/" +
                eff_dt.getYear());
</SCRIPT>
```

How It Works

When the HTML document is modified, the document's lastModified property is set to the date and time when the change occurred. The document's writeln method is used to place the lastModified date into the document input stream. This is done when the document is loaded into the browser. The browser uses the document input stream to determine text placement on the screen. Therefore, the document always displays the last modified date as the price effective date. The page uses a system property instead of hardcoding the price effective date inside the document body. This approach is acceptable because the two dates are identical.

Comments

The ability to establish dynamic HTML expressions represents one of the key features of the JavaScript language. Through JavaScript, Web developers have access to a wide variety of information relating to a user's interaction with a Web page.

COMPLEXITY
INTERMEDIATE

14.2 How do I...
Set the layout of a document at runtime?

COMPATIBILITY: NAVIGATOR 2.X NAVIGATOR 3.X EXPLORER 3.X

Problem

There are situations when a document's layout is dependent on the factors that persist when the document is loaded into the browser. How can I use JavaScript to change how a document is laid out at runtime?

Technique

By embedding JavaScript code into the middle of an HTML document, a document's layout can become dependent on runtime conditions. The JavaScript language contains the standard conditional and looping logical expressions found in most block level languages. Logical expressions are distinguished from other expressions by the fact that they alter a program's normal execution sequence. A predicate is used to choose between one of two paths. Predicates are the Boolean elements of JavaScript logical expressions that return either a true or false value. By using JavaScript's logical expressions, alternative execution paths can be established.

The predicate will contain the "rules" that determine how a document is to be laid out. Predicate expressions should be based on the runtime-dependent information, such as the current day of the week, that influences the layout rule. Each path will contain a unique set of write and writeln method calls designed to establish different layout patterns for the document. The following code displays a different HTML expression depending on the day of the week in which the interaction occurred.

```
if (today.getDay() == TUESDAY) {
    document.write("Show TIEriffic Tuesday Prices");
} else {
    document.write("Show Regular Prices");
}
```

If today is Tuesday, the expression "Show TIEriffic Tuesday Prices" will be displayed. Otherwise the expression "Show Regular Prices" will be displayed. Under no circumstances will both expressions be displayed to the user at the same time.

Steps

For this example, you will modify the home page created in How-To 14.1. Because this document was a work-in-progress, an "under construction" image was displayed in place of the list of tie prices. Tie Die has a standard price list for its products. On Tuesdays, Tie Die runs a special promotion called TIEriffic Tuesday where ties are sold at a discount price. This example will show you how to use the current date to conditionally display HTML expressions based on the day of the week. To make this example simple, you should assume that the time the document was loaded into the browser determines which prices will be used. Therefore, if the user begins an interaction on Tuesday, but submits an order on Wednesday, the promotion price will still be valid.

From Navigator 2.0+ or Explorer, use the File/Open menu option to load the HT1402.HTM document into memory. If you are viewing this document on a Tuesday, the document shown in Figure 14-2 will appear inside the browser's document viewing area. Otherwise, the document shown in Figure 14-3 will be displayed.

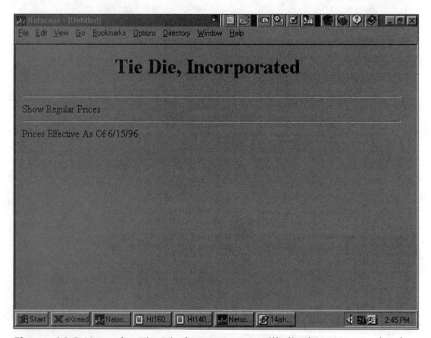

Figure 14-2 How the Tie Die home page will display on Tuesdays

Figure 14-3 How the Tie Die home page will display on any day but Tuesday

1. Remove the <IMG> tag used to display the under construction image. In its place, insert the following JavaScript code. This code uses the date method, invoked without a parameter, to store the current date inside the variable named *today*. The Date object's getDay method is used to determine which day of the week the document was loaded into the browser. The getDay method is normalized on Sunday, returning a value of 0. Therefore, if the current day is a Tuesday, this method will return a value of 2. As a temporary measure, the write method will be used to display an HTML expression that indicates the price list that should be displayed to the user. Save the document as HT1402.HTM.

```
<SCRIPT LANGUAGE="JavaScript">

var TUESDAY = 2;    // TUESDAY is Day 2 of the week
var today = new Date();   // Get today's date from the system

// Based On The Day Of The Week, Display The Appropriate Price.
//    On Tuesday, Show TIEriffic Tuesday Prices

if (today.getDay() == TUESDAY) {
   document.write("Show TIEriffic Tuesday Prices");
} else {
   document.write("Show Regular Prices");
}
</SCRIPT>
```

How It Works

This page uses a conditional statement to select the dynamic HTML statement that will be displayed inside the document's body. The JavaScript code must choose between two candidate statements. The two statements are mutually exclusive, meaning that only one statement will be visible at a time. The conditional's predicate uses the current date to determine which statement to display.

Comments

In addition to conditionals, looping constructs could also be used to repeatedly display the statements to the screen. This may be appropriate for arrays in which each element is inserted as a new statement.

COMPLEXITY
INTERMEDIATE

14.3 How do I...
Specify a format for a dynamic HTML expression?

COMPATIBILITY: NAVIGATOR 2.X NAVIGATOR 3.X EXPLORER 3.X

Problem

Because write and writeln can be used to create dynamic HTML expressions, can I include format tags in these expressions that will alter their appearance on the screen?

Technique

The String object contains a set of text format methods that will place the proper format tags inside the calling String object. These methods can be used with dynamic HTML expressions to establish alternative display formats. The complete list of text format methods is shown in Table 14-1.

METHOD	HTML TAG	DESCRIPTION
big	<BIG>	Text displayed using a big font
blink	<BLINK>	Causes text to blink
bold	<B>	Text displayed as bold
fixed	<TT	Text displayed in fixed-pitch font
fontcolor	<FONT COLOR=color>	Causes text to be displayed in the specified color
fontsize	<FONTSIZE=size>	Causes text to be specified in the specified font size
italics	<I>	Text is italicized
small	<SMALL>	Causes text to be displayed in a small font
strike	<STRIKE>	Text is displayed as struck out text
sub	<SUB>	Text is displayed in subscript
sup	<SUP>	Text is displayed in subscript

Table 14-1 String object's text format methods

The majority of these methods do not take a parameter. Input is based on the calling String object. That object's text is encased inside the appropriate HTML format tags. Merely calling the format tags will not change a text's appearance on the screen. The output of each method must be sent to the write or writeln methods for inclusion on the layout stream. Format tags, embedded inside text placed onto the layout stream, serve to flush the stream. Flushing means that information contained in the stream is displayed on the screen when a format tag is encountered. Therefore, the write methods are dependent on the fact that any text it receives has been properly formatted for display. If the format method is invoked following the text being written to the stream, then the text will be displayed in the default format. The following example demonstrates how to use the bold method to format a text string.

```
var THE_EXEC = "The Executive Tie";
var exec_txt = THE_EXEC.bold();
```

The following text represents the output of the bold method in the example above.

```
<B> The Executive Tie </B>
```

Now that the text has been properly formatted, it is ready to be pushed onto the layout stream. This is accomplished by passing the text as a parameter to either the write or writeln routine.

```
document.write("<LI> " + exec_txt + " Price $12 " + promo_txt);
```

Two text format methods, fontcolor and fontsize, require a single parameter. In the case of fontsize, the parameter is a value between 0 and 7. The value indicates the desired font size to use. The lower the number, the smaller the font size. When an integer value is passed as the parameter, the calling object's text is resized to one of seven predefined sizes. If a string is passed as the parameter, the font size is adjusted relative to the size specified in the <BASEFONT> tag.

The parameter passed to the fontcolor method defines the text's foreground color. Colors can be defined as hexadecimal red-green-blue (RGB) values or as one of the predefined color value literals. The fontcolor method will override the document's text property. The following code demonstrates how to pass an RGB and color value parameter to this method. Both calls to the fontcolor method will set the text color to blue.

```
eff_dt_txt.sup().fontcolor("blue"));
eff_dt_txt.sup().fontcolor("0000FF"));
```

Chaining Format Methods

Because the output of all text format methods is a string containing the original text encased inside the appropriate HTML format tag, the technique of chaining can be used to apply multiple formats to a single line of text. Chaining involves using the output of one method as the input of another method. The following code uses chaining to apply both bold and big formats to the text "The Executive Tie".

```
var THE_EXEC = "The Executive Tie";
var exec_txt = THE_EXEC.bold().big();
```

The following text represents the output of the bold method in the example above.

```
<B> The Executive Tie </B>
```

In the example, the bold method is applied before the big method. The output string, with embedded bold format tags, is then passed to the big method as input. The input takes place through the calling object which invokes the big method. The following text represents the output of the big method.

```
<BIG> <B> The Executive Tie </B> </BIG>
```

Now that the text has been properly formatted, it is ready to be pushed onto the layout stream.

```
document.write("<LI> " + exec_txt + " Price $12 " + promo_txt);
```

Steps

For this example, you will modify the home page created in the How-To 14.2. The previous example demonstrated how to conditionally create HTML expressions based on the day of the week. In this example, you will replace the stubbed text, displayed in How-To 14.2, with the HTML expressions required to display a list of available ties. These HTML expressions will use the String object's text format methods to format the list of ties using standard HTML format tags.

From Navigator 2.0+ or Explorer, use the File/Open menu option to load the HT1403.HTM document into memory. If you are viewing this document on a Tuesday, the document shown in Figure 14-4 will appear inside the browser's document viewing area. Otherwise, the document shown in Figure 14-5 will be displayed.

1. In the JavaScript code, created in How-To 14.1, Step 2, replace the document.writeln method with the following piece of code. This code is used to display the effective date for tie prices. The new code stores the HTML

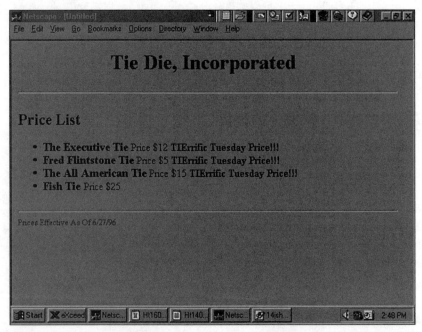

Figure 14-4 How the Tie Die home page will display on Tuesdays

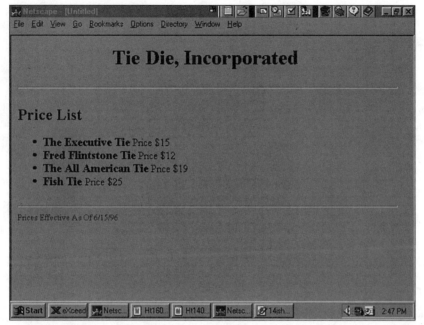

Figure 14-5 How the Tie Die home page will display on any day but Tuesday

expression in a variable. Text format methods, sup and fontcolor, are used to display the effective date text using the <SUP> and <FONTCOLOR="blue"> tags.

```
var eff_dt_txt = "Prices Effective As Of " + (eff_dt.getMonth() + 1) + ⇐
"/" +
                eff_dt.getDate() + "/" +
                eff_dt.getYear();

document.writeln(eff_dt_txt.sup().fontcolor("blue"));
```

2. Immediately following the first horizontal rule <HR> tag, create the shell for an unordered list. This list will be used to hold all ties available for sale. Use the <H2> tag to establish a header for the list. The list is called Price List. Insert a single list item <LI> into the list. This item represents a single product whose price is unaffected by the promotion.

```
<H2> Price List </H2>
<UL>
<LI> <B> <BIG> Fish Tie </BIG> </B> Price $25
</UL>
```

3. Replace the JavaScript code, created in How-To 14.2, Step 1, with the following code. This code establishes a set of contents that will be used in this piece of code. Most of the constants represent tie names that will be stored in the unordered list, created in Step 2.

```
<SCRIPT LANGUAGE="JavaScript">

var TUESDAY = 2;     // TUESDAY is Day 2 of the week
var THE_EXEC = "The Executive Tie";
var FLINT = "Fred Flintstone Tie";
var AMERICA = "The All American Tie";
var PROMO = "TIErrific Tuesday Price!!!";

</SCRIPT>
```

4. Beneath the contents, created in Step 3, insert the following code. This code uses the String object's text format methods, big and bold, to format the tie names. These methods are chained together to apply multiple text formats to the tie names. The output of the text format methods is stored inside JavaScript variables. The variables contain the same values as the corresponding string constants, with the exception that the values are contained within a set of HTML tags. A promotion string is also created by this code. The promotion tag will display blinking text next to any product whose prices have been lowered by the promotion. The ability to have the promotion text blink will bring attention to the fact that the price has been lowered.

```
var exec_txt = THE_EXEC.bold().big();
var flint_txt = FLINT.bold().big();
var amer_txt = AMERICA.bold().big();
var promo_txt = PROMO.blink().bold();
```

5. Beneath the code inserted in Step 4, place the following code. This code is similar to the code used in How-To 14.2 Step 1. The current day will determine the document's text. The stub messages have been replaced with multiple write methods which will output the formatted tie names and prices. The text is defined as a list item belonging to the unordered list created in Step 2. For promotional prices, a blinking message, indicating the special prices, will be displayed after a tie's price.

```
// Based On The Day Of The Week, Display The Appropriate Price.
//    On Tuesday, Show TIEriffic Tuesday Prices

var today = new Date();    // Get today's date from the system

if (today.getDay() == TUESDAY) {


   document.write("<LI> " + exec_txt + " Price $12 " + promo_txt);
   document.write("<LI> " + flint_txt + " Price $5 " + promo_txt);
   document.write("<LI> " + amer_txt + " Price $15 " + promo_txt);
} else {
   document.write("<LI> " + exec_txt + " Price $15");
   document.write("<LI> " + flint_txt + " Price $12");
   document.write("<LI> " + amer_txt + " Price $19");
}
```

How It Works

The String object's text format methods are used to insert HTML format tags before and after dynamic statements. The format tags result in the dynamic lines being displayed in a manner different than normal text.

Comments

The existence of the text format methods does not prohibit you from concatenating the tags onto the ends of a text string. The write and writeln methods will properly push the formatted text on the layout stream no matter which method you choose. Therefore, the following code would have produced the same layout as the examples in How-To 14.3.

```
document.write("<LI> <BIG> <B> " + exec_txt + " </B> </BIG> Price $12 " ⇐
+ promo_txt);
```

COMPLEXITY
INTERMEDIATE

14.4 How do I...
Dynamically create an HTML anchor?

COMPATIBILITY:

Problem

One of the important parts of an HTML document is the ability to establish anchors which can be referenced by hypertext links. There may be several reasons that I need to dynamically create an anchor object, including adding an anchor to a dynamically created document and changing the location of an anchor. How can I dynamically create an HTML anchor?

Technique

In addition to the text format methods, discussed in How-To 14.3, the String object also contains an anchor method which can be used to dynamically create an HTML anchor. Like the format methods, the output of the anchor method is properly formatted HTML text that will set up an anchor inside a document. The output must be passed to either the write or writeln methods to make it onto the layout stream.

The anchor method accepts a single parameter. This parameter is a string that represents the anchor's name. This string will be assigned to the anchor's NAME property inside the output string. The anchor encases the text stored inside the calling String object. The following example dynamically creates an anchor named EXEC.

```
var THE_EXEC = "The Executive Tie";
var THE_EXEC_ANC = "EXEC"
THE_EXEC.anchor(THE_EXEC_ANC)
```

The following text represents the output of the call to the anchor method above.

```
<A NAME="EXEC"> The Executive Tie </A>
```

The output of the anchor method must be passed onto the layout stream in order for it to appear inside the document.

```
document.writeln("<H3>" + THE_EXEC.anchor(THE_EXEC_ANC) + "</H3>");
```

Steps

For this example, you will modify the home page created in the How-To 14.3. A list of ties has been added to the page, but no description of ties exists anywhere on the page. For this example, you will create these descriptions and add an anchor that marks the beginning of each description. In How-To 14.5, you will convert each tie in the unordered list from simple text to a hypertext link. The anchors that are created in this How-To will serve as the reference point for these anchors. The result will be a list of ties whose descriptions can be seen if the user clicks on the appropriate product.

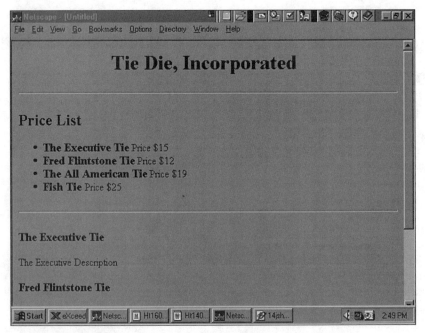

Figure 14-6 Tie Die home page with product descriptions

From Navigator 2.0+ or Explorer, use the File/Open menu option to load the HT1404.HTM document into memory. If you are viewing this document on a Tuesday, the document shown in Figure 14-4 will appear inside the browser's document viewing area. Otherwise, the document shown in Figure 14-5 will be displayed. Scroll to the bottom of the document, and it will appear similar to Figure 14-6. Although not visible to a normal user, anchors reside underneath each product description header. In How-To 14.5, you will create links to reference these anchors.

1. Within the list of variable definitions at the top of the first JavaScript code segment, add the following variable declarations. These declarations represent anchor names that will be used by both the anchor and links for a particular product description.

```
var THE_EXEC_ANC = "EXEC"
var FLINT_ANC = "FLINT"
var AMER_ANC = "AMER"
```

2. Convert the list header from static HTML expressions to dynamic HTML expressions. Place the following code before the condition which checks to see if today is a Tuesday. This code is being converted in an effect to create a dynamic document that will be used later in the chapter.

```
document.writeln("<H2> Price List </H2>");
document.writeln("<UL>");
```

3. Convert the last tie description from static HTML expressions to dynamic HTML expressions. Place the following code immediately after the condition which checks to see if today is a Tuesday. This code is being converted in an effect to create a dynamic document that will be used later in the chapter.

```
document.writeln("<LI> <B> <BIG> Fish Tie </BIG> </B> Price $25");
document.writeln("</UL>");
```

4. Place the following code at the end of the first JavaScript code fragment. This code will create a product description section where a detailed description of each tie can be seen. Each description will have a header that also serves as a anchor. The anchor can be used by hypertext links to point to this area of the document. Save the document as How-1404.HTM.

```
document.writeln("<HR>");
document.writeln("<H3>" + THE_EXEC.anchor(THE_EXEC_ANC) + "</H3>");
document.writeln("<P> The Executive Description </P>");
document.writeln("<H3>" + FLINT.anchor(FLINT_ANC) + "</H3>");
document.writeln("<P> Flintstone Description </P>");
document.writeln("<H3>" + AMERICA.anchor(AMER_ANC) + "</H3>");
document.writeln("<P> The All American Description </P>");
```

How It Works

The String object's anchor method is used to dynamically create HTML anchors inside the body of an HTML document. The anchor method takes a single property that defines the anchor's name. This allows links to point to this particular anchor. The String's value property is used as the link's text. The anchor method needs the writeln method to insert the newly created anchor into the document's body.

Comments

In addition to dynamically creating anchors, you can also dynamically insert hypertext links into the document's body. How-To 14.5 discusses how to do this.

COMPLEXITY
INTERMEDIATE

14.5   How do I...
Dynamically create a hypertext link?

COMPATIBILITY: NAVIGATOR 2.X   NAVIGATOR 3.X   EXPLORER 3.X

Problem

I may need to dynamically create a link object under several circumstances, including adding a link to a dynamically created document, changing where a link references, and changing the location of a link. How can I dynamically create an HTML link?

Technique

The String object contains a link method which can be used to dynamically create an HTML link. Like the format and anchor methods, the output of the link method is properly formatted HTML text that will establish a hypertext link inside a document. The output of the link method must be passed to either the write or writeln methods to make it onto the layout stream.

The link method accepts a single parameter. This parameter is a string that represents the document or anchor which the link references. The single parameter represents the link's HREF property. The link will contain all text stored inside the calling String object. The following example dynamically creates an anchor named EXEC.

```
var THE_EXEC = "The Executive Tie";
var THE_EXEC_ANC = "EXEC"
THE_EXEC.link("#" + THE_EXEC_ANC);
```

The following text represents the output of the call to the link method above.

```
<A HREF="#EXEC"> The Executive Tie </A>
```

The output of the link method must be passed onto the layout stream in order for it to appear inside the document.

```
document.writeln("<LI>" + THE_EXEC.link("#" + THE_EXEC_ANC));
```

Steps

For this example, you will modify the home page created in How-To 14.4. The unordered list of ties will be converted from simple text to hypertext links. These links will point to the anchors created in How-To 14.4

From Navigator 2.0+ or Explorer, use the File/Open menu option to load the HT1405.HTM document into memory. If you are viewing this document on a day other than Tuesday, the document shown in Figure 14-7 will appear inside the browser's document viewing area. On Tuesdays, the document in Figure 14-5 will appear with the product list containing links versus regular text. Click on the "Fred Flintstone Tie" link and notice the document adjust so that the related product description becomes visible.

1. Turn the product list items from simple text to hypertext links by adding a call to the link method in the section of code which establishes the list item format. This code was created in How-To 14.3, Step 4. The new links will reference the anchors established in How-To 14.4, using the variables

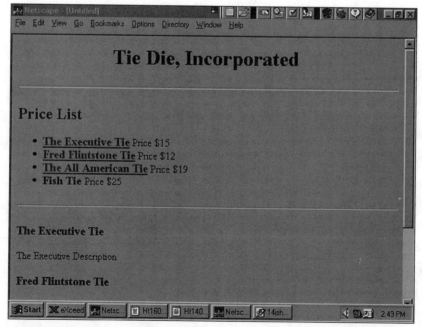

Figure 14-7 Tie Die home page with tie product list containing links to product descriptions

which hold the anchor names. To identify the links that reference anchors, as opposed to documents, the "#" character will be concatenated to the beginning of the anchor names. The single parameter to the link method is synonymous with the string assigned to the HREF attribute for an HTML anchor object. Save the document as HT1405.HTM.

```
var exec_txt = THE_EXEC.bold().big().link("#" + THE_EXEC_ANC);
var flint_txt = FLINT.bold().big().link("#" + FLINT_ANC);
var amer_txt = AMERICA.bold().big().link("#" + AMER_ANC);
```

How It Works

The String object's link method is used to dynamically create hypertext links into the body of an HTML document. The link method takes a single property which is the URL of a referenced document. This parameter will initialize the link's HREF attribute. The String's value property is used as the link's text. The link method requires the writeln method to insert the newly created link into the document's body.

Comments

So far, you have seen techniques for embedding dynamic, formatted text inside the middle of a static document. How-To 14.6 will demonstrate how to create from scratch a new dynamic document that will replace the document in the current window.

COMPLEXITY
ADVANCED

14.6 How do I...
Display a dynamically created HTML document?

COMPATIBILITY: NAVIGATOR 2.X NAVIGATOR 3.X EXPLORER 3.X

Problem

The previous How-Tos demonstrated how to embed dynamic HTML expressions inside an existing HTML document. Suppose I want to use a dynamic document whose entire structure is determined at runtime. How can I have my dynamic document replace the current document inside the browser's viewing area.

Technique

A new layout stream can be opened by invoking the Document object's open method. The stream will collect the output of write and writeln methods which will establish the text displayed inside the new document. New documents require a new layout stream which will contain their page specific text. The layout stream is a memory buffer used to accumulate information to reduce the cost of I/O system calls.

By including a call to the open method inside an event handler, a Web developer implies that they are opening a new document. This assumption is based on the fact that event handlers are executed after the current document's stream has been closed. Once closed, a stream cannot be reopened. Therefore any call to the open method will imply that a new document is being defined.

If write or writeln methods are called from an event handler, without having been preceded by a call to the open method, the browser will assume a new document is being opened with a mime type of text/html. Mime types indicate the class of information that is being viewed by the browser. The open method accepts a single optional parameter which defines the mime type of the new document. Example mime types are defined in Table 14-2.

MIME TYPE	DESCRIPTION
text/html	ASCII Text With HTML Format Tags
text/plain	Regular ASCII Document
image/gif	GIF Image
image/jpeg	JPEG Image
image/x-bitmap	Bitmap Image

Table 14-2 Example mime types

If the mime type is text or an image, the stream is opened as a layout stream; otherwise a plug-in is used. As the write and writeln methods are inserting text into the stream, the layout stream is occasionally flushed when an HTML format tag is encountered. To close the document, invoke the Document object's close method. For layout streams, the close method will force all remaining text to display to the screen. The "Document:Done" message will appear inside the status bar.

Steps

For this example, you will modify the home page created in How-To 14.5. An initial page will be added which asks users to select their state of residence. A button is then clicked which dynamically builds the entire home page. The JavaScript and HTML code from the previous How-Tos have been integrated inside a new JavaScript function. The output of this function is the dynamic document that will replace the current document in the browser's viewing area.

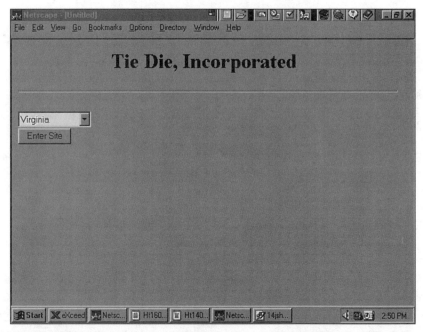

Figure 14-8 Initial screen displayed when entering Tie Die's Web site

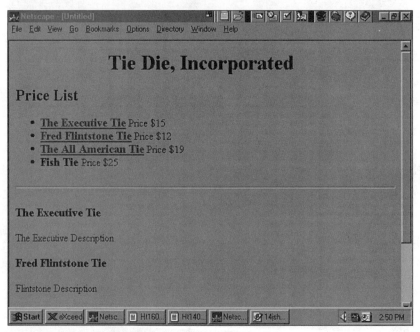

Figure 14-9 Dynamically created Tie Die home page displayed in the browser's viewing area

From Navigator 2.0+ or Explorer, use the File/Open menu option to load the HT1406.HTM document into memory. The document in Figure 14-8 will display inside the document viewing area. Activate the "Enter Site" button, and the document in Figure 14-9 will replace the calling document inside the browser's viewing area. This document was dynamically created by the display_page function created in Step 2.

1. Move both JavaScript code fragments outside of the document body. The code should be moved to the document's heading section, identified by the <HEAD> tag. Combine both code fragments into a single section of code. Because this code has been moved outside the document's body, it no longer influences how the browser will layout the document.

2. Set up a function display_page that will contain all the JavaScript code, moved in Step 1. The creation of this function will allow an event handler to invoke this function. The function will create a dynamic HTML document that will replace the current document inside the browser's viewing area. The current document is replaced because the Write and writeln methods inside this function still access the current window's open document.

```
function display_page() {}
```

3. In the display_page function, add the following code before the first call to the write or writeln methods. The open method will create a data stream, also called a buffer, that will hold the output of subsequent Write and writeln methods.

```
document.open();
```

4. In the display_page function, add the following code after the last call to the write or writeln method. The close method will force the browser to lay out the dynamic HTML expressions inside the document viewing area.

```
document.close();
```

5. Add the following HTML code to the document's body. This code will display a list of states where Tie Die is authorized to do business as the opening screen in the company's home page. This information will be used in How-To 14.8 to determine whether or not sales tax should be computed when this user orders a tie. A button element is added to allow the user to enter the site.

```
<CENTER> <H1> Tie Die, Incorporated </H1> </CENTER>
<HR>
<FORM>
<SELECT NAME="state">
<OPTION VALUE="VA"> Virginia
<OPTION VALUE="MD"> Maryland
<OPTION VALUE="DL"> Delaware
<OPTION VALUE="WV"> West Virginia
```

continued on next page

continued from previous page

```
<OPTION VALUE="NC"> North Carolina
</SELECT>
<BR>
<INPUT TYPE="button" VALUE="Enter Site">
</FORM>
```

6. Add an onClick event handler to the "Enter Site" button. This event handler
will invoke the display page function created in Step 2. When the user
clicks on this button, the display page will replace the current document
with a dynamically created HTML document whose structure is determined
at runtime. Save the document as HT1406.HTM.

```
<INPUT TYPE="button" VALUE="Enter Site" onClick="display_page()">
```

How It Works

The new document is established by a call to the Document object's open method.
Any calls to the write and writeln methods, following the creation of a new document, will insert content into the new document. The close method indicates that
all content has been placed inside the document's input stream. The browser will
use this information to display the new document on the screen.

Comments

This example demonstrated how to display dynamic HTML documents displayed
inside the current window. How-To 14.7 will discuss how to display dynamic documents inside a new popup window.

COMPLEXITY
ADVANCED

14.7 How do I...
Display a dynamically created HTML document inside a new window?

COMPATIBILITY: NAVIGATOR 2.X NAVIGATOR 3.X EXPLORER 3.X

Problem

Instead of displaying a dynamically created document inside the browser's viewing
area, I would like for it to display inside a new popup window. How can I do this
in JavaScript?

Technique

The window object's open method can be used to pop up the new window. As with each window object, the document property represents the document that is displayed inside the window. By invoking the open method for the new window's document, a new layout stream is created. All text inserted into the stream by the write and writeln methods will be displayed inside the new window. After the stream is closed, the layout buffer is flushed to display any remaining text in this window.

Steps

For this example, you will modify the home page created in How-To 14.6. This example will display the tie catalog document inside a newly created popup window instead of the browser's document viewing area. This enables multiple documents to be concurrently displayed to the user.

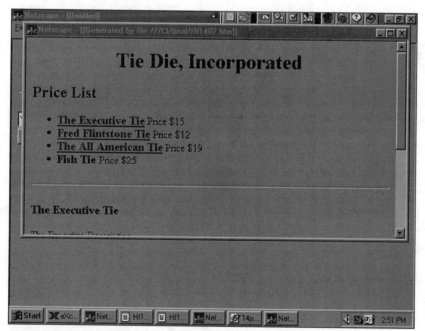

Figure 14-10 Dynamically created Tie Die home page displayed in a new window

From Navigator 2.0+ or Explorer, use the File/Open menu option to load the HT1407.HTM document into memory. The document in Figure 14-8 will display inside the document viewing area. Activate the "Enter Site" button, and the document in Figure 14-10 will appear inside a new popup window. The new window was created by the display_window function coded in Step 3.

1. Add a parameter to the display page function. The parameter, named doc, will be used by the write and writeln methods to indicate the document where dynamic expressions will be displayed.

```
function display_page(doc) {}
```

2. Replace all references to the current document with references to the doc parameter. This change is facilitated by the fact that previous How-Tos wrote dynamic expressions to the current window's document. In this example, a new window will be used to view the dynamic document. Because the new window's document is only accessible after the window is created, the document must be passed as a parameter to the display_page routine.

3. Add the following JavaScript function to the document header. This function will create the new window and then invoke the display_page method which sets up the layout of the window's document.

```
function display_window() {
    var new_win = window.open("", "Products",
        "scrollbars=yes,resizeable=yes,width=600,height=300");
    display_page(new_win.document);
}
```

4. Change the event handler, established in How-To 14.6, Step 6, so that the display_window function is called instead of the display_page function. Save the document as HT1407.HTM.

```
<INPUT TYPE="button" VALUE="Enter Site" onClick="display_window()">
```

How It Works

The Window object's open method is used to display the new window on the screen. Each window already contains a Document object. By accessing the Document object, the write and writeln methods can be used to display the new document inside the popup window.

Comments

The previous two examples represent some of the most complicated and powerful capabilities of the JavaScript language. If you understand the logic of these examples, then proceed to the last part of the chapter. Otherwise, you may want to review these sections before trying to understand "cookies." The next two examples make frequent use of dynamic HTML in demonstrating the concept of a cookie.

COMPLEXITY
ADVANCED

14.8 How do I...
Store persistent information in an HTTP cookie?

COMPATIBILITY: NAVIGATOR 2.X NAVIGATOR 3.X EXPLORER 3.X

Problem

I have a piece of data which needs to be accessed from multiple documents. How can I use JavaScript to store the persistent information in an HTTP cookie?

Technique

Since the World Wide Web is a connectionless environment, server-side persistence is limited. HTTP cookies have been developed as a client-side data persistence mechanism. A cookie is a small piece of information that needs to be persistent throughout the user's interaction with a site. The Navigator browser stores cookie data on the client machine, inside the cookie.txt file. Cookies are typically used by server processes to store persistent information on the client machine. The cookie data is contained within the HTTP header. The Set-Cookie request is used to establish persistent information on the client machine. The format for a Set-Cookie request is Set-Cookie: NAME=VALUE. Notice that cookies use the same NAME/VALUE scheme as input parameters. Any postings to the server will cause the appropriate cookie data to be transmitted to the server. The cookie data is contained inside the cookie section of the HTTP request header.

A cookie's properties can be used to restrict a cookie's scope.

Restrictions can be based on the time the request was issued and directory where the requested object is stored.

The JavaScript language was designed to reduce a client's dependency on the server. Although the JavaScript language provides client-side persistence, there are certain circumstances where a cookie is the easiest way to transfer information between pages. To account for the limited dependency on server-side processes, JavaScript gives Web developers access to HTTP cookies. The document object contains a cookie property which contains any data stored in cookies on the host machine. In addition to server processes, JavaScript code can also assign a syntactically correct cookie expression to this property. Cookie expressions follow this general format:

```
NAME=VALUE;expires=DATE;path=PATH;domain=DOMAIN_NAME;secure
```

This property can also be referenced to gain access to a persistent date stored using the cookie mechanism. The following code demonstrates how the cookie named SALES_TAX can be assigned to the document's cookie property.

```
document.cookie = "SALES_TAX=Y";
```

Other cookies are established by assigning a value to the cookie property. Assigning new cookies to this property will not override any existing cookies that have already been established. In this manner, the cookie property behaves differently than other JavaScript properties.

Because JavaScript can access cookie information, it is important that you understand how to access this data. The only mandatory element in a cookie expression is the NAME=VALUE piece. As you may notice, the NAME+VALUE pair, contained inside HTTP requests, also is used for HTTP cookies. The NAME label is a logical representation for the individual cookie's name. The VALUE label represents the critical information needed by a server process.

The remaining cookie elements are considered optional. If some are unspecified when the cookie is established, then a default for each element is used. These optional elements define the a cookie's scope. Before a client submits a cookie to the server, it must fall within the scope specified by these elements.

The expires element is used to bound a cookie's timeframe. A cookie remains valid, which means that it will remain stored as long as the expiration date has not passed. Unlike other JavaScript properties, a cookie cannot be removed by simply assigning a new value to the property. To delete a cookie, set the expiration date to a date and time in the past. If the expire element is not defined, a cookie is valid until the user's session is completed.

The domain element can be used to restrict cookie submission to servers that belong to a particular domain. The path element is used to restrict cookie submission to requests that access files from a particular directory branch. The secure property can be used to restrict cookie submission to communication channels that use a secure channel.

Steps

For this example, you will modify the home page created in How-To 14.7. In How-To 14.6, a new initial page was constructed that prompted to the user to indicate his or her state of residence. Up to this point, we have not used the information that was provided. This example will use this information to set an HTTP cookie named SALES_TAX. The SALES_TAX cookie will be used by other documents to determine whether or not to add sales tax to a customer's order. Because Tie Die, Incorporated resides in Warsaw, VA, only Virginia residents are required to pay sales tax.

From Navigator 2.0+ or Explorer, use the File/Open menu option to load the HT1408.HTM document into memory. The document in Figure 14-8 will display inside the document viewing area. Activate the "Enter Site" button, and the document in Figure 14-10 will appear inside a new popup window. Type the URL mocha:document.cookie into the location field. The value appearing in Figure 14-11 will appear in the browser's viewing area.

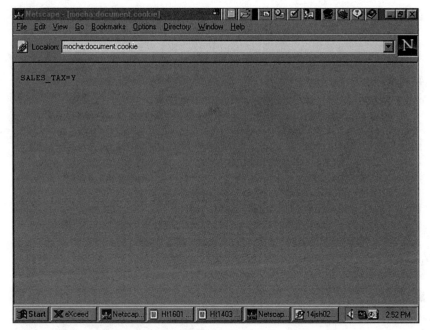

Figure 14-11 Current HTTP cookie string

1. Add the parameter from the display_window function created in How-To 14.7, Step 3. The "Enter Site" button will pass a reference to its form when the onClick event handler calls this function. The form must be passed into the function so that it has access to the "state" select element. The state selection will determine whether or not sales tax should be added to a tie order.

```
function display_window(form) {}
```

2. Add the following JavaScript code to the beginning of the display_window function. The SALES_TAX cookie will be used by other pages to determine whether or not to add the appropriate sales tax to this customer's tie orders. If the user selects Virginia, the SALES_TAX cookie will be set to Y; otherwise, it will have a default value of N.

```
// Set The SALES_TAX Cookie To Indicate To Server Processes
// That Sales Tax Must Be Added To Any Order

if (form.state.options[form.state.selectedIndex].value == "VA") {
   document.cookie = "SALES_TAX=Y";
} else {
   document.cookie = "SALES_TAX=N";
   }
```

3. Add the following JavaScript code to the display_page function. This code will be placed immediately after the check for current day being a Tuesday. This code will create a cookie named PROMO, if today is a Tuesday, to TIErriffic Tuesday.

```
// Set PROMO Cookie To Indicate To Server Processes That
// This Promotion Is In Effect

window.document.cookie = "PROMO=TIErrifficTuesday";
```

4. Add the following JavaScript code before the code created in Step 3. This code will coerce the date variable today to midnight Tuesday night. This is the time when the TIErriffic Tuesday promotion expires. The code will allow the PROMO cookie's expiration date to be established. This means that users who enter the site Tuesday night and hesitate to place an order until early Wednesday morning will not receive the promotion price.

```
today.setHours(23);
today.setMinutes(59);
today.setSeconds(59);
```

5. Modify the cookie assignment code, inserted in Step 3, to include an expiration date. The expiration date is defined by the JavaScript contained in Step 4.

```
window.document.cookie = "PROMO=TIErrifficTuesday;expires="
                + today.toGMTString();
```

How It Works

This example implements two cookies designed to contain persistent information needed by multiple documents. The cookies are established by making an assignment to the Document object's cookie property. The SALES_TAX cookie is a flag which indicates that the customer is a resident of the state of Virginia. Because TieDie is a Virginia company, sales tax must be computed on any order made by this individual. The SALES_TAX cookie is set in the opening window. The user's selection from the state input will determine whether this cookie is set to (N)o or (Y)es.

The second cookie, PROMO, is used on Tuesdays to indicate that TieDie is running a special promotion. Because multiple pages will have special content for this promotion, the PROMO flag indicates which content should be displayed. Without the PROMO cookie, each document would have to check the system clock to determine if the current date was Tuesday. Besides the additional overhead associated with a system call to get the current date and time, the PROMO allows the promotion date to be changed with minimal impact to the system. The PROMO cookie serves as a single decision point that can be changed, if need be, by the site's Webmaster. Because the promotion is only valid on Tuesday, the cookie is set to expire at 11:59:59 Tuesday night.

Comments

Now that the cookies have been set, How-To 14.9 will discuss techniques for extracting the information from inside a cookie.

COMPLEXITY
ADVANCED

14.9 How do I...
Access persistent information stored in an HTTP cookie?

COMPATIBILITY: NAVIGATOR 2.X NAVIGATOR 3.X EXPLORER 3.X

Problem

Now that I have stored some persistent data in an HTTP cookie, how can I extract this information when I need to access the data within another document?

Technique

The Document object's cookie property is also used to access cookie data. The format of the cookie property is dictated by the number of established cookies and properties defined for each cookie. If a process needs to access a specific cookie, that cookie's name can be used to locate a cookie inside this property. The String object's indexOf method can be used to locate the cookie name. The following example uses the indexOf method to locate the SALES_TAX cookie inside the cookie property.

```
var index = document.cookie.indexOf("SALES_TAX");
```

If this method returns a value greater than 0, then the cookie exists. Take the output of the indexOf method and offset it by the length of the name string, as well as an extra location to account for the equal character. The following code positions the index variable at the beginning of the value string.

```
index += ("SALES_TAX".length + 1);
```

If the value is a single character, as is the case with the SALES_TAX cookie, the String object's charAt method can be used to return the value. Otherwise use the substring method to return a value whose length is greater than one. The following code extracts the single character value stored at the index position.

```
var tax = document.cookie.charAt(index);
```

For more information on the String object's charAt and indexOf methods, proceed to Chapter 6, "Built-In Objects." This chapter covers many of the String object's methods.

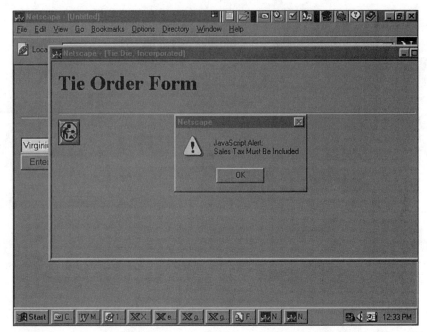

Figure 14-12 Order form for a customer who resides in the state of Virginia

Steps

For this example, you will modify the home page created in How-To 14.8. This How-To established several cookies that will persist throughout the user's interaction with a site. In this example, you will create the skeleton for an order form to be displayed inside in the new window. The order form will need to access the SALES_TAX cookie when computing a customer's bill. For this example, it will display an alert dialog, indicating whether or not sales tax should be computed, when the order form is displayed on the screen.

From Navigator 2.0+ or Explorer, use the File/Open menu option to load the HT1409.HTM document into memory. The document in Figure 14-8 will display inside the document viewing area. Activate the "Enter Site" button, and the document in Figure 14-10 will appear inside a new popup window. Activate the "Order Form" link, and the document displayed in Figure 14-12 will be displayed inside the popup window. Close this window. Change the state on the opening screen to "Delaware". Activate the "Enter Site" button, and the document in Figure 14-10 will appear inside a new popup window. Activate the "Order Form" link, and the document displayed in Figure 14-13 will be displayed inside the popup window.

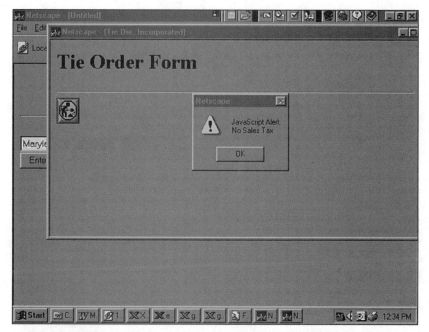

Figure 14-13 Order form for a customer who resides outside the state of Virginia

NOTE
If the wrong Sales Tax alert is displayed inside the order form, type the URL mocha: document.cookie into the browser's location field. This URL displays the entire cookie string. Go back to the previous page and try pulling up the order form. The correct alert should be displayed on the screen. There appears to be a bug in Netscape's implementation of HTTP cookies.

1. Add a new link to the tie catalogue document. Save this document as HT1409.HTM.

```
doc.writeln("Order Form".Link("file:///C|/book/code/chapter.14/ ⇐
HT14091.htm"));
```

2. Using the following code, create the outline for a new HTML document. This document will be used to display a product order form.

```
<HTML>
<HEAD> <TITLE> Tie Die, Incorporated </TITLE> </HEAD>
<BODY>
<H1> Tie Order Form </H1>
<HR>
<IMG SRC="Atwork.gif">
</BODY>
</HTML>
```

3. In the document header, use the following code to create the sales_tax method. This method will be invoked by an onLoad event handler. The output of sales_tax is an alert dialog which indicates whether or not sales tax will be computed on customer orders.

```
<SCRIPT LANGUAGE="JavaScript">
function sales_tax() {

    // Extract The SALES_TAX Cookie From The Cookie Property
    var index = document.cookie.indexOf("SALES_TAX");
    index += ("SALES_TAX".length + 1);
    var tax = document.cookie.charAt(index);

    // As A Temporary Measure, Display A Prompt Indicating
    // Whether Or Not Sales Tax Should Be Included
    if (tax == 'Y') {
        alert("Sales Tax Must Be Included");
    } else {
        alert("No Sales Tax");
    }
}
</SCRIPT>
```

4. Add an onLoad event handler to the <BODY> tag created in Step 2. The event handler will invoke the sales_tax function, created in Step 3. Save the document as HT1409A.HTM.

```
<BODY onLoad="sales_tax()">
```

How It Works

The cookie property contains a string which is a concatenation of all unexpired cookie specifications. The cookie property is implemented as a String object. Therefore, String methods, such as charAt, substring, and indexOf can be used to locate individual cookies with the main cookie string. These methods are designed for location and removal of information embedded inside a formatted text. The cookie string contains individual cookie tokens separated by a semicolon (;). Within individual cookies, the equal (=) character is used to separate the cookie name from the value.

Comments

NOTE

The <mocha:> tag is only available if you are using Navigator2.X or 3.X.

The <mocha:> tag, introduced in How-To 1.5, is an excellent way to determine what cookies have been set up in your browser. As you begin to use sites that implement cookies, the <mocha:> tag is a valuable debugging tool that will show the values of individual cookies. This technique is better than displaying an alert dialog set to the cookie string. The alert dialog would have to be added and removed each time you debug a piece of code.

CHAPTER 15
ADVANCED FEATURES

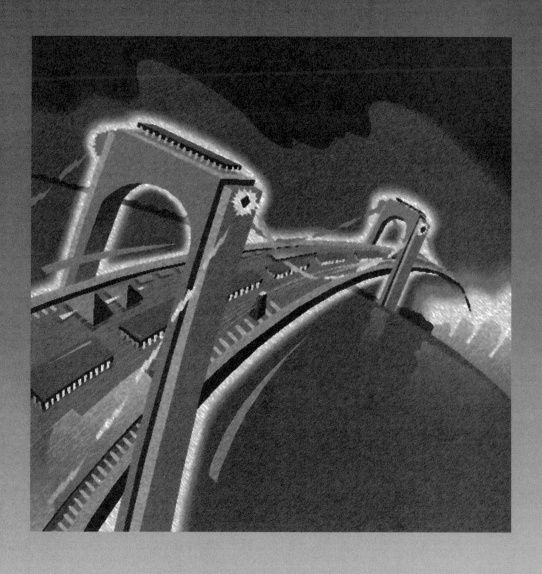

ADVANCED FEATURES

How do I...

JavaScript is by its very nature dynamic, but only to a point. You have probably found that if you issue a writeln() method call to your current document, the current contents are erased. However, if you open a new document you can embed graphics into it using the document write() or writeln() methods. In addition, you can use the eval() built-in function to evaluate and implement JavaScript expressions or statements that have been created at run-time. With the newest version of Navigator, 3.0, you can access and modify images in the current document after it has been displayed.

Within your current window and your current document, you can use JavaScript to implement a scrolling banner in the window status bar or in a text field. Additionally, if your document has multiple forms, you can access data from all of them and coordinate efforts between forms. An important feature of JavaScript is the ability to intercept the submission of a form and to verify the form contents before the form is submitted. Once this occurs, JavaScript uses the Form object method submit() to send the data to the HTTP server.

Probably one of the most useful extensions to the HTML standard is the plug-in. A plug-in gives you the ability to embed an object directly into your HTML document. When your document is opened or the line containing the <EMBED> tag is evaluated, the plug-in is loaded into memory and processes the object. With JavaScript you can dynamically add plug-in objects to your Web pages. You can also open and write directly to some plug-ins, such as the Netscape Live3D VRML (Virtual Reality Modeling Language) plug-in.

15.1   Handle images

Images stored in GIF or JPG format can be created in a document using the JavaScript write() or writeln() Document object methods. This How-To demonstrates how you can use these methods to embed images dynamically.

15.2   Change images in the current document

With the release of Navigator 3.0, you can access and manipulate images in the current document in the currently displayed window after its layout has occurred. This How-To demonstrates this capability.

15.3   Dynamically create and evaluate a JavaScript expression

Ever wonder what the result of your JavaScript statement would be while you are creating it? This How-To provides the steps to build a dynamic JavaScript evaluation page that allows you to test JavaScript before you place it into your document. One example builds a JavaScript statement from choices selected on a form, the other provides a totally unconstrained entry of a statement.

15.4   Use timer to create a progress bar

JavaScript has built-in functions to start and stop a timer. A JavaScript timer will run only once and must be called again if you want additional timer events. This How-To demonstrates the use of this built-in function to provide a text-based and a graphical-based progress bar. The graphical progress bar uses the new Image object from Navigator 3.0.

15.5   Display a scrolling banner

An increasingly popular use of JavaScript is to create a scrolling banner in the Windows' status bar. This How-To demonstrates a fairly simple method to do this. Additionally, the How-To demonstrates an alternative approach by scrolling to a text field.

15.6   Use the Navigator object to check the installed plug-ins

The Navigator object stores information about the version and application the Web page reader is currently using. With Navigator 3.0, Netscape also includes information about the plug-ins currently installed, as this How-To will demonstrate.

15.7   Handle elements and data stored in multiple forms

You could have a single document with multiple forms, such as a case in which customer information is input in one form and the items being ordered are input into the second form. With this type of set up, you will need the ability to coordinate information between the forms. This How-To demonstrates this technique.

15.8   Submit data back to the HTTP server

Once you have data in a form and you have used JavaScript to verify its content, you will need to send the data to the HTTP server. This How-To demonstrates the form submit() method.

15.9   Work with VRML worlds by using embedding and by writing to a VRML plug-in using the Write and writeln commands

With plug-ins, a file of a certain type can be embedded in an HTML document and the application that can process the file type is automatically loaded when the file type is encountered. The plug-in can open directly in the document, as is demonstrated in this How-To, or in a separate window. Additionally, you can open the document using the plug-in mimeType specification and write appropriate commands to the file using JavaScript Write() and writeln() methods. This How-To demonstrates the use of this technology to build an ad hoc VRML world generator.

COMPLEXITY
INTERMEDIATE

15.1   How do I...
Handle images?

COMPATIBILITY: NAVIGATOR 2.X   NAVIGATOR 3.X   EXPLORER 3.X

Problem

I am generating a new HTML document, and I want to place graphic images into the document. How do I do this with JavaScript?

Technique

The document methods Write() or writeln() can be used to embed a GIF or JPG file into a document and to set its attributes directly. The statements can be used when the HTML document is created or can be issued dynamically.

Steps

Open the file IMAGE.HTM. The document that is displayed contains the cliché "April Showers Bring May Flowers" with a little graphical illustration, as shown in Figure 15-1. This example hard codes the names of the graphic files directly into the code of the generating document. The steps to create these examples follow.

1. Create a new empty HTML file.

2. Start a HEAD and JavaScript section by typing the code below.

```
<HEAD><TITLE> Images </TITLE>

<SCRIPT LANGUAGE="JavaScript">
<!--- hide script from old browsers

// JavaScript Global Variables

// JavaScript Functions
```

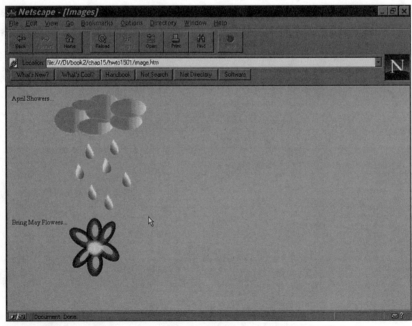

Figure 15-1 Image.HTM after opening

3. Set the background and text color properties of the current document and begin the BODY section by typing in the following statements.

```
// set document properties and start BODY
document.bgColor="#ADD8E6"
document.fgColor="#00008B"
document.write('<BODY>')
```

4. Type in the statements to create a text string in the document and to embed a GIF file. The file is embedded using the <IMG> tag, and the attributes are set so that the graphic is aligned with the top of the text string that is on the current line and displayed to the right of the string.

```
// add images and words
document.write("<p>April Showers...")
document.writeln
  ('<IMG SRC="rain.gif" ALIGN=TOP ALIGN=RIGHT WIDTH=184 HEIGHT=221>')
```

5. The next text string and graphic image are created in the document using the same JavaScript writeln() method calls that were used to create the first text string and graphic image.

```
document.writeln('<p>Bring May Flowers...')
document.write
  ('<IMG SRC="smflowr.gif" ALIGN=TOP WIDTH=100 HEIGHT=111>')
```

6. The document is finished by typing in the following code.

```
// end hiding from old browsers -->
</SCRIPT>
</HEAD>
```

7. Close your document file and save it as IMAGE.HTM. Test the code by opening the document in your browser.

8. An additional technique is to dynamically build the statement that is used in the write() or writeln() method calls. This allows you to dynamically change the graphic that appears. To see this demonstrated, open the file OPENGRPH.HTM in your browser. The window consists of five frames, one larger across the top and four smaller frames of equal size at the bottom, as shown in Figure 15-2. Open a graphic file in the first of the graphics frames by typing the name of the graphic file, "rain.gif" in the first text field, entering 1 into the field requesting the frame number, selecting blue as the background color, and entering a height and a width of 125 and 100 respectively. Press the Open Graphic button and the results should look similar to those shown in Figure 15-3. Continue to fill in the remaining slots by opening up other graphic files, both GIF and JPEG image types, in the frames as shown in Figure 15-4.

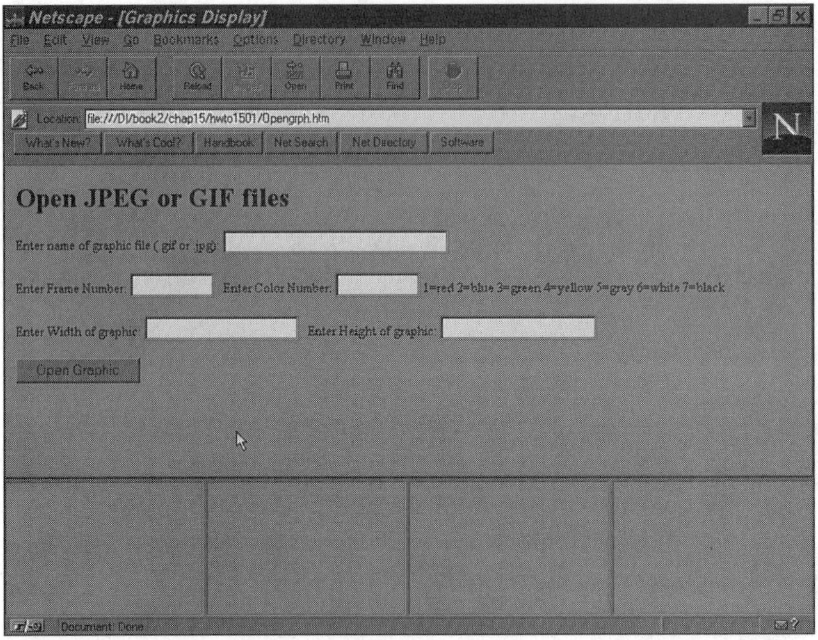

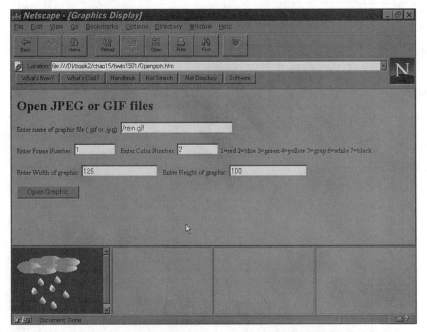

Figure 15-2 OPENGRPH.HTM after opening

Figure 15-3 OPENGRPH.HTM after opening RAIN.GIF in first graphics frame

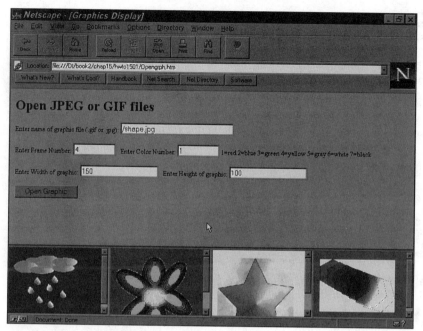

Figure 15-4 OPENGRPH.HTM after opening graphic files in all four graphics frames

9. Create this sample by creating a blank HTML document that will be modified at run-time. Start by opening a new HTML document.

10. Type in the following code and close and save the document as BLANK.HTM.

```
<HTML>
<HEAD><TITLE> Working Window </TITLE></HEAD>
<BODY></BODY>
</HTML>
```

11. Create a second HTML document that will create the Frameset document. Start with an empty HTML document.

12. Type in the code to create two Framesets. The first has two rows, and the second has four columns.

```
<HTML>
<HEAD>
<TITLE>Graphics Display</TITLE>
</HEAD>
<FRAMESET ROWS="70%, *">
   <FRAME SRC=open.htm NAME="Open">
   <FRAMESET COLS="25%, 25%, 25%, *">
   <FRAME SRC=blank.htm NAME="Frame1">
   <FRAME SRC=blank.htm NAME="Frame2">
```

continued on next page

continued from previous page

```
    <FRAME SRC=blank.htm NAME="Frame3">
    <FRAME SRC=blank.htm NAME="Frame4">
    </FRAMESET>
</FRAMESET>
</HTML>
```

13. The first frame has OPEN.HTM as its source, which will be created in the next steps. The rest of the frames use the BLANK.HTM file as their source. They are named Frame1 through Frame4. The frames have to be named in order to access the contents of the frame.

14. Close and save the document as OPENGRPH.HTM.

15. Create a last HTML document by creating a new document file.

16. Start a HEAD and JavaScript section by typing the following.

```
<HTML>
<HEAD><TITLE> Opening a Graphic Image </TITLE>

<SCRIPT LANGUAGE="JavaScript">
<!--- hide script from old browsers
```

17. Add the MakeArray JavaScript function. This function originated with Netscape and enables JavaScript authors to create arrays of values.

```
// MakeArray originated at Netscape
// and is probably include in most if not all HTML
// documents that use JavaScript
//
// MakeArray will create a generic array object with
 function MakeArray(n)
 {
        this.length = n;
        for (var i = 1; i <= n; i++)
        { this[i] = 0 }
        return this
  }
```

18. Create a function with no parameters called WriteGraphic. Access the graphic file, frame number, color, and width and height from the current document form.

```
// WriteGraphic
// Function will get the name of the graphic
// the frame number, the color, and the width and
// height - it will then
// open document and write to stream
// at the end of the document is closed to flush
// the stream and display the results
//
function WriteGraphic() {
    var sObject = document.DocumentForm.GrphFile.value
    var iFrame = document.DocumentForm.Number.value
    var sColor = document.DocumentForm.Color.value
    var iHeight = parseFloat(document.DocumentForm.GrphHeight.value)
    var iWidth = parseFloat(document.DocumentForm.GrphWidth.value)
```

19. The function uses parseFloat to convert the result to a number. If the value is not a number (NaN), the result will be NaN. Verify that the Web page reader has entered correct values by typing the following.

```
// check for correct frame number
   if (iFrame < 1 || iFrame > 4) {
   alert("You must specify a frame number between 1 and 4")
   return
   }
```

```
// check for correct width and height
   if (isNaN(iHeight) || isNan(iWidth)) {
   alert("You have entered an incorrect width and height")
   return
   }
```

20. Add in the statements to open the document in the target frame, set its background color, and write out a statement that will embed the graphic in the window with the specified width and height. The document is then closed to force the document to display.

```
// get background color based on frame number
parent.frames[iFrame].document.open()
parent.frames[iFrame].document.writeln
("<HTML><HEAD></HEAD>")
parent.frames[iFrame].document.writeln
    ("<BODY BGCOLOR=" + sColor + ">")
parent.frames[iFrame].document.writeln
("<IMG SRC='" + sObject +
    "' WIDTH=" + iWidth + " HEIGHT=" + iHeight + ">")
parent.frames[iFrame].document.writeln
("</BODY></HTML>")
parent.frames[iFrame].document.close()
}
```

21. End the JavaScript and HEAD sections.

```
// end hiding from old browsers -->
</SCRIPT>

</HEAD>
```

22. Create the BODY section and include in it a form. The form will have five text fields, one for the graphic file name, one for the frame number, one for the color choice, and two for the graphic width and height. The form will also have a button, with the onClick event of the button trapped and the WriteGraphic function called when the event occurs.

```
<BODY>

<H1> Open JPEG or GIF files </H1>

<FORM NAME="DocumentForm" >
Enter name of graphic file (.gif or .jpg):
```

continued on next page

continued from previous page

```
<INPUT TYPE="text" Name="GrphFile" size=30>
<p>
Enter Frame Number:
<INPUT TYPE="text" Name="Number" size=10>
<p>
Enter Color Name or Hexidecimal Value (including #):
<INPUT TYPE="text" Name="Color" size=20>
<p>
Enter Width of graphic:
<INPUT TYPE="text" Name="GrphWidth">  
Enter Height of graphic:
<INPUT TYPE="text" Name="GrphHeight">
<p>
<INPUT TYPE="button" VALUE="Open Graphic"onClick="WriteGraphic()">
</FORM>
</BODY>
</HTML>
```

23. Close the file and save it as OPEN.HTM. Test your new files by loading OPENGRPH.HTM in your browser and trying out various JPEG and GIF files.

How It Works

The Write() and writeln() methods of a Document object allow you to write out any HTML statements including those that embed and position graphic files such as GIF and JPG files. If you use this technique, you will want to specify a width and a height. Failing to do so can cause some browsers to fail or produce unexpected results.

Comments

Notice in the examples that the filename for the figures, as shown in Figure 15-3, does not specify a fully qualified URL. The HTML and the graphic file both reside locally on the machine where the testing occurs, and the fully qualified pathname is not necessary. Note also that the function IsNaN and the Not a Number constant NaN are now available for all platforms, including Windows.

COMPLEXITY
ADVANCED

15.2 How do I ...
Change images in the current document?

COMPATIBILITY:

Problem

I need to be able to change the images in the document I currently have loaded, but I don't want to have to generate new document statements, and I don't want to have to reload the document. How can I dynamically change images in my currently loaded and displayed document?

Technique

Beginning with Navigator 3.0, you can now access and modify images in a document using the new Image object. This object is a property of the Document object and allows you to create a new Image object to cache for future use, or to access and modify the images currently displayed. The displayed images can be found in an image array that contains the images in the order in which they were loaded in the document.

Steps

Open the CHGIMG.HTM file in your browser. This file contains four graphics at the top, a text field for entering graphic numbers, and a listbox that displays the names of the four graphic files, as shown in Figure 15-5. Modify the graphics by changing the first graphic to RAIN.GIF and the last graphic to SMFLOWR.GIF, as shown in Figure 15-6. You can change a graphic by specifying the graphic number in the text field and then clicking on the file in the list. The steps to create this application follow.

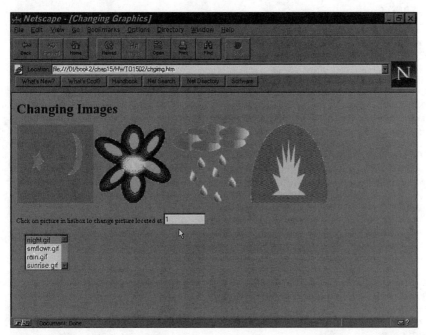

Figure 15-5 CHGIMG.HTM after opening and with original graphic files

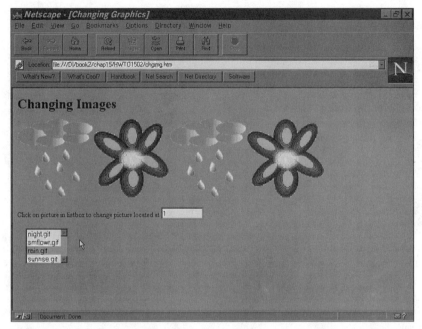

Figure 15-6 CHGIMG.HTM after dynamically changing two of the graphic files

1. Create a new HTML document.

2. Start a HEAD and a JavaScript section by typing the following code.

```
<HTML>
<HEAD><TITLE> Changing Graphics </TITLE>
<SCRIPT LANGUAGE="JavaScript">
<!--- hide script from old browsers

// JavaScript Global Variables

// JavaScript functions
```

3. Create a function called ChangeGraphic that takes one parameter, the form, and accesses the selected graphic source file. This file information is then used to change the image in the position the Web page reader specifies.

```
// create display window for document
//
// Open document and write to stream
function ChangeGraphic(GrphForm) {

    var iIndex = GrphForm.Picture.value
    sSelected =
        GrphForm.Graphic.options[GrphForm.Graphic.selectedIndex].text
    var sImage = ""

    sSelected = "/" + sSelected
    iIndex--
```

```
document.images[iIndex].src = sSelected
}
```

4. Close out the JavaScript and HEAD sections.

```
// end hiding from old browsers -->
</SCRIPT>

</HEAD>
```

5. Start the BODY section and add four images.

```
<body>

<H1> Changing Images </H1>
<p>
<IMG SRC="night.gif" width=150 height=150>
<IMG SRC="smflowr.gif" width=150 height=150>
<IMG SRC="rain.gif" width=150 height=150>
<IMG SRC="sunrise.gif" width=150 height=150>
```

6. Create a form and place in it a text field for accessing the graphic figure number.

```
<p>
<FORM NAME="FormValue" >
Click on picture in listbox to change picture located at
<INPUT TYPE="text" Name="Picture" Value=1 size=10>
```

7. Create a listbox using the SELECT statement. For the options specify the names of the four graphics files used to create the original document. Trap the onChange event and provide an event handler that will call the newly created ChangeGraphic function, passing in the Form object. Close out the BODY section.

```
<p>
<FORM>
    
<SELECT SIZE=4 NAME="Graphic"
  onChange="ChangeGraphic(this.form)">
<OPTION SELECTED> night.gif
<OPTION> smflowr.gif
<OPTION> rain.gif
<OPTION> sunrise.gif
</SELECT>

</FORM>
</BODY>
</HTML>
```

8. Close and save the file as CHGIMG.HTM. Test the application by loading the file into your browser and changing the graphic in each of the positions.

How It Works

The Image object was defined beginning with Navigator 3.0. This object will allow you to create a new Image object by using the new keyword. A new image can be used to cache an image for access at a later time after the document is loaded. The Image object is also the type of a new property for the Document object and instantiated as images. This property holds the images that are currently loaded and displayed in the document. With this capability the properties of the image can be accessed and changed dynamically without having to reload the document.

COMPLEXITY
ADVANCED

15.3 How do I...
Dynamically create and evaluate a JavaScript expression?

COMPATIBILITY: NAVIGATOR 2.X   NAVIGATOR 3.X   EXPLORER 3.X

Problem

I would like to be able to dynamically build a JavaScript statement based on the Web page reader's actions and other factors. How can I do this and have the JavaScript implemented?

Technique

You can build JavaScript statements into a string and then use the JavaScript built-in function eval() to evaluate and implement the statements. If the string expression contains a numeric expression, a result is returned from the function. If the expression contains valid JavaScript statements, the statements are implemented.

Steps

Open the file BLDPRNT.HTM in your browser. The document contains four Radio buttons and a text field. The Radio buttons will generate a specific JavaScript statement that will change the background color of the document, add a heading, an image, or add a hypertext link. Each button has an associated dialog that will ask for additional information. Clicking on the Color button opens the Color information dialog, as shown in Figure 15-7. Clicking the yellow Radio button will close the dialog and return the result, which will then generate the JavaScript statement. Pushing the Evaluate button will cause the statement to be evaluated and the results targeted to the second frame window, as shown in Figure 15-8. Clicking the Heading button will open the Heading dialog, as shown in Figure 15-9; clicking the Image button will open the Image dialog, as shown in Figure 15-10; and clicking the Link dialog will open the Link dialog, as shown in Figure 15-11. Returning from any of the dialogs will trigger generation of JavaScript statement, which is placed in the text field, as shown in Figure 15-12. The result is implemented in the second frame, as shown in Figure 15-13. The steps to create this example follow.

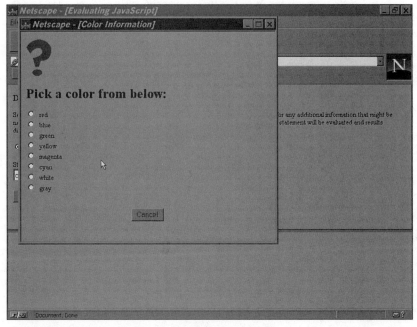

Figure 15-7 Color dialog from BLDPRNT.HTM

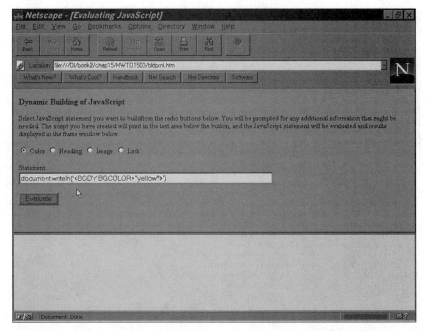

Figure 15-8 The results after evaluation of the JavaScript command to change the background color

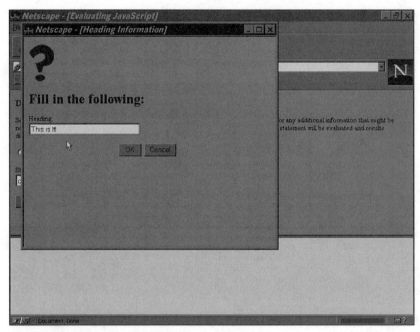

Figure 15-9 The Heading dialog

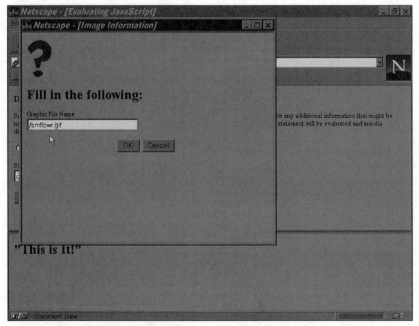

Figure 15-10 The Image dialog

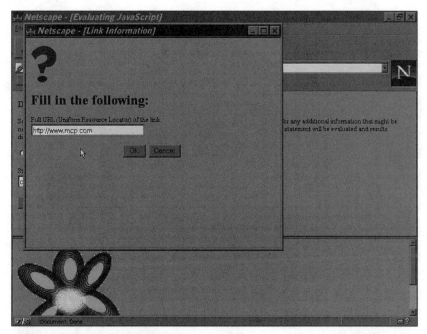

Figure 15-11 The Link dialog

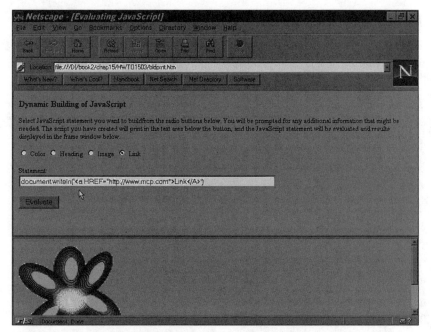

Figure 15-12 The BLDPRNT.HTM document with a generated
JavaScript statement

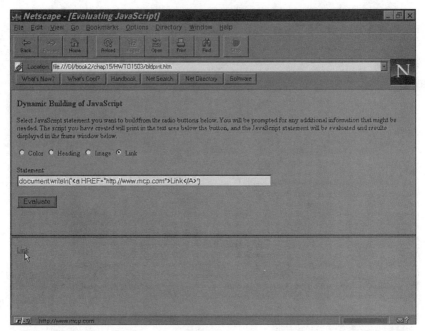

Figure 15-13 The BLDPRNT.HTM after a Link has been generated

1. Create the color dialog file. Start with an empty HTML document.

2. Type the following code to start the HEAD and JavaScript sections, and create a global variable called prevWindow. Set the value of this variable to null.

```
<HTML>
<HEAD><TITLE> Color Information</TITLE>

<SCRIPT LANGUAGE="JavaScript">
<!--- hide script from old browsers

// JavaScript Global Variables
prevWindow = null
```

3. Create a JavaScript function called SetInformation. This function will call a function defined in the window set to the prevWindow variable. The function gets a color string, which it passes on to FinishStmt(). Close the JavaScript and HEAD sections.

```
// SetInformation
//
// function will get input values
// and set to calling window
function SetInformation(sColor) {
```

```
        prevWindow.FinishStmt(sColor)
        window.close()


        }

// end hiding from old browsers -->
</SCRIPT>

</HEAD>
```

4. Create the BODY section, with a form containing eight Radio buttons. The buttons will trap the onClick event and pass the button value to the SetInformation function.

```
<BODY>
<IMG SRC="question.gif" width=50 height=70>

<H1>Pick a color from below:</H1>
<p>
<FORM NAME="DiagForm">
<INPUT type="radio" Value="red" Name="Color"
    onClick="SetInformation(this.value)">  red<br>
<INPUT type="radio" Value="blue" Name="Color"
    onClick="SetInformation(this.value)">  blue<br>
<I   PUT type="radio" Value="green" Name="Color"
    onClick="SetInformation(this.value)">  green<br>
<INPUT type="radio" Value="yellow" Name="Color"
    onClick="SetInformation(this.value)">  yellow<br>
<INPUT type="radio" Value="magenta" Name="Color"
    onClick="SetInformation(this.value)">  magenta<br>
<INPUT type="radio" Value="cyan" Name="Color"
    onClick="SetInformation(this.value)">  cyan<br>
<INPUT type="radio" Value="white" Name="Color"
    onClick="SetInformation(this.value)">  white<br>
<INPUT type="radio" Value="gray" Name="Color"
    onClick="SetInformation(this.value)">  gray<br>

<p><CENTER>
<INPUT type="button" Value="Cancel" onClick="window.close()">
</CENTER>
</FORM>

</BODY>
</HTML>
```

5. Close and save the file as BKGNCLOR.HTM.

6. Create a second empty HTML document.

7. Create a JavaScript and a HEAD section, and create a global variable called prevWindow.

```
<HTML>
<HEAD><TITLE> Heading Information</TITLE>
```

continued on next page

continued from previous page

```
<SCRIPT LANGUAGE="JavaScript">
<!--- hide script from old browsers

// JavaScript Global Variables
prevWindow = null
```

8. Create a JavaScript function called SetInformation. This function will set the value of a text field contained in a form, which is contained in the window that is set in prevWindow. The function will then close the dialog. Close the HEAD and JavaScript sections.

```
// SetInformation
//
// function will get input values
// and set to calling window
function SetInformation() {

    prevWindow.FinishStmt(document.DiagForm.Head.value)
    window.close()

    }

// end hiding from old browsers -->
</SCRIPT>
```

9. Create the BODY section with a form containing a text field and two buttons, one labeled OK and the other labeled Cancel. The OK button will capture the onClick event and call the SetInformation function.

```
</HEAD>
<BODY>
<IMG SRC="question.gif" width=50 height=70>

<H1>Fill in the following:</H1>
<p>
<FORM NAME="DiagForm">
Heading:
<br><INPUT type="text" size=30 Name="Head">
<p><CENTER>
<INPUT type="button" Value="  OK   "
    onClick="SetInformation()">
 
<INPUT type="button" Value="Cancel" onClick="window.close()">
</CENTER>
</FORM>

</BODY>
</HTML>
```

10. Close and save the file as HEADDIAG.HTM.

11. Create a third HTML document.

12. As with the other two documents, create a HEAD and a JavaScript code section.

```
<HTML>
<HEAD><TITLE> Image Information</TITLE>

<SCRIPT LANGUAGE="JavaScript">
<!--- hide script from old browsers

// JavaScript Global Variables
prevWindow = null
```

13. Create the SetInformation function for this document, which will set the value of the form text field in the window that is contained in the prevWindow variable.

```
// SetInformation
//
// function will get input values
// and set to calling window
function SetInformation() {

    prevWindow.FinishStmt(document.DiagForm.Figure.value)
    window.close()

  }
// end hiding from old browsers -->
</SCRIPT>
```

14. Create the BODY section containing a form with a text field and two buttons. The OK button will trap the onClick event and call the SetInformation function. The Cancel button will close the window.

```
<BODY>
<IMG SRC="question.gif" width=50 height=70>

<H1>Fill in the following:</H1>
<p>
<FORM NAME="DiagForm">
Graphic File Name:
<br><INPUT type="text" size=30 Name="Figure">
<p><CENTER>
<INPUT type="button" Value="  OK   "
     onClick="SetInformation()">
 
<INPUT type="button" Value="Cancel" onClick="window.close()">
</CENTER>
</FORM>

</BODY>
</HTML>
```

15. Close the document and save it as GRPHDIAG.HTM.

16. Create a fourth, empty HTML document to serve as a placeholder document.

17. Type in the following code and close and save the document as BLANK.HTM.

```
<HTML>
<HEAD><TITLE> Working Window </TITLE></HEAD>
<BODY></BODY>
</HTML>
```

18. Create a fifth HTML document and type in the following code to create a Frameset with two rows.

```
<HTML>
<HEAD>
<TITLE>Evaluating JavaScript</TITLE>
</HEAD>

<FRAMESET ROWS="65%, 35%">
    <FRAME SRC=bldjava.htm NAME="Open">
    <FRAME SRC=blank.htm NAME="workFrame">
</FRAMESET>

</HTML>
```

19. Close and save the document as BLDPRNT.HTM.

20. Create a last empty document and start a HEAD and a JavaScript section with four global variables. These variables will hold the current statement being evaluated, whether it is quoted, a final statement, or a timer.

```
<HTML>
<HEAD><TITLE> Building JavaScript </TITLE>
<SCRIPT LANGUAGE="JavaScript">
<!--- hide script from old browsers

// JavaScript Global Variables
sStatement = ""
sEndStatement = ""
msgTime = null
bQuoted = false

// JavaScript functions
```

21. Create a JavaScript function that will set the prevWindow variable of the window referenced in the newWindow variable to the current window. This function is called as a result of a timer operation, so clear the timer first.

```
// SetProperty
//
// Function will set window
// of old window in new
function SetProperty() {

    newWindow.prevWindow = this
    clearTimeout(msgTime)

}
```

22. Create a second function, CallDialog, which will call the appropriate statement dialog based on the type of statement. The function will then open the appropriate dialog and set the timer. The timer insures that the window is open before the variable contained in the window is accessed.

```
// CallDialog
// call appropriate dialog to get
// extra information
function CallDialog(sStmt) {

    var sDiag = ""

    // check for stmt type
          if (sStmt == "Color")
       sDiag = "bkgnclor.htm"
    else if (sStmt == "Heading")
         sDiag = "headdiag.htm"
    else if (sStmt == "Link")
         sDiag = "linkdiag.htm"
    else
       sDiag = "grphdiag.htm"

    newWindow=window.open(sDiag,"",
       "toolbar=no,directories=no,width=500,height=400")

    msgTime=setTimeout("SetProperty()", 3000)

    }
```

23. Create a function called Evaluate, which will evaluate the statement passed to it. The results will be targeted to the document in the second frame.

```
// create display window for document
//
// Open document and write to stream
function Evaluate(sExpression) {
   parent.workFrame.document.open("text/html")
   sExpression = "parent.workFrame." + sExpression
   eval(sExpression)
   parent.workFrame.document.close()
   }
```

24. Create a function called BuildStmts, which will accept a statement type. Based on the type, the appropriate statement beginning and the appropriate statement ending are generated. The CallDialog function is called with the statement.

```
// BuildStmts
//
// function will access checkboxes and
// build JavaScript statments
// These will be sent to Evaluate
// for implementation

function BuildStmts(sStmt) {

    // setup statment based on statement type

    sStatement = "document.writeln"
```

continued on next page

continued from previous page

```
        if (sStmt == "Color") {
     sStatement = sStatement +
     "('<BODY BGCOLOR="
     sEndStatement = ">')"
     bQuoted=true
     }
  else if (sStmt == "Heading") {
     sStatement = sStatement +
     "('<H1> "
     sEndStatement = "</H1>')"
     }
  else if (sStmt == "Link") {
     sStatement = sStatement +
     "('<a HREF="
     sEndStatement = ">Link</A>')"
     bQuoted=true
     }
  else {
     sStatement = sStatement +
     "('<IMG SRC="
     sEndStatement = " width=200 height=200>')"
     bQuoted=true
     }

  CallDialog(sStmt)
  }
```

25. Create a last function called FinishStmt, which will finish the statement generation by appending quotes if appropriate and adding any ending statement.

```
// FinishStmt
//
// function will finish building statement
// after return from information dialog
function FinishStmt(sValue) {

   if (bQuoted) {
      sStatement = sStatement + '"'
      sEndStatement = '"' + sEndStatement
      }

   // add to existing statement and end stmt
   sStatement = sStatement + sValue + sEndStatement
   document.FormValue.Stmt.value=sStatement

   }
// end hiding from old browsers -->
</SCRIPT>
</HEAD>
```

26. Create the BODY section with a form, four Radio buttons, a text field, and a button. The onClick event of the Radio buttons will result in a call to the BuildStmts function. The onClick event of the button will call the Evaluate function to evaluate the generated JavaScript.

```
<body>
<H3> Dynamic Building of JavaScript </H3>
```

```
<p>
Select JavaScript statement you want to buildfrom the
radio buttons below. You will be prompted for any additional
information that might be needed. The script you have created will
print in the text area below the button, and the
JavaScript statement will be evaluated and results
displayed in the frame window below.
<p>
<FORM NAME="FormValue" >
<p>
<INPUT type="radio" Name="Choice" Value="Color"
   onClick="BuildStmts(this.value)"> Color 
<INPUT type="radio" Name="Choice" Value="Heading"
   onClick="BuildStmts(this.value)"> Heading 
<INPUT type="radio" Name="Choice" Value="Image"
   onClick="BuildStmts(this.value)"> Image 
<INPUT type="radio" Name="Choice" Value="Link"
   onClick="BuildStmts(this.value)"> Link 
<p>
Statement:
<br><INPUT TYPE="text" Name="Stmt" size=70>
<p>
<INPUT TYPE="button" VALUE="Evaluate"
   onClick="Evaluate(document.FormValue.Stmt.value)">
</FORM>

</BODY>
</HTML>
```

27. Close and save the file as BDLJAVA.HTM. Test the code by opening BLDPRNT.HTM in your browser and trying out the different options.

28. Another option for a dynamic JavaScript evaluation application is to create one that evaluates any statement entered by the Web page reader. To see this open the file EVALPRNT.HTM in your browser. In this page you can enter any valid JavaScript statement as shown in Figure 15-14. Once the statement has been entered, you can press the Evaluate button and the results will be displayed in the second frame, as shown in Figure 15-15.

29. To create this second example you will be re-using the BLANK.HTM file you created in Step 17.

30. Create a new HTML document and type in the following code to create a Frameset.

```
<HTML>
<HEAD>
<TITLE>Evaluating JavaScript</TITLE>
</HEAD>

<FRAMESET ROWS="45%, 65%">
   <FRAME SRC=evaljava.htm NAME="Open">
   <FRAME SRC=blank.htm NAME="workFrame">
</FRAMESET>

</HTML>
```

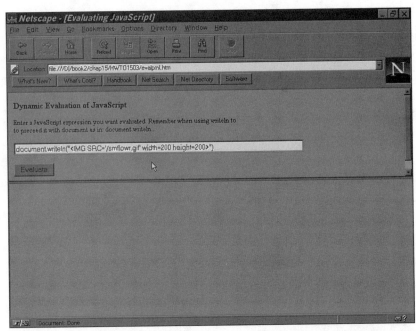

Figure 15-14 EVALPRNT.HTM with image file JavaScript statement

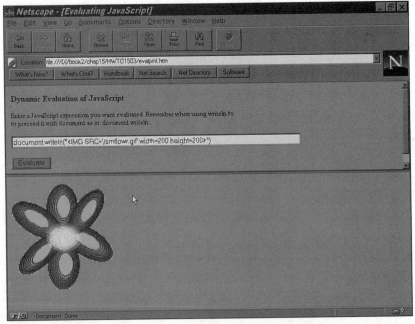

Figure 15-15 EVALPRNT.HTM after JavaScript statement has been evaluated

31. Save the file as EVALPRNT.HTM.

32. Create another blank HTML document and type in the code to start a
HEAD and a JavaScript section.

```
<HTML>
<HEAD><TITLE> Evaluating JavaScript </TITLE>
<SCRIPT LANGUAGE="JavaScript">
<!--- hide script from old browsers

// JavaScript Global Variables

// JavaScript functions
```

33. Create the Evaluate function and end the JavaScript and HEAD sections.
Evaluate will call the JavaScript eval() function to process the expression
from the form.

```
// Evaluate
// Evaluate JavaScript statement
// and display in second frame
//
// Open document and write to stream
function Evaluate() {
   var sExpression = document.FormValue.expr.value
   parent.workFrame.document.open("text/html")
   sExpression = "parent.workFrame." + sExpression
   eval(sExpression)
   parent.workFrame.document.close()
   }

// end hiding from old browsers -->
</SCRIPT>

</HEAD>
```

34. Create the BODY section with a form with a text field and a button. Capture
the onClick event of the button and call the Evaluate function.

```
<body>
<H3> Dynamic Evaluation of JavaScript </H3>

<FORM NAME="FormValue" >
Enter a JavaScript expression you want evaluated. Remember when using⇐
writeln to<br>
to preceed it with document as in: document.writeln...<p>

<p>
<INPUT TYPE="text" NAME="expr" size=80>
<p>
<INPUT TYPE="button" VALUE="Evaluate"
   onClick="Evaluate()">
</FORM>
</BODY>
</HTML>
```

35. Close and save the file as EVALJAVA.HTM. Test this second example by loading EVALPRNT.HTM into your browser and trying out several JavaScript statements.

How It Works

The eval() built-in function will evaluate one or more JavaScript statements and expressions. If the string contains an arithmetic expression, eval() returns a numeric result. If the string contains valid JavaScript statements, the statements are implemented. If the JavaScript method to be evaluated is a method for a particular object, you will need to include this in the string being evaluated.

COMPLEXITY
ADVANCED

15.4 How do I...
Use timer to create a progress bar?

COMPATIBILITY: NAVIGATOR 2.X   NAVIGATOR 3.X   EXPLORER 3.X

Problem

When I am performing JavaScript processing, I want to provide a visual cue to the Web page reader that some processing is under way. How can I display a progress bar?

Technique

You can open a separate popup window using the open() window function, and you can create a progress bar using the built-in setTimeout() function to modify the graphics that are displayed. Additionally, beginning with Navigator 3.0, you can also change a graphic in a document after it has been displayed. With these functions you can also create a progress bar that uses graphics and is embedded directly in the document.

Steps

Open the STATUS.HTM file in your browser. The page contains a text input field and a button, as shown in Figure 15-16. Press the button and a new window opens containing the string from the text field and 10 dashes (-), as shown in Figure 15-17. The images change color from left to right over time, emulating a progress bar. A second example can be found by opening STATUS2.HTM. This page contains several subdued colored boxes and a button, as shown in Figure 15-18. Pressing the button in this page will start the timer and start changing the boxes to ones that are lighter in hue, as shown in Figure 15-19. To create both of these examples, follow these steps.

1. Create an empty HTML file.

2. Create a HEAD section and a JavaScript code section. In the JavaScript code section several global variables are created.

```
<HTML>
<HEAD><TITLE> Open PopUp Status Window </TITLE>
<SCRIPT LANGUAGE="JavaScript">
<!--- hide script from old browsers

// JavaScript Global Variables
var iDot = 1
var tmID = null
var newwindow = null
var sMessage = ""

// JavaScript Functions
```

3. Create a JavaScript function called OpenStatusWindow. Type in code to set the document color on the window and begin the BODY section.

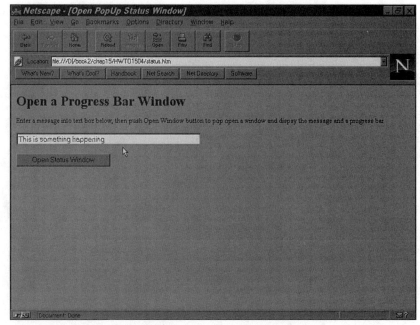

FIGURE 15-16 STATUS.HTM before pressing button

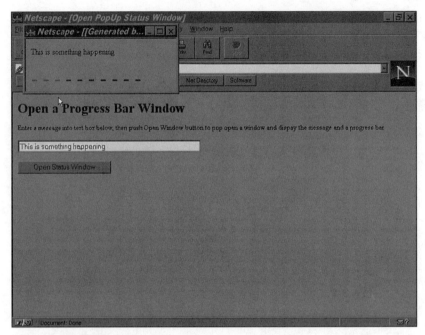

FIGURE 15-17 STATUS.HTM with progress window

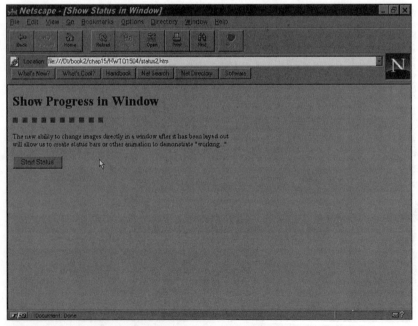

FIGURE 15-18 STATUS2.HTM after opening

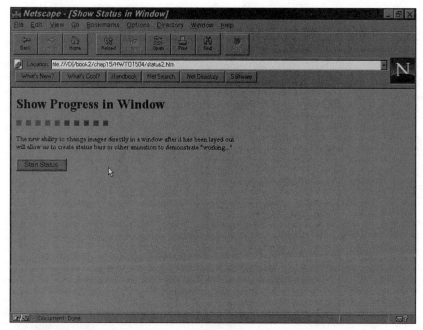

FIGURE 15-19 STATUS2.HTM with progress bar in action

```
// OpenStatusWindow
// Function will open a new window
// using URL passed to it
function Progress() {
    newwindow.document.open()
    newwindow.document.writeln("<HEAD></HEAD>")
    newwindow.document.bgColor="#C0C0C0"
    newwindow.document.writeln("<BODY><BIG>" + sMessage + "</BIG><p>")
```

4. Type in two loops that will first write out the bright graphics based on the global variable, iDot, and then will write out the darker graphics.

```
    // write out light dots
newwindow.document.writeln("<FONT COLOR='#FF0000' size=10>")
for (i=1; i < iDot; i++) {
    newwindow.document.writeln("-")
    }
newwindow.document.writeln("</FONT>")

newwindow.document.writeln("<FONT COLOR='#0000C0' size=10>")
// write out dark dots
for (i=iDot; i <= 10; i++) {
    newwindow.document.writeln("-")
    }
newwindow.document.writeln("</FONT>")
```

5. Close the document body. This will cause the document to be drawn and increment the dot counter. If the counter is over 11, close the progress window and reset the dot counter back to one and return from the function. If the dot counter is not over 11, reset the timer.

```
// close body and reset timer
newwindow.document.writeln("</BODY>")
newwindow.document.close()

// incr dot counter
iDot ++

if (iDot > 11 ) {
    newwindow.close()
    iDot = 1
    return
    }

tmID = setTimeout("Progress()", 1000)
}
```

6. Create a second new JavaScript function that will open the new window and start the display and timer process.

```
function OpenStatusWindow() {
    sMessage = document.OpenWindow.Message.value
    newwindow = window.open("","newWin",
        "toolbar=no,directories=no,width=300,height=100")
    Progress()
    }
```

7. Close the JavaScript code section, create a heading, and close the HEAD section.

```
// end hiding from old browsers -->
</SCRIPT>
<H1> Open a Progress Bar Window</H1>
</HEAD>
```

8. Create the document BODY with a form that has an input text field and a button. Trap the onClick event for the button and call a new OpenStatusWindow function.

```
<BODY>
Enter a message into text box below, then push Open Window button to
pop open a window and dispay the message and a progress bar
<FORM NAME="OpenWindow"
<p><INPUT TYPE="text" NAME="Message" VALUE="Hello!" size=50>
<p><INPUT TYPE="button" NAME="OpenWin" VALUE="Open Status Window"
    onClick="OpenStatusWindow()">
</FORM>
</BODY>
</HTML>
```

9. Close the document and save it as STATUS.HTM. Test your document by loading it into your browser and pressing the Open Status Window button.

10. For the second example, create a second HTML document file.

11. Again, create a HEAD and a JavaScript function and create several global variables as shown below.

```
<HTML>
<HEAD><TITLE> Show Status in Window </TITLE>
<SCRIPT LANGUAGE="JavaScript">
<!--- hide script from old browsers

// JavaScript Global Variables
var iDot = 0
var tmID = null
var imgNew = new Image
imgNew.src = "/light.gif"

// JavaScript Functions
```

12. Create a function called Progress, which will change the graphic source of the image that can be found in the images array object at the location given in the variable iDot. Continue the timer if the count of iDot is less than nine. Otherwise, kill the timer and return from the function.

```
// Progress
// Function will change the graphic
// depending on where it is in the count
function Progress() {

    document.images[iDot].src=imgNew.src

    // incr dot counter
    iDot ++

    if (iDot > 9 ) {
        iDot = 0
        clearTimeout(tmID)
        return
        }

    tmID = setTimeout("Progress()", 1000)
    }


// end hiding from old browsers -->
</SCRIPT>
</HEAD>
```

13. Create the BODY section and put in 10 copies of the same graphic file. This will also populate the Images Array object of the Document object with 10 image references.

```
<BODY>
<H1> Show Progress in Window</H1>
<RIGHT>
<IMG SRC="dark.gif" width=10 height=10>  
<IMG SRC="dark.gif" width=10 height=10>  
```

continued on next page

continued from previous page

```
<IMG SRC="dark.gif" width=10 height=10>  
<IMG SRC="dark.gif" width=10 height=10>  
<IMG SRC="dark.gif" width=10 height=10>  
<IMG SRC="dark.gif" width=10 height=10>  
<IMG SRC="dark.gif" width=10 height=10>  
<IMG SRC="dark.gif" width=10 height=10>  
<IMG SRC="dark.gif" width=10 height=10>  
<IMG SRC="dark.gif" width=10 height=10>  
</RIGHT>
```

14. Finish the document by creating a form with one button. The onClick event of the button will be trapped and the Progress function called when the event is triggered.

```
<p>
The new ability to change images directly in a window
after it has been layed out
<br>
will allow us to create
status bars or other animation to demonstrate "working..."
<p>
<FORM>
<INPUT type="button" Value="Start Status"
    onClick="Progress()">
<p>
</BODY>
</HTML>
```

15. Close and save the file as STATUS2.HTM. Test your document by loading it into your browser and pressing the "Start Status" button.

How It Works

The timer built-in function setTimeout() will start a timer and will set up the function or property of an object to be called or modified when the timer event occurs. The function is contained in an expression that is passed to the event as the first parameter. This expression could contain the property of an object or a function call as the example has demonstrated. Once the timer event has been triggered the timer will not run again. If you wish it to run you must call the setTimeout function again.

Comment

Repeated calls to setTimeout() in a recursively called function can cause problems with certain versions of some browsers. A workaround is to stop the timer at certain intervals and re-start it.

COMPLEXITY
ADVANCED

15.5   How do I...
Display a scrolling banner?

COMPATIBILITY: NAVIGATOR 2.X   NAVIGATOR 3.X   EXPLORER 3.X

Problem

I have seen scrolling banners in status bars at some Web sites. How can I implement a scrolling banner using JavaScript?

Technique

You can implement a scrolling banner by implementing a timer and creating a message string that is decremented by one letter each time the message is set into the status bar. When the message string is empty, it is reset to the full message. An alternative method can set the scrolling message to a text field in a form.

Steps

Open the file SCROLL1.HTM page in your browser. At the bottom of the window you will see a banner scrolling across the status bar as shown in Figure 15-20. To see scrolling in a text field, open the file SCROLL2.HTM and instead of scrolling in the status bar, the message scrolls in the text field, as shown in Figure 15-21. To create a Web page with a scrolling banner using either technique, follow these steps.

1. Create an empty HTML file.

2. Create a HEAD section and begin a JavaScript code section by typing the following code. You will be creating two global variables, one to hold the message you wish to display and one to hold the count of letters that will be clipped from the front of the message.

```
<HTML>
<HEAD><TITLE> Scrolling Status </TITLE>

<SCRIPT LANGUAGE="JavaScript">
<!--- hide script from old browsers

// JavaScript Global Variables
var iPos = 0
var sMessage = ""

// JavaScript functions
```

3. Next, create a function called StartScrolling. This function will grab a substring from the message string based on the value of the position of the

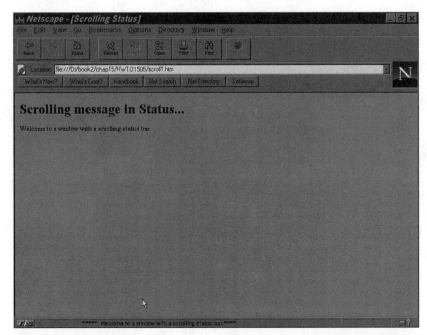

Figure 15-20 SCROLL1.HTM with scrolling banner in the status bar

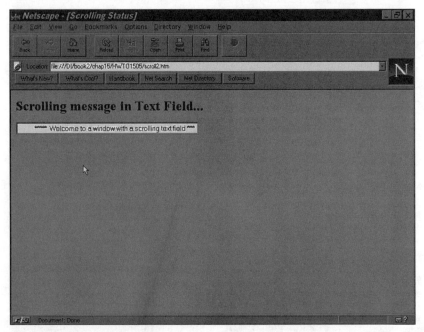

Figure 15-21 SCROLL2.HTM with scrolling banner in a text field

starting character and the length of the string. This new string will be set to the status bar, and the timer will be reset.

```
// JavaScript Functions
function StartScrolling() {

   // modify message
   var sOut = sMessage.substring(iPos, sMessage.length)
   status=sOut

   iPos++
   if (iPos > sMessage.length) {
      iPos = 1
      }

   setTimeout("StartScrolling()", 100)
   }
```

4. Create a second JavaScript function and call it SetupMessage. This function will create the base message that will be displayed in the banner. The message is padded on the left with blanks to allow for more of a scrolling effect.

```
function SetupMessage() {
   sMessage = ""
   for (i = 1; i <= 100; i++) {
      sMessage = sMessage + " "
      }

   sMessage = sMessage + "Welcome to a window with"
   sMessage = sMessage + " a scrolling status bar"

   // start timer
   StartScrolling()
   }
```

5. Close the HEAD section and create the BODY section. This section has a string message only.

```
// end hiding from old browsers -->
</SCRIPT>

<H1> Scrolling message in Status...</H1>
</HEAD>
<BODY onLoad="SetupMessage()">
Welcome to a window with a scrolling status bar
</BODY>
</HTML>
```

6. Close the file and save it as SCROLL1.HTM. Test your scrolling banner by loading the document into your browser.

7. Create the second example by creating a second HTML document.

8. Start the JavaScript and HEAD sections by again typing the following code.

```
<HTML>
<HEAD><TITLE> Scrolling Status </TITLE>
```

continued on next page

continued from previous page

```
<SCRIPT LANGUAGE="JavaScript">
<!--- hide script from old browsers

// JavaScript Global Variables
var iPos = 0
var sMessage = ""

// JavaScript functions
```

9. Create the function StartScrolling. In this example the function will output to a text field.

```
// JavaScript Functions
// Function will scroll through message
// pulling off characters through each
// iteration.
//
function StartScrolling() {

    // modify message
    var sOut = sMessage.substring(iPos, sMessage.length)
    document.ScrollForm.StatusBar.value=sOut

    iPos++

    // reset
    if (iPos > sMessage.length)
       iPos = 1

    setTimeout("StartScrolling()", 100)
    }
```

10. Create the SetupMessage function again, but decrease the number of spaces as the text field is much smaller than the status bar.

```
// SetupMessage
// Function will create original message and
// start timer
//
function SetupMessage() {
    sMessage = ""
    for (i = 1; i <= 50; i++) {
       sMessage = sMessage + " "
       }


    sMessage = sMessage + "*****  Welcome to a window with"
    sMessage = sMessage + " a scrolling text field ****"

    // start timer
    StartScrolling()
    }


// end hiding from old browsers -->
</SCRIPT>
</HEAD>
```

11. Create the BODY section with a form containing one text field.

```
<BODY onLoad="SetupMessage()">
<H1> Scrolling message in Text Field...</H1>
<FORM Name="ScrollForm">
<INPUT TYPE="text" Name="StatusBar" size=50>
</FORM>
</BODY>
</HTML>
```

12. Close and save this file as SCROLL2.HTM. Test this document by loading it into the browser.

How It Works

With the use of the timer and by truncating a string using the String object method of substring(), you can create a scrolling banner in the status bar. After you print out each message you must reset the timer as it will not run again automatically.

The advantage of scrolling text to a text field is that you will not be in competition with the browser for the use of the status bar. Any browser messages will go into the status bar and the scrolling banner could overwrite them before the Web page reader has a chance to read them.

COMPLEXITY
ADVANCED

15.6 How do I...
Use the Navigator object to check the installed plug-ins?

COMPATIBILITY: NAVIGATOR 2.X   NAVIGATOR 3.X   EXPLORER 3.X

Problem

How can I query which plug-ins are installed and display their data and file extension types?

Technique

With Navigator 3.0, the Navigator object now has a new property, which is an object called Plugin. With this object you can display information about the application associated with the plug-in and the plug-in description. You can also refer to the Plugin object as an array, and query each file extension and description.

Steps

Open the file NAVIG.HTM in your browser. This document will list every plug-in currently installed with your browser and provide information about each plug-in,

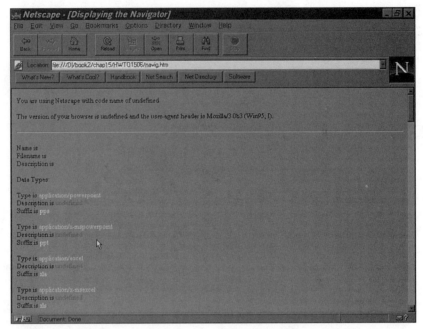

Figure 15-22 NAVIG.HTM with display of information from Plugin object

including its associated mime types, as shown in Figure 15-22. To create this document, follow the steps below.

1. Create an HTML document.

2. Create and close the HEAD section and start the BODY section. Also start a JavaScript section.

```
<HTML>
<HEAD><TITLE> Displaying the Navigator </TITLE></HEAD>
<BODY>

<SCRIPT LANGUAGE="JavaScript">
<!--- hide script from old browsers
```

3. Write out the Navigator application name, code name, version, and user-agent from the Navigator object. The user-agent is sent with the HTTP protocol between client and server.

```
// write out navigator structure information
document.write("You are using " + navigator.appName)
document.writeln(" with code name of " + navigator.appCodName + ".<p>")

document.write("The version of your browser is " + navigator.version)
document.writeln(" and the user-agent header is " +
    navigator.userAgent + ".<p>")
```

4. Query the number of plug-ins installed on the system and use this in a *for* loop. Access each plug-in and assign it to a local variable.

```
// write out plugin information

var iplugins = navigator.plugins.length

// for each plugin write out structure information
// and iterate through each of it's datatypes
for (icount = 0; icount < iplugins; icount++) {

        var current = navigator.plugins[icount];
```

5. Write out information that is singular for each plug-in, which is the plug-in name, filename, and description.

```
document.write("<HR><p>");
document.write("Name is <FONT COLOR='#FF0000'>" + current.name)
document.writeln("</FONT><br>")
document.write("Filename is <FONT COLOR='#00FF00'>"
    + current.filename)
document.writeln("</FONT><br>")
document.write("Description is <FONT COLOR='#0000FF'>" +
    current.description)
document.writeln("</FONT><p>Data Types:<p>")
```

6. Access the Plugin object as an array and iterate through each of the array elements. Write out the mime type, description, and associated suffix (file extension).

```
// iterate through types
for (itype = 0; itype < current.length; itype++)
    {
    var mmtype = current[itype]

    if (mmtype)  {
       document.write("Type is <FONT COLOR='#FFFF00'>" +
       mmtype.type)
    document.writeln("</FONT><br>")
       document.write
       ("Description is <FONT COLOR='#FF00FF'>"
       + mmtype.description.filename)
       document.writeln("</FONT><br>")
       document.write("Suffix is <FONT COLOR='#FFFFFF'>" +
       mmtype.suffixes)
       document.writeln("</FONT><p>")
       }
    }
}
```

7. Close out the BODY section.

```
// end hiding from old browsers -->
</SCRIPT>

</BODY>
</HTML>
```

8. Close the file and save it as NAVIG.HTM. Test the document by running it in your browser.

How It Works

The Navigator object existed prior to version 3.0, but with this version, information about the plug-ins can now be found as properties of this object. You can verify the existence of a Plugin by iterating through the plug-ins and testing the mime type or suffix against the one you will use in your HTML document.

COMPLEXITY
ADVANCED

15.7   How do I...
Handle elements and data stored in multiple forms?

COMPATIBILITY:    NAVIGATOR 2.X   NAVIGATOR 3.X   EXPLORER 3.X

Problem

I want to create an order form for my Web page, but I have some data that the Web page reader need enter only once and other data that must be entered several times. In this case the reader enters his or her name once and then enters several items. I would like to implement this with two forms. How can I coordinate data between two forms?

Technique

You can create several forms in one document and use JavaScript to coordinate between them. Each form can be accessed either by its name or by its entry in the Forms array, which is a property of the document.

Steps

Open the file FORMS.HTM in your browser. This document has two forms. The first is for the customer name and address; the second is for the item shown in Figure 15-23. Enter a customer name into the top form and select the Radio button labeled Junk Food. This will update the Item Category field in the second form. Enter your junk food item, in this case chocolate (an essential food item), as shown in Figure 15-24. When done press the Submit Query button. You can see from the Location field that the query has been submitted and the data string created. Note from the string that the customer name, a value from the first form, has been added to the data in the second form, as shown in Figure 15-25. This was accomplished using a hidden form field. To find out how to re-create this form, follow these steps.

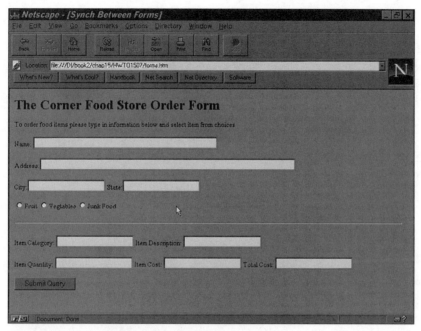

Figure 15-23 FORMS.HTM after opening

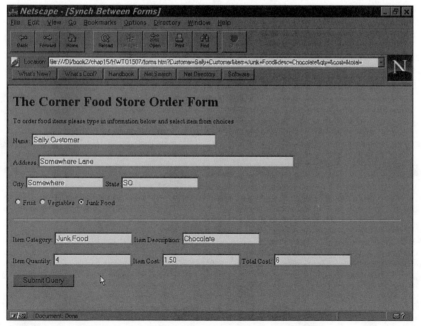

Figure 15-24 FORMS.HTM after entering a category

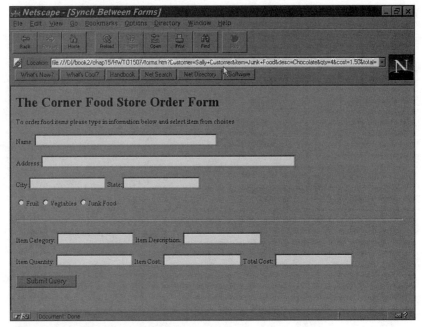

Figure 15-25 After form submission

1. Create a new HTML document file.

2. Start a HEAD and a JavaScript code section by typing in the following code.

```
<HTML>
<HEAD><TITLE> Synch Between Forms </TITLE>
<SCRIPT LANGUAGE="JavaScript">
<!--- hide script from old browsers

// JavaScript Global Variables

// JavaScript Functions
```

3. Create a new function called NewItem. This function will set the value of the item field in the second form named Item with the value passed as a parameter. Note that the form is accessed using the generic forms array, which is a property of a Document object.

```
// NewItem(sItem)
// Function will set item
// in Item form to parameter
function NewItem(sItem) {

    // set item and customer
    document.forms[1].item.value = sItem
    }
```

4. Create a second JavaScript function called NewCost. This function will calculate a third field by multiplying two other fields. The items and form are all addressed by name.

```
// NewCost
// Compute total cost
function NewCost() {
    var iCost = parseFloat(document.Item.cost.value)
    var iQty = parseInt(document.Item.qty.value)

    var iTotal = iCost * iQty
    document.Item.total.value = iTotal
    }
```

5. End the JavaScript and HEAD sections and begin the BODY section by typing the following.

```
// end hiding from old browsers -->
</SCRIPT>

</HEAD>

<BODY>
<H1> The Corner Food Store Order Form</H1>
```

6. Create a form called "PersonForm" and place in it four text fields and three Radio buttons. Trap the onChange event for the Name field and set the value of the Customer field in the second form to this new value. Additionally, trap the onClick event for the Radio buttons and call the JavaScript NewItem function.

```
To order food items please type in information below and select
item from choices

<FORM NAME="PersonForm">
<p>Name: <INPUT TYPE="text" NAME="Name" size=50
    onChange="document.Item.Customer.value=this.value">
<P>Address:<INPUT TYPE="text" NAME="Address" size = 70>
<p>City:<INPUT TYPE="text" Name="City">
State:<INPUT TYPE="text" Name="State">
<p> <INPUT TYPE="radio" Name="Items" Value="Fruit"
    onClick="NewItem(this.value)">Fruit
<INPUT TYPE="radio" Name="Items" Value="Vegtables"
    onClick="NewItem(this.value)">Vegtables
<INPUT Type="radio" Name="Items" Value="Junk Food"
    onClick="NewItem(this.value)">Junk Food
</FORM>
```

7. Type in a horizontal rule to create a break between the two forms.

```
<p>
<hr>
<p>
```

8. Create a second form named "Item." This form will have five text fields and a standard Submit object. A Submit object will create a button labeled Submit Query, which will automatically submit the form based on what is defined for the form's ACTION property when the button is pressed. Close out the BODY section.

```
<FORM NAME="Item">
<INPUT TYPE="hidden" NAME="Customer" Value="">
<p>Item Category: <INPUT TYPE="text" Name="item" Value="">
Item Description: <INPUT TYPE="text" Name="desc" Value="">
<p>Item Quantity: <INPUT TYPE="text" Name="qty">
Item Cost: <INPUT TYPE="text" Name="cost"
        onChange="NewCost()">
Total Cost: <INPUT TYPE="text" Name="total">
<p><INPUT TYPE="submit">
</FORM>
</BODY>
</HTML>
```

9. Save your file as FORMS.HTM. Load this into your browser and test by entering different data and pressing the submit button.

How It Works

A form becomes an accessible property of a document, and most properties of the Document object are accessible in JavaScript code. You can coordinate data between several forms in different windows as long as the window and the document reference are stored in variables that can be accessed when access to the form is needed.

In addition, you can create Hidden objects in any one form. A Hidden object will allow you to store a name-value pair with the form. You can use this capability to coordinate the data between different forms by placing a unique identifier in the hidden field. If you need to have more than one value to identify the form uniquely, create multiple hidden fields.

The Submit Query button on this form would submit only the second form. You could place a submit button on each of your forms, or you could have one button to capture the submission. This capture could be used to verify the code, and the forms could be submitted individually. The example in How-To 15.8 will explain this in more detail.

COMPLEXITY
ADVANCED

15.8 How do I...
Submit data back to the HTTP server?

COMPATIBILITY: NAVIGATOR 2.X   NAVIGATOR 3.X   EXPLORER 3.X

Problem

I have more than one form, and I want to verify their results before I submit them. How can I verify the form data and submit more than one form?

Technique

The Submit button embedded in a form is not the only means for submitting a form. The submit() method for the form will perform the same action as this button. The data is gathered from the form and sent to the HTTP server using the method specified in the form declaration.

Steps

Open the file FORMSUB.HTM in your browser. This form is for a food store that sells three types of items: vegtables, fruit, and junk food. Enter an item but do not enter your name. Press the Send Order button, and you will be notified that you need to type in your name, as shown in Figure 15-26. Do this and press the button again. A new Web page, as shown in Figure 15-27, informs you that your order has been received. If you look in the Location field of the browser, you will see the data that was sent when the order was submitted. The steps to re-create this page follow.

1. Create a new empty HTML file.

2. Type the following code to start both a HEAD section and a JavaScript code section.

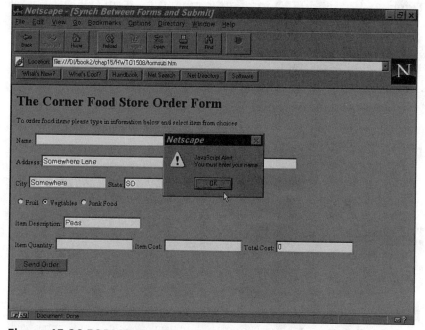

Figure 15-26 FORMSUB.HTM with message about missing data

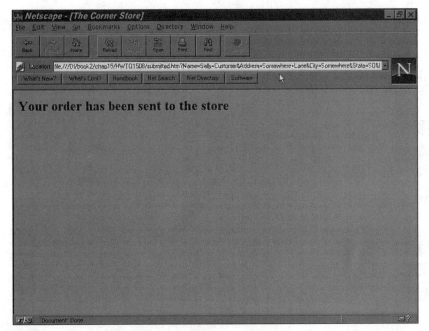

Figure 15-27 SUBMITTED form after submitting form FORMSUB.HTM

```
<HTML>
<HEAD><TITLE> Synch Between Forms and Submit </TITLE>
<SCRIPT LANGUAGE="JavaScript">
<!--- hide script from old browsers

// JavaScript Global Variables

// JavaScript Functions
```

3. Next, create a function called NewCost. This function will generate a value for a third form field by multiplying two other form fields.

```
// NewCost will
// calculate cost of qty and item
function NewCost() {
  var iCost = parseFloat(document.Item.cost.value)
  var iQty = parseInt(document.Item.qty.value)

  var iTotal = iCost * iQty
  document.Item.total.value = iTotal
  }
```

4. Create a second function called SendData. This function will verify that the customer did enter his or her name. If no name is entered an alert message is shown and the process is stopped. If the validation succeeds, the form data is submitted using the submit() method.

```
// submit order
function SendOrder() {

   // validate data
   if (document.Item.Name.value == "") {
      alert("You must enter your name")
      return
      }
   document.Item.submit()
   }
```

5. Close out the JavaScript and HEAD sections and begin the BODY section.

```
// end hiding from old browsers -->
</SCRIPT>

<H1> The Corner Food Store Order Form</H1>
</HEAD>

<BODY>
```

6. Create a form called Item. In the form tag modify the (address) code and replace it with the full address of the location where you will create the SUBMITTED.HTM file. This file will be created in later steps. This form will have several text input fields and three Radio buttons. An event handler is coded for the onChange event for the field named "cost". This handler will call the JavaScript function NewCost. Instead of a submit button on the form you will create your own, which will call the SendOrder function when the button is clicked.

```
To order food items please type in information below and select
item from choices

<FORM NAME="Item"
   ACTION=" file:///(address)submitted.htm">
<p>Name: <INPUT TYPE="text" NAME="Name" size=50" Value="">
<P>Address:<INPUT TYPE="text" NAME="Address" size = 70>
<p>City:<INPUT TYPE="text" Name="City">
State:<INPUT TYPE="text" Name="State">

<p> <INPUT TYPE="radio" Name="Items" Value="Fruit">Fruit
<INPUT TYPE="radio" Name="Items" Value="Vegtables">Vegtables
<INPUT Type="radio" Name="Items" Value="Junk Food">Junk Food

<p>Item Description: <INPUT TYPE="text" Name="desc" Value="">
<p>Item Quantity: <INPUT TYPE="text" Name="qty">
Item Cost: <INPUT TYPE="text" Name="cost"
      onChange="NewCost()">
Total Cost: <INPUT TYPE="text" Name="total" Value=0>

<p><INPUT TYPE="button" Value="Send Order"
   onClick="SendOrder()">
</FORM>
</BODY>
</HTML>
```

7. Close your file and save it as FORMSUB.HTM.

8. Create a second blank HTML document.

9. In this document, create a basic HTML document that contains only a heading.

```
<HTML><TITLE> The Corner Store </TITLE></HEAD>
<BODY>
<H1> Your order has been sent to the store </H1>
</BODY>
```

10. Close and save this document as SUBMITTED.HTM.

11. To test the document, make sure that the SUBMITTED.HTM file is in the subdirectory that you coded into FORMSUB.HTM. Load FORMSUB.HTM into your browser and test it by entering data and submitting it.

How It Works

You can use the submit form item to submit form data, or your can create your own button and JavaScript function. With this latter technique you can verify the form contents and then submit by using the Form Submit() method.

COMPLEXITY
ADVANCED

15.9 How do I...
Work with VRML worlds by using embedding and by writing to a VRML plug-in using the Write and writeln commands?

COMPATIBILITY:

Problem

I want to modify a document dynamically by embedding a Plugin object into it. How can I do this and make sure that the object is played by the plug-in application? Also, can I send data directly to a plug-in?

Technique

You can embed a Plugin object as easily as you would a graphic. You will need to make sure that the Plugin is installed with your browser and in the plug-in subdirectory. Then, all you have to do is use the EMBED tag to place the object into the document. When the tag is parsed in the document, the plug-in application is loaded and the object is read or played, whichever is appropriate.

You can also open a document as the plug-in type and communicate directly with the plug-in using the Write() and writeln() methods. The plug-in will process the data as if it had opened a file of the mime type associated with the plug-in directly.

Steps

The plug-in used in this example is the Live3D VRML plug-in from Netscape. VRML is the language used to create three-dimensional interactive worlds which in turn allow you to create realistic images that you can then manipulate. If you do not have this plug-in, you can download it from Netscape or you can copy it from the CD that came with this book. Install the plug-in using the installation program.

After you have installed the plug-in, open the WRLDPRNT.HTM document in your browser. The page has a button that can be used to test for the plug-in, a text field where the Web page reader can enter a VRML world file (extension of .wrl), and a button to create the document shown in Figure 15-28. Test for the plug-in by pressing the test button. If the plug-in is successfully installed, you should see the message shown in Figure 15-29. If you did not receive this message, try installing the plug-in again.

After the test, type in the name of a VRML world. There is one on the CD with this book called first.wrl which you can use for this test. After you type this in, click the Display in Window button and the VRML world will open, embedded in the second frame, as shown in Figure 15-30. As can be seen in Figure 15-31, you can click the right mouse button over the displayed VRML file, and the options available for this type of plug-in are displayed. You can also use the navigation controls to move around the world, as seen in Figure 15-32.

You can also create a VRML world dynamically by opening an empty document using the plug-in mime type. You can see this by opening the file OPENWRLD.HTM in your browser. This window has several controls, which allow you to draw, color, and apply several geometric transformations to a shape, as shown in Figure 15-33. Select the cone shape and color it cyan. Apply the translation transformation to the object, which will move it along both the X and the Y axes. Last, apply a rotation transform along the X axis, as shown in Figure 15-34. Press the button to display the window and you will see a separate window open, as shown in Figure 15-35 where the VRML world you just specified is created. You can modify the scene by changing the shape and color of the VMRL world as shown in Figure 15-36. Also note that the VRML code is listed in the text field at the bottom of the form.

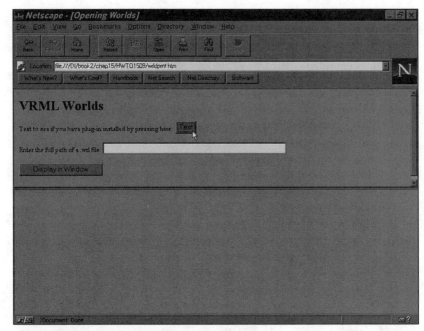

Figure 15-28 WRLDPRNT.HTM after opening

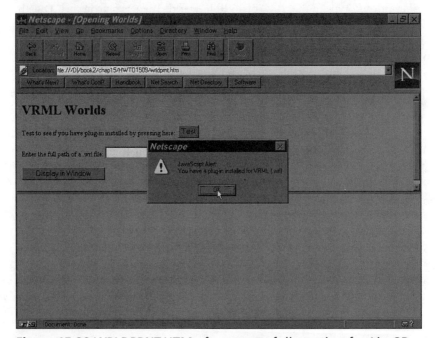

Figure 15-29 WRLDPRNT.HTM after successfully testing for Live3D plug-in

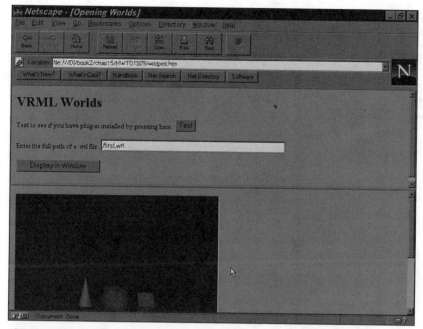

Figure 15-30 WRLDPRNT.HTM after displaying VRML world

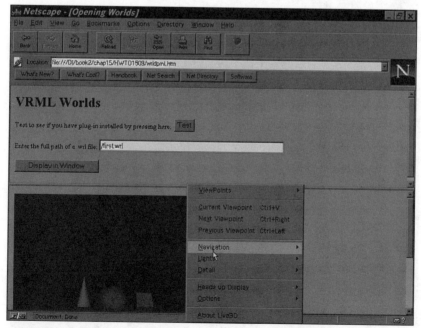

Figure 15-31 Right mouse button menu listing options for VRML embedded object

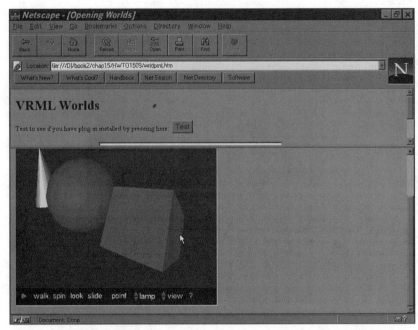

Figure 15-32 Demonstration of navigation capability of VRML object

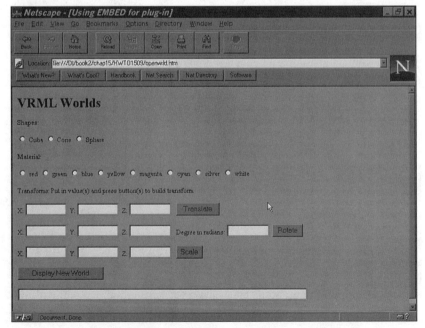

Figure 15-33 OPENWRLD.HTM after opening

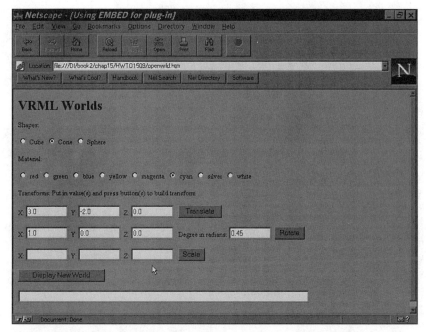

Figure 15-34 OPENWRLD.HTM after entering several fields for new VRML world

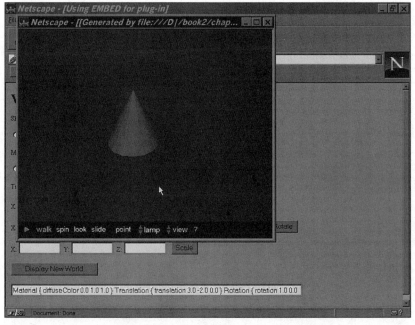

Figure 15-35 The newly defined VRML world, generated using JavaScript

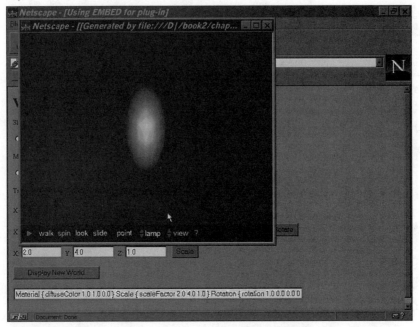

Figure 15-36 New VRML world with different shape

To create both of these examples follow the steps below.

1. Create an HTML document to use as a work document. Type in the following code.

```
<HTML>
<HEAD><TITLE> Working Window </TITLE></HEAD>
<BODY></BODY>
</HTML>
```

2. Close the document and name it BLANK.HTM.

3. Create a second document that will create a Frameset as shown in the code below.

```
<HTML>
<HEAD>
<TITLE>Opening Worlds</TITLE>
</HEAD>

<FRAMESET ROWS="40%, 66%">
   <FRAME SRC=showwrld.htm NAME="Open">
   <FRAME SRC=blank.htm NAME="workFrame">
</FRAMESET>

</HTML>
```

4. Close and save this document as WRLDPRNT.HTM. Create a new document.

5. Type in code to start a HEAD section and a JavaScript section.

```
<HTML>
<HEAD><TITLE> Using EMBED for plug-in</TITLE>
<SCRIPT LANGUAGE="JavaScript">
<!--- hide script from old browsers

// JavaScript Global Variables
testWindow = ""

// JavaScript Functions
```

6. Create a function that will test for the existence of the plug-in using a method defined by Netscape.

```
// TestPlugin
// function will test if plug-in exists
// and provide message accordingly
//
// code concept is from Netscape JavaScript
// Authoring Guide
function TestPlugIn() {
   var testWindow = window.open("", "Test", "width=1,height=1")
   if (testWindow != null) {
      if (testWindow.document.open("x-world/x-vrml") != null) {
         alert("You have a plug-in installed for VRML (.wrl)")
   }
      else {
       alert("You do not have a plug-in installed for VRML.")
       }
      }
   testWindow.close()
   }
```

7. Next, create a second function that will use JavaScript to add an EMBED statement to the work document, using the name of the source passed to the function. The embedded object is opened with a default size of 400 units width and 400 units height. You must specify a size when using an EMBED tag.

```
// create display window for document
//
// Embed .wrl file in document which
// will trigger plug-in
function DisplayWorld(sExpression) {
   parent.workFrame.document.open("text/html")
   parent.workFrame.document.writeln
   ("<EMBED SRC='" + sExpression + "' WIDTH='400' HEIGHT='400'>")
   parent.workFrame.document.close()
   }


// end hiding from old browsers -->
</SCRIPT>
</HEAD>
```

8. Create the BODY section, which will contain a form with two buttons and a text field. The first button will call the TestPlugIn function when it is clicked, and the second button will call the DisplayWorld function, passing the value in the text field to the function.

```
<body>
<H1> VRML Worlds </H1>
<p>
<FORM NAME="FormValue" >
Test to see if you have plug-in installed by pressing here: 
<INPUT TYPE="button" Value="Test" onClick="TestPlugIn()">

<p>Enter the full path of a .wrl file:
 <INPUT TYPE="text" NAME="expr" size=50>

<p>
<INPUT TYPE="button" VALUE="Display in Window"
   onClick="DisplayWorld(document.FormValue.expr.value)">
</FORM>
</BODY>
</HTML>
```

9. Close and save the file as SHOWWRLD.HTM. Test your new documents by opening WRLDPRNT.HTM in your browser.

10. This last example was a nice demonstration of an embedded plug-in, but it did not show the real power that JavaScript can give you with plug-ins. If you have the ability to write the commands or language that a plug-in understands in a write() or writeln() document method function, you can manipulate the plug-in dynamically. The next example demonstrates this.

11. Create a new HTML document file.

12. Start a HEAD and a JavaScript section, and create several global variables.

```
<HTML>
<HEAD><TITLE> Using EMBED for plug-in</TITLE>

<SCRIPT LANGUAGE="JavaScript">
<!--- hide script from old browsers


sShape = ""
sMaterial = ""
sTranslate = ""
sRotate = ""
sScale = ""

// JavaScript Functions
```

13. Create a function that will write out the VRML code for a Cone object with a height of eight units and a radius of six units. All parts of the code will be generated.

```
//
// Following functions create the shapes
```

```
// CreateCone
//
// Generate VRML to draw a cone
function CreateCone() {

    sShape = "Cone { height=8.0 radius=6.0 parts=ALL } "

    }
```

14. Create a second function that will generate a VRML cube with a height of eight units and a width of four units.

```
// CreateCube
//
// Generate VRML to draw a cube
function CreateCube() {

    sShape = "Cube { height=8.0 width=4.0 } "

    }
```

15. Create a third shape function for the Sphere object with a radius of six units.

```
// CreateSphere
//
// Generate VRML to draw a sphere
function CreateSphere() {

    sShape = "Sphere { radius=6.0 } "

    }
```

16. Next, you will create a function that will generate the material of the object. The material determines the object's color, transparency, and other aspects of its surface appearance. The function will receive the color as a parameter.

```
// following function creates the material

// CreateMaterial
//
// Generate VRML to create the material
function CreateMaterial(sColor) {

    sMaterial = "Material { diffuseColor " +
    sColor + " } "

    }
```

17. You will create the transformation function next, starting with the translation function. This function will access its X, Y, and Z values directly from the document form.

```
/* following functions create the Translation,
   rotation, and scale */
```

continued on next page

continued from previous page

```
// CreateTranslate
//
// Generate VRML for translations
function CreateTranslate() {
    var tX = document.ValueForm.TX.value
    var tY = document.ValueForm.TY.value
    var tZ = document.ValueForm.TZ.value

    sTranslate = "Translation { translation " +
        tX + " " + tY + " " + tZ + " } "
}
```

18. Next, create the Rotation function. Rotation will move an object around its axis by the degree given. Which axis the object is being rotated around and the degree of rotation, expressed as radians, are accessed from fields in the document form.

```
// CreateRotation
//
// Generate VRML for translations
function CreateRotation() {

    var rX = document.ValueForm.RX.value
    var rY = document.ValueForm.RY.value
    var rZ = document.ValueForm.RZ.value
    var rDeg = document.ValueForm.Deg.value

    sRotate = "Rotation { rotation " +
        rX + " " + rY + " " + rZ + " " +
        rDeg + " } "
}
```

19. The last of the transform functions will scale the object by a factor along the X, Y, or Z axis. The values for these factors are again accessed directly from the document form.

```
// CreateScale
//
// Generate VRML for scale
function CreateScale() {

    var sX = document.ValueForm.SX.value
    var sY = document.ValueForm.SY.value
    var sZ = document.ValueForm.SZ.value

    sTranslate = "Scale { scaleFactor " +
        sX + " " + sY + " " + sZ + " } "
}
```

20. The next function, WritePlugIn, will take the values from creating the shape, applying a material, and applying a transform. It will form one string expression containing the whole. If no value is given for any one of the options, an empty string is added to the expression.

```
// WritePlugIn
// function will open a document of the type of
// plug-in and write directly to it
function DisplayWorld() {

   var sExpression = sMaterial + sTranslate + sRotate
      + sScale + sShape
```

21. The expression string is assigned to a text field in the form for display, and a new window is opened. In the window a new document of the mime type of the plug-in is opened and the string expression is written to it using the document writeln() method. Finally, the document is closed to enable the new document to process the string.

```
document.ValueForm.Result.value=sExpression

   var newWindow = window.open("", "World",
   "scrollbars=yes,width=500,height=400")

   newWindow.document.open("x-world/x-vrml")
   newWindow.document.writeln("#VRML V1.0 ascii")
   newWindow.document.writeln(sExpression)
   newWindow.document.close()
}
```

22. The HEAD section is ended and the BODY section is begun. A form is created and the first set of controls are Radio buttons for the shape.

```
// end hiding from old browsers -->
</SCRIPT>

</HEAD>
<body>
<H1> VRML Worlds </H1>
<p>
<FORM NAME="ValueForm" >
Shapes:<p>
<INPUT type="radio" Name="Shape"
   onClick="CreateCube()"> Cube 
<INPUT type="radio" Name="Shape"
   onClick="CreateCone()"> Cone 
<INPUT type="radio" Name="Shape"
   onClick="CreateSphere()"> Sphere 
<p>
```

23. The next set of controls are Radio buttons for the material color.

```
Material:<p>
<INPUT type="radio" Name="Material" Value="1.0 0.0 0.0"
   onClick="CreateMaterial(this.value)"> red 
<INPUT type="radio" Name="Material" Value="0.0 1.0 0.0"
   onClick="CreateMaterial(this.value)"> green 
<INPUT type="radio" Name="Material" Value="0.0 0.0 1.0"
   onClick="CreateMaterial(this.value)"> blue 
<INPUT type="radio" Name="Material" Value="1.0 1.0 0.0"
   onClick="CreateMaterial(this.value)"> yellow 
```

continued on next page

continued from previous page

```
<INPUT type="radio" Name="Material" Value="1.0 0.0 1.0"
    onClick="CreateMaterial(this.value)"> magenta 
<INPUT type="radio" Name="Material" Value="0.0 1.0 1.0"
    onClick="CreateMaterial(this.value)"> cyan 
<INPUT type="radio" Name="Material" Value="0.75 0.75 0.75"
    onClick="CreateMaterial(this.value)"> silver 
<INPUT type="radio" Name="Material" Value="1.0 1.0 1.0"
    onClick="CreateMaterial(this.value)"> white 
<p>
```

24. The next controls handle the translation transformation. Pressing the button associated with this grouping will call the CreateTranslate function, which will create the translation VRML.

```
Transforms: Put in value(s) and press button(s) to build transform<p>
X: <INPUT type="text" size=10 Name="TX"> 
Y: <INPUT type="text" size=10 Name="TY"> 
Z: <INPUT type="text" size=10 Name="TZ">  
<INPUT TYPE="button" Value="Translate"
    onClick="CreateTranslate()">
<p>
```

25. The next set of controls are for the rotation transformation.

```
X: <INPUT type="text" size=10 Name="RX"> 
Y: <INPUT type="text" size=10 Name="RY"> 
Z: <INPUT type="text" size=10 Name="RZ">  
Degree in radians: <INPUT type="text" size=10 Name="Deg">
  <INPUT TYPE="button" Value="Rotate"
    onClick="CreateRotation()">
```

26. The next set of controls are for the scaling transformation.

```
<p>
X: <INPUT type="text" size=10 Name="SX"> 
Y: <INPUT type="text" size=10 Name="SY"> 
Z: <INPUT type="text" size=10 Name="SZ">  
<INPUT TYPE="button" Value="Scale"
    onClick="CreateScale()">
<p>
```

27. Last, a text field to display the VRML and a button are created. The onClick event of the button will generate the VRML and create the VRML world.

```
<INPUT TYPE="button" VALUE="Display New World"
    onClick="DisplayWorld()">
<p>
<INPUT TYPE="text" size=80 Name="Result">
</FORM>

</BODY>
</HTML>
```

28. Close and save the file as OPENWRLD.HTM. Test the results in your browser.

How It Works

Plug-ins are, in most cases, no different than graphics in that they can be embedded directly into an HTML document. You will always need to specify a width and a height or your page will most likely generate an error. In addition, some plug-ins require that you specify other information such as a file subcomponent. Check the plug-in document for this.

A more powerful combination of plug-in and JavaScript is one that allows you to open a document using the plug-in type and to send commands dynamically and directly to the plug-in. In this way, you can create plug-in content that is influenced or even generated by the use. The downside of this type of use is that you may not be able to write out the language that the plug-in, such as one that takes graphic file data, can understand.

LIVECONNECT

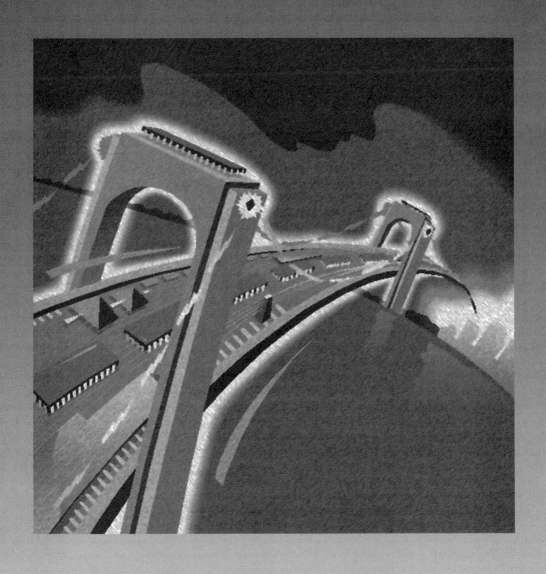

16

LIVECONNECT

How do I...

16.1   **Add a Java applet to an HTML document?**

16.2   **Control a Java applet from JavaScript?**

16.3   **Access data returned by a Java method?**

16.4   **Access data contained inside a Java class?**

16.5   **Use a Java constructor to initialize a JavaScript variable?**

LiveConnect is the name of a new capability, introduced in Netscape Navigator 3.0, which integrates JavaScript, Java, and plug-ins into a comprehensive interactive environment. Figure 16-1 represents the LiveConnect architecture.

Before LiveConnect, the Web's three primary interactive environments operated independently of one another. LiveConnect permits transfer of both data and control from one environment to another. LiveConnect allows JavaScript developers to:

- Use Java constructors to instantiate new JavaScript objects
- Control applets and plug-ins from JavaScript functions
- Establish JavaScript functions as callbacks invoked by plug-in events
- Store Java attributes and method-return data in JavaScript variables

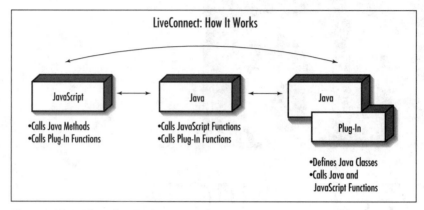

Figure 16-1 The LiveConnect environment

With LiveConnect, JavaScript code can invoke public attributes and methods belonging to a Java object. If you are not familiar with Java, you can still take advantage of LiveConnect through the ever-expanding library of reusable Java applets. As the LiveConnect technology matures, the quantity and scope of reusable applets will continue to grow. Through Java's class library, JavaScript developers have access to features not available in the JavaScript language, such as primitive graphics, audio, video, and image manipulation. JavaScript developers can also control plug-ins defined by a proxy Java object. Navigator 3.0 comes with three JavaScript-compliant plug-ins: Live Audio, Live Video, and Live 3D.

> **NOTE**
>
> At the time of publishing, the LiveConnect environment and Navigator 3.0 were in beta release. Because of this, the JavaScript/plug-in connection will not be covered in this chapter. All examples in this chapter were developed and tested using Navigator Gold version 3.0b4Gold. Because these examples are based on a beta release, they may not work with other versions of the Navigator browser.

16.1   Add a Java applet to an HTML document

This How-To will demonstrate how to embed a Java applet inside an HTML document.

16.2   Control a Java applet from JavaScript

Through the LiveConnect technology introduced in Navigator 3.0, JavaScript code can invoke public Java methods belonging to an applet. Learn how to access the properties of the JavaScript applet object.

16.3 Access data returned by a Java method

Many Java methods return data to the calling function. This How-To will demonstrate how to store this data in a JavaScript variable.

16.4 Access data contained inside a Java class

This How-To will teach you how to access the information contained in objects returned by a Java method.

16.5 Use a Java constructor to initialize a JavaScript variable

Learn how to use Java constructors to create new JavaScript objects.

COMPLEXITY
ADVANCED

16.1 How do I...

Add a Java applet to an HTML document?

COMPATIBILITY: NAVIGATOR 2.X NAVIGATOR 3.X EXPLORER 3.X

Problem

Besides JavaScript, the Java language, created by Sun Microsystems, represents another tool for creating interactive applications for the World Wide Web. How can I embed Java programs, known as applets, into the body of an HTML document?

Technique

The Java language differs from JavaScript in that the source code does not reside inside the HTML document. Java source code is stored in separate files, identified by a .Java extension. This means that Java code is physically separate from the HTML documents which use it. The Java compiler, which comes with the Java Developer's Kit (JDK), converts Java source code into "byte codes" stored in an object file with a .class extension. Byte codes are platform-independent executable statements that adhere to the Java Virtual Machine specification.

The <APPLET> tag is used to embed a Java applet inside an HTML document. The <APPLET> tag is a container that must be closed by a </APPLET> tag. This tag lets the browser know which applet should be downloaded from the server and executed on the client machine. No additional step is required to start an applet's execution. The following code demonstrates how to use the <APPLET> tag to embed the applet Weather inside an HTML document.

```
<APPLET CODE=Weather>
```

The <APPLET> tag's CODE attribute is assigned the name of the .class containing the desired applet subclass. Java code is organized into classes containing attributes and methods. At least one class must inherit from the java.applet.Applet class, provided as part of the JDK framework, for an applet to exist. Applets are event driven, which means that functionality is contained inside event handlers executed by certain system- and user-initiated actions. The java.applet.Applet class defines the minimum set of event handlers a Java applet must define.

Along with the CODE attribute, all <APPLET> tags must have their HEIGHT and WIDTH attributes set. These attributes specify the number of pixels assigned to the applet's display area. The ALIGN attribute establishes where the applet will appear inside the display area. Valid values include left, right, top, texttop, middle, absmiddle, baseline, bottom, and absbottom. The CODEBASE attribute specifies a uniform resource locator (URL), where the applet's .class file is stored. If this attribute remains unassigned, the browser attempts to locate the applet inside the document base location. The ALT attribute establishes content that will be displayed to the user if an error prevents an applet from being initialized. This message will not be displayed inside non-Java-compatible browsers. The following code demonstrates an <APPLET> tag that defines most of its valid attributes.

```
<APPLET CODE=Weather ALIGN=middle WIDTH=300 HEIGHT=300>
```

Java-compatible browsers will ignore anything inside an <APPLET> container except for the <PARAM> tag. This tag is used to define a series of parameters that will be passed to the applets upon initialization. The <PARAM> tag's NAME attribute specifies a parameter's name, which is used to identify the parameter. The VALUE attribute represents the actual parameter value returned by the Applet class's getParameter() method. The VALUE attribute should be changed to alter the way an applet behaves. The following code demonstrates how the <PARAM> tag can be used to establish a parameter named SEQUENCE_INTERVAL, with a value of 275.

```
<PARAM NAME=SEQUENCE_INTERVAL VALUE=275>
```

Steps

This example will create an HTML document that contains an embedded Java applet. The applet will loop through a time series display of satellite images taken over the continental United States. The images show weather patterns for an eight-hour period. The eight images that comprise the sequence are in Graphical Interchange Format (GIF) format. The applet will loop through all eight images, pause, and then start the loop again. Looping will be performed by a background thread.

From Navigator 3.0, open the file HT1601.HTM. After 5 to 10 seconds, notice the satellite image displayed in Figure 16-2 appear. The applet takes a few seconds to load because it is opening and reading eight GIF raster image files. When eight images are loaded into memory, the applet will begin to execute a continuous animation loop. This loop is executed on a background thread. Each frame sequence involves the display of all eight images with the background thread pausing after each image is displayed. The amount of time that the system pauses or sleeps is passed to the applet in two parameters, SEQUENCE_INTERVAL and FRAME_INTERVAL.

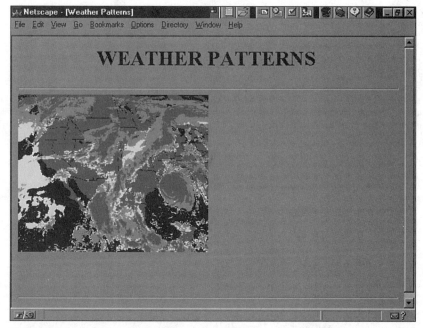

Figure 16-2 The weather pattern applet

1. The following Java code can be used to create the Weather applet .class file. This applet contains an animation loop, running as a background thread, which will run through a series of satellite images. These images show weather patterns over the United States.

2. Underneath your working directory, create a new subdirectory called java. If you do not have access to the JDK, make sure that the Weather.class and igs*.gif files have been moved from the CD to the java subdirectory before continuing.

If you have access to JDK and have not used the java compiler, create a new file based on the following code. This file will be saved in your working directory under the name Weather.java. From the command line type "javac Weather.java". Be sure the JDK bin directory resides in your path. The javac compiler will create a new file named Weather.class. This file contains the "byte codes" pertaining to the Weather applet.

```
import          java.applet.Applet;
import          java.awt.Graphics;
import          java.awt.Image;
import          java.net.URL;
import       java.awt.MediaTracker;

public class Weather extends Applet implements Runnable {
  static int sequence_interval;
```

continued on next page

continued from previous page

```java
static int frame_interval;
static int num_images = 7;

Thread  animationThread = null;
Image frame[] = new Image[num_images];
MediaTracker mt;
int cur = 1;

  public void init() {
  sequence_interval = Integer.parseInt(getParameter("SEQUENCE_INTERVAL"));
  frame_interval = Integer.parseInt(getParameter("FRAME_INTERVAL"));

  mt = new MediaTracker(this);

  for (int i = 0; i < num_images; i++) {
      try {
          frame[i] = getImage(new URL(getCodeBase(),
                              "iga28q" + (i+1) + "0.gif"));
          mt.addImage(frame[i], 1);
      } catch(Exception e) {}
  }
  }

  public void start() {
  if (animationThread == null) {
      animationThread = new Thread(this);
  }
  animationThread.start();
  }

  public void stop() {
  animationThread.stop();
  }

  public void run() {

  try {
      mt.waitForAll();
  } catch (Exception e) {}

      Thread me = Thread.currentThread();
      me.setPriority(Thread.MIN_PRIORITY);

      for (;;) {
      for (cur = 1; cur <= num_images; cur++) {
                  repaint();
          try {
                              Thread.sleep(frame_interval);
          } catch(Exception e) { }
                  }
      try {
          Thread.sleep(sequence_interval);
          } catch(Exception e) {}
      }
  }
```

```
    public void update(Graphics g) {
        paint(g);
    };

    public void paint(Graphics g) {
    g.drawImage(frame[cur], 0, 0, this);
    }
}
```

3. Open an editor and use the following HTML code to create the shell for a new Web page. The title and header for this page is Weather Patterns.

```
<HTML>
<HEAD> <TITLE> Weather Patterns </TITLE> </HEAD>
<BODY>
<CENTER> <H1> WEATHER PATTERNS </H1> </CENTER>
<HR>
<HR>
</BODY>
</HTML>
```

4. In between the two <HR> tags, add the following HTML code, which is used to download and execute the Weather applet. The applet is allocated a 300x300 pixel square where the weather images will be displayed. Two parameters are passed to the Weather applet. The SEQUENCE_INTERVAL, assigned the value of 275, indicates the amount of time the system sleeps following the display of the final frame and before the first frame is displayed in the new sequence. The FRAME_INTERVAL, initialized to 75, defines the pause interval between each frame.

```
<APPLET CODEBASE=./java CODE=Weather ALIGN=middle WIDTH=300 HEIGHT=300>
<PARAM NAME=SEQUENCE_INTERVAL VALUE=275>
<PARAM NAME=FRAME_INTERVAL VALUE=75>
</APPLET>
```

How It Works

The <APPLET> tag is used to embed the Weather applet inside an HTML document. The CODE attribute indicates the name of the applet that should be downloaded from the server and executed on the client. Two parameters, SEQUENCE_INTER-VAL and FRAME_INTERVAL, are used to modify the behavior of the Weather applet.

Comments

Netscape's JavaScript language is closely tied to Sun Microsystems' Java language, which can also be used to add interactive content to the Web. The close relationship between the two languages, which were developed independently, is the result of a cooperative agreement between Netscape and Sun.

Although both languages give developers the ability to add interactive content to HTML documents, Java and JavaScript have vastly different implementations. The main difference between the two environments revolves around the size and complexity of the application required to perform similar processing. Think of Java as a 3GL and JavaScript as a 4GL.

JavaScript is heavily dependent on HTML's current capabilities, which allow developers to set up input forms. JavaScript developers leverage off the fact that they have access to a wide array of predefined classes. These classes are automatically instantiated into objects when a document is loaded into the browser. HTML input elements are automatically instantiated in memory when an input form is loaded. Because these objects are available for a JavaScript developer to use, a JavaScript program is largely oriented toward data manipulation based on the values stored in these objects' properties. Although Java developers have access to a wide range of predefined classes, in the AWT package, it is up to the developer to instantiate these classes into objects. Other differences between the two languages are that JavaScript is a more loosely typed language and JavaScript code is not compiled.

COMPLEXITY
ADVANCED

16.2 How do I...
Control a Java applet from JavaScript?

COMPATIBILITY: | NAVIGATOR 2.X | NAVIGATOR 3.X | EXPLORER 3.X |

Problem

I understand that LiveConnect permits JavaScript code to invoke Java methods. How can I use this new technology to exercise control over the execution of a Java applet?

Technique

As mentioned earlier, proxy JavaScript objects are automatically instantiated for many Web-related objects when an HTML document is loaded into a browser. Proxy objects contain information and functionality needed by JavaScript developers to exercise control over Web objects ranging from input elements to frames. Navigator 2.0 did not instantiate proxy JavaScript objects for Java applets embedded within a document. This meant that JavaScript developers could not exercise control over an applet. With the release of Navigator 3.0, Proxy objects are also created for applets. This means that JavaScript developers can now invoke an applet's methods or store one of its attributes in a JavaScript variable. Because HTML documents can contain more than one applet, Applet objects are stored inside an applets array belonging to the corresponding Document object. Like all JavaScript arrays, the member sequencing is based on the applet's position inside a document. Because documents are laid out from top to bottom, the topmost applet is the first applet in the array. The array's length property indicates the number of applets embedded in a document. The following code demonstrates how to use the applets array to invoke the topmost applet's Stop method:

```
document.applets[0].stop()
```

Initializing the <APPLET> tag's NAME attribute gives JavaScript developers an alternative method for referencing a Java applet. The following code demonstrates how to use the applet name Weather to invoke that applet's Stop method. This code is logically equivalent to the example above.

```
document.applets["weather"].stop()
document.weather.stop()
```

The Applet object differs from other JavaScript objects in that its interface, which contains the object's attributes and methods, is determined at runtime . The interface is composed of an applet's public properties. In Java, all properties belong to a class definition. Each property is assigned an access modifier. Access modifiers specify whether or not the property can be accessed from a method external to the native class or package. The primary Java access modifiers are public, private, and protected. JavaScript developers are only concerned with public properties. These properties are accessible to all external objects, including JavaScript objects. JavaScript developers can look through the source code of a Java applet to determine which properties they can access. The following Java code demonstrates how a public member function will be defined inside a class specification.

```
public void stop() {
    animationThread.stop();
}
```

Because applet subclasses inherit from the java.applet.Applet class, all JavaScript applet objects will possess a minimal set of properties. Table 16-1 lists the public properties belonging to the java.applet.Applet class. Because Java is an object-oriented language, it is hard to pinpoint the exact behavior of each public method. This is because subclasses can override the behavior of an inherited method.

PUBLIC METHOD	DESCRIPTION
public void int()	Invoked when applet execution begins in the client machine. Used to perform applet initialization.
public void start()	Invoked when a new applet is loaded or the user moves back to the page containing the document from another page. This method is used to launch background threads in animation applets.
public void stop()	Invoked when the user leaves the Web page containing an applet. This method is used to halt execution of a background thread.
public void destroy()	Invoked when the user exits the Web browser. This method typically performs clean-up of system resources.

Table 16-1 Applet public methods

In addition to the public methods inherited from the java.applet.Applet class, applet subclasses can define additional public properties. Therefore, Table 16-1 represents a subset of all properties accessible to a JavaScript developer. You should check with an applet's author, documentation, or source code to compile a complete list of properties for a specific JavaScript applet object.

Steps

This example will use the time-sequenced weather display introduced in How-To 16.1. Users will be given two buttons, Start and Stop, which will allow them to control the background thread. This will allow them to start and stop the animation from an HTML document.

From Navigator 3.0, open the file HT1602.HTM. This example appears the same as Figure 16-1 except that two control buttons now appear at the bottom of the screen. The modified page appears as in Figure 16-3. The animation control buttons will call JavaScript event handlers, which will use LiveConnect to control the Weather java applet. That applet's Start and Stop public methods will be used to control the animation loop.

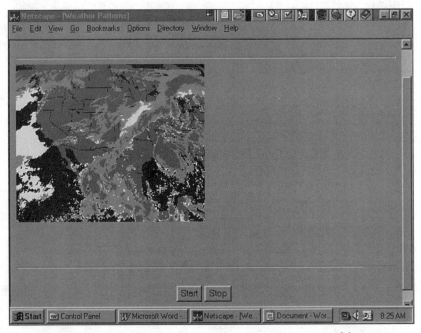

Figure 16-3 The Weather applet with animation control buttons

1. Open an editor and use the following HTML document created in How-To 16.1. This file is called HT1601.HTM. Modify the <APPLET> tag so that the NAME attribute is assigned the name "Weather". JavaScript developers can now access this applet's public methods either through the applets array or the applet name.

```
<APPLET NAME="weather" CODEBASE=./java CODE=Weather ALIGN=middle WIDTH=300⇐
HEIGHT=300>
```

2. Beneath the second <HR> tag, create an input form based on the following HTML code. This form will contain push buttons that will eventually control the execution of the Weather applet.

```
<FORM>
<CENTER>
<INPUT TYPE="button" VALUE="Start">
<INPUT TYPE="button" VALUE="Stop">
</CENTER>
</FORM>
```

3. Add onClick event handlers to the push buttons created in Step 2. The "Start" button's onClick handler uses the applet name "weather" to invoke that applet's Start method. The "Stop" button's onClick handler uses the applets array to call that applet's Stop method. Save the document as HT1602.HTM.

```
<INPUT TYPE="button" VALUE="Start" onClick="document.weather.start()">
<INPUT TYPE="button" VALUE="Stop" onClick="document.applets[0].stop()">
```

How It Works

The applets array is used by JavaScript code to control the execution of the Weather applet. This applet creates a background thread, which runs continuously in the background. The Weather applet's Stop method can be used to stop the background thread. This results in the animation loop being paused. The Start method creates a background thread, if one is not already defined, and starts execution of the background thread. Both the Start and Stop methods are inherited methods of the java.applet.Applet class and are public methods of the Weather applet.

Comments

Now that you have seen how to invoke Java methods from JavaScript, How-To 16.3 will demonstrate how to assign the return value of a Java method to a JavaScript variable.

COMPLEXITY
ADVANCED

16.3 How do I...
Access data returned by a Java method?

COMPATIBILITY: NAVIGATOR 2.X   NAVIGATOR 3.X   EXPLORER 3.X

Problem

Many Java methods return data to the calling function. Can I access this data inside my JavaScript code?

Technique

The return data from a Java method can be stored inside a JavaScript variable. The following code demonstrates how to assign the return data from the Color class's getRed method to a text field's value string:

```
form.red.value = document.color.color.getRed();
```

Because the JavaScript language has weak data typing, much detail about the language binding between Java and JavaScript can be ignored by a developer. Language binding defines the data type conversions required when moving data from one environment or language to another. Because Java and JavaScript do not have the same set of data types, certain rules have been established for moving data between disparate data types. In the example above, the integer returned by the getRed method is assigned to the text field's value property, defined as a string. Once the return data is assigned to a JavaScript object, it can be used throughout a JavaScript function.

Steps

This example will allow a user to have a visual representation of the color defined by a given Red/Green/Blue (RGB) color specification.

From Netscape Navigator version 3.0, open the file HT1603.HTM. The form shown in Figure 16-4 will appear on the screen. Enter a value between 0 and 255 into the Red, Green, and Blue text fields. Click on the "Apply New Color" button and notice the background of the applet change to the specified color. Click on the "Red" button. The applet's background changes color and the Red, Green, and Blue text fields are updated to 255, 0, and 0.

1. The following Java code can be used to create the ColorApplet applet .class file. The ColorApplet will display a background set to a given RGB color specification. This allows users to see the color produced by various RGB combinations.

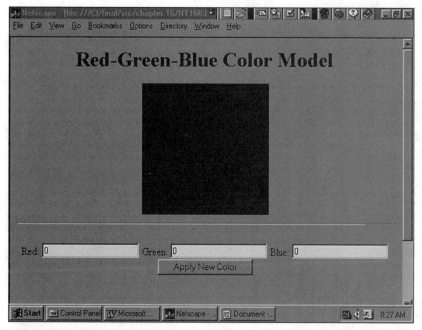

Figure 16-4 The Color applet

Underneath your working directory, create a new subdirectory called java. If you do not have access to the Java Developer's Kit, make sure the ColorApplet.class has been moved from the CD to the java subdirectory before continuing.

If you have access to JDK and have not used the java compiler, create a new file based on the following code. This file will be saved in your working directory under the name "ColorApplet.java". From the command line type "javac ColorApplet.java". Be sure the JDK bin directory resides in your path. The javac compiler will create a new file named ColorApplet.class. This file contains the "byte codes" pertaining to the ColorApplet applet.

```
import java.applet.Applet;
import java.awt.Color;
import java.awt.Graphics;
import java.awt.Rectangle;

public class ColorApplet extends Applet {
    public Color color = new Color(0,0,0);

    public void changeColor(int red, int green, int blue) {
        color = new Color(red,green,blue);
        repaint();
    }
```

continued on next page

continued from previous page

```
    public void turnBlack() {
        color = Color.black;
        repaint();
    }

    public void turnBlue() {
        color = Color.blue;
        repaint();
    }

    public void turnCyan() {
        color = Color.cyan;
        repaint();
    }
    public void turndarkGray() {
        color = Color.darkGray;
        repaint();
    }
    public void turnGray() {
        color = Color.gray;
repaint();
    }
    public void turnGreen() {
        color = Color.green;
        repaint();
    }
    public void turnlightGray() {
        color = Color.lightGray;
        repaint();
    }
    public void turnMagenta() {
        color = Color.magenta;
        repaint();
    }
    public void turnOrange() {
        color = Color.orange;
        repaint();
    }
    public void turnPink() {
        color = Color.pink;
        repaint();
    }
    public void turnRed() {
        color = Color.red;
        repaint();
    }
    public void turnWhite() {
        color = Color.white;
        repaint();
    }
    public void turnYellow() {
        color = Color.yellow;
        repaint();
    }
    public void paint(Graphics graphics) {
        graphics.setColor(color);
```

```
      Rectangle outline = bounds();
      graphics.fillRect(outline.x, outline.y,
                                  outline.width, outline.height);
   }
}
```

2. Open an editor and use the following HTML code to create the shell for a new Web page. Designate the title and header for this page as Red-Green-Blue Color Model.

```
<HTML>
<HEAD> <TITLE> Red-Green-Blue Color Model </TITLE>
</HEAD>
<BODY>
<CENTER> <H1> Red-Green-Blue Color Model </H1> </CENTER>
<HR>
</BODY>
</HTML>
```

3. Add the following <APPLET> tag before the <HR> tag. This HTML code will download and execute a Java applet stored in ColorApplet.class. This applet is named "color" and occupies a 200x200 pixel space on the screen.

```
<APPLET CODEBASE=.\java CODE="ColorApplet" NAME="color" WIDTH=200⇐
HEIGHT=200>
</APPLET>
```

4. Following the <HR> tag, use the following HTML code to create an input form. This form will contain three text fields where the user can enter a red, green, or blue attribute for a color. By clicking the Apply button, the background of the applet, created in Step 3, will change to the corresponding color. Predefined color buttons, at the bottom of the form, will use static color objects to set the applet's background.

```
<FORM>
<CENTER>
Red: <INPUT TYPE NAME="red" LENGTH=3>
Green: <INPUT TYPE NAME="green" LENGTH=3>
Blue: <INPUT TYPE NAME="blue" LENGTH=3>
<INPUT TYPE="button" NAME="apply" VALUE="Apply New Color">
</CENTER> <BR>
<CENTER> <H3> Predefined Colors </H3> </CENTER>
<CENTER>
<INPUT TYPE="button" NAME="Black" VALUE="Black">
<INPUT TYPE="button" NAME="Blue" VALUE="Blue">
<INPUT TYPE="button" NAME="Cyan" VALUE="Cyan">
<INPUT TYPE="button" NAME="DarkGray" VALUE="Dark Gray">
<INPUT TYPE="button" NAME="Gray" VALUE="Gray">
<INPUT TYPE="button" NAME="Green" VALUE="Green">
<INPUT TYPE="button" NAME="LightGray" VALUE="Light Gray">
<INPUT TYPE="button" NAME="Magenta" VALUE="Magenta">
<INPUT TYPE="button" NAME="Orange" VALUE="Orange">
<INPUT TYPE="button" NAME="Pink" VALUE="Pink">
<INPUT TYPE="button" NAME="Red" VALUE="Red">
```

continued on next page

continued from previous page

```
<INPUT TYPE="button" NAME="White" VALUE="White">
<INPUT TYPE="button" NAME="Yellow" VALUE="Yellow">
</CENTER>
</FORM>
```

5. Before the </HEAD> tag, add the following JavaScript code to create the changeColor function. This function will extract the red, green, and blue values entered into the three text fields. The function verifies that values have been entered into the text fields. If the values are valid, then the "color" applet's changeColor is invoked. The changeColor method is defined inside the ColorApplet applet. Compare this to the methods in How-To 16.2, which were inherited and defined inside an existing Java superclass. The changeColor accepts the RGB values, stored in JavaScript variables, as parameters.

```
<SCRIPT LANGUAGE="JavaScript">
function changeColor(form) {
    var r = parseInt(form.red.value);
    var g = parseInt(form.green.value);
    var b = parseInt(form.blue.value);

    if ((r < 0) || (r > 255)) alert("ERROR\n
                                     Red Not Between 0 and⇐
255");
    else if ((g < 0) || (g > 255)) alert("ERROR\n
                                     Green Not Between 0 and⇐
255");
    else if ((b < 0) || (b > 255)) alert("ERROR\n
                                     Blue Not Between 0 and⇐
255");
    else document.color.changeColor(r,g,b);

}
</SCRIPT>
```

6. Beneath the changeColor function created in Step 5, use the following JavaScript code to create the resetRGB function. This function uses the Java Color class's public methods getRed, getGreen, and getBlue to set the three RGB text fields. If one of the canned color buttons is clicked, this function can be used to change the RGB text field values to the new color.

```
function resetRGB(form) {
    form.red.value = document.color.color.getRed();
    form.green.value = document.color.color.getGreen();
    form.blue.value = document.color.color.getBlue();
}
```

7. Add an onClick event handler to the Apply button. This handler calls the changeColor JavaScript function created in Step 4.

```
<INPUT TYPE="button" NAME="apply" VALUE="Apply New Color"⇐
onClick="changeColor(this.form)">
```

8. Add onClick event handlers to the canned color buttons. These handlers
call the ColorApplet public methods designed to change the applet's background color. The JavaScript function resetRGB is then called to update the
three RGB text fields to the new color's attributes. Store the document as
HT1603.HTM.

```
<INPUT TYPE="button" NAME="Black" VALUE="Black"⇐
onClick="document.color.turnBlack(); resetRGB(this.form);">
<INPUT TYPE="button" NAME="Blue" VALUE="Blue"⇐
onClick="document.color.turnBlue(); resetRGB(this.form);">
<INPUT TYPE="button" NAME="Cyan" VALUE="Cyan"⇐
onClick="document.color.turnCyan(); resetRGB(this.form);">
<INPUT TYPE="button" NAME="DarkGray" VALUE="Dark Gray"⇐
onClick="document.color.turndarkGray(); resetRGB(this.form);">
<INPUT TYPE="button" NAME="Gray" VALUE="Gray"⇐
onClick="document.color.turnGray(); resetRGB(this.form);">
<INPUT TYPE="button" NAME="Green" VALUE="Green"⇐
onClick="document.color.turnGreen(); resetRGB(this.form);">
<INPUT TYPE="button" NAME="LightGray" VALUE="Light Gray"⇐
onClick="document.color.turnlightGray(); resetRGB(this.form);">
<INPUT TYPE="button" NAME="Magenta" VALUE="Magenta"⇐
onClick="document.color.turnMagenta(); resetRGB(this.form);">
<INPUT TYPE="button" NAME="Orange" VALUE="Orange"⇐
onClick="document.color.turnOrange(); resetRGB(this.form);">
<INPUT TYPE="button" NAME="Pink" VALUE="Pink"⇐
onClick="document.color.turnPink(); resetRGB(this.form);">
<INPUT TYPE="button" NAME="Red" VALUE="Red"⇐
onClick="document.color.turnRed(); resetRGB(this.form);">
<INPUT TYPE="button" NAME="White" VALUE="White"⇐
onClick="document.color.turnWhite(); resetRGB(this.form);">
<INPUT TYPE="button" NAME="Yellow" VALUE="Yellow"⇐
onClick="document.color.turnYellow(); resetRGB(this.form);">
```

How It Works

JavaScript variables should be used to store data returned by Java methods invoked
by a JavaScript function. Once the variable assignment is made, the variable can be
used throughout the function like any other JavaScript variable.

Comments

Besides returning scalar values, Java methods can also return Java objects. How-To
16.4 will demonstrate how to store returned Java objects in a JavaScript variable.

16.4 How do I...
Access data contained inside a Java class?

COMPATIBILITY: NAVIGATOR 3.X

Problem

In How-To 16.3, I learned that return data from Java methods can be assigned to JavaScript objects. If the method returns a Java object, can I access the information contained inside the object?

Technique

Objects returned by Java methods can be stored in JavaScript variables. The class definition for these objects was defined using the Java language. Despite this fact, the interface for Java objects is identical in both the JavaScript and Java environments. Similar to applets, an object's public properties can be referenced by the JavaScript functions and event handlers. The following code stores the java.awt.Graphic object, returned by the java.applet.Applet getGraphics method, in a JavaScript variable named Graphics:

```
var Graphics = Applet.getGraphics();
```

The getGraphics method returns the applet's graphic content. This object contains all the Java primitive vector drawing methods. Following this line of code, the Graphics variable is synonymous to a java.awt.Graphics object. This means that the public method clearRect, which belongs to this class, can be used to manipulate the applet's graphic context. The following call demonstrates how to invoke this Java method on the Graphics variable.

```
Graphics.clearRect(25,25,125,125);
```

Steps

This example uses the ColorApplet application, created in How-To 16.3. The JavaScript code is modified to leverage off some of the Java graphics library utilities. These utilities return Java objects to the JavaScript program. The reader will learn how to access information, from JavaScript, contained within a Java object.

From Netscape Navigator version 3.0, open the file HT1604.HTM. The form displayed in Figure 16-5 will appear on the screen. Click on the Clear Middle button, and notice the center of the applet turns to white. The color change is the result of the Java Graphic's class clearRect method. JavaScript does not possess functional-

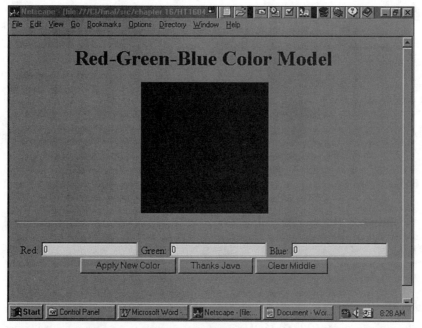

Figure 16-5 The Enhanced Color applet

ity to perform primitive vector graphic manipulation such as drawing lines and polygons, but JavaScript developers using Java's graphic capabilities have access to enhanced functionality not provided by the JavaScript language. Click on the Thanks Java button and see a Thank You message in the browser's status bar.

1. Open an editor and use the HTML document created in How-To 16.3. This file is called HT1603.HTM. Beneath the Apply button, add two new buttons. These buttons will add additional capabilities to the RGB Color Document.

```
<INPUT TYPE="button" NAME="thanks" VALUE="Thanks Java">
<INPUT TYPE="button" NAME="clear" VALUE="Clear Middle">
```

2. Inside the <SCRIPT> container, use the following JavaScript code to create the clearMiddle function. This function will use the applet's getGraphics method to obtain access to the Web browser's graphic context. The Java Graphic's object is stored inside the JavaScript variable called Graphics. As with applets, JavaScript developers have access to public properties of returned Java classes. The Graphic object's public method clearRect is then called to "whiten out" the middle of the ColorApplet.

```
function clearMiddle() {
    var Applet = document.color;
    var Graphics = Applet.getGraphics();
    Graphics.clearRect(25,25,125,125);
}
```

3. Inside the <SCRIPT> container, use the following JavaScript code to create the displayThanks function. This function uses the applet class's showStatus method to assign a message to the browser's status bar. This method performs the same functionality as assigning the same string to the JavaScript Document object's status property.

```
function displayThanks() {
   document.color.showStatus("Thanks Java For Letting Me Use Your⇐
SHOWSTATUS
                            Method, Even Though I Can Do The Same Thing
                            With My DOCUMENT.STATUS Property");
}
```

4. Modify the two buttons created in Step 1 to contain event handlers that call the JavaScript functions created in Steps 2 and 3.

```
<INPUT TYPE="button" NAME="thanks" VALUE="Thanks Java"⇐
onClick="displayThanks()">
<INPUT TYPE="button" NAME="clear" VALUE="Clear Middle"⇐
onClick="clearMiddle()">
```

How It Works

The getGraphics method of the ColorApplet applet is used to get a handle to the applet's graphics context. This method returns a java.awt.Graphics object. Once this object is stored in a JavaScript variable, any public method belonging to the class can be invoked from JavaScript.

Comments

In the previous examples, you learned how to access existing Java objects from JavaScript. In each example, the objects were instantiated inside the Java or JavaScript framework. How-To 16.5 will teach you how to use Java constructors to instantiate new JavaScript objects.

COMPLEXITY
ADVANCED

16.5 How do I...
Use a Java constructor to initialize a JavaScript variable?

COMPATIBILITY: NAVIGATOR 2.X   NAVIGATOR 3.X   EXPLORER 3.X

Problem

If LiveConnect allows JavaScript code to invoke Java functions, can it also be used to create new JavaScript objects based on Java constructor functions?

Technique

When an object is created in Java, a function called a *constructor* is called upon to initialize properties to their default state. In addition to public member functions, LiveConnect also gives JavaScript developers access to a class's constructors. In Java class definitions, constructors are discriminated by the fact that they return no value and they possess the same name as the class they belong to. Within the context of Java and JavaScript programs, constructors are differentiated from other functions by the fact that they are preceded by the new operator and do not require an object reference. The new operator is similar to its JavaScript cousin in that it is used to dynamically allocate memory off the system heap.

As discussed in How-To 16.2, JavaScript uses a concept similar to constructors when creating objects not included as part of the JavaScript framework. The dissimilarity between the two approaches is that JavaScript constructors define the properties of an object. With Java, class definitions specify an object's makeup.

To reference a Java constructor, you must call the function immediately following a reference to the new operator. This combination serves to dynamically allocate memory and initialize the object in a single JavaScript statement. If the constructor is contained within a java package, the package name must precede the constructor. Because Java allows developers to establish package hierarchies, multiple package names may precede the constructor function. The following example creates a Stack object, defined in the Java framework as part of the java.util package, whose reference is stored in the JavaScript variable stack.

```
var stack = new java.util.Stack();
```

Now that the stack variable has been established as a java.util.Stack object, any of the class's public properties can be accessed within JavaScript. The following code calls the public method *push* to add a token onto the top of the stack.

```
stack.push(token);
```

Notice the power this capability gives JavaScript developers. The JavaScript language does not possess a Stack object as part of its default framework. Without this capability, a Stack object would have to be created and tested using JavaScript to provide similar functionality. By giving JavaScript developers the ability to instantiate Java classes, a reuse library of domain-specific and generic Java classes can be created. This library can be used by both Java and JavaScript developers to quickly build powerful Web-based applications.

Steps

This example gives the user a simplified calculator. This calculator accepts only numeric computations defined using Reverse Polish notation. Reverse Polish notation has a format equal to

```
operand1    operand2    operator
```

The algorithm for analyzing Reverse Polish notation expressions uses a Stack. Stacks are Last In First Out (LIFO) data structures. This means that the last data stored in Stack will be the first data popped off Stack. The algorithm specifies that all operands and return values are placed on the Stack. If a binary operator is located, then the last two values are popped off the Stack. For unary operators, the last value is popped off the Stack.

From Netscape Navigator version 3.0, open the file HT1605.HTM. The form shown in Figure 16-6 will appear inside the browser's document viewing area. Enter the numeric expression 2 4 + 2 2 + * into the Expression text field. This expression is in Reverse Polish format and equates to the regular numeric expression (2 + 4) * (2 + 2). See the number 24 appear inside the Answer text field. The following computational steps will appear inside the Steps text area:

*** Push Number 2 *** Push Number 4 --- Perform Computation 2 + 4 === Answer 6 *** Push Number 2 ** Push Number 2 --- Perform Computation 2 + 2 === Answer 4-- Perform Computation 6 * 4 == Answer 24

This example uses existing capabilities in the Java class library or framework to manipulate a stack and string tokenizer. For evaluating numeric expressions represented as strings, this example takes advantage of the Evaluation method contained in the JavaScript framework.

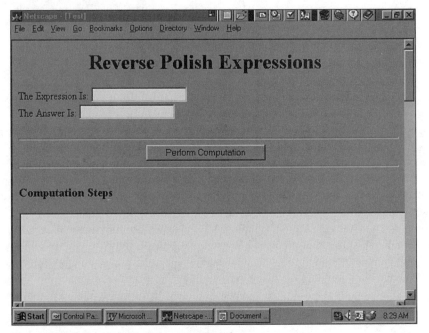

Figure 16-6 Reverse Polish notation form

1. Open an editor and use the following HTML code to create the shell for a new Web page. Designate the title and header for this page as "Reverse Polish Expressions."

```
<HTML>
<HEAD> <TITLE> Reverse Polish Expressions </TITLE>
</HEAD>
<BODY>
<CENTER> <H1> Reverse Polish Expressions </H1> </CENTER>
</BODY>
</HTML>
```

2. Immediately following the <BODY> tag, use the HTML code below to create an input form. This form contains two text fields, one push button, and a text area. The Expression text field is where users will enter numeric expressions in Reverse Polish notation. When the button is clicked, the Reverse Polish expression will be evaluated and the result displayed inside the Answer text field. The computational steps taken to evaluate the numeric expression will be displayed inside the Steps text area.

```
<FORM NAME="count">
The Expression Is: <INPUT NAME="expression"> <BR>
The Answer Is: <INPUT NAME="answer"> <BR>
<HR>
<CENTER> <INPUT TYPE="button" NAME="compute"
<H3> Computation Steps </H3>
<TEXTAREA NAME="steps" ROWS=100 COLS=100 WRAP=logical>
</TEXTAREA>
</FORM>
```

3. Preceding the </HEAD> tag, enter the following code to create the shell for a JavaScript function named computeReversePolishExpression(). When this function is completed, it will contain the logic required to evaluate syntactically correct Reverse Polish numeric expressions.

```
<SCRIPT LANGUAGE="JavaScript">
function computeReversePolishExpression() {
}
</SCRIPT>
```

4. In the body of the computeReversePolishExpression function created in Step 3, enter the variable declaration JavaScript code at the end of this section. This code utilizes LiveConnect to create JavaScript objects based on existing Java class definitions. By using the new operator in combination with existing Java constructors, this code defines two JavaScript variables whose memory allocations and initializations are based on Java classes. The tokenizer variable is defined as a java.util.StringTokenizer object. Notice that the full package name, java.util, must be used in order to locate the desired class. The JavaScript code can access the information stored in this object through the public attributes and methods of the java.util.StringTokenizer class. The stack variable is defined as a java.util.Stack object.

This ability to create JavaScript objects based on Java constructors allows JavaScript developers to use the existing Java framework provided with the Java Developer's Kit for certain complex tasks that cannot be performed with the existing JavaScript framework. Without LiveConnect, JavaScript code would have to be developed to perform processing similar to the java.util.StringTokenizer and java.util.Stack classes. This new capability exists in Navigator 3.0 because JavaScript is now included as part of the Java environment.

```
// Use JAVA Constructers To Build A Tokenizer
// (Based On The Expression Text Field) And A Stack

var tokenizer =
            new⇐
java.util.StringTokenizer(document.count.expression.value);
    var stack = new java.util.Stack();
```

5. After the variable declarations in Step 4, add the following JavaScript code to the bottom of the computeReversePolishExpression function. This code uses the StringTokenizer object to extract one token at a time from the numeric expression. If the token is a number, push it onto the top of the Stack. If the token is an operator, build the regular numeric expression by enclosing the operator inside two operands popped off the top of the Stack. Use the JavaScript eval function, which will evaluate numeric expressions represented as strings to determine the resulting answer. Display the answer in the "answer" text field. Push the answer back onto the Stack. At every step in the computational process, display a description of the step in the Step text area.

```
// Clear Out Steps Text Area

document.count.steps.value = "";

// Loop Which Extracts One Token At A Time

while(tokenizer.hasMoreTokens()) {
    var token = tokenizer.nextToken();

    // Turn Token Into A Number To Determine Data Type

    var num = parseInt(token);

    // If Number, Then Push Onto Stack, Else Perform Computation And
    // Push Answer Onto Stack

    if (num != 0) {
        document.count.steps.value = document.count.steps.value +
                            "*** Push Number " + token;
        stack.push(token);
    } else {

        // Build Numeric Expression And Use JavaScript EVAL Method To
        // Perform Numeric Computation
```

```
                    var expression = stack.pop() + token + stack.pop();
                    var answer = eval(expression);
                    document.count.steps.value = document.count.steps.value +
                                    "--- Perform Computation " + expression;

                    // Push Answer Back Onto The Stack

                    stack.push(answer);
                    document.count.steps.value = document.count.steps.value +
                                    "=== ANSWER " + answer;
                }
        }

        // Display The Final Answer In The Answer Text Field

        document.count.answer.value = stack.pop();
```

6. In the input form created in Step 2, add an onClick event handler to the Compute button. This handler will invoke the computeReverse PolishExpression function, created in Steps 3 through 5. Adding this event handler will cause the expression analysis to occur when the Compute button is clicked. Save the HTML document as HT1605.HTM.

```
<INPUT TYPE="button" NAME="compute" VALUE="Perform Computation"
    onClick="computeReversePolishExpression()"> </CENTER>
```

How It Works

The algorithm to evaluate Reverse Polish notation numeric expressions is very straightforward. A string tokenizer is used to read one token at a time from a syntactically correct Reverse Polish notation expression. If a number is encountered, then this value is pushed onto a Stack. When a binary numeric operator is encountered, two values are popped off the Stack and combined with the binary operator to form a regular numeric expression. The result is pushed back onto the Stack.

The JavaScript framework does not possess a native Stack or StringTokenizer class. With Netscape Navigator version 2.0, this functionality would have to be developed from scratch. However, with LiveConnect, JavaScript developers can take advantage of the fact that the java.util package contains both Stack and StringTokenizer classes. By using the new operator in connection with the appropriate constructor, new JavaScript objects are created that give the developer access to the needed functionality. The Web page is built in a fraction of the time it would take had the Stack and StringTokenizer not existed.

Comments

Now you know how Java and JavaScript are integrated in Netscape Navigator version 3.0. The LiveConnect technology represents a powerful new feature that gives Web developers flexibility in building interactive Web sites.

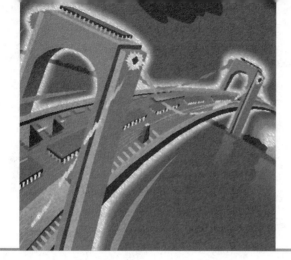

INDEX

C

CaclulateDecimal function, 130-131

calculators
  Button object, 285-289
  classes, 171-172
  Math object, 165-171
  URL-based, 23-25

calling functions, 119-122

CGI scripts
  ATM form, 259
  Hidden Text objects, 255-256

CGIs, 117-118

Change function (looping statements), 151-152

Change Operator button (VARIABLES.HTM), 123-127

ChangeColors function, 70-71
  links, 74-75

ChangeImage function, 89-92

Characters (String object), 180-182
  changing case, 188-190
  locating position, 182-185

CharAt method (returning characters), 180-182

Checkboxes
  building, 242-246
  changing selected, 311-316
  determining states of, 241-242
  forms, 229
  properties, 242

Checked attribute (checkboxes), 242

Checked property
  changing radio box/checkbox selections, 312-316
  checkboxes, 245-246
  radio buttons, 251
  Radio object, 247
  selection lists, 316-322

Child frames
  global variables, 404-408
  sibling properties, 409-412

Class (Java data), 576-578

Class constructor (Date object), 190-193

Class properties
  Math object, 162-163
  With container, 163-164

classes, 328
  defining, 329-334
  Math object calculators, 171-172

Clear Comments button, 17-19

clear text (passwords), 260

Click event handler, 12-13, 284-289
  links (target windows), 440-444
  object arrays, 367-368
  object classes, 334
  radio buttons, 249-250
  selection lists selections, 317-322

Click method (changing selections), 311-312

Client-side image maps (targeting), 451-454

Close method, 62-63

CloseDocument function, 61-63

Closing (HTML documents), 59-64

ClrNum function (Math object calculators), 168

CODE attribute (APPLET tag), 561-562

code blocks
  executing conditionally, 140-143
  if...else statements, 144
  looping, 144-152

code fragments (String objects), 179

CODEBASE attribute (APPLET tag), 562

color arrays, 129-131

color control radio buttons (VRML), 553

colors
  code blocks, 140-143
  looping HTMs, 145-149, 151-152
  HTML documents, 67-71
  links, 71-75
  text, 71
  VRML objects, 551

COLS (sizing frames), 378-380

comments (JavaScript code), 153-155

Common Gateway Interfaces, *see* CGIs

ComputeBinary function (Math object calculators), 169-170

ComputeUnary function (Math object calculators), 170

concatenating
  converting numbers to strings, 207-210
  multiple string objects, 175-177

Concatenation operator, 175-177
  polymorphism, 177

CONDIT.HTM, 140-143

conditional if...else statements, 142-144

conditional loops, 144-152

conditionally executing code blocks, 140-143

cone object (VRML), 550-551

Confirm method, 16-19

Confirmation dialog boxes, 15-16
  modifying Reader Feedback forms, 17-19

Books have a substantial influence on the destruction of the forests of the Earth. For example, it takes 17 trees to produce one ton of paper. A first printing of 30,000 copies of a typical 480-page book consumes 108,000 pounds of paper, which will require 918 trees!

Waite Group Press™ is against the clear-cutting of forests and supports reforestation of the Pacific Northwest of the United States and Canada, where most of this paper comes from. As a publisher with several hundred thousand books sold each year, we feel an obligation to give back to the planet. We will therefore support organizations that seek to preserve the forests of planet Earth.

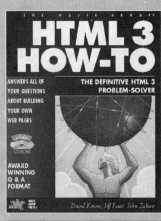

Message from the
Publisher

WELCOME TO OUR NERVOUS SYSTEM

Some people say that the World Wide Web is a graphical extension of the information superhighway, just a network of humans and machines sending each other long lists of the equivalent of digital junk mail.

I think it is much more than that. To me, the Web is nothing less than the nervous system of the entire planet—not just a collection of computer brains connected together, but more like a billion silicon neurons entangled and recirculating electro-chemical signals of information and data, each contributing to the birth of another CPU and another Web site.

Think of each person's hard disk connected at once to every other hard disk on earth, driven by human navigators searching like Columbus for the New World. Seen this way the Web is more of a super entity, a growing, living thing, controlled by the universal human will to expand, to be more. Yet, unlike a purposeful business plan with rigid rules, the Web expands in a nonlinear, unpredictable, creative way that echoes natural evolution.

We created our Web site not just to extend the reach of our computer book products but to be part of this synaptic neural network, to experience, like a nerve in the body, the flow of ideas and then to pass those ideas up the food chain of the mind. Your mind. Even more, we wanted to pump some of our own creative juices into this rich wine of technology.

TASTE OUR DIGITAL WINE

And so we ask you to taste our wine by visiting the body of our business. Begin by understanding the metaphor we have created for our Web site—a universal learning center, situated in outer space in the form of a space station. A place where you can journey to study any topic from the convenience of your own screen. Right now we are focusing on computer topics, but the stars are the limit on the Web.

If you are interested in discussing this Web site or finding out more about the Waite Group, please send me e-mail with your comments, and I will be happy to respond. Being a programmer myself, I love to talk about technology and find out what our readers are looking for.

Sincerely,

Mitchell Waite

Mitchell Waite, C.E.O. and Publisher

200 Tamal Plaza
Corte Madera, CA 94925
415-924-2575
415-924-2576 fax

Website:
http://www.waite.com/waite

CREATING THE HIGHEST QUALITY COMPUTER BOOKS IN THE INDUSTRY

Waite Group Press

Come Visit
WAITE.COM
Waite Group Press
World Wide Web Site

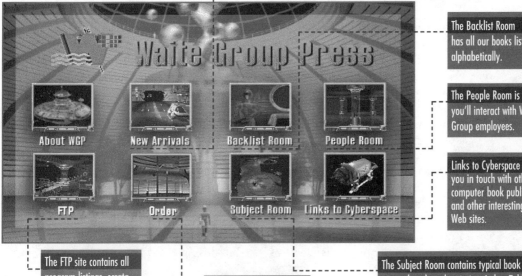

Now find all the latest information on Waite Group books at our new Web site, **http://www.waite.com/waite**. You'll find an online catalog where you can examine and order any title, review upcoming books, and send e-mail to our authors and editors. Our FTP site has all you need to update your book: the latest program listings, errata sheets, most recent versions of Fractint, POV Ray, Polyray, DMorph, and all the programs featured in our books. So download, talk to us, ask questions, on **http://www.waite.com/waite**.

The New Arrivals Room has all our new books listed by month. Just click for a description, Index, Table of Contents, and links to authors.

The Backlist Room has all our books listed alphabetically.

The People Room is where you'll interact with Waite Group employees.

Links to Cyberspace get you in touch with other computer book publishers and other interesting Web sites.

About WGP

New Arrivals

Backlist Room

People Room

FTP

Order

Subject Room

Links to Cyberspace

The FTP site contains all program listings, errata sheets, etc.

The Order Room is where you can order any of our books online.

The Subject Room contains typical book pages that show description, Index, Table of Contents, and links to authors.

World Wide Web:

COME SURF OUR TURF—THE WAITE GROUP WEB

http://www.waite.com/waite
Gopher: gopher.waite.com
FTP: ftp.waite.com

This is a legal agreement between you, the end user and purchaser, and The Waite Group®, Inc., and the authors of the programs contained in the disk. By opening the sealed disk package, you are agreeing to be bound by the terms of this Agreement. If you do not agree with the terms of this Agreement, promptly return the unopened disk package and the accompanying items (including the related book and other written material) to the place you obtained them for a refund.

SOFTWARE LICENSE

1. The Waite Group, Inc. grants you the right to use one copy of the enclosed software programs (the programs) on a single computer system (whether a single CPU, part of a licensed network, or a terminal connected to a single CPU). Each concurrent user of the program must have exclusive use of the related Waite Group, Inc. written materials.

2. The program, including the copyrights in each program, is owned by the respective author and the copyright in the entire work is owned by The Waite Group, Inc. and they are therefore protected under the copyright laws of the United States and other nations, under international treaties. You may make only one copy of the disk containing the programs exclusively for backup or archival purposes, or you may transfer the programs to one hard disk drive, using the original for backup or archival purposes. You may make no other copies of the programs, and you may make no copies of all or any part of the related Waite Group, Inc. written materials.

3. You may not rent or lease the programs, but you may transfer ownership of the programs and related written materials (including any and all updates and earlier versions) if you keep no copies of either, and if you make sure the transferee agrees to the terms of this license.

4. You may not decompile, reverse engineer, disassemble, copy, create a derivative work, or otherwise use the programs except as stated in this Agreement.

GOVERNING LAW

This Agreement is governed by the laws of the State of California.

LIMITED WARRANTY

The following warranties shall be effective for 90 days from the date of purchase: (i) The Waite Group, Inc. warrants the enclosed disk to be free of defects in materials and workmanship under normal use; and (ii) The Waite Group, Inc. warrants that the programs, unless modified by the purchaser, will substantially perform the functions described in the documentation provided by The Waite Group, Inc. when operated on the designated hardware and operating system. The Waite Group, Inc. does not warrant that the programs will meet purchaser's requirements or that operation of a program will be uninterrupted or error-free. The program warranty does not cover any program that has been altered or changed in any way by anyone other than The Waite Group, Inc. The Waite Group, Inc. is not responsible for problems caused by changes in the operating characteristics of computer hardware or computer operating systems that are made after the release of the programs, nor for problems in the interaction of the programs with each other or other software.

THESE WARRANTIES ARE EXCLUSIVE AND IN LIEU OF ALL OTHER WARRANTIES OF MERCHANTABILITY OR FITNESS FOR A PARTICULAR PURPOSE OR OF ANY OTHER WARRANTY, WHETHER EXPRESS OR IMPLIED.

EXCLUSIVE REMEDY

The Waite Group, Inc. will replace any defective disk without charge if the defective disk is returned to The Waite Group, Inc. within 90 days from date of purchase.

This is Purchaser's sole and exclusive remedy for any breach of warranty or claim for contract, tort, or damages.

LIMITATION OF LIABILITY

THE WAITE GROUP, INC. AND THE AUTHORS OF THE PROGRAMS SHALL NOT IN ANY CASE BE LIABLE FOR SPECIAL, INCIDENTAL, CONSEQUENTIAL, INDIRECT, OR OTHER SIMILAR DAMAGES ARISING FROM ANY BREACH OF THESE WARRANTIES EVEN IF THE WAITE GROUP, INC. OR ITS AGENT HAS BEEN ADVISED OF THE POSSIBILITY OF SUCH DAMAGES.

THE LIABILITY FOR DAMAGES OF THE WAITE GROUP, INC. AND THE AUTHORS OF THE PROGRAMS UNDER THIS AGREEMENT SHALL IN NO EVENT EXCEED THE PURCHASE PRICE PAID.

COMPLETE AGREEMENT

This Agreement constitutes the complete agreement between The Waite Group, Inc. and the authors of the programs, and you, the purchaser.

Some states do not allow the exclusion or limitation of implied warranties or liability for incidental or consequential damages, so the above exclusions or limitations may not apply to you. This limited warranty gives you specific legal rights; you may have others, which vary from state to state.

SATISFACTION REPORT CARD

Please fill out this card if you wish to know of future updates to
JavaScript How-To, or to receive our catalog.

rst Name: _____   Last Name: _____

reet Address: _____

ty: _____   State: _____   Zip: _____

mail Address _____

aytime Telephone: (   ) _____

te product was acquired: Month   Day   Year   Your Occupation:

---

erall, how would you rate *JavaScript How-To*?

Excellent   ☐ Very Good   ☐ Good
Fair   ☐ Below Average   ☐ Poor

hat did you like MOST about this book? _____

_____

_____

hat did you like LEAST about this book? _____

_____

_____

ase describe any problems you may have encountered with
talling or using the disk: _____

_____

w did you use this book (problem-solver, tutorial, reference...)?

_____

at is your level of computer expertise?

New   ☐ Dabbler   ☐ Hacker
Power User   ☐ Programmer   ☐ Experienced Professional

at computer languages are you familiar with?_____

_____

ase describe your computer hardware:

nputer _____   Hard disk _____

" disk drives _____   3.5" disk drives_____

o card _____   Monitor _____

ter _____   Peripherals _____

d Board _____   CD ROM_____

Where did you buy this book?

☐ Bookstore (name):_____

☐ Discount store (name):_____

☐ Computer store (name):_____

☐ Catalog (name):_____

☐ Direct from WGP   ☐ Other _____

What price did you pay for this book? _____

What influenced your purchase of this book?

☐ Recommendation   ☐ Advertisement

☐ Magazine review   ☐ Store display

☐ Mailing   ☐ Book's format

☐ Reputation of Waite Group Press   ☐ Other

How many computer books do you buy each year?_____

How many other Waite Group books do you own?_____

What is your favorite Waite Group book?_____

_____

**Is there any program or subject you would like to see Waite
Group Press cover in a similar approach?**_____

_____

Additional comments?_____

_____

_____

Please send to: **Waite Group Press**
                    200 Tamal Plaza
                    Corte Madera, CA 94925

☐ **Check here for a free Waite Group catalog**